JULIUS CAESAR

THE NEW CAMBRIDGE SHAKESPEARE

Romeo and Juliet, edited by G. Blakemore Evans
The Taming of the Shrew, edited by Ann Thompson
Othello, edited by Norman Sanders
King Richard II, edited by Andrew Gurr
A Midsummer Night's Dream, edited by R. A. Foakes
Hamlet, edited by Philip Edwards
Twelfth Night, edited by Elizabeth Story Donno
All's Well That Ends Well, edited by Russell Fraser
The Merchant of Venice, edited by M. M. Mahood
Much Ado About Nothing, edited by F. H. Mares
The Comedy of Errors, edited by T. S. Dorsch
Julius Caesar, edited by Marvin Spevack

JULIUS CAESAR

Edited by
MARVIN SPEVACK
Professor of English, University of Münster

CAMBRIDGE UNIVERSITY PRESS
Cambridge
New York Port Chester
Melbourne Sydney

Published by the Press Syndicate of the University of Cambridge
The Pitt Building, Trumpington Street, Cambridge CB2 1RP
32 East 57th Street, New York, NY 10022, USA
10 Stamford Road, Oakleigh, Melbourne 3166, Australia

First published 1988
Reprinted 1989

Printed in Great Britain by
the University Press, Cambridge

British Library cataloguing in publication data

Shakespeare, William
Julius Caesar. – (The New Cambridge
Shakespeare).
I. Title II. Spevack, Marvin
822.3'3 PR2808

Library of Congress cataloguing in publication data

Shakespeare, William, 1564–1616
Julius Caesar / edited by Marvin Spevack
p. cm. – (The New Cambridge Shakespeare)
Bibliography: p.
ISBN 0 521 22220 6 ISBN 0 521 29408 8 (pbk.)
1. Caesar, Julius – Drama. I. Spevack, Marvin. II. Title.
III. Series: Shakespeare, William, 1564–1616. Works.
1984. Cambridge University Press.
PR2808.A2S64 1988 822.3'3 – dc19 87–27238 CIP

ISBN 0 521 22220 6 hard covers
ISBN 0 521 29408 8 paperback

WV

THE NEW CAMBRIDGE SHAKESPEARE

The *New Cambridge Shakespeare* succeeds *The New Shakespeare* which began publication in 1921 under the general editorship of Sir Arthur Quiller-Couch and John Dover Wilson, and was completed in the 1960s, with the assistance of G. I. Duthie, Alice Walker, Peter Ure and J. C. Maxwell. *The New Shakespeare* itself followed upon *The Cambridge Shakespeare*, 1863–6, edited by W. G. Clark, J. Glover and W. A. Wright.

The New Shakespeare won high esteem both for its scholarship and for its design, but shifts of critical taste and insight, recent Shakespearean research, and a changing sense of what is important in our understanding of the plays, have made it necessary to re-edit and redesign, not merely to revise, the series.

The *New Cambridge Shakespeare* aims to be of value to a new generation of playgoers and readers who wish to enjoy fuller access to Shakespeare's poetic and dramatic art. While offering ample academic guidance, it reflects current critical interests and is more attentive than some earlier editions have been to the realisation of the plays on the stage, and to their social and cultural settings. The text of each play has been freshly edited, with textual data made available to those users who wish to know why and how one published text differs from another. Although modernised, the edition conserves forms that appear to be expressive and characteristically Shakespearean, and it does not attempt to disguise the fact that the plays were written in a language other than that of our own time.

Illustrations are usually integrated into the critical and historical discussion of the play and include some reconstructions of early performances by C. Walter Hodges. Some editors have also made use of the advice and experience of Maurice Daniels, for many years a member of the Royal Shakespeare Company.

Each volume is addressed to the needs and problems of a particular text, and each therefore differs in style and emphasis from others in the series.

PHILIP BROCKBANK
General Editor

For DIANNE AND BILLY

CONTENTS

ILLUSTRATIONS

ACKNOWLEDGEMENTS

I am privileged to acknowledge the help I have received from students and colleagues, friends and strangers, who contributed their expertise and goodwill to this enterprise. I take pleasure in the fact that my debt is great and to many on both sides of the Atlantic.

In seminars in Münster and New Mexico (where I spent the academic year 1985–6) I was able to profit from the remarks of the prospective users of a work of this kind: the reactions of students to the necessity and nature of the Commentary. In Münster, my thanks to Sabine Ulrike Bückmann-de Villegas, Peter Hellfeuer, Michael Hiltscher, Thomas Pago, Ulrich Paul, Elisabeth Pirke, Clemens Sorgenfrey, Elke Stracke, Krishnan Venkatesh, Martin Wolny, and Angela Zatsch. In Albuquerque, to Mohamed Ali, Mary Lou Fisk, David Kreuter, Catherine Mecklenburg, Linda Oldham, and Jon Tuttle.

For help in the preparation of the manuscript in Albuquerque, I am indebted to Marta Field and K. T. Martin, for administrative encouragement to Hamlin C. Hill, and for computer support to Harry C. Broussard; in Münster, to Lydia Remke for typing and Carsten Ehmke and Bernhard Friederici for computing. Marga Munkelt, as always, provided ready solutions to many and varied scholarly problems. Special credit is due to Elisabeth Pirke, who worked on all aspects in Münster and Albuquerque, and to Sabine Ulrike Bückmann-de Villegas, who saw to all the final details as well as writing the section of the Introduction dealing with the stage history.

For the selection of illustrations, I was able to draw on the experience of J. W. Binns, Hildegard Hammerschmidt-Hummel, Fortunato Israël, Julian-Matthias Kliemann, Vera Liebert, Giorgio Melchiori, Sylvia Morris, Karl Noehles, Robert Rockman, and Robert Smallwood.

For their unfailing assistance on individual questions I thank G. Blakemore Evans, C. Walter Hodges, Helga Spevack-Husmann, Michael Steppat, and Hans-Jürgen Weckermann. Brian Gibbons read the manuscript with professional crispness and courtesy. Paul Chipchase supplied the necessary editorial consistency and concern. I am particularly grateful to John W. Velz, who went to great trouble checking the collation and making available, in countless ways, his profound knowledge of this play, and to Krishnan Venkatesh, who was a source of sensitivity, insight, and common sense all along the way.

M.S.

Münster

ABBREVIATIONS AND CONVENTIONS

Shakespeare's plays, when cited in this edition, are abbreviated in a style modified slightly from that used in the *Harvard Concordance to Shakespeare.* Other editions of Shakespeare are abbreviated under the editor's surname (Ridley, Sanders) unless they are the work of more than one editor. In such cases, an abbreviated series name is used (Cam.). When more than one edition by the same editor is cited, later editions are discriminated with a raised figure (Rowe[2]). References to Abbott's *Shakespearian Grammar* are to paragraph numbers. All quotations from Shakespeare, except those from *Julius Caesar*, use the text and lineation of *The Riverside Shakespeare*, under the general editorship of G. Blakemore Evans.

1. Shakespeare's plays

Ado	*Much Ado about Nothing*
Ant.	*Antony and Cleopatra*
AWW	*All's Well That Ends Well*
AYLI	*As You Like It*
Cor.	*Coriolanus*
Cym.	*Cymbeline*
Err.	*The Comedy of Errors*
Ham.	*Hamlet*
1H4	*The First Part of King Henry the Fourth*
2H4	*The Second Part of King Henry the Fourth*
H5	*King Henry the Fifth*
1H6	*The First Part of King Henry the Sixth*
2H6	*The Second Part of King Henry the Sixth*
3H6	*The Third Part of King Henry the Sixth*
H8	*King Henry the Eighth*
JC	*Julius Caesar*
John	*King John*
LLL	*Love's Labour's Lost*
Lear	*King Lear*
Mac.	*Macbeth*
MM	*Measure for Measure*
MND	*A Midsummer Night's Dream*
MV	*The Merchant of Venice*
Oth.	*Othello*
Per.	*Pericles*
R2	*King Richard the Second*
R3	*King Richard the Third*
Rom.	*Romeo and Juliet*
Shr.	*The Taming of the Shrew*
STM	*Sir Thomas More*
Temp.	*The Tempest*
TGV	*The Two Gentlemen of Verona*

Tim.	*Timon of Athens*
Tit.	*Titus Andronicus*
TN	*Twelfth Night*
TNK	*The Two Noble Kinsmen*
Tro.	*Troilus and Cressida*
Wiv.	*The Merry Wives of Windsor*
WT	*The Winter's Tale*

2. Other works cited and general references

Abbott	E. A. Abbott, *A Shakespearian Grammar*, 3rd edn, 1870
Alexander	*Works*, ed. Peter Alexander, 1951
Anon.	anonymous
Appian	*Shakespeare's Appian*, ed. Ernest Schanzer, 1956
apud	in
Badham	Charles Badham, 'The text of Shakespeare', *Cambridge Essays*, vol. 2, 1856, pp. 261–91
Becket	Andrew Becket, *Shakespeare's Himself Again*, 2 vols., 1815
Bevington	*Works*, ed. David Bevington, 1980
Blair	*Works*, ed. Hugh Blair, 1753
Blake	N. F. Blake, *Shakespeare's Language: An Introduction*, 1983
Boswell	*Plays & Poems*, ed. James Boswell, 1821
BSUF	*Ball State University Forum*
Bulloch	John Bulloch, *Studies on the Text of Shakespeare*, 1878
Bullough	Geoffrey Bullough (ed.), *Narrative and Dramatic Sources of Shakespeare*, vol. 5, 1964
CahiersE	*Cahiers Elisabéthains*
Cam.	*Works*, ed. William George Clark and William Aldis Wright, 1863–6 (Cambridge Shakespeare)
Capell	*Comedies, Histories, and Tragedies*, ed. Edward Capell, [1768]
Capell MS.	MS. holograph of Capell's edition, before 1751 (Trinity College Library, Cambridge)
Cartwright	Robert Cartwright, *New Readings in Shakspere*, 1866
Charney	*Julius Caesar*, ed. Maurice Charney, 1969 (Bobbs-Merrill Shakespeare Series)
Collier	*Works*, ed. John Payne Collier, 1842–4
Collier^2	*Plays*, ed. John Payne Collier, 1853
Collier^3	*Comedies, Histories, Tragedies, and Poems*, ed. John Payne Collier, 1858
Collier^4	*Plays and Poems*, ed. John Payne Collier, 1875–8
Collier MS.	MS. notes by J. P. Collier in a copy of F2 (Perkins Folio in the Huntington Library), before 1852
conj.	conjecture
Craig	*Works*, ed. W. J. Craig, [1891] (Oxford Shakespeare)
Craik	*The English of Shakespeare*, ed. George L. Craik, 1857
Daniel	Peter A. Daniel, *Notes and Conjectural Emendations of Certain Doubtful Passages in Shakespeare's Plays*, 1870
Deighton	*Julius Caesar*, ed. Kenneth Deighton, 1890 (Grey Cover Shakespeare)
Delius	*Werke*, ed. Nicolaus Delius, 1854–[61]
Dent	R. W. Dent, *Shakespeare's Proverbial Language: An Index*, 1981 (references are to numbered proverbs)

Dorsch	*Julius Caesar*, ed. T. S. Dorsch, 1955 (Arden Shakespeare)
Douai MS.	Douai MS. 7.87, *c.* 1694 (Douai Public Library)
DR	*Dalhousie Review*
Dyce	*Works*, ed. Alexander Dyce, 1857
Dyce²	*Works*, ed. Alexander Dyce, 1864–7
EDH	*Essays by Divers Hands*
EIC	*Essays in Criticism*
ELH	*Journal of English Literary History*
ELN	*English Language Notes*
Evans	*The Riverside Shakespeare*, ed. G. Blakemore Evans *et al.*, 1974
F1	*Mr. William Shakespeares Comedies, Histories, and Tragedies*, 1623 (First Folio)
F2	*Mr. William Shakespeares Comedies, Histories, and Tragedies*, 1632 (Second Folio)
F3	*Mr. William Shakespear's Comedies, Histories, and Tragedies*, 1663–4 (Third Folio)
F4	*Mr. William Shakespear's Comedies, Histories, and Tragedies*, 1685 (Fourth Folio)
Farmer	Richard Farmer, contributor to Steevens (1773 edn) and Steevens² (1778 edn)
Folger MS.	Folger Shakespeare Library MS. V.a.85, *c.* 1665
Franz	Wilhelm Franz, *Die Sprache Shakespeares in Vers und Prosa*, 4th edn, 1939
Furness	*Julius Caesar*, ed. Horace Howard Furness, Jr, 1913 (New Variorum Shakespeare)
Globe	*Works*, ed. William George Clark and William Aldis Wright, 1864 (Globe Edition)
Hall	'Mr. Hall' mentioned in Thirlby
Halliwell	*Works*, ed. James O. Halliwell, 1853–65
Hanmer	*Works*, ed. Thomas Hanmer, 1743–4
Heraud	John A. Heraud, contributor to Cam. (1863–6 edn)
Herr	J. G. Herr, *Scattered Notes on the Text of Shakespeare*, 1879
Hudson	*Works*, ed. Henry N. Hudson, 1851–6
Hudson²	*Works*, ed. Henry N. Hudson, 1880–1 (Harvard Edition)
Hulme	Hilda M. Hulme, *Explorations in Shakespeare's Language: Some Problems of Lexical Meaning in the Dramatic Text*, 1962
Humphreys	*Julius Caesar*, ed. Arthur Humphreys, 1984 (Oxford Shakespeare)
John Hunter	*Julius Caesar*, ed. John Hunter, [1869] (Hunter's Annotated Shakespeare)
Joseph Hunter	Joseph Hunter, *New Illustrations of the Life, Studies, and Writings of Shakespeare*, 2 vols., 1845
Mark Hunter	*Julius Caesar*, ed. Mark Hunter, 1900 (College Classics Series)
Irving	*Works*, ed. Henry Irving and Frank A. Marshall, 1888–90 (Henry Irving Shakespeare)
J.D.	J.D., 5 *N&Q* 8 (1877), 262–3
JEGP	*Journal of English and Germanic Philology*
Jennens	*Julius Caesar*, ed. Charles Jennens, 1774
Jervis	Swynfen Jervis, *Proposed Emendations of the Text of Shakspeare's Plays*, 1860

Johnson	*Plays*, ed. Samuel Johnson, 1765
Johnson^2	*Plays*, ed. Samuel Johnson, 1765
S. F. Johnson	*Julius Caesar*, ed. S. F. Johnson, 1960 (Pelican Shakespeare)
S. F. Johnson^2	*Julius Caesar*, ed. S. F. Johnson, 1969 (Pelican Shakespeare)
Thomas Johnson	*Plays*, ed. Thomas Johnson, 1711
Thomas Johnson^2	*Plays*, ed. Thomas Johnson, *c.* 1720
Keightley	*Plays*, ed. Thomas Keightley, 1864
Kittredge	*Works*, ed. George Lyman Kittredge, 1936; *Julius Caesar*, 1939
Knight	*Comedies, Histories, Tragedies, & Poems*, ed. Charles Knight, [1838–43] (Pictorial Edition)
Lettsom	William Nanson Lettsom, 'New readings in Shakespeare', *Blackwood's Edinburgh Magazine* 74 (Aug. 1853), 181–202
Linthicum	M. Channing Linthicum, *Costume in the Drama of Shakespeare and his Contemporaries*, 1936
Littledale	Richard Frederick Littledale, contributor to Macmillan (1902 edn)
Macmillan	*Julius Caesar*, ed. Michael Macmillan, 1902 (Arden Shakespeare)
Malone 1780	Edmond Malone, Supplement to Steevens^2 (1778 edn), 2 vols., 1780
Malone	*Plays & Poems*, ed. Edmond Malone, 1790
Mason	John Monck Mason, *Comments on the Last Edition of Shakespeare's Plays*, 1785
Mason 1919	*Julius Caesar*, ed. Lawrence Mason, 1919 (Yale Shakespeare)
Mitford	John Mitford, 'Conjectural emendations on the text of Shakspere', *Gentleman's Magazine* n.s. 22 (1844), 451–72
MLN	*Modern Language Notes*
MLR	*Modern Language Review*
Morley	Henry Morley, contributor to Mark Hunter (1900 edn)
N&Q	*Notes and Queries*
Nicholson	Brinsley M. Nicholson, contributor to William Aldis Wright, MS. Notes (Add. MS. b.58) in Trinity College Library, Cambridge
OCD	*The Oxford Classical Dictionary*, ed. N. G. L. Hammond and H. H. Scullard, 2nd edn, 1970
OED	*The Oxford English Dictionary*, ed. James A. H. Murray *et al.*, 12 vols. and supplement, 1933
Onions	C. T. Onions, *A Shakespeare Glossary*, revised by Robert D. Eagleson, 1986
Pauly	August Friedrich von Pauly, *Real-Encyclopaedie der classischen Altertumswissenschaft*, ed. Georg Wissowa *et al.*, 33 vols. and supplement, 1893–1978
PBSA	*Publications of the Bibliographical Society of America*
Platner/Ashby	Samuel Ball Platner, *A Topographical Dictionary of Ancient Rome*, completed and revised by Thomas Ashby, 1929
Plutarch	*The Lives of the Noble Grecians and Romanes*, translated by Sir Thomas North, 1579 (page references are to the extracts given in the Appendix, pp. 154–83 below)
PMLA	*Publications of the Modern Language Association of America*
Pope	*Works*, ed. Alexander Pope, 1723–5
Pope^2	*Works*, ed. Alexander Pope, 1728
PQ	*Philological Quarterly*
Q (1684)	*Julius Caesar* quarto

Q (1691)	*Julius Caesar* quarto
QU1, QU2, QU3, QU4	Undated quartos of *Julius Caesar* issued between the late seventeenth and early eighteenth centuries
Rann	*Dramatic Works*, ed. Joseph Rann, 1786–[94]
Reed	*Plays*, ed. Isaac Reed, 1803
RenD	*Renaissance Drama*
RES	*Review of English Studies*
Ridley	*Julius Caesar*, ed. M. R. Ridley, 1935 (New Temple Shakespeare)
Ripley	John Ripley, *'Julius Caesar' on Stage in England and America, 1599–1973*, 1980
Ritson	Joseph Ritson, contributor to Steevens³ (1793 edn)
Rowe	*Works*, ed. Nicholas Rowe, 1709
Rowe²	*Works*, ed. Nicholas Rowe, 1709
Rowe³	*Works*, ed. Nicholas Rowe, 1714
Sanders	*Julius Caesar*, ed. Norman Sanders, 1967 (New Penguin Shakespeare)
Schmidt	Alexander Schmidt, *Shakespeare-Lexicon*, 2 vols., 1874–5
SD	stage direction
SH	speech heading
S.St.	*Shakespeare Studies*
S.Sur.	*Shakespeare Survey*
Singer	Samuel W. Singer, contributor to Cam. (1863–6 edn) and Hudson² (1880–1 edn)
Singer	*Dramatic Works*, ed. Samuel W. Singer, 1826
Singer²	*Dramatic Works*, ed. Samuel W. Singer, 1856
Singer 1858	Samuel W. Singer, 2 *N&Q* 5 (1858), 289–90
Sisson	*Works*, ed. Charles Jasper Sisson, [1954]
SJ	*Shakespeare-Jahrbuch*
Spurgeon	Caroline F. E. Spurgeon, *Shakespeare's Imagery and What It Tells Us*, 1935
SQ	*Shakespeare Quarterly*
Staunton	*Plays*, ed. Howard Staunton, 1858–60
Staunton²	*Works*, ed. Howard Staunton, 1864
Steevens	*Plays*, ed. Samuel Johnson and George Steevens, 1773
Steevens²	*Plays*, ed. Samuel Johnson and George Steevens, 1778
Steevens³	*Plays*, ed. Samuel Johnson and George Steevens, 1793
subst.	substantively
Suetonius	*Suetonius: Lives of the Caesars*, trans. J. C. Rolfe, The Loeb Classical Library, 2 vols., revised 1951
Theobald 1730	Lewis Theobald, letter to William Warburton (14 Feb. 1729/30)
Theobald	*Works*, ed. Lewis Theobald, 1733
Theobald²	*Works*, ed. Lewis Theobald, 1740
Theobald³	*Works*, ed. Lewis Theobald, 1752
Theobald⁴	*Works*, ed. Lewis Theobald, 1757
Thirlby	Styan Thirlby, MS. Notes in eighteenth-century editions of Shakespeare, 1723–51
Tilley	Morris Palmer Tilley, *A Dictionary of the Proverbs in England in the Sixteenth and Seventeenth Centuries*, 1950 (references are to numbered proverbs)
Tyrwhitt	Thomas Tyrwhitt, contributor to Steevens² (1778 edn)
Upton	John Upton, *Critical Observations on Shakespeare*, 1746

Walker	William Sidney Walker, *A Critical Examination of the Text of Shakespeare*, ed. W. Nanson Lettsom, 3 vols., 1860
W. S. Walker	William Sidney Walker, *Shakespeare's Versification*, 1854
Warburton 1734	William Warburton, letter to Lewis Theobald (2 June 1734)
Warburton	*Works*, ed. William Warburton, 1747
Wells and Taylor	*Works*, ed. Stanley Wells and Gary Taylor, 1986 (Oxford Shakespeare)
White	*Works*, ed. Richard Grant White, 1857–66
White[2]	*Comedies, Histories, Tragedies, and Poems*, ed. Richard Grant White, 1883 (Riverside Shakespeare)
Wilson	*Julius Caesar*, ed. John Dover Wilson, 1949 (New Shakespeare)
Wordsworth	*Historical Plays*, ed. Charles Wordsworth, 1883
Wright	*Julius Caesar*, ed. William Aldis Wright, 1878 (Clarendon Press Series)

INTRODUCTION

Date

There is little doubt among scholars today that *Julius Caesar* was written in 1599. Although the play appeared in print for the first time in the First Folio (1623) – see the Textual Analysis, p. 148 below – there is no entry for it in the Stationers' Register, and the earliest estimates (starting with those of Edward Capell and Edmond Malone in the late eighteenth century and continuing for about a hundred years) placed it among the later plays, about 1607.[1] The evidence for the precise earlier dating is considerable and varied. Direct and indirect, external and internal, it reflects many of the facets of the procedure for determining the chronology of Shakespeare's plays.

The *terminus a quo*, it must be admitted, has been established on the basis of rather scant, even negative, evidence. The play is not mentioned in Francis Meres's *Palladis Tamia* (1598) among the comedies and tragedies for which '*Shakespeare* among the English is the most excellent', a fact which many find revealing, considering how popular a play *Julius Caesar* evidently was.[2] But Meres also fails to mention other plays which had preceded the publication of his work: the *Henry VI* trilogy, *The Taming of the Shrew*, *The Merry Wives of Windsor*, perhaps even *2 Henry IV*. And there is little reason to believe that Meres purported to be exhaustive or even accurate: his choice of six comedies and six tragedies, for example, seems to suggest rhetorical balance rather than an attempt to list Shakespeare's complete works.

Attempts to find clues in contemporary works that Shakespeare may have echoed have been frequent but not wholly accepted. Most often cited are lines from Samuel Daniel's *Musophilus*, published in 1599:

> And who in time knowes whither we may vent
> The treasure of our tongue, to what strange shores
> This gaine of our best glorie shal be sent,
> T'inrich vnknowing Nations with our stores?
> VVhat worlds in th'yet vnformed Occident
> May come refin'd with th'accents that are ours? –

which are thought to resemble Cassius's

> How many ages hence
> Shall this our lofty scene be acted over
> In states unborn and accents yet unknown! (3.1.111–13)

[1] A convenient recapitulation of opinions up to 1910 is to be found in Furness, p. 292.

[2] Evidence of its popularity is most often deduced from the commendatory verses by Leonard Digges, which are believed to have been intended for inclusion in the Folio but appeared later in the 1640 edition of Shakespeare's *Poems*.

And from John Davies's *Nosce Teipsum* (1599), especially the comparison of

> Mine *Eyes*, which view all obiects, nigh and farre,
> Looke not into this litle world of mine,
> Nor see my face, wherein they fixed are

with Shakespeare's 1.2.51–8. If this 'parallel' were not already questionable, Dover Wilson's (p. 109) adding of further examples of the same idea in the same poem strains the credibility of the attempt:

> All things without, which round about we see,
> We seeke to know, and how therewith to do:
> But that whereby we *reason, liue, and be,*
> Within our selues, we strangers are thereto...
>
> Is it because the minde is like the eye,
> (Through which it gathers knowledge by degrees,)
> Whose rayes reflect not, but spread outwardly,
> Not seeing it selfe, when other things it sees?

These examples only help establish the sentiment as a commonplace, one not unsurprisingly found in Tilley and Dent (see Commentary, 1.2.52–3). Recent additions to Wilson's list are perforce likewise highly speculative.[1] Finally, even while suggesting parallels between lines 1995–6 of the anonymous *A Warning for Faire Women* (1599) and the wounds that will speak (3.1.259–61, 3.2.215–16), Humphreys sensibly admits that the 'simile was not uncommon and its occurrence in both plays may be mere coincidence' (p. 2).

Stylistic or internal evidence, by nature less conclusive than hard facts or other external evidence, is of slight help. In analysing Shakespeare's vocabulary, for example, Alfred Hart notes many peculiarities: '*Julius Caesar* has a smaller vocabulary than any other play of Shakespeare except *Two Gentlemen* and *Comedy of Errors*, which is seven hundred lines shorter. It has the lowest number of both peculiar and compound words and makes a contribution to the vocabulary of the poet smaller than that made by any other play except *Pericles* and *Henry VIII*; both of these plays are only Shakespeare's in part.' However, he sees no connection with the chronology of the plays, except somewhat indirectly in attributing the spareness to Shakespeare's coming 'about 1598–9 ... for a time under the influence of Jonson and his theories of dramatic art and literary composition'.[2] A study of line length is equally unrewarding. 'In that singular tragedy, *Julius Caesar*, the upwelling spring of the poet's plenty seems to have dried up, but the drought may have been intentional',[3] Hart concludes, but although he does not hesitate to alter Chambers's chronology – for example, placing *The Merry Wives* after *Henry V* and before *Julius Caesar* – he accepts the position of *Julius Caesar*. Given the nature of this kind of evidence, it is not surprising that the play may be considered 'very early' because some passages are very 'stiff',[4] somewhat later because of the just-mentioned influence

[1] See, for example, Gary Taylor, '*Musophilus*, *Nosce Teipsum*, and *Julius Caesar*', *N&Q* 229 (1984), 191–5.
[2] Alfred Hart, 'Vocabularies of Shakespeare's plays', *RES* 19 (1943), 135.
[3] Alfred Hart, 'The growth of Shakespeare's vocabulary', *RES* 19 (1943), 254.
[4] E. H. C. Oliphant, 'Shakspere's plays: an examination. III', *MLR* 4 (1908–9), 191.

of Jonson, or even as late as 1607 because of its resemblance to the other Roman plays (a view first advocated by Capell) or its similarity to (or confusion with) other plays of the time, like Malone's mentioning of William Alexander's *Julius Caesar* or the anonymous *Caesar's Revenge*.

Metrical analyses have also been inconclusive or noncommittal. Kerrl places the first act of *Julius Caesar* after *The Merchant of Venice* and perhaps at the same time as *2 Henry IV*, but Acts 2–5 between *Henry V* and *Hamlet*;[1] according to the criteria of Ingram, however, *Julius Caesar* belongs between *Measure for Measure* and *Othello*.[2] In the most recent detailed study, Dorothy Sipe summarises stylistic, phonological, and lexical implications, but makes no assertions at all about chronology (even, for the sake of coherence with the *OED*, being obliged to accept its now questionable chronological order).[3] Likewise, although *Julius Caesar* has fewer lines of rhyme (24) than any other play in the canon, no convincing attempt has been made to apply the data to the chronology: Ness's conclusion is that 'Shakespeare came to reserve rhyme for particular effects. Where the play seemed to require these effects, there the rhyme was used, whether the play was written in 1600 or in 1610.'[4] Finally, imagery studies deal but slightly with *Julius Caesar* since it is generally agreed that it contains relatively few images or image patterns or clusters: Spurgeon devotes little more than a page to the entire play; Armstrong cites it but five times.[5] As a rule, the recurrence of the content and structure of imagery throughout Shakespeare's career is studied rather than its use as a marker for a particular period.

A stronger case has been made for the *terminus ad quem*, for the external evidence is considerable, even if not totally verifiable. The main document is the report of the Swiss traveller Thomas Platter, who visited England from 18 September to 20 October 1599: 'On the 21st of September, after dinner, at about two o'clock, I went with my party across the water; in the straw-thatched house we saw the tragedy of the first Emperor Julius Caesar, very pleasingly performed, with approximately fifteen characters.'[6] Chambers's evaluation of this information as 'fairly definitely' fixing the date of production has been accepted by almost all scholars in this century: 'He [Platter] does not name the Globe, but the theatre was south of the river, and the Swan was probably not in regular use. The Rose no doubt was, but as the Admiral's had new Caesar plays in 1594–5 and again in 1602, they are not very likely to have been staging one in 1599. Platter's "at least fifteen characters" agrees fairly with *Julius Caesar*, on the assumption that he disregarded a number of inconspicuous parts.'[7] Ernest Schanzer's 'word of caution about the use of

[1] Anna Kerrl, *Die metrischen Unterschiede von Shakespeares King John und Julius Caesar: Eine chronologische Untersuchung*, 1913, p. 152.

[2] John K. Ingram, 'On the "weak endings" of Shakspere, with some account of the history of the verse-tests in general', *New Shakspere Society Transactions* 1 (1874), 450.

[3] Dorothy L. Sipe, *Shakespeare's Metrics*, 1968.

[4] Frederic W. Ness, *The Use of Rhyme in Shakespeare's Plays*, 1941, p. 109.

[5] Edward A. Armstrong, *Shakespeare's Imagination*, 1946.

[6] The literal translation appears in Ernest Schanzer, 'Thomas Platter's observations on the Elizabethan stage', *N&Q* 201 (1956), 466. The German text, reprinted by E. K. Chambers, *William Shakespeare*, 2 vols., 1930, II, 322, is first discussed by Gustav Binz, 'Londoner Theater und Schauspiele im Jahre 1599', *Anglia* 22 (1899), 462.

[7] Chambers, *Shakespeare*, I, 397.

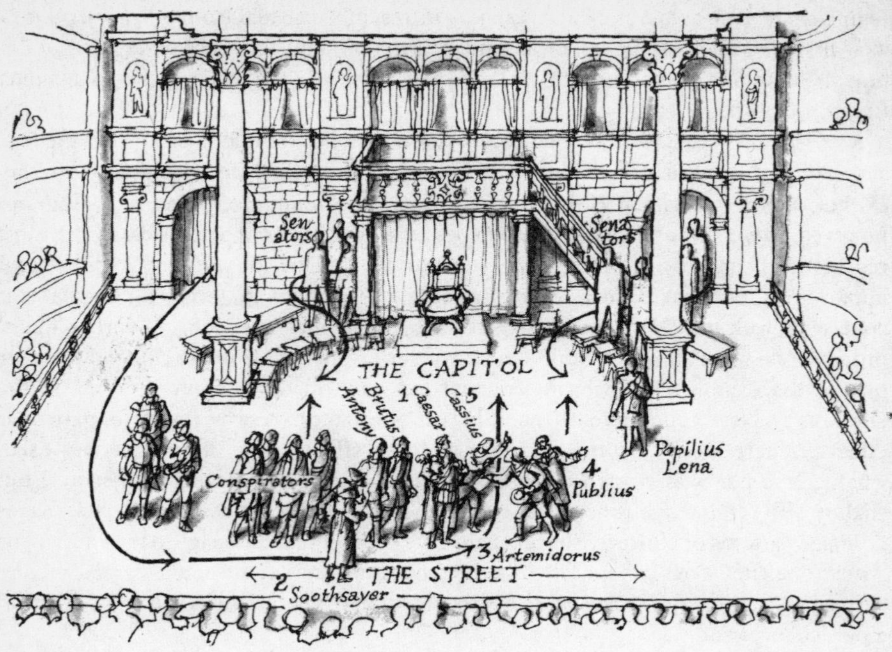

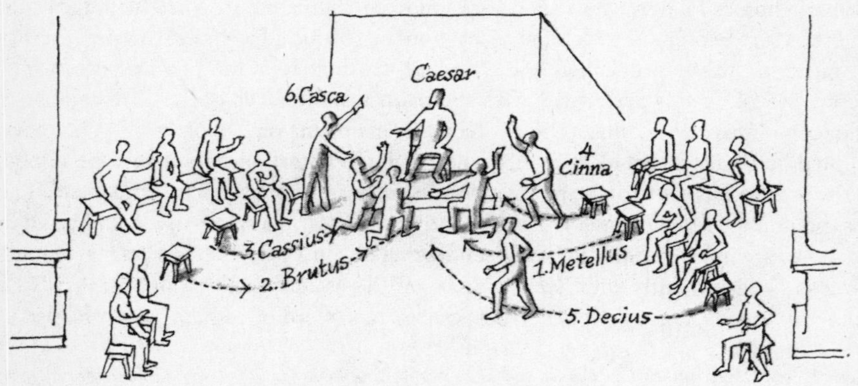

1 A likely Elizabethan staging of Act 3, Scene 1, drawn by C. Walter Hodges

a Caesar's way towards the Capitol: (1) The Ides of March are come. (2) Ay, Caesar, but not gone. (3) Hail, Caesar! Read this schedule. (4) Sirrah, give place. (5) What, urge you your petitions in the street? Come to the Capitol. (6) I wish your enterprise today may thrive

b The Senate being seated, the conspirators approach Caesar from their places one by one

Platter's evidence in attempting to date the composition and first performances' (p. 466) – based on his view that the Rose might also fit the description, that the Admiral's might well have had Caesar plays if they were so popular, and that Shakespeare's play has over forty speaking parts – has led at best to a certain qualification rather than a challenging of Chambers's conclusion.

All agree with Chambers that the 'date of 1599 fits in well with other evidence',[1] which consists in the main of an ever-increasing number of possible allusions – called rather indiscriminately 'echoes', 'quotations', 'paraphrases', 'reminiscences', 'parallels', and the like – to *Julius Caesar* found in contemporary works. Halliwell (p. 374) was the first to mention lines from John Weever's *Mirror of Martyrs*, published in 1601 but which, as its dedication avers, was 'some two yeares agoe ... made fit for the Print':

> The many-headed multitude were drawne
> By *Brutus* speach, that *Caesar* was ambitious,
> When eloquent *Mark Antonie* had showne
> His vertues, who but *Brutus* then was vicious?

A bit later, F. G. Fleay, arguing unconvincingly that Ben Jonson altered and abridged Shakespeare's play,[2] may have inadvertently instigated what is considered by many as telling confirmation: in a mocking context in *Every Man Out of His Humour* (5.6.79) Jonson seems to be repeating Shakespeare's unhistorical '*Et tu, Brute*' (3.1.77). A second reference from the same play of 1599, '*Reason long since is fled to animals*' (3.4.33), is now almost unhesitatingly accepted as an 'obvious quotation' if not a parody of Shakespeare's 'O judgement, thou art fled to brutish beasts, / And men have lost their reason' (3.2.96–7). Dorsch (pp. viii–x) summarises the host of further allusions from works written within a few years after *Julius Caesar*: among them are Jonson's *Cynthia's Revels*, *Timber*, and *A Staple of News*, as well as the anonymous *The Wisdom of Dr Dodypoll* (1600), Samuel Nicholson's poem *Acolastus his Afterwitte* (1600), Michael Drayton's *The Barons' Wars* (1603), Philip Massinger and John Fletcher's *T[ragedy] of Sir John Van Olden Barnavelt*. Among numerous others, Wilson (NS, p. x) adds lines 26–8 of the prologue of Act 5 of *Henry V*, to suggest that Shakespeare was 'studying' Plutarch in 1599.

Ironically, the more allusions offered, the less convincing the attempt to fix the date. For one thing, there is little agreement on the exact nature of the illustrations: Chambers, for example, calls the second Jonson reference a 'quotation',[3] Dorsch an 'echo' (p. viii), Evans a 'paraphrase' (p. 53). For another, there is not always agreement on the evaluation of the allusions: in one of many instances, Simpson considers the second Jonson reference 'less certain',[4] whereas Chambers finds it 'obvious'.[5] Finally, the content of the allusions tends to be general, almost proverbial or axiomatic. The widespread appearance of such passages may be attributable to Shakespeare's

[1] Chambers, *Shakespeare*, I, 397.

[2] F. G. Fleay, 'On two plays of Shakspere's: Part II. *Julius Caesar*', *New Shakspere Society Transactions* I (1874), 357–66.

[3] Chambers, *Shakespeare*, I, 245.

[4] Percy Simpson, 'The date of Shakspeare's "Julius Caesar"', *N&Q* 54 (1899), 106.

[5] Chambers, *Shakespeare*, I, 397.

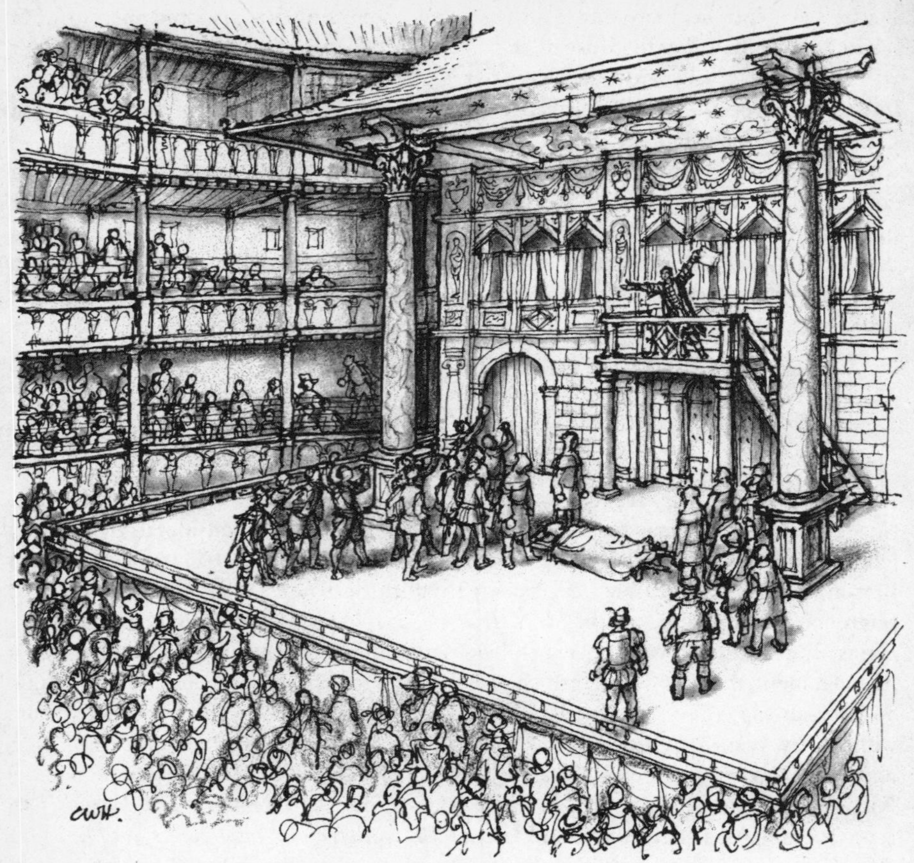

2 'You will compel me then to read the will?' Antony's funeral oration, Act 3, Scene 2: a suggested Elizabethan staging, by C. Walter Hodges

popularity, but it may just as well be the result of the Elizabethan fondness for commonplaces and *sententiae*.

Though abundant and various, the direct evidence for the precise dating of *Julius Caesar* is not completely conclusive. The weight of the evidence is, however, undeniable. The necessary caveat, 'in all probability', having been supplied or not, scholars seem determined to have 1599 as the year in which *Julius Caesar* was written. There is no reason to disagree.

Sources

Dealing with Shakespeare's sources calls to mind Diogenes' stroll across the market-place: he was pleasantly surprised, it is said, that there were so many articles he had no need of. That Shakespeare employed sources is indisputable; that he employed or was

3 'Most noble brother, you have done me wrong.' The meeting of Brutus and Cassius, Act 4, Scenes 2 and 3: a possible Elizabethan staging, by C. Walter Hodges

influenced by as many as have been proposed is, however, another matter. Or, to put it another way, distinctions are necessary if the contours of Shakespeare's craft are to be sharply defined and the contributions of the prodigious industry of Shakespearean scholarship fairly evaluated. As with many other concerns, less may in the long run be more.

The indisputable main source of *Julius Caesar* is Sir Thomas North's translation of Plutarch's *Lives of the Noble Grecians and Romanes* (1579), more specifically, the lives of Caesar and Brutus (large sections of which are reproduced in the Appendix, pp. 154–83 below) and to a much slighter extent of Antony and perhaps Cicero. That they were directly and consciously used by Shakespeare, that they may be called 'sources', is clear not merely from the events portrayed but especially from the structuring, phrasing, vocabulary, and other stylistic characteristics which Shakespeare seems to have consciously adopted or modified. The distinction between sheer content and particular style must be stressed because, obviously, historical information of the kind that Shakespeare most frequently uses – the 'story', as it were – was part of the common heritage; in the unlikely event that Shakespeare did not know the broad outlines of the assassination of Caesar and its consequences, if he had been asleep on the school benches of Stratford, he could have had recourse to the 'story' in any number of contemporary histories or dramas.

Unfortunately, simplicity is not always in favour. The scholarship dealing with

Shakespeare's possible 'sources' is voluminous: W. C. Hazlitt's modestly sized six-volume *Shakespeare's Library* (1875) has given way in this century to Geoffrey Bullough's generous eight-volume *Narrative and Dramatic Sources of Shakespeare* (1957–75); whole volumes have been devoted to single influences, like *Shakespeare's Holinshed*, *Shakespeare's Ovid*, *Shakespeare's Plutarch*, *Shakespeare's Appian*, and to particular subjects, like *Shakespeare and the Classics*, *Shakespeare and the Greek Romance*, *Classical Mythology in Shakespeare*, *Shakespeare's Biblical Knowledge.* There are book-length studies dealing, each in its own way, with Shakespeare's treatment of 'sources': T. W. Baldwin's *William Shakspere's Small Latine & Lesse Greeke* (1944), Virgil Whitaker's *Shakespeare's Use of Learning* (1953), Kenneth Muir's *The Sources of Shakespeare's Plays* (1977; supplanting his *Shakespeare's Sources*, 1957), relevant sections of Reuben A. Brower's *Hero & Saint: Shakespeare and the Graeco-Roman Heroic Tradition* (1971), Emrys Jones's *The Origins of Shakespeare* (1977), Robert S. Miola's *Shakespeare's Rome* (1983).

The matter is a difficult one. Who can decide what books Shakespeare actually had in his hand, what pages he turned, and what he made direct use of? Who can estimate what he actually read, retained, and assimilated, copying it out or drawing it up when needed from the recesses of memory? Who can say what was just 'in the air', what conversations, events, acquaintances, experiences contributed to his work? Who can say with certainty what were simply commonplaces, clichés, locutions of the trade if not of the time? Who can draw the line between 'foreground' and 'background'? What is a 'source', what is an 'influence'? What is fact, what is speculation? Those seminal questions cannot be answered here,[1] but they reflect the directions which Shakespeare scholarship has taken and must preface a discussion of the 'sources' of *Julius Caesar* or any other Shakespeare play for that matter.

The heaviest concentration of research has, naturally, been on Shakespeare's use of North's translation of Plutarch's lives of Caesar and Brutus. More than a hundred years of almost microscopic comparison – Stapfer (1880), Delius (1882), MacCallum (1910), Honigmann (1959), Schanzer (1963), Bullough (1964), Maguin (1973), Homan (1976),[2] among many others, as well as extensive treatment in numerous editions, like Macmillan (1902), Wilson (1949), Dorsch (1955), Humphreys (1984) – has shown such detailed and convincing overlapping that it is easy to understand Muir's frank 'there is little new to be said on the subject'.[3] Indeed, all the nooks and crannies have been

[1] They have been discussed by various critics. See, for example, G. K. Hunter, 'Shakespeare's reading', in *A New Companion to Shakespeare Studies*, ed. Kenneth Muir and S. Schoenbaum, 1971, pp. 55–66. F. P. Wilson, 'Shakespeare's reading', *S.Sur.* 3 (1950), 14–21, gives an instructive example of the commonplace that is Hamlet's 'There is nothing either good or bad, but thinking makes it so' (p. 19). The most recent and probing treatment is Robert S. Miola, 'Shakespeare and his sources: observations on the critical history of *Julius Caesar*', *S.Sur.* 40 (1987), 69–76.

[2] Paul Stapfer, *Shakespeare and Classical Antiquity*, trans. Emily J. Carey, 1880; Nicolaus Delius, 'Shakespeare's Julius Caesar und seine Quellen im Plutarch', *SJ* 17 (1882), 67–81; M. W. MacCallum, *Shakespeare's Roman Plays and their Background*, 1910; E. A. J. Honigmann, 'Shakespeare's Plutarch', *SQ* 10 (1959), 25–33; Ernest Schanzer, *The Problem Plays of Shakespeare*, 1963; Geoffrey Bullough, *Narrative and Dramatic Sources of Shakespeare*, 8 vols., 1957–75; Jean-Marie Maguin, 'Preface to a critical approach to *Julius Caesar*', *CahiersE* 4 (1973), 15–49; Sidney Homan, 'Dion, Alexander and Demetrius – Plutarch's forgotten *Parallel Lives* – as mirrors for *Julius Caesar*', *S.St.* 8 (1976), 195–210.

[3] Kenneth Muir, *Shakespeare's Sources*, 1957, p. 187. In the 1977 version, *The Sources of Shakespeare's Plays*, Muir omits the assertion.

searched and illuminated. And the long selections reprinted in the Appendix (pp. 154–83 below) should make Shakespeare's debt immediately obvious and also illuminate the special talents and insights of both the popular dramatist and the moral historian, for it is natural that many treatments of Shakespeare and Plutarch tend to highlight differences, showing Shakespeare at work, the artist absorbing, adapting, modifying, departing within the inescapable frame of historical precedent. For Shakespeare's task (like Plutarch's) was not mainly to reconstruct the past but to superimpose the past upon the present, to make it a contemporary event, a kind of play-within-the-play, a piece of theatre within the *theatrum mundi*.

It is agreed that North's translation of Plutarch was Shakespeare's most carefully, almost pedantically, followed source. History is history – at least in its general outlines. Thus Shakespeare had no choice but to follow the general outlines of the well-known story (a story found in other easily available works as well, like Appian and Suetonius) from the triumph of Munda in October 45 BC to the suicide of Brutus in October 42 BC. But story is not identical with plot: whereas Plutarch is chronological, Shakespeare is causal. Shakespeare creates and shapes *his* plot by selection, expansion, and dramatic spotlighting. He makes direct use of roughly the last quarter of Plutarch's life of Caesar, the last days of Caesar. Omitted are the events which made Caesar the 'foremost man of all this world', the 'noblest man / That ever livèd in the tide of times': the great military campaigns in Gaul, in England, in Asia, in Africa; the intrigues and discord in Rome with Cicero and Cato and Pompey and others; the adventures with pirates, the disguises, the romances, the feasts and fasts – in short, the cinemascope Caesar in Technicolor.

Shakespeare makes more extensive use of the life of Brutus, which is itself more concentrated than that of Caesar, focussing on the conspiracy after devoting only about half a dozen pages to the events of Brutus's life up to the point of Cassius's 'temptation'. But closer analysis reveals that a good part of the detail is likewise to be found in the life of Caesar. The overlapping signals Shakespearean (as well as Plutarchan) highlights, like the 'temptation' scene between Brutus and Cassius in 1.2, the scene between Caesar and Calpurnia on the eve of the assassination (2.2), the assassination itself (3.1), the mob's treatment of Cinna the Poet (3.3), and the appearance of the ghost of Caesar to Brutus in 4.3, among others. The focus is sharpened in a number of ways. It is usually said that Shakespeare compresses the action from three years to five or six days. But compression is a misleading word. Granted, certain events are telescoped: the triumph of Munda, which took place in October 45 BC, is moved to 15 February 44 BC, whereas in Plutarch intervening events, like Caesar's being named 'perpetual Dictator', the dedication of the Temple of Clemency for Caesar's 'courtesy', his plans for enlarging the Roman empire, his reform of the calendar, etc., are related; the proscriptions of November 43 BC seem to follow immediately after the Cinna the Poet episode, whereas in Plutarch the account of the rivalry between Antony and Octavius separates the events; Shakespeare's brief fifth act – a bare 354 lines covering the two pitched battles at Philippi and the suicides of Cassius and Brutus – contrasts sharply with Plutarch's two dozen pages of military and other detail.

This kind of treatment is not so much a matter of compression as of concentration. For it is concentration, combined with repetition, which gives the real contours of the plot. A few examples will suffice. The action of the play consists of uninterrupted conflict situations, personal and political, or personal-political: the presentation of violence, ranging from the serio-comic altercation between the tribunes and the plebeians to the bloody assassination, the burning of Rome, civil war, two majestic battles, and two significant suicides. When there is no actual fighting, there are quarrels; when there are no public meetings, there is conspiracy or precaution. The violence is physical and verbal. And it is extended beyond the level of the activity of the public figures. Shakespeare focusses the plot by, on the one hand, giving greater and more continuous prominence to the plebeians than Plutarch does, thereby stressing a socio-political polarisation and underlining the disastrous consequences of self-interest, if not the unreliability and uncontrollability of all human desires; and, on the other hand, by complementing the public and private levels with the portentous inscrutability of the supernatural both in and outside of Rome. Thus Shakespeare achieves greater concentration by anticipation and repetition, not so much by reordering the events of the narrative as by stressing certain of them, if need be by inventing them (as is the case with the plebeians, especially the expansion of their encounter with Cinna the Poet), by conflating them (as in the two episodes in Plutarch before and after Lupercalia, which in Shakespeare take place in the Forum), and by repeating them (as in the stringing out of the portents over the course of the play).

One kind of Shakespearean spotlighting is attributable, of course, to the very nature of the genres. Plutarch's prose narrative is laced with dialogue, an obvious technique for actualising and stressing certain events. But in the material Shakespeare worked from, Plutarch uses direct discourse only rarely and in the main briefly, in one-line utterances or single-line exchanges. These bits of dialogue, many coming at the end of a little scene, are part of Plutarch's system, a way of enlivening and indeed punctuating dramatic moments. As such, they indicate certain priorities, situations and sentiments which Plutarch deemed important. It is interesting, therefore, to see, for one thing, which are taken over or ignored by Shakespeare and, for another, which bare statements are developed into dramatic units by Shakespeare. Surprisingly, perhaps, Plutarch's little scenes tend to highlight private and personal conflicts and tribulations, the most developed being Portia's desire to share her husband's plans and fate (p. 166 below), and surprising too is Plutarch's use of dialogue in what are for Shakespeare relatively unimportant situations (like the concern of uneasy conspirators) or characters (like Lucius Pella or Lucilius). Shakespeare, for his part, not only dramatises personal situations as well as mainly political scenes lightly sketched in Plutarch, as in Cassius's 'temptation' in 1.2.25–177 (compare pp. 157, 164 below), and in the opening encounter of Murellus and Flavius with the plebeians, but also combines the personal and the political in scenes not found in Plutarch – among the most famous being Brutus's soliloquy at the beginning of the second act.

Perhaps the greatest area of dramatic concentration is the treatment of character, the feature which has received the most critical attention. The difference of genre, as well as of intent, makes comparisons difficult. Since the Shakespearean characters will be discussed below within the total context of the play, perhaps a few distinctions will suffice here. Shakespeare's expansion of the 'temptation' by Cassius from bare outlines in

Plutarch and invention of soliloquies in 2.1 help to create a more doubting and introvert Brutus. He is also more charismatic than in Plutarch, exercising greater authority and influence, as in his 'oath' speech at 2.1.114–40 (Shakespeare's touch), his decision not to kill Cicero (in Plutarch the decision of all the conspirators) or Antony (moved by Shakespeare into this scene), and his being visited by the sick Ligarius (whereas in Plutarch it is Brutus who visits Ligarius). The presentation of Caesar by both authors is more elusive. Plutarch's Caesar, however, is portrayed favourably over a long and illustrious career. It is easy to understand the widespread view that Shakespeare's Caesar, so little speaking and seen, is to a large extent the creation of the personages around him. Shakespeare polarises his strength and weakness: Cassius condemns his weakness, Antony celebrates his strength, whereas in Plutarch Caesar's falling sickness and great exploits go together as mutually reinforcing, ultimately compatible traits. Brutus's soliloquy at 2.1.10–34, among other utterances, underlines the poise of opposites and to a certain extent their incompatibility. Cassius is much easier to deal with. Shakespeare tellingly omits Plutarch's simple motivation: 'But Cassius being a choleric man and hating Caesar privately, more than he did the tyranny openly' (p. 163 below). From no more than outlines in Plutarch Cassius becomes in Shakespeare a full-blown Elizabethan figure: friend, patriot, rebel, egotist, difficult to like or dislike. Casca appears to be all Shakespeare's, but for the name. And Antony, the remaining major figure, emerges in Shakespeare from a position approaching subservience in 1.2 to a powerful controller of forces such as the mob, such as destiny, which are almost impossible to control; his position is made stronger, among other ways, by Shakespeare's imbuing him with great rhetorical gifts and downplaying his rivalry with Octavius.

The source is apparent not only in plot manipulation and character drawing but in direct quotations and verbal echoes. To mention but a few: the 'wonderful' portents before Caesar's death (1.3.15 ff.; Plutarch, p. 158); Caesar's depiction of the 'fat, sleek-headed men' and the 'lean and hungry' Cassius (1.2.192–5; Plutarch, p. 158); Portia's assertion of her obligations as Brutus's wife and not his 'bedfellow and companion in bed and at board only' (2.1.279–87; Plutarch, p. 166); Brutus's declaration to Ligarius of 'A piece of work that will make sick men whole' (2.1.327; Plutarch, p. 165); Artemidorus's exhortation that Caesar read his 'bill' (3.1.3–9; Plutarch, p. 159); Brutus's response to the 'evil spirit': 'then I shall see thee again' (4.3.284; Plutarch, p. 174); Brutus's calling Cassius the 'last of all the Romans' (5.3.99; Plutarch, p. 179).

What is perhaps more interesting than the simple verbal quotations is the influence of certain key words in Plutarch on the thematic focus and structure of *Julius Caesar*. Although such stylistic elements will be discussed in detail below, it might be well to illustrate one in the present context. The word 'constant' and its inflected forms 'constancy' and 'constantly' occur more often in *Julius Caesar* (eight times) than in any other work of Shakespeare's. It is also a frequent and crucial word in Plutarch, where it appears (in the reproduced excerpts) five times in the life of Brutus and refers to five different persons or groups: to Brutus (p. 163), to Portia (p. 166), to the conspirators (p. 167), to the 'unconstant' multitude (p. 171), and to mankind in general (p. 177). Shakespeare parallels Plutarch in applying it ('constancy') to the conspirators (2.1.227) and to Portia (2.1.299, 2.4.6), but then has Brutus address it to Cassius (3.1.22) and

Cassius apply it to himself (5.1.91) in a way not unlike the last instance cited in Plutarch, 'To meet all perils very constantly' in the Stoic manner. Most striking of all is Shakespeare's giving it three times to Caesar (3.1.60, 72, 73) in his ironic and hubristic insistence on his 'constant' position and attitude just a few lines before he is struck down. (The contrast with the additional marginal gloss in Plutarch praising the '*wonderful constancy of Brutus* in matters of justice and *equity*' is drastic.)

The indisputable reliance of Shakespeare on North's translation of the lives of Caesar and Brutus, as well as relevant smaller parts of the life of Antony and perhaps Cicero, has not hindered critics from proposing other works as 'sources'. Since this literature is extensive and at times not uncontroversial, it might be best here to survey the type of influence and indicate summarily the main recent advocates. Since much – if not most – of the criticism of *Julius Caesar* has dealt with character, it is not surprising that major attention has been paid to this feature in source study: Geoffrey Bullough's introduction to his excerpts from what he terms sources, possible sources, and analogues is in large measure organised according to character. To illuminate details of individual characters as well as the 'triple group-relationship' (v, 56) of Caesar, Brutus, and Antony, he reprints, although admitting there is no proof Shakespeare read them, selections of various lengths from Roman historians: *The Histories of Sallust* (whom Shakespeare 'may possibly have read' (v, 8)), Velleius's *Roman History* (for information on Caesar), Lucan's *Pharsalia*, Tacitus's *Annals* (especially for the portrayal of Augustus), Suetonius's *History of the Twelve Caesars* (which 'contributed to the balanced view of the dictator' (v, 14)), Appian's *Civil Wars* (for details about the motivation of Caesar, Brutus, and 'most striking[ly]' Antony (v, 14–15)), and Florus's *Roman Histories* (for a favourable picture of Caesar and an 'antagonistic' one of Brutus, Cassius, and Antony (v, 15)). For further details of events and character, Bullough suggests that Shakespeare 'may have read' Plutarch's lives of Cicero and Cato (v, 36). In fact, other lives have been proposed for the understanding of characters: Honigmann draws attention to the 'Comparison of Dion with Brutus' as throwing light on Brutus; Homan concurs, adding the Life of Alexander (for, among other things, a passage on Caesar's deafness) and the 'Comparison of Demetrius and Antony' (for traits of Antony's character).

Among contemporary works Shakespeare 'probably used', Bullough reprints selections from Sir Thomas Elyot's *Governour* (for illustrations in Caesar of 'several qualities of a good prince' – physical prowess, industry, learning, diligence – as well as Caesar's 'fault in withdrawing from Affability' or embodying Ambition (v, 22–3)) and – although 'there is no evidence that Shakespeare used it' – selections from *The Mirror for Magistrates* as an 'example of pre-Shakespearian moralizing' (v, 24–5).

Verbal parallels beyond those in Plutarch's lives of Caesar and Brutus are likewise abundant. Despite G.K. Hunter's accurate perception that the 'wisdom of the Elizabethans was nearly all traditional wisdom'[1] and, it must be added, traditionally phrased, critics have been active in finding clusters of verbal similarities as well as single instances, which they group under 'sources', from authors as far apart as Cicero and Samuel Daniel. Among the many instances of clusters, Honigmann sees connections

[1] G.K. Hunter, 'Shakespeare's reading', p. 55.

between Plutarch's 'Comparison of Dion with Brutus' and 2.1.10–21 of *Julius Caesar*, his 'Pompeius' and Murellus's long speech at 1.1.31–54, and his 'Cicero' and 2.1.150–2.[1] Bush, Maxwell, and Bullough present the case for Sir Thomas Elyot;[2] Schanzer, Muir, Bullough, and Pearson for the anonymous *Caesar's Revenge*;[3] Rees for Daniel's *Civil Wars* and Taylor for his *Musophilus* and *Letter from Octavia*;[4] Cairncross for the *Hystorie of Hamblet*;[5] Wilson (p. x) and Taylor for Davies's *Nosce Teipsum*;[6] Brooks, Muir, and Bullough for the *Mirror for Magistrates*.[7] Among those to identify single parallels are Muir (for echoes of the portents in Ovid, Virgil, Lucan, and others);[8] Bullough (for Cicero's *De Claris Oratoribus* and the orations in 3.2);[9] Tobin (for Apuleius's *Golden Ass* and the description of Lepidus at 4.1.12–40);[10] and Humphreys (pp. 24–5) (for a summary of the various implications of *Et tu, Brute*). As a whole, these attempts are so numerous and varied in quality that it is impossible to do more here than point in their direction. And one can do even less for a second ring of 'influences' representing Roman and Elizabethan historiography (like Appian and other Roman historians; Machiavelli, Bodin, and Montaigne) and also contemporary and native dramatic traditions (like the French Senecans, Thomas Kyd's *Cornelia*, Pescetti's *Il Cesare*, and Eedes's *Caesar Interfectus*). Except, of course, to mention their existence and, in doing so, to close the circle by repeating how difficult it is to define 'source'. As F. P. Wilson has written: 'Shakespeare knew when to stop even if his critics do not. North's Plutarch was sufficient for his Roman play.'[11] And Shakespeare's dependence on Plutarch is, it should be clear, the measure of his independence.

The play

In the discussion of the date and sources of *Julius Caesar*, as well as in the Textual Analysis, some of the main literary aspects have been touched on: stylistic influences in establishing the date, comparison with Plutarch in defining the Shakespearean focus and structure, bibliographical elements in deducing Shakespeare's conception and revision of his dramatic and poetic intentions. These approaches are essentially external, using evidence drawn from contemporary records, authors, printing practices, and the like to help establish an informed perception of Shakespeare's text. Not surprisingly, however, the analysis of the Shakespearean corpus offers perhaps the strongest evidence for the

1 Honigmann, 'Shakespeare's Plutarch', pp. 26–7, 29, 30.
2 Douglas Bush, '*Julius Caesar* and Elyot's *Governour*', *MLN* 52 (1937), 407–8; J. C. Maxwell, '"Julius Caesar" and Elyot's "Governour"', *N&Q* 201 (1956), 147; Bullough, *Sources*, v, 166–8.
3 Ernest Schanzer, 'A neglected source of "Julius Caesar"', *N&Q* 199 (1954), 196–7; Muir, *Sources*, 1977, pp. 120–1; Bullough, *Sources*, v, 196–211; Jacqueline Pearson, 'Shakespeare and *Caesar's Revenge*', *SQ* 32 (1981), 101–4.
4 Joan Rees, 'Shakespeare's use of Daniel', *MLR* 55 (1960), 79–82; Taylor, '*Musophilus*', pp. 191–5.
5 Andrew S. Cairncross, 'A source for Antony', *ELN* 13 (1975), 4–6.
6 Taylor, '*Musophilus*', pp. 194–5.
7 Harold Brooks (in Dorsch, notes on 2.3.1–5, 3.1.1–2, 6–10, 77); Muir, *Sources*, 1977, pp. 121–2; Bullough, *Sources*, v, 168–73.
8 Muir, *Sources*, 1977, pp. 123–5.
9 Bullough, *Sources*, v, 7.
10 J. J. M. Tobin, 'Apuleius and the proscription scene in *Julius Caesar*', *Archiv* 216 (1979), 348–50.
11 F. P. Wilson, 'Shakespeare's reading', p. 18.

understanding of the play and the author. As G. K. Hunter wisely remarks, in a single sentence easily overlooked in his discussion of the intricacies involved in assessing Shakespeare's reading: 'Nor should we forget the amount that Shakespeare copied from himself.'[1] Indeed, by the end of 1599 Shakespeare had written 21 plays and the entire body of non-dramatic poetry: if not much is known about his person, certainly the impress of his work is unmistakable. For all the talk of its 'singularity' *Julius Caesar* is very recognisably Shakespearean.

THE FRAME

Broadly seen, Shakespeare's concern with the private sphere is most evident in his comedies and poetry, with the public sphere in the history plays. Had Shakespeare not resumed writing tragedies with *Julius Caesar*, the two tragedies which preceded it, *Titus Andronicus* and *Romeo and Juliet*, might *mutatis mutandis* be assigned to the histories and comedies respectively. But the question of genre need not be stretched or stressed. What is apparent from the Yorkist and Lancastrian tetralogies and *King John* is Shakespeare's interest in public affairs, in problems of power and rule, in the qualities of the ideal governor, in the confrontation of ideologies, in the clash of armies, in civil conflict, in the collision of the high and low members of the body politic, in history *qua* history. What is even more apparent, and very typical of Shakespeare, is the crystallisation of character in history, the emergence of individual personalities, and thus the inextricability of public and private affairs. This focus, especially since it involves a leading figure who is the key to the fate of all the others, serves to illuminate his individualised psychological features as they emerge from or respond to overt bustle and battle, secret conspiracy and counsel, society and isolation. This inexorable mixture of concerns is in itself a record of human events, one of the major forms of historiography. And the interest in individual responses is also an added structural device for perceiving and ordering the episodes of history. In other words, chronology is complemented by psychology, both contributing to, but not entirely constituting, the overall *Weltanschauung* of *Julius Caesar*, for what else emerges with the regularity of ritual – and thus a further structural device – is a sense of the national past, present, and future: that continuity which takes the form of consciousness of one's forefathers, patriotism towards the existing state, responsibility to posterity for the outcome of events. Heritage, in fact, is coupled with destiny, whether personal or national. And destiny, an enveloping dimension, involves more than the accurate report of an individual plight or the dramatisation of the tide of the times. For Shakespeare blends in the extra-sensory: portents, visions, and dreams. He employs metadramatic allusions, analogies between the theatre and the world, playing and being: in the individual, by such means as the distancing use of apostrophes and the large store of mnemonic devices; in the action, by the presence of allegory and the enactment of ritual. Interfused with and yet crowning all is the super-natural: the reference to, if not the superimposed presence of, something 'outside': the interplay of a superlunary realm, the operations of fate, the gods, mysterious and undeniable metaphysical forces.

[1] G. K. Hunter, 'Shakespeare's reading', p. 59.

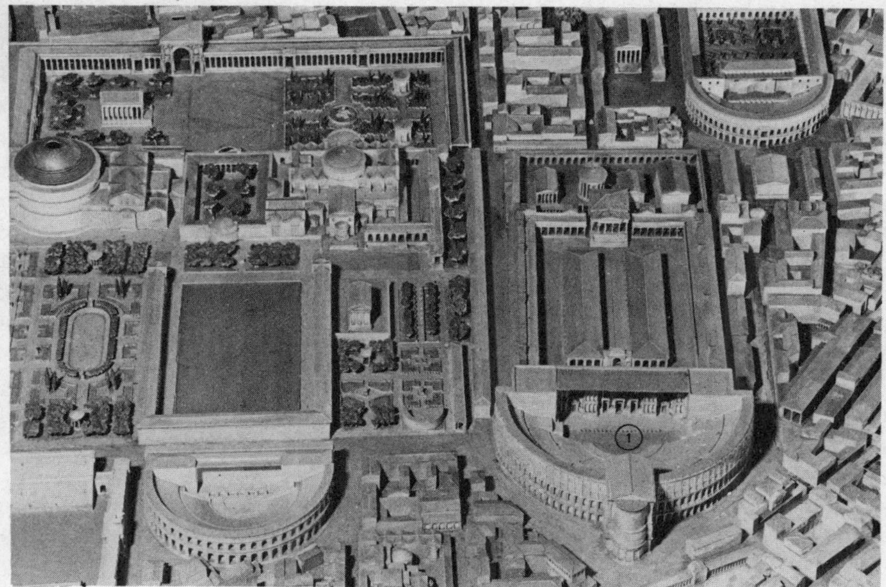

4 Model of Imperial Rome, showing the Theatre and Portico of Pompey (1), where Caesar was assassinated, and buildings of later date

STRUCTURE

Despite the fact that the action of *Julius Caesar* is chronological, a shadowing of the historical events outlined in Plutarch and other sources with some distinctive highlighting by Shakespeare, some critics have drawn attention to what appears to be a 'two-peak' action. Fleay was among the first to remark on the sharp division between the first three acts and the last two.[1] The first part portrays a steadily increasing tension beginning with the quarrel between the tribunes and the plebeians, which not only opens but also foreshadows the ensuing dissension, as do the supernatural omens and portents on a parallel level; continuing with the 'temptation' of Brutus by Cassius and the solitary self-questioning and self-divisiveness of Brutus; mounting with the resoluteness and consolidation of the conspirators set against the menacing power and isolation of Caesar; growing complicated with the ambiguities of assessing persons and interpreting events and prophecies; coming to a crescendo in a ritual of assassination which takes place almost privately in the confines of the Capitol; then reverberating in the public display of the body, the perversion of the plebeians, the dispersal of the conspirators, and the burning of Rome – with the disposing of Cinna the Poet in 3.3 as a devastatingly ironic rendition of all that has led up to the climax.[2] The second part, beginning with the

[1] Frederick Gard Fleay, *A Chronicle History of the Life and Work of William Shakespeare*, 1886, p. 215.

[2] Nicholas Brooke, *Shakespeare's Early Tragedies*, 1968, p. 158, calls it a 'final emblem ... the brutal little farce'; John W. Velz, '"If I were Brutus now...": role-playing in Julius Caesar', *S.St.* 4 (1968), 153, a 'pathetic microcosm of the assassination'. For an attempted application in Christian terms, see Norman N. Holland, 'The "Cinna" and "Cynicke" episodes in *Julius Caesar*', *SQ* 11 (1960), 439–44.

likewise devastatingly ironic proscription scene (which rehearses in but a few lines the earlier manœuvring and ruthlessness and foreshadows personal and public conflicts to come), also mounts to a resolution, albeit in another key: the increasing political and military unrest and dissension reflected in the altercation and ultimate impossibility of reconciliation of Brutus and Cassius; the growing isolation of Brutus; the swift ascent and yet almost programmed decline of Antony against the growing prominence of a new young man, Octavius; the climactic battles with their ambiguous outcomes and mistaken consequences (like Cassius's suicide); and the final submission of Brutus (like the assassination of Caesar), at once a defeat and a victory – with the whole action of Acts 4 and 5, as in the first part, permeated by reminders of the past, portents regarding the present, and in the presiding ghost of Caesar the personal, political, and cosmological interactions and consequences of human actions.[1]

Fleay interpreted this structure formally, as the result of a combining of two plays, *Caesar's Tragedy* and *Caesar's Revenge.* Although few would agree with his attribution of the structure to dual authorship and the pressure of contemporary dramatic fashions, many do remark that the structure is somehow striking and unusual, for them another indication of the singularity of *Julius Caesar.* Still, the contours of the action, the dramatic and tragic structure, accord with normal critical as well as Shakespearean modes. The major climax or climaxes in roughly the middle of the play are standard Shakespearean practice in comedy, history, and tragedy; critics from Aristotle to Freytag to Frye would approvingly agree. The apparent anti-climax of what is roughly the fourth and early parts of the fifth acts is not only Shakespearean but also quite natural. Certainly, apart from what is often a convulsive and frantic resolution at the very end, it is hardly surprising that the intensity of the central climaxes cannot be matched: the strain would be too great for audience and author alike. Besides, it is not that there is a lull in the action but that a certain deepening of effect and reorganisation of forces take place. Thus *Julius Caesar* shares with *Romeo and Juliet*, recently finished, and *Hamlet*, in progress, a second half which is marked by the growing isolation of the hero, his estrangement from all around him, indeed his physical displacement to a foreign context (Romeo from Verona, Brutus from Rome, Hamlet from Denmark); by a series of smaller but nonetheless passionate altercations, acts of frustration leading (strangely) to a kind of resoluteness; by a feeling, after the main climaxes, of let-down, of chances missed or mismanaged or misadventured; by a growing awareness of the irreversibility of events and an acceptance of that situation: 'I am fortune's fool', Romeo admits; 'There's a divinity that shapes our ends', Hamlet acknowledges; 'Julius Caesar, thou art mighty yet', Brutus concedes. The catastrophes and dénouements are, in their outlines, so similar as to be ritualistic: a final burst of energy – be it in a graveyard, on the field of battle, in a royal palace – an explosive physical action marked by error or misconception, an action so precipitate that the death of the hero seems self-willed, a suicide. And then the words of reconciliation, the

[1] The interrelationship – repetitions, parallels, mirrorings, pairings, and foreshadowings – of the first three and the last two acts has from the beginning been one of the favourite subjects of *Julius Caesar* criticism – see, for example, Albert Lindner, 'Die dramatische Einheit im Julius Cäsar', *SJ* 2 (1867), 90–5; John Palmer, 'Marcus Brutus', in his *Political Characters of Shakespeare*, 1945, pp. 1–64, esp. pp. 33–46; Adrien Bonjour, *The Structure of 'Julius Caesar'*, 1958, p. 30, n. 33; R. A. Yoder, 'History and the histories in *Julius Caesar*', *SQ* 24 (1973), 309–27, esp. pp. 311–14.

apparent personal and public harmony in a final eulogy, the stillness and rest after the fray.

What is perhaps more precisely characteristic of Shakespearean tragedy, more striking and significant in *Julius Caesar* than in earlier tragedies, is the reversibility of public and private scenes. It is not so much that there are public and private scenes or that there is a conflict between a public and a private self as that the public scenes tend to develop private concerns as well as public ones, and that the private scenes are simultaneously public ones in intent and result. Notwithstanding modern designations of *Julius Caesar* – Roman play, revenge play, problem play, or whatever – this inside-out effect is certainly derived from the practice and indeed very nature of Shakespeare's history plays. Richard III's wooing of Lady Anne, widow of the heir to the throne, and Henry V's of Katherine, Princess of France, both employing the conventional military/sexual imagery of the courtship of comedy, are obvious and literal enactments of military and political victories, both soldier-kings portrayed as conqueror-husbands. Lady Anne's acceptance of Richard's ring after he has put up his sword and made his peace and the princess's serio-comic English lessons may be construed as signals of submission, as prefiguring the fall of the House of Lancaster to York in the one instance, the fall of France to England in the other. The lamenting choric diatribes against the 'hell-hound' Richard by the three mourning queens (*Richard III* 4.4.35 ff.), the garden scene (3.4) in *Richard II*, the tavern scenes in *1* and *2 Henry IV*, to cite but three further examples from many, are public scenes in the guise of private ones. In *Julius Caesar* the great scenes between Brutus and Cassius are private in that the two are alone – as in 1.2.25–177 and, mirror-like, in 4.3.1–123 – and asserting their personal, almost domestic claims on each other and yet public in their issues (the first encounter being played against the public celebration of Lupercalia and the second within the context of the military campaign against Octavius and Antony). Their subject is always self and society, not by turns but simultaneously.

Most prominent are two domestic events derived from Plutarch but very typically Shakespearean in the direct presentation of immediately recognisable intimate scenes. Rulers who are uneasy about their crowns are the subjects of Shakespeare's histories and tragedies. They are characteristically sleepless, a state which portrays less their agitation or weakness or self-doubt than their isolation. In such instances Webster may have shown the skull beneath the skin, but Shakespeare is likely to show first the nightcap beneath the crown.[1] Both Brutus and Caesar, in the night, alone and awake, are joined by their sleepless wives, Portia and Calpurnia, in adjoining scenes, 2.1 and 2.2, the mighty Caesar in his nightgown. Portia's concern for her husband's strange behaviour, the possibility of his catching cold in the dank morning, her desire to know his 'secret' may be traceable to her marriage vow, 'Which did incorporate and make us one' (2.1.273), just as it may explain Lady Hotspur's lighter inquisitiveness about her husband's likewise strange and secretive behaviour (*1 Henry IV* 2.3.37 ff.): both husbands have left the marriage bed, both wives are alarmed by the 'portents' signified by the odd

[1] *The Tatler* (no. 53, 11 August 1709; reprinted in Anglistica & Americana 100, 1970, p. 33) finds Caesar's appearance in his nightgown in no way diminishing that 'great soul'; on the contrary, it is enhanced since 'his genius was above ... mechanic methods of showing greatness'.

behaviour, both use the adjective 'heavy' to describe the situation. The argument about husband and wife being 'incorporate' – made one – is likewise used by both wives (as it had been from the beginning of Shakespeare's career in Adriana's 'undividable incorporate' (*Comedy of Errors* 2.2.122)). What is remarkable about the private scene is its inflection of the public theme: an inquiry into the nature of man's relationship to himself and to the world about him, of rulers to subjects, of nobles to nobles, of husbands to wives.[1] The key words are 'unity', 'incorporate', 'one' – to which may be added even the polarities of disposition and weather, 'ungentle' against 'gentle', the 'dank morning' against the 'wholesome bed', among many others. And with special reference to the conspiracy as well is the resounding of the concern for secrecy, disclosure, keeping counsel. Above all, the keystone of personal and political behaviour, as of marriage, receives its fullest expression in the dominant word 'constancy', from the beginning to the end of Shakespeare's career, in poems, comedies, histories, and tragedies, at the heart of the Shakespearean ethic.

The nocturnal scene between Caesar and Calpurnia, which follows directly, deepens the concern. Like Portia, Calpurnia is worried about her husband's well-being. She too, who 'never stood on ceremonies' (2.2.13), is made uneasy by portents and omens. She has had bad dreams. Like others in the play – the Soothsayer, Decius, Antony – she is an interpreter and, more important perhaps, a proposer of action based on her assessment of 'these things ... beyond all use' (25). She knows her husband: 'Your wisdom is consumed in confidence' (49). Her judgement, however, is not merely a wife's; it is the judgement of the conspirators. It is the judgement, further, upon which is based that tragedy, formal and human, of the fall of princes. Her reaction to a world of uncertainty and change is traditional: 'And I do fear them' (26), echoing or anticipating what constitutes a Shakespearean commonplace, as in 'Be wary then, best safety lies in fear', Laertes' caution to Ophelia (*Hamlet* 1.3.43). Calpurnia's specific advice is not unlike that which Brutus says must govern the conspirators: 'Hide it [the "monstrous visage" of conspiracy] in smiles and affability' (2.1.82). Calpurnia's attitude is climaxed in the last words she speaks in the play: they constitute a political message in a private formula. Emphasising Caesar's decision not to go to the Capitol, she instructs Decius to 'Say he is sick' (2.2.65).

The simultaneity of public and private concerns implies still another overlapping of structural and thematic consequence. By most medieval and Renaissance historians and poets, history was regarded as a window to the past, the present, and the future. More accurately, perhaps, it was, on the one hand, continuous – updating, the adding of new figures and new scenes, was the standard practice. It was, on the other hand, still to a good measure figural – omnitemporal ('synchrony' might be a better translation than 'omnitemporalness' of Erich Auerbach's *Jederzeitlichkeit*), if not in the view that all events in universal history are contained in the one great Christian drama from the Creation to the Last Judgement, then at least in the general habit of thinking and organising human experience in this manner, as is evident – *inter alia* – in the persistence of mythical or legendary personages and events in Elizabethan historiography and of course in the

[1] Robert S. Miola, *Shakespeare's Rome*, 1983, p. 97: 'These two wives represent forces and ideals crucial to the city ... Their anguish conveys Shakespeare's increasingly critical conception of Rome and Roman values.'

popularity of allegory.[1] This penchant towards synchrony is apparent in various ways in *Julius Caesar*, affecting structure, theme, and style.

A dominant concern in the play is time. For various dramatic reasons Shakespeare, as has been mentioned earlier, takes liberties with time: it is his general practice to modify, to compress or expand, time as need be. Within the play, moreover, there is an inordinate interest in time, the vocabulary of which is extensive, the major word-classes amply represented. Apart from the obvious but powerful employment of night and day (affording a context, setting off and emphasising many of the polarities in the play) and the frequent references to the time of day (literally and symbolically useful for events dependent upon synchronisation and precision, like conspiracies, assassinations, battles), the characters and action are not simply looking at an event but are looking back and looking forward in time. Looking back is not a nostalgic view of Rome in the good old days or an easy appeal to patriotic sentiments. For one thing, the Brutus 'once that would have brooked / Th'eternal devil to keep his state in Rome' (1.2.159–60) is not merely Brutus's ancestor, he is also his namesake – a neat way of superimposing the past upon the present.[2] For another, history superimposes other ancestors, legendary figures of identification, like Aeneas (ever-recurring in Elizabethan times), even larger than life- or legend-size figures, like the Colossus. Similarly, looking forward is not a short-sighted view of Rome in the time of or just after Caesar, concentrating on political and military matters, on 'who's in, who's out'; it involves more than what will happen tomorrow, on the Ides of March. The future finds expression in omens and prophecies. The future is connected with the present, as with the past, but not simply by the ceaseless movement of the clock – 'from hour to hour, we ripe and ripe, / And then from hour to hour, we rot and rot', as Touchstone puts it (*As You Like It* 2.7.26–7) – but by 'irrational' and unpredictable forces. The portents and predictions, signs and spirits – the whole assembly of melodramatic clap-trap devices and appearances – are more than Shakespeare's employment of the paraphernalia of the revenge play or some other fashion of the time: they are his expression of something beyond as well as within. In the seemingly cold and calculating Roman world, and for all the rational planning and logical deductions, they prove an undeniable and inexorable force of the future in the present. For the future is not what is to come but the working out of destiny in the moment.

Given this context, it is not necessary to fault Shakespeare for using anachronisms (like the clock striking at 2.1.191) or to apologise for him by pointing out that some are

[1] Although a distinction is to be made between medieval and Renaissance historiography, it is undeniable that they co-existed, to one degree or another, in the time of Shakespeare. See, for example, R. G. Collingwood, *The Idea of History*, 1946, pp. 46–58; Irving Ribner, 'The Tudor history play: an essay in definition', *PMLA* 69 (1954), 591–609 (esp. p. 602), and his *The English History Play in the Age of Shakespeare*, 1957, esp. pp. 21–6; and J. G. A. Pocock, 'The sense of history in Renaissance England', in *William Shakespeare: His World, His Work, His Influence*, ed. John F. Andrews, 3 vols., 1985, I, 143–57; for views of Roman history in Shakespeare's time, T. J. B. Spencer, 'Shakespeare and the Elizabethan Romans', *S.Sur.* 10 (1957), 27–38, and J. Leeds Barroll, 'Shakespeare and Roman history', *MLR* 53 (1958), 327–43. It is self-evident that Shakespeare was very much in the tradition of the older, providential view of history. H. B. Charlton, *Shakespearian Tragedy*, 1948, pp. 72–4, finds evidence for this view both in Philemon Holland, Plutarch's Elizabethan translator, and indeed in Plutarch's *Morals*.

[2] Ralph Berry, 'Julius Caesar: a Roman tragedy', *DR* 61 (1981), 327, mentions the 'obsessive awareness of ancestry' as an important feature of the Romanness, the 'communal identity' of the Romans: 'what the Romans imitate is their ancestry; what they aspire to be is the reflection of the dead' (335).

found in North and Amyot or that he was too concerned with more important matters to be bothered by trifles or that he was habitually careless. They are as natural to the historiography he was reflecting as they were to the dramatic tradition which he inherited, as, indeed, to the visual arts around him and of course to the architecture of theatres (not to mention the name and motto of his own theatre) as well as to matters ranging from theatrical gesture and enunciation to staging and costuming.[1] In all, there was hardly purity or singleness of form or focus, the age itself tending towards practical eclecticism or at least the co-existence of various styles, even opposites, which marks an age of transition. Seen both within the immediate dramatic context and the larger historiographic one, the discussion of anachronisms as lapses or curiosities is by and large irrelevant.

A further dimension, connecting the structural with the stylistic, is to be found in inflections of a self-conscious historicity practised by the characters themselves. They are not merely characters in a play but characters who seem, at crucial moments, to be aware of the fact that they are characters performing and that what they are performing is being viewed by others and will be so in the future.[2] This added dimension, which conveys a certain historical verisimilitude, takes various forms: in actions, stance, even grammar and vocabulary.

Actions of this kind are to be found in enacted rituals, like the Lupercalia, in which the actors assume roles; in Antony's historical identification of Caesar – 'Thou art the ruins of the noblest man / That ever livèd in the tide of times' (3.1.256–7) – and then his assumption of the role of augurer in interpreting the wounds 'Which like dumb mouths do ope their ruby lips / To beg the voice and utterance of my tongue' (3.1.260–1); in Brutus's abstracting and transforming the literal event – 'Let's be sacrificers, but not butchers, Caius' (2.1.166)[3] – and in Cassius's famous prophetic utterance in which the ritual becomes the mythic:

How many ages hence
Shall this our lofty scene be acted over
In states unborn and accents yet unknown! (3.1.111–13)

To which Brutus replies, with some irony (Shakespeare can seldom resist the temptation to make fun of his profession) about the way the scene will be played: 'How many times shall Caesar bleed in sport'. Actions of this kind are also to be found in the numerous plays-within-plays, most obviously in Cassius's re-enacting (in 1.2), with dialogue and stage business, his saving of the drowning Caesar; and in the quadruple presentation of Caesar's refusing the crown in 1.2: its historicity is confirmed in the first instance by off-

[1] G. Wilson Knight, *The Imperial Theme*, 1931, pp. 35–6, feels many of the anachronisms referring to 'ordinary things' contribute to a 'peculiar sensitiveness to human appearance and human "spirit": a vivid apprehension of human life' (p. 34).

[2] For various views on the function of role-playing, Velz, 'Role-playing in Julius Caesar', p. 150: 'Numerous characters ... adopt, or consider adopting, roles which other characters have played'; Thomas F. Van Laan, *Role-Playing in Shakespeare*, 1978, p. 153: 'the *act* of projecting a representation of the self which is superior to the reality is ... without doubt the most characteristic act of the play'; Berry, 'Julius Caesar', p. 329: 'The Romans are playing the roles, not of others, but of themselves.'

[3] The most often mentioned treatment of ritual and ceremony is Brents Stirling, '"Or else this were a savage spectacle"', *PMLA* 66 (1951), 765–74.

stage sounds commented on by Cassius and Brutus and, in the second, by the playlet of Casca, who re-enacts the scene he has witnessed, supplying it synaesthetically with the sight, sound, smell, feel, and taste of the off-stage event. Among many other examples – randomly chosen from some not often noticed – are the ominous and unusual events surrounding and thus punctuating the literal actions: the universal perspective of 'The heavens themselves blaze forth the death of princes' (2.2.31); Brutus's assurance to the plebeians that 'The question of [Caesar's] death is enrolled in the Capitol' (3.2.32–3); the strikingly ritualistic and self-conscious flyting, even the formula describing it, 'Words before blows' (5.1.27); Cassius's reference to the conquered being 'led in triumph / Through the streets of Rome' (5.1.108–9); the action-within-the-action of Pindarus's report of Titinius's plight (5.3.28–32); and Brutus's delivering posterity's eulogy of himself for the act of suicide he is about to perform:

I shall have glory by this losing day
More than Octavius and Mark Antony
By this vile conquest shall attain unto. (5.5.36–8)

These performed or visualised actions-within-the-actions are complemented by a certain histrionic stance and expression. Quite apart from Shakespeare's obvious intention to write a noble, a Roman, play[1] (the remoteness of the original event and the glamour of the illustrious characters adding an immediate statuesqueness to their presence), Shakespeare employs certain linguistic devices to stress the distance of the characters from the event. Inset speeches, notably the funeral orations of Brutus and Antony, are, as various analyses have shown,[2] rhetorical exercises following traditional models, not the characters' normal discourse. A further dimension is added, in the one, by the fact that Brutus's oration is delivered almost in a vacuum of formality, and the reaction of the plebeians appropriately mechanical; and, in the other, by Antony's vigorously self-conscious awareness that he is delivering a speech, his attention to the effect of his speech as he delivers it, indeed his comments during his speech on the response of his audience. Another form of distancing is evident in the numerous images and references from the theatre itself: actors and players acting parts, plays, scenes, shows, spectacles in a theatre to audiences who applaud, clap, hiss, hoot. Still another form of distancing is to be found in the numerous apostrophes, especially those beginning with 'O' and addressing abstractions – 'O grief' (1.3.111), 'O conspiracy' (2.1.77), 'O constancy' (2.4.6), 'O judgement' (3.2.96), 'O murd'rous slumber'

[1] Chambers, *Shakespeare*, I, 399, speaks for the many: 'Shakespeare is deliberately experimenting in a classical manner, with an extreme simplicity both of vocabulary and of phrasing.' For the style of Plutarch and its connection to Shakespeare, see Reuben A. Brower, 'The discovery of Plutarch: *Julius Caesar*', in his *Hero & Saint: Shakespeare and the Graeco-Roman Tradition*, 1971, pp. 204–38.

[2] See, for example, Walther Azzalino, 'Stilkundliche Betrachtung der Reden des Brutus und des Antonius in Shakespeares "Julius Caesar" (III, 2)', *Neuphilologische Monatsschrift* 11 (1940), 249–71; for Brutus's Forum speech based on the principles of Quintilian and Cicero, Maria Wickert, 'Antikes Gedankengut in Shakespeares Julius Cäsar', *SJ* 82/83 (1948), 11–33; for wider ranging applications: Jean Fuzier, 'Rhetoric *versus* rhetoric: a study of Shakespeare's *Julius Caesar*, act III, scene 2', *CahiersE* 5 (1974), 25–65; John W. Velz, '*Orator* and *Imperator* in *Julius Caesar*: style and the process of Roman history', *S.St.* 15 (1982), 55–75; Anne Barton, '*Julius Caesar* and *Coriolanus*: Shakespeare's Roman world of words', in *Shakespeare's Craft*, ed. Philip H. Highfill, Jr, 1982, pp. 24–47.

(4.3.267), 'O hateful error' (5.3.67), 'O error' (5.3.69) – as well as personalising places, as in 'O Rome, I make thee promise' (2.1.56) and 'O world' (3.1.207, 208).

The use of the third person in reference to oneself serves likewise to supplement the actual person with another whose being and actions are somehow separate and observable, co-existing, but on another level of the action. This dissociation – not necessarily pathological but certainly stressing the simultaneity of public and private selves – is not solely evident in Caesar, though practised by the historical Caesar in his own writings (as it was by Thucydides) to give them an official or objective character. It is more than just the royal prerogative: 'The Queen is not amused' may be taken lightly, but the captured Richard II's 'What must the king do now?' is quite another matter. Caesar may refer to himself as Caesar nineteen times in the play – almost always evoking a negative response in critics[1] – but others, interestingly enough, refer to themselves in the third person as well: among the major characters, Antony three times, Brutus thirteen times, Casca once, Cassius fourteen times, and Portia once.[2] In addition to the psychological and other implications,[3] the overall effect is a certain stateliness, a classical look, a consciousness on the part of the actors that they are acting in a not so everyday context. The audience too is constantly reminded that it is in the theatre, that it is not witnessing the action through the naturalistic invisible fourth wall, and in fact that it is observing actions which are themselves being observed, and, given these conditions, that these actions are not so much literal as exemplary: that, in other words, 'the purpose of playing', as Hamlet, who should know, puts it, 'whose end, both at the first and now, was and is, to hold as 'twere the mirror up to nature: to show virtue her feature, scorn her own image, and the very age and body of the time his form and pressure' (*Hamlet* 3.2.20–4).

Hamlet's characterisation implies more than a literal rendition in what is usually called a naturalistic manner. The 'nature' he refers to is general nature, the recognisable and repeated outlines of the human experience. It is not surprising that Shakespeare adapts his style to frame and enforce, through moralising didacticism, the enacted events. At times he takes a small hint from Plutarch and phrases it in the manner of a sententious statement. Plutarch's explanation for Caesar's not consenting to 'have a guard for the safety of his person' is to report that Caesar 'said it was better to die once than always to be afraid of death' (p. 155); Shakespeare doubles the sentiment:

[1] Already evident in earlier critics, like Edward Dowden, *Shakspere: A Critical Study of His Mind and Art*, 1897, p. 285: 'He is a *numen* to himself, speaking of Caesar in the third person, as if of some power above and behind his consciousness.' This stylistic feature, illeism, which Shakespeare 'may have thought characteristically Roman', is mentioned in John W. Velz, 'The ancient world in Shakespeare: authenticity or anachronism? A retrospect', *S.Sur.* 31 (1978), 9–10, in his larger treatment of what Rome was to Shakespeare (7–12).

[2] The exact references are to be found in the concordances to the speakers' parts, in volume 3 of my *Complete and Systematic Concordance to the Works of Shakespeare*, 9 vols., 1968–80. The statistics mentioned do not include the instances of ambiguity between the third person in direct discourse and the vocative discussed in the Commentary at 2.1.255, 3.1.76, 3.1.77.

[3] For various functions of names, see, for example, R. A. Foakes, 'An approach to *Julius Caesar*', *SQ* 5 (1954), 265–8; Lawrence Danson, *Tragic Alphabet: Shakespeare's Drama of Language*, 1974, pp. 61–3; Berry, 'Julius Caesar', p. 328.

Cowards die many times before their deaths,
The valiant never taste of death but once.
Of all the wonders that I yet have heard
It seems to me most strange that men should fear,
Seeing that death, a necessary end,
Will come when it will come.
(2.2.32–7)

In Plutarch, Caesar, 'talk falling out amongst them, reasoning what death was best ... cried out aloud: "Death unlooked for"' (p. 158); Shakespeare transfers the sentiment to Brutus and transforms it tellingly: 'That we shall die we know: 'tis but the time, / And drawing days out, that men stand upon' (3.1.99–100). Brutus, sententiously, becomes the main spokesman for the philosophical and tragic locus of the play. In responding to Messala's report of the death of Portia, Brutus (in a much-discussed and often misunderstood response[1]) says

We must die, Messala.
With meditating that she must die once,
I have the patience to endure it now.
(4.3.190–2)

Before the fateful battle, Brutus intones:

O, that a man might know
The end of this day's business ere it come!
But it sufficeth that the day will end,
And then the end is known.
(5.1.122–5)

THEME

The purpose of the *sententiae* is not confined to theatrical distancing by means of mnemonic phrasing, nor to didactic moralising. The stylistic devices serve to inflect the all-embracing theme of the play – the tension between the 'tide of times' and 'the necessary end'. In *Julius Caesar* change is so often inflected and stressed that the play becomes, on all levels, a dramatisation not merely of instances of change, however drastic, but of uncertainty and instability in the affairs of men. From the opening scene, with its emphasis as much on the change of heroes (from Pompey to Caesar) as on the changeability of the plebeians, to the confusion over the outcome of the battle at Philippi and the 'mistaken' suicide of Cassius, there is hardly an action or scene which does not give evidence of change. It may be in alchemical images, as in Cassius's appraisal of Brutus – 'I see / Thy honourable metal may be wrought / From that it is disposed' (1.2.297–9) – or Casca's 'His countenance, like richest alchemy, / Will change to virtue and to worthiness' (1.3.159–60), both echoes of the tribunes' indictment of the fickle commoners: 'See where their basest metal be not moved' (1.1.60). It may be in the countless references to standing and falling, ebbing and flowing, and the 'full circle of events'.[2] It is found in the construction of scenes which often consist of opposing

[1] See below, p. 149.

[2] See, for example, Bonjour, *Structure*, pp. 62–73; John W. Velz, 'Undular structure in "Julius Caesar"', *MLR* 66 (1971), 21–30; Foakes, 'An approach', p. 260.

interpretations of a particular issue or event: portents and omens, for example, are normally interpreted in dramatically opposite ways, either by being ignored ('He is a dreamer', says Caesar of the Soothsayer) or by being advocated by two or more juxtaposed characters (as in Calpurnia's and Decius's advice to Caesar to avoid or not to avoid going to the Capitol). Or apparent incompatibles are presented side by side, producing not simply a lack of clarity or an ambiguity but an inevitable collision and even impossibility: Pompey may give way to Caesar, Caesar to the conspirators, Brutus and Cassius to Octavius and Antony, Antony to Octavius, each change doubtful in its stated or implied motivation. Neither ambiguity *per se* nor irony alone will suffice for the concurrence of Caesar, 'the foremost man of all this world' (4.3.22), of Brutus, 'the noblest Roman of them all' (5.5.68), and Cassius 'The last of all the Romans ... It is impossible that ever Rome / Should breed thy fellow' (5.3.99–101).

The fluidity and unpredictability of the action is reinforced by Shakespeare's minute attention to the motivation of the characters. Of course, the much-discussed and widely accepted discussion of a deliberate ambiguity of response (see below, pp. 27–30) supplies some part of the explanation. But it focusses largely on the response of the audience, not on a character's own response to his situation. Caesar may be an enigma: to some critics he is an arrogant tyrant, to others he is more sinned against than sinning.[1] But Caesar himself has few doubts about his role. Even Brutus, whom Cassius does not so much tempt as confirm in that which has already been in his thoughts, has doubts not so much about the assassination as about how it is to be done and how it is to be linguistically phrased so as to be publicly (as well as personally) acceptable. What seems to unite all the characters, to be the motor of their thoughts and actions, is self-justification, which serves both for self-characterisation and, most important here, as a way of structuring the overall unsatisfactory – that is, unstable – situation. The important characters tend to define themselves in terms of a fixed trait. And that trait, which is to focus and clarify, to shackle accidents, to stem the tide, is constancy. Whether used naïvely or shrewdly, simply or ironically, constancy – like 'true' in *1 Henry IV* – is the major dramatic, psychological, social, and political ideal, whatever its ultimate consequences.[2] Caesar's repeated application of it to himself is answered by the repeated stabs

[1] The literature on the subject is vast, discussed by practically all the works on the Reading List (p. 184 below). For a survey of the way Caesar was viewed in the dramatic, especially Senecan, tradition in the Renaissance, see Harry Morgan Ayres, 'Shakespeare's *Julius Caesar* in the light of some other versions', *PMLA* 25 (1910), 183–227, and T. J. B. Spencer, '*Julius Caesar* and *Antony and Cleopatra*', in *Shakespeare: Select Bibliographical Guides*, ed. Stanley Wells, 1973, pp. 203–15. For the Caesar 'Mythos' from his time to the Renaissance, see Bullough, *Sources*, v, 4–25.

[2] For 'the presence of opposite implications within the single word' – among them 'constant' – see Robert C. Reynolds, 'Ironic epithet in *Julius Caesar*', *SQ* 24 (1973), 330. To the list may be added a number of abstractions, like 'virtue', 'honour', and 'humour'. For the Elizabethan 'ambivalence toward the ancient virtue of constancy', see Ruth M. Levitsky, '"The elements were so mix'd..."', *PMLA* 88 (1973), 244. A recent discussion of the simultaneity of opposites is Jan H. Blits, 'Caesar's ambiguous end', in his *The End of the Ancient Republic: Essays on 'Julius Caesar'*, 1982, pp. 63–91. Constancy, especially in connection with Stoicism, is focussed on by, for example, John Anson, 'Julius Caesar: the politics of the hardened heart', *S.St.* 2 (1966), 11–33; and Marvin L. Vawter, '"Division 'tween our souls": Shakespeare's Stoic Brutus', *S.St.* 7 (1974), 173–95. The inaccurate and contradictory use of the term 'Stoic' in discussions of the play is summarised and criticised by Gilles D. Monsarrat, *Light from the Porch: Stoicism and English Renaissance Literature*, 1984, pp. 139–44.

of the conspirators, and his '*Et tu, Brute*' seems his surprised, puzzled, and certainly disappointed response to Brutus's lack of constancy. Brutus's constancy to his Roman heritage binds him to a course involving an act resembling regicide, if not parricide. Cassius's constancy to his own course is the basis of his bond to Brutus and at the same time the cause of their estrangement. Antony emerges as individual and leader when he recognises his constancy to Caesar. Portia, in her nocturnal scene with Brutus, apostrophises constancy as the key to all human relationships. Brutus's last and most comforting awareness, the crowning assertion of the unchanging value of constancy, is the prologue to his suicide: 'Countrymen, / My heart doth joy that yet in all my life / I found no man but he was true to me' (5.5.33–5). The absoluteness of the statement – 'in all my life', 'no man', 'true' – is less the result of Brutus's naïve or blind idealism, less an ironic reflection on his unsuccessful action, than the assertion of the only satisfactory answer to the way the world is: This above all . . .

Between the prevalence of change and the desire for constancy lies the world which is Rome. One response to the gap, a major psychological and existential one, is fear. Plutarch's not infrequent use of the word and its inflections (a total of seventeen times in the extracts given in the Appendix) is expanded by Shakespeare to 41 instances spoken by no fewer than sixteen characters and covering the semantic spectrum from timorousness to concern to apprehension to dread. In the entire canon this total is surpassed only by *Macbeth* (45) and *Richard III* (43). Since all but three occurrences are in the first three acts, in which are found all the usages by the two leading practitioners, Cassius (nine) and Caesar (seven), the effect on the portrayal of Rome needs little discussion. Another major mode of response, perhaps less noticed but also to be found in Plutarch and emphasised by Shakespeare, is the verb 'prevent', the noun 'prevention'. It appears at six crucial moments: it is uttered by Brutus in soliloquy as his answer to the 'question' of Caesar's nature being changed if he is crowned: 'So Caesar may. / Then lest he may, prevent' (2.1.27–8); it is spoken again by Brutus in his soliloquy on conspiracy: 'Not Erebus itself were dim enough / To hide thee from prevention' (2.1.84–5); it is used twice by Cassius, once as justification for the murder of Antony as well as Caesar (2.1.158–61) and again, just before the assassination, as he nervously urges Casca to 'be sudden, for we fear prevention' (3.1.19) and elicits Brutus's 'Cassius, be constant' (22); it is spoken by Caesar urging Cimber not to kneel, but, ironically perhaps, has the effect of a kind of prelude to the hubristic utterances (punctuated by the repetition of 'constant') which programme his death; and finally and climactically it is characterised by Brutus as the opposite of his Stoic philosophy: 'But I do find it cowardly and vile, / For fear of what might fall, so to prevent / The time of life' (5.1.103–5). 'Prevent' – to anticipate and take precautions, to act before or more quickly than another – is essentially a defensive reaction to a real or imaginary threat, reflecting insecurity and characterising a world of poised tensions and dangerous instability. It is the mark of a world of mistrust and conspiracies. It is the ally of fear, the enemy of constancy.

On a larger scale the opposition in the play which embraces 'fear–prevent' and 'constant' is between the rational and the irrational. Rome may be cold and sober and calculating, with marble columns and statues, and in the fields of Philippi the battles are drawn up and ordered in the formal Roman manner, but both Rome and Philippi are beset with 'things that do presage', which wondrously and irresistibly come true. Against the plots and fears and preventions are the portents and omens and prophecies. Against conspirators are set soothsayers; against soldiers, seers; against arithmetic, alchemy; against calculation, coincidence; against arrangement, accident; against counsel, ceremony; and against ratiocination, divination. If constancy is the desired end – and there is little doubt that it is – then the answer to the turbulence which marks the action of the play lies, paradoxically perhaps, not in the rational but in the irrational. For reason, be it in Brutus's attempts to justify his part in the assassination or in Antony's to justify his seizure of power, is essentially limited. It cannot foresee or prevent miscalculations or mischances. And it may itself be suspect, be not so much ratiocination as rationalisation, a way of phrasing one's behaviour in a manner which is publicly and personally agreeable: as in the motivation of the conspirators, in which the line between personal grievance and public policy is difficult to discern, in the impossibility of their separating Caesar the man from Caesar the tyrant (despite Brutus's rather stiff and contrived attempt), in the response of the plebeians to Antony's demagoguery (they receive 'reasons' – the physical testimony of the will, the parks and money – for supporting Caesar with which to cover their fickleness and greed), and in the majestically 'rational' madness of the mob which dispatches Cinna the Poet: after rejecting the 'reason' that Cinna the Poet is not Cinna the Conspirator, they find the 'reason' for their actions in the quality of his verse.

What truth, what permanence, what constancy exists in the play is connected with the 'irrational'. The omens and portents and prophecies are ambiguous only when men attempt to explain them rationally. To the seers they are clear. They come true. And it must be added that among the soothsayers are Calpurnia, whose advice, which is drawn from 'things . . . beyond all ůse' (2.2.25) – she is often played as a Cassandra-type figure – would have preserved Caesar, had he followed it; Antony, who, wondrously inspired by the wounds of Caesar, recognises his destiny; and in the end Brutus himself, who realises that his fate is in the hands of the *spirit* of Caesar

> The ghost of Caesar hath appeared to me
> Two several times by night, at Sardis once
> And this last night here in Philippi fields.
> I know my hour is come. (5.5.17–20)

It is the power of the *spirit* that Brutus acknowledges:

> O Julius Caesar, thou art mighty yet,
> Thy spirit walks abroad and turns our swords
> In our own proper entrails. (5.3.94–6)

The might of the dead Caesar is continuous: 'yet' spans then and now and to be. It reverses the rational attempts of man: their swords are turned against themselves. It dictates, as the *ultima ratio*, as the means of overcoming chance and the limitations of reason, suicide. Against the harshness and meanness of the world – its jaggedness stressed in a dominant cluster of verbs describing carving, chopping, cutting, dismembering, hacking, hewing, piercing, plucking, pricking, quartering, rending, riving, running through, scratching, splitting, spurring, stabbing, stinging, striking, tearing, thrusting, whetting, wounding; its aggressiveness evident in the frequent images of strife and storm; its garish ugliness in the semantic fields of fire and blood;[1] its infirmity in references to sickness[2] – against all this, and furthermore against the impact of impending time and the urgency of action, against agitation and prevention, only the tranquillity of death assures constancy. It is more than the necessary end: it is the noble end. It is the act which is best described by the often repeated patrician adjective 'gentle'.

The continuity with Richard II, Romeo, and Hamlet – in terms both of person and of play – is obvious. In *Julius Caesar* the essential tragedy of the human condition is once again unflinchingly depicted: all are fortune's fools. In a larger sense all the characters share the same destiny. For *Julius Caesar*, which begins with references to the supplanting of Pompey by Caesar and ends with the supplanting of Brutus by the newly arrived Octavius (who, in still another of the many successions, is apparently edging out the not quite established Antony), contains many tragedies or rather victims of relentless change. No one is spared in the explicit *Zusammenschau* (to use Auerbach's term) which contains all the tragedies. Plutarch's lives are, in contrast, 'parallel' and sequential. Tragedy is implicit at best, for in Plutarch human affairs can be managed in different ways by different personalities; opposites can be resolved in composites. Both Caesar and Brutus can be praised: they exist side by side; preferences are not prescriptive. For Shakespeare the essential unmanageability of human affairs is the core of tragedy; opposites are polarised and irreconcilable except in death. Caesar and Brutus are entangled; choice is obligatory.

PERSONS AND POLITICS

In this light it is perhaps not surprising that so much critical attention has been paid to the question of who the hero of the play is. But the discussion is nevertheless puzzling. For it cannot seriously be doubted that Brutus is the focus – dramatically, psychologically, politically, and morally. It is no accident that he is present throughout: in the beginning he is the motor of the action; in the end his death resolves the action. Further proof, though abundant, would be tedious. And little is to be gained by such well-meaning Solomonic distinctions as 'Caesar is the titular hero, Brutus the dramatic hero': naming a play after a character does not necessarily confer hero status, as a handful of Shakespeare's histories demonstrates. That many of his plays are named for the main characters or characters who do turn out to be the heroes or heroines does not of itself solve the problem of the title of this play. What is really at issue in the matter of the hero, especially since it is Caesar or Brutus who is proposed, is politics. Hudson's often-quoted appraisal, made more than a hundred years ago, is still relevant and typical: 'As here represented, [Caesar] is indeed little better than a grand, strutting piece of puff-paste; and when he speaks, it is very much in the style of a glorious vapourer and braggart, full of lofty airs and mock-thunder.'[3] Putting aside the question of how

[1] See, for example, Knight, *The Imperial Theme*, pp. 45–50, and Foakes, 'An approach', pp. 261–2.
[2] See, for example, Knight, *The Imperial Theme*, pp. 40–2.
[3] H. N. Hudson, *Shakespeare: His Life, Art, and Characters*, 2 vols., 1872, II, 234.

The ambiguity of Caesar:
five sixteenth-century versions

5 *The Emperor Julius Caesar on Horseback.* An engraving by Antonio Tempesta from *The First Twelve Roman Caesars* (Rome, 1596)

6 Julius Caesar. An engraving by Marcantonio Raimondi from the series *The Twelve Caesars* (*c.* 1520)

7 Julius Caesar. An engraving by Martino Rota from *Twenty-Four Portraits of Roman Emperors* (Venice, 1570)

8 Julius Caesar. An engraving by Egidius Sadeler (*c.* 1593) after Titian's series *Roman Emperors*

9 *The Triumphator Julius Caesar on his Chariot.* From *The Triumphs of Caesar* by Andrea Mantegna at Hampton Court (late fifteenth century)

Caesar's minuscule speaking part and his undistinguished vocabulary could account for this portrait, or the question of how critics can talk of the play's classical dignity and manner[1] in the light of a thrasonical[2] Caesar, or how an infatuate could be eulogised by Brutus, worried about by Calpurnia, and revered by Antony – putting aside such questions, Hudson attempts to account for the 'contradiction between Caesar as known and Caesar as rendered' by musing that he 'sometimes thought that the policy of the drama may have been to represent Caesar, not as he was indeed ["that colossal man"], but as he must have appeared to the conspirators ... For Caesar was literally too great to

[1] See above, p. 21.

[2] A favourite appellation, perhaps but not convincingly traceable to the braggart Hercules of the Senecan tradition; see Ayres, '*Julius Caesar*', esp. pp. 202–12.

be seen by them.'[1] From this view – which conveniently serves as well to clear the way for the hero Brutus – it is but a step towards the depersonalising of Caesar. 'The real man Caesar disappears for himself under the greatness of the Caesar myth',[2] writes Edward Dowden a short while later – from which Paul Stapfer develops the formula for a major portion of ensuing criticism: 'It is not the spirit of any one man, but the spirit of a new era about to begin – the spirit of *Cæsarism* – that fills Shakespeare's play and gives it its unity and moral significance.'[3] Indeed, much of the discussion of the conflicting claims on behalf of Caesar and Brutus as hero has in reality dealt with the conflict between monarchism and republicanism, tyranny and freedom, dictatorship and democracy, or any of the political polarities which, not unexpectedly, frame practically all stage presentations. Caesar as Hitler, Brutus as Che Guevara, are no longer uncommon.

This is not to say, however, that Marx has replaced Freud. On the contrary, perhaps the major technical achievement of the play is its remarkable sense of individual character and the interaction of characters (unlike Plutarch, who tends to concentrate on one, subordinating the others often to the point of reducing or even eliminating the contours of their personalities). And the attractive complexity of Brutus is the most interesting aspect of the play, for it combines all the qualities associated with heroes – adjectives like 'noble' and 'gentle'; an inner life made known through soliloquy, which as it delineates also separates; self-doubts and rationalisations; the inevitable attempt to impose a personal set of values on a public one. Above all, Brutus is the only character to whom the heroic criterion, a moral sense, is searchingly and deeply applied. Those who reject him do so on the basis of moral failings, but they have no other serious candidate. Or they propose that there is no hero at all.[4] Or that plot is of major importance, not character.[5] Or, as is the case with the difficulty of pinpointing the political intent of the play, they make a virtue of the difficulty of defining characters or their relationships. Not untypical is Mark Hunter's view that the 'personal interest in this play, the appeal of individual character, is not concentrated, as it is in the normally constructed tragedies, on one dominating figure which overshadows all the rest. It is distributed.'[6] Very early on, many critics have responded by proposing that ambiguity is the major intent, if not theme, of the play: from Gustav Freytag (commenting on actors' different interpretations of the same character: 'Who is right? Each of them'[7]) and Michael Macmillan ('The poet's aim was to produce ... an even balance in our sympathies, so that they should waver to and fro, inclining alternately to Caesar and the conspirators', p. xxv) to Ernest Schanzer (treating *Julius Caesar* as a 'problem' play, one which evokes 'uncertain and divided responses ... in the minds of the audience'[8]) and Mildred Hartsock ('*Julius*

[1] Hudson, *Shakespeare*, II, 237.

[2] Dowden, *Shakspere*, p. 285.

[3] Stapfer, *Classical Antiquity*, p. 328.

[4] See, for example, Waldo F. McNeir, *Shakespeare's 'Julius Caesar': A Tragedy without a Hero*, 1970, p. 52.

[5] See, for example, Foakes, 'An approach', p. 270.

[6] Mark Hunter, 'Politics and character in Shakespeare's "Julius Caesar"', in *EDH*, *Transactions of the Royal Society of Literature*, n.s. 10 (1931), 114.

[7] Gustav Freytag, *Die Technik des Dramas*, 1894, p. 221. The German text reads: 'Wer hat Recht? Jeder von ihnen.'

[8] Ernest Schanzer, *The Problem Plays of Shakespeare*, 1963, p. 6 (developed from his 'The problem of *Julius Caesar*', *SQ* 6 (1955), 297–308).

Caesar is not a problem play, but a play about a problem: the difficulty – perhaps the impossibility – of knowing the truth of men and of history'[1]). This drift, it is important to note, emphasises the inextricability of character and politics, as is evident in the personalising adjectives applied to a political situation in so typical a formulation as Hartsock's 'Is Caesar an egocentric, dangerous dictator – a genuine threat to Rome; or is he the "noblest man / That ever lived"?'[2]

Whether the entire presentation is indeed ambiguous or whether the view is mainly based on a modern relativistic reaction away from either/or solutions or from solutions altogether, the critical discussion of 'good', 'bad', or 'mixed' characters and political constellations has been relentless.[3] The answer, in short, is elusive. This is no small tribute to a 'simple', 'straightforward' and yet 'singular' play.

Julius Caesar on the stage

Julius Caesar was probably performed for the first time on 21 September 1599 at the Globe Theatre.[4] Although there exist only three more records of performances for the time up to the closing of the theatres in 1642, contemporary references to the play testify to a popularity far greater than this number would suggest, and the play has continued to attract audiences after the Restoration and up to the present time.

Julius Caesar has been performed in England and America with only minor interruptions for almost four centuries mainly because the characters and situation are sufficiently complex, if not ambiguous, for each age to extract what best suits its taste or circumstances: actor-managers and directors could use the play as a star vehicle, stress its patriotic and nationalistic features, indulge their audiences' enthusiasm for Rome (although this was often directed more towards imperial Rome than the Republican era) or for elocution and rhetoric, and relate it to contemporary political events. By twentieth-century standards, this easy adaptability was often achieved at a great cost. Shakespeare's text was freely tampered with in the eighteenth and nineteenth centuries, the reasons for cutting, adding, rewriting, and redistributing speeches ranging from economical ones (decreasing the original cast of 40 speaking parts, for instance) to attempts at clarifying

1 Mildred E. Hartsock, 'The complexity of *Julius Caesar*', *PMLA* 81 (1966), 61.

2 *Ibid.*, p. 56. Hartsock summarises some of the leading views of Caesar as person and political force (pp. 56–7).

3 A useful brief summary of opinions concerning Brutus, for example, is given by Spencer, '*Julius Caesar* and *Antony and Cleopatra*', p. 208. More recent and representative views may be found in Levitsky, '"The elements"', p. 241: 'We repeatedly see in Brutus the purity of motive, steadfastness of purpose, and strength of will characteristic of the Stoic, mixed with a tendency toward human passion and compassion which render him more vulnerable to suffering but also more lovable than the obdurate Caesar'; in J. L. Simmons, *Shakespeare's Pagan World: The Roman Tragedies*, 1974, p. 69: 'The moral schizophrenia that Brutus manifests when he translates the ideal into action seems to be derived from Plutarch's inchoate paradox'; in E. A. J. Honigmann, *Shakespeare: Seven Tragedies*, 1976, p. 33: 'Shakespeare turned Brutus into an intellectual hideously corrupted by high-mindedness'; and in Richard A. Levin, 'Brutus: "Noblest Roman of them all"', *BSUF* 23 (1982), 16: 'Brutus merely has too much of the natural human desire to think well of oneself; refusing to see his own faults, he lets them run free . . . satisfying his conscience . . . by protesting his virtue too strongly and by finding socially approved forms for his destructive emotions; his public-mindedness conceals personal envy.'

4 This survey is greatly indebted to John Ripley's detailed study *'Julius Caesar' on Stage in England and America, 1599–1973*, 1980. For the date of the first performance, see p. 3 above.

syntax, preserving decorum (as in the omission of supposedly anachronistic references to nightgowns, cloaks, hats, and the like), heightening the tragic effect, and imposing a unity, supposedly lacking, on the play. Ludwig Tieck, visiting London and the London theatres in 1817, wrote of the 'carelessness' of the English in preparing Shakespeare's texts for the stage and complained about their lack of 'the sense of the play as a whole', resulting in what Sprague has called a 'scenes-from-Shakespeare-heavily-upholstered type of production'.[1]

The slender evidence we have of seventeenth-century productions suggests that actors spoke a text close to the Folio. But towards the end of the century, when Thomas Betterton took over the role of Brutus, elimination of minor characters and redistribution of speeches – a great number of passages amplifying Casca's and Trebonius's parts, regardless of their being in character or not – had already begun. Betterton established the interpretation of Brutus as philosopher and patriot and thus continued the earlier tendency to regard *Julius Caesar*, despite its title, as more appropriately the tragedy of Brutus, a tradition that was dominant through most of the nineteenth century. Cassius seems to have been portrayed as basically a man of emotion, whose rash temper served as a foil to Brutus's equanimity in the quarrel scene (4.3) which emerged as the prominent one of the play.[2] Eighteenth-century actors followed the trends set by their predecessors, supported in their endeavours by acting-versions of the text that eliminated ambiguities in Shakespeare's character portrayals and accelerated the pace of the action. In addition to further juggling of characters and speeches – merging the roles of Artemidorus and the Soothsayer, for instance, and cutting 3.3, the scene in which Cinna the Poet meets his death – and, in accordance with eighteenth-century rationalism, reducing extensive references to the supernatural to a minimum, the so-called Dryden–Davenant version of 1719 produced a Brutus purged of expressions and sentiments unsuited to a tragic hero and, most of all, endowed him with a more dignified death, an 'improvement' actors were not willing to dispense with before the present century: in 5.5, Brutus invites only one of his followers, whose name varies in different texts, to kill him,[3] and when he is refused Brutus proceeds to commit suicide without external help after delivering a death-speech appropriate for a patriot and tragic hero. Leading actors, with the notable exception of Garrick – and Kean, Irving, and Olivier in the following centuries – took the parts of Brutus, Antony, and Cassius while the play's titular hero Caesar received no special attention and was generally played as a stock stage tyrant without individuality or even majesty. It is a noteworthy feature of eighteenth-century productions that the mob, so important in 3.2 – 3.3 being cut – consisted of an average of six actors, often comedians, who were not really called upon to interact.[4]

[1] Ludwig Tieck, *Dramaturgische Blätter*, 3 vols., 1826, III, 3–4; Arthur Colby Sprague, *Shakespeare and the Actors*, 1948, p. xxii.

[2] For a contemporary account of Betterton's acting powers, see *An Apology for the Life of Colley Cibber*, ed. B. R. S. Fone, 1968, pp. 59–70; the passage on Betterton's rendering of Brutus, quoted by Ripley, p. 20, can be found on p. 62 of the *Apology*.

[3] Some texts follow the original in having Brutus address two friends in turn, but follow the Dryden–Davenant version in making the essential alteration of having both reject Brutus's request.

[4] Ripley quotes Francis Gentleman, who recalled an instance of 'wretched buffoonery' on the part of the comedians: to while away their time on stage they diverted themselves and the audience with taking Antony's metaphorical language during the Forum speech – 'lend me your ears!' (3.2.65), for instance – literally (p. 37).

10 *Brutus and the Ghost of Caesar.* A drawing of 1806 by William Blake, from an extra-illustrated Second Folio

The nineteenth century radically changed this tradition, filling – and sometimes crowding – the stage with supers whose number could vary from 79 to 250 and who were often employed for purely visual effects.[1] Historical accuracy of costumes and scenery was no tenet of the seventeenth and eighteenth centuries, actors wearing more or less imaginary Roman dress, whereas the nineteenth-century actor-managers considered authenticity a major asset. Often this did not hinder them, however, from reproducing the splendour of Imperial Rome instead of the more austere buildings of the Republican era. Two major productions – John Philip Kemble's at Covent Garden and Herbert Beerbohm Tree's at Her Majesty's – mark the beginning and the end of the nineteenth century and serve as examples of changing ideas and interpretations. Kemble, who staged *Julius Caesar* in 1812, created the 'grand style' of acting, characterised by its special emphasis on visual effects – splendour of scenery and costume, colourful and stately processions, statuesque groupings of performers – and elevation of the action on to the plane of the ideal. The aesthetic principles governing this conception paralleled closely those laid down by Sir Joshua Reynolds in his *Discourses on Art* in which he advised young artists to strive for 'perfect form' and 'ideal beauty' but reminded them at the same time not to forget the 'nobleness of conception' and the 'art of animating and dignifying the figures with intellectual grandeur, of impressing the appearance of philosophick wisdom, or heroick virtue'. Only the combination of these aspects could bring forth a painting in what he termed 'great style'.[2]

In order to fit these preconceived ideas Kemble subjected Shakespeare's text to a new and drastic revision which became, with only minor alterations, the standard one for the first half of the century. Not surprisingly, reduction of speaking parts, cutting and reallocation of speeches were again the methods employed to tighten the structure of the play and smooth out inconsistencies in action and characterisation. The attempt at presenting a straight-line interpretation was carried far beyond anything essayed in the eighteenth century. For Kemble, who played Brutus, his beau idéal Roman's dominant quality was stoic discipline. Philosophy enabled him to stifle any personal considerations and to be guided and motivated in his actions almost exclusively by his profound patriotism. In his death-speech, influenced by its eighteenth-century predecessors, Brutus was allowed to drive home this point forcefully, apostrophising his 'Beloved country!'[3] Cassius, played by Charles Mayne Young, underwent the same kind of simplification and became once again a man characterised by an explosive temper. The two conspirators were opposed by Charles Kemble's Antony, a young and athletic nobleman motivated only by the purest motives. Anything smacking of ruthlessness or

[1] Samuel Phelps, who had only a modest budget at his disposal for his productions at Sadler's Wells from 1846 to 1862, nevertheless felt he could not do without '32 plebeians, 6 boys, 4 priests, 6 senators . . . 12 guards with spears, 12 guards with fasces, and 7 ladies' (Ripley, p. 96). Herbert Beerbohm Tree's record number of approximately 250 supers on the stage of Her Majesty's in 1898 was surpassed in this century only by a gigantic *Julius Caesar* at the Beechwood Amphitheatre near Los Angeles, which was forced to make use of multiple stages in order to accommodate 5,000 actors and supers (see *The Christian Science Monitor* of 23 May 1916, referred to in Ripley, pp. 221, 338).

[2] Ed. Robert R. Wark, 1959, no. 3, pp. 44–5, 50.

[3] Kemble inserts this apostrophe at 5.5.50, retaining the second half of the line ('Caesar . . . still') and the following one. For the entire death-speech, see Ripley, p. 54. There is also a facsimile reproduction of Kemble's 1814 acting-version published in 1970.

opportunism was banned from the text – the proscription scene (4.1) disappearing entirely, of course – and what remained was Caesar's youthful friend and revenger. Kemble's preoccupation with visual effects and impressive groupings induced him to bring his supers into play almost everywhere; they even remained on stage during the assassination scene, silent spectators of a ritualised, ballet-like killing of the titular hero.[1] Kemble's text and style of production strongly influenced his successors in the following decades, even though they restored some humanity to his over-dignified Romans. The only important and trend-setting innovation was made by William Charles Macready, who, feeling a need for more realistic action, rescued his supers from the fate of passive onlookers; in the Forum scene, the plebeians finally became in deed a decisive force.

The company of the Duke of Saxe-Meiningen, which brought their German production of *Julius Caesar* to London in 1881, carried on and expanded Macready's new design. The Meininger were known for disciplined and realistic ensemble acting and they turned the Forum scene into the climax of the play, displacing the assassination and the long-popular quarrel scene.[2] From this performance Herbert Beerbohm Tree took his cue when he staged *Julius Caesar* at Her Majesty's in 1898. The newly acquired prominence of the Forum scene and the persuasiveness of the actor who had played Antony convinced Tree that Antony was the leading role. He did not hesitate to break with a centuries-long tradition and heavily blue-pencilled Shakespeare's text in order to substantiate Antony's claim to stardom. In an attempt to prevent Acts 4 and 5 from becoming utterly anti-climactic, a fate that had attended the Meiningen performance, he retained only Antony's appearances and the parts necessary in terms of plot movement. The result of this tailoring was a three-act play – Act 2 taken up entirely by the Forum scene – with a tableau curtain for Antony at the end of each act. It is a curious feature that Tree, despite his relegating Brutus to an unrewarding second place, continued to concede him the time-honoured suicide, though without Kemble's patriotic death-speech. Tree approached his production of *Julius Caesar* in the firm belief that his audiences expected scenic realism and spectacle and he was prepared to fulfil these wishes which happily coincided with his own conviction that Rome and its people were of a far greater importance than earlier producers had admitted. His portrayal of daily life before the tribunes enter in 1.1 is probably unique in the stage history of *Julius Caesar*,[3] and in the Forum scene he had his plebeians force Antony to exert himself to the utmost in order to draw them over to his side. Tree's sumptuous scenery, for the most part historically accurate, the extraneous stage business he felt free – and indeed obliged – to insert,[4] and his deliberate accelerating or slowing down of the action helped to

[1] The comparison of the assassination to a formal ballet was made by Ludwig Tieck in 1817 and can be found in *Dramaturgische Blätter*, III, 10–11. He thought the staging of this scene 'most strange' and 'grotesque', but sought the reason for this arrangement partly in the depth and height of the stage.

[2] For the Saxe-Meiningen company, see Robert Speaight, *Shakespeare on the Stage*, 1973, pp. 108–12, but esp. p. 108, and Michael R. Booth, 'The Meininger Company and English Shakespeare', *S.Sur.* 35 (1982), 13–20.

[3] For a detailed account of this scene, see Ripley, pp. 155–7.

[4] For instance, Tree had Calpurnia enter as Antony prepared to carry Caesar's body out of the Senate, seemingly imploring him through her gestures to revenge her husband's violent death – a device which, as George Bernard Shaw conceded, produced an 'effective curtain', even if it seemed slightly melodramatic (*Our Theatres in the Nineties*, 3 vols., 1932, III, 300–1).

11 The assassination of Julius Caesar, Act 3, Scene 1. Herbert Beerbohm Tree's production at Her Majesty's Theatre in 1898. Set designed by Lawrence Alma-Tadema

underscore his aim. Even if the acting did not earn the same applause as the mob orchestration and the scenery – Shaw called the set-designer Lawrence Alma-Tadema 'the real hero of the revival'[1] – and even if he greatly overstated Antony's importance and simplified Shakespeare's ambiguous character, Tree deserves credit for releasing him from the restraints of the beau idéal tradition, for firmly establishing the crowd as meriting attention in the performance, and for choosing an actor for the role of Caesar – Charles Fulton – who gave this character a human dignity he had not often been endowed with.

American productions of the nineteenth century were mainly stock performances, catering to audiences steeped in revolutionary ideals but coming to the theatre mainly in search of fine declamation and great stars.[2] Oratory being an important factor in American politics in the nineteenth century, *Julius Caesar* with its many rhetorical passages would have seemed to be ideally suited, but only one production, Edwin Booth's New York revival in 1871, deserves special mention.[3] Booth did not conceive of the action as continuous and linear but as a sequence of separate events, with a linkage

1 *Our Theatres*, III, 302.

2 In her study, *Shakespeare in America*, 1939, pp. 132–48, Esther Cloudman Dunn analyses the mentality and expectations of the American playgoer of the first half of the nineteenth century.

3 In addition to Ripley, pp. 115–39, see Charles H. Shattuck, *Shakespeare on the American Stage*, 1976, pp. 145–7.

12 'Grand Square in Rome': setting for the opening scene of Edwin Booth's New York production of 1871. A watercolour by the set-designer, Charles Witham

provided by the characters, and he accordingly divided the play into six acts, Acts 3 and 4 being dedicated to the assassination and Forum scenes respectively. On the whole he followed Kemble's emphasis on visual effects, but instead of neo-classical grandeur his *Julius Caesar* displayed romantic overtones, most poignantly in the portrayal of a Brutus whose sensibility and idealism were particularly stressed and whose aversion to violent action was made palpable in his reluctance to strike at Caesar in the assassination scene. This sentimentalised Brutus, seconded by a vigorous and passionate Cassius and a purely noble Antony, found such favour with his audiences that Booth was assured of a long-standing popularity although reviewers invariably remarked that his physical appearance was completely at odds with a convention that demanded a tall, heroic-looking Roman.[1]

In the stage history of *Julius Caesar* at Stratford, the turn of the century was marked by Frank Benson's productions. Between 1892 and 1915, the Shakespeare Memorial Theatre saw eleven revivals of this play, adhering, as far as text and acting style were concerned, to the nineteenth-century heroic conception and declamation, but turning away from the sumptuous scenery that had threatened to smother the text. Benson did not feel authorised to rewrite speeches or interpolate new ones, sharply differing from the older actor-managers in this, or to cut the text in order to set off one character, as Tree had not hesitated to do, but he blue-pencilled with abandon in order to achieve structural clarity, leaving the text as mutilated as ever, only differently so. His Brutuses and Antonys were of the Kemble breed, but the Caesars struck out in a new direction. The portrayal of Caesar as a man whose former strength and power are clearly declining

[1] See Shattuck, *American Stage*, p. 146.

but who preserves his dignity and is still a force to be reckoned with was an innovation later productions took notice of.

Benson's successor at Stratford, William Bridges-Adams, a director, not actor-manager, strongly influenced by William Poel and Harley Granville-Barker, brought to his production of *Julius Caesar* notions that differed as much as possible from those of Tree or Benson. For the first time since the Restoration a near full-text production of the play was seen in performance, putting an end to straight-line interpretations, a change that affected most strongly the role of Antony. After a century's absence the proscription scene (4.1) returned to the stage, among many other important passages, but Cinna the Poet continued to be omitted owing to the inexperience of the available supers.[1] Bridges-Adams altered the traditional stage, using almost exclusively the fore-stage for action. He eliminated all the extraneous stage business and the emphasis on one or two star roles so dear to his predecessors, replaced their sumptuous and rather static set with a less elaborate and more flexible one, and accelerated the pace of speech and acting in order to accommodate the considerably longer text to the usual length of performance. For a number of years the diametrically opposed approaches of Tree and Bridges-Adams co-existed on the British stage, until the latter's style of production carried the day. Directors like Robert Atkins and Harcourt Williams, who put on *Julius Caesar* at the Old Vic during the 1920s, continued the trend set by Bridges-Adams – Williams laying special emphasis on psychological character studies, a notion he had gained from Granville-Barker's *Prefaces*.

But it was in America that *Julius Caesar* was given a completely new direction. In 1937, Orson Welles staged a highly personal vision of the play, subtitled 'Death of a Dictator', in which he drove home contemporary parallels by stressing 'the issues of political violence and the moral duty of the individual in the face of tyranny'.[2] Welles must have considered Shakespeare's Roman tragedy simply as a vehicle for his ideas about the effective theatrical realisation of a burning political issue, for he mercilessly hacked the text. His almost exclusive concentration on Caesar, Brutus, and the mob produced something even farther removed from the original than its eighteenth- and nineteenth-century predecessors. In this political context the masses in all their fickleness, easy persuadability, and unreflecting cruelty acquired an unsurpassed prominence, with the Cinna the Poet scene (3.3) – in a complete reversal of a centuries-long tradition – as a haunting experience. Welles obviously had to play in modern dress – Fascist uniforms and everyday clothes – and, with a sure instinct for producing spectacular impressions, made extensive use of cinematic lighting effects. His production set a precedent never to be forgotten by later directors.

Welles's immediate followers in Britain, however, came up with two rather grotesque versions. A 1938 production in Cambridge, drastically modernising, presented Caesar breakfasting on grapefruit and coffee and telephoning the augurers, and compressed the supernatural events into a *Daily Express* article. A year later at the Old Vic Henry Cass's actors donned a mixture of Spanish, British, and SS uniforms and confronted their audience with sensationalised melodrama. More than twenty years had passed when in

[1] See Ripley, p. 200, for Bridges-Adams's explanation of this cut.
[2] Quoted in Ripley, p. 222.

13 Antony's funeral oration, Act 3, Scene 2, from Orson Welles's modern-dress production at the Mercury Theatre, New York, in 1937. Antony was played by George Coulouris

1962 the Greek director Minos Volanakis approached *Julius Caesar*, parting from the conviction that Shakespeare in this play had been exploring 'the possibility of salvation through politics'.[1] His Rome was a gloomy and spellbound place on the brink of a new era; his Brutus, a man whose attempt to save the old ideals backfired on him, unleashing precisely those dark forces he was fighting. Because Volanakis's Old Vic production sacrificed characterisation to the abstract message, the experiment eventually backfired on him: 'a plain text and provocative commentary in an insecure binding', as Trewin remarked.[2] John Blatchley staged the play at Stratford a year later but his understanding of *Julius Caesar* as portraying the dirty business of politics at any given time found equally little favour with critics, who complained about monochrome scenery, a hodge-podge of costumes, and an incredibly slow pace.[3] But Blatchley had placed Caesar firmly at the centre of the tragedy and in this respect he was followed by Trevor Nunn in 1972. With the titular hero a compelling personality and powerful character, Brutus's nervousness, his impatience, and sometimes violent outbursts did not prove too successful an interpretation, although some critics hailed it as the one Shakespeare had intended.[4] Nunn drew overt parallels to Fascism while staging *Julius Caesar* as part of his 'Roman cycle', which sought to exemplify 'the rise and fall of the Roman state from "tribalism to authoritarianism, to colonialism, to decadence"'.[5] If Nunn failed in his attempt to link the plays thematically, Octavius certainly profited. He was allowed to emerge from his hitherto marginal position in order to foreshadow his role in *Antony and Cleopatra* as a real match for his fellow triumvir.

Directors in the late 1970s and 1980s obviously felt a need for more immediate contemporary parallels and turned to different countries and models. Gerald Freedman at the Stratford, Connecticut, Shakespeare Festival in 1979 conceived of Caesar as a Latin American dictator and of the crowd as tourists brandishing cameras, but on the whole he employed modern elements rather eclectically. The connection with Latin America had been made ten years earlier by Edward Payson Call in Minneapolis, but his costumes, ranging from Aztec-style to contemporary military dress, had made it of all times and no time at all. At Belfast in 1981, Leon Rubin sought a new and striking association with current events and hit on the idea of drawing a parallel with the assassination of the Egyptian president Sadat and with the plight of Latin American countries. This interpretation must have suited Jerry Turner, for he adopted it a year later at the Oregon Shakespeare Festival. His Caesar reminded one reviewer of Che Guevara; the Soothsayer was turned into a 'bag lady' or female tramp and Casca into 'a

[1] Ripley, p. 260. See also Samuel L. Leiter (ed.), *Shakespeare Around the Globe: A Guide to Notable Postwar Revivals*, 1986, pp. 271–2.

[2] J. C. Trewin, 'The Old Vic and Stratford-upon-Avon, 1961–1962', *SQ* 13 (1962), 510.

[3] Trewin's remark was especially devastating – '*Julius Caesar* ... seemed to be about some minor plot in an unimportant hole or corner' (*Shakespeare on the English Stage 1900–1964*, 1964, p. 250) – but Robert Speaight considered speech and characterisation unfairly condemned, although he too criticised a good many aspects ('Shakespeare in Britain', *SQ* 14 (1963), 425–7).

[4] See, for instance, Benedict Nightingale, *The New Statesman and Nation*, 12 May 1972, quoted in Leiter, *Around the Globe*, p. 274.

[5] Leiter, *Around the Globe*, p. 274.

cigarette-smoking, pistol-packing, female revolutionary' whose striking at Caesar had sexual overtones.[1]

While a number of directors thus succumbed to the pressure of ever more modernising *Julius Caesar*, no doubt in order to enhance its relevance to contemporary audiences, others struck out in the opposite direction and tried their skill at producing the play Elizabethan-style. At the Westminster Theatre in 1953, Michael MacOwan, one of the first, was unsuccessful owing to the inadequacy of his resources – actors, properties, and stage. Deficient scenery or a modern proscenium stage were not problems Michael Langham had to contend with two years later. At the Canadian Stratford Festival he employed a thrust stage, seated the audience on three sides of it, and had his actors make their entrances and exits passing among the audience along five aisles. His view of *Julius Caesar* as chronicle rather than tragedy prepared the ground for unbroken, fast-paced movement; Renaissance costumes, a lavish but functional use of supers, and some memorable and meaningful stage business (like having the sleeping soldiers shudder and groan in the presence of Caesar's ghost) proved further assets of this production, but Shakespeare's poignant characterisation eluded the director and this seriously marred the otherwise successful attempt. More recent productions sometimes confined the 'Elizabethanness' to Renaissance costumes or fell prey to a fate similar to MacOwan's.[2] The most drastic of all Elizabethan approaches was probably a student production at Cambridge in 1952. Under John Barton, later a director of the Royal Shakespeare Company, the Marlowe Society set out to recreate the architecture and atmosphere of Shakespeare's Globe, and even to approximate Elizabethan pronunciation: Casca met 'a lay-on' near the Capitol (1.3.20), Cassius bared his 'boozim to the thoonder sto-erm' (1.3.49), Caesar was warned of the 'Ades of March', and 'Breutus' became 'an hounerable mun' (3.2).[3] The experiment was generally applauded, but when Barton revived *Julius Caesar* with the RSC in 1968, his aims had become quite different. He concentrated on character study, stressing negative facets in Brutus and Cassius and bringing out the ambiguous and conflicting in Antony through costume changes and some telling business, like his appearing at Caesar's house in 2.2 visibly marked by the excesses of the previous night. Ripley found himself reminded of 'a veritable portrait gallery, paying lip service to a warts-and-all vision, but specializing in warts',[4] while Speaight confessed himself very much impressed.[5] Brewster Mason's Caesar was a real threat and his commanding personality continued to dominate the play even after his death so that Barton's allowing the ghost two more appearances – crossing the battlefield after 5.1 and looming over the dead Brutus – seemed rather superfluous.

One of the outstanding productions of this century was certainly the 1950 Stratford revival under the direction of Anthony Quayle and Michael Langham. A conservative staging in that fewer than a hundred lines were cut and togas and Roman military dress

[1] W. R. Streitberger, 'Shakespeare in the Northwest: Ashland and Seattle', *SQ* 34 (1983), 348.
[2] See J. C. Trewin, 'Shakespeare in Britain', *SQ* 29 (1978), 218, for one such failed attempt.
[3] See Leiter, *Around the Globe*, p. 264.
[4] Ripley, p. 266.
[5] Speaight, 'Shakespeare in Britain', *SQ* 19 (1968), 373–4.

employed, this *Julius Caesar* was convincing because pure acting skill brought Shakespeare's complex characters alive. John Gielgud clearly made Cassius the driving force; his conspirator's nature was a mixture of frustrated ambition, envy, amazing energy, awareness of the ingredients of 'Realpolitik', and nobility. If, against his better judgement, he gave way to Brutus in important matters, he thereby only recognised the other's moral superiority. Octavius, often considered such a minor figure as to deserve no special attention, became in Alan Badel's portrayal 'the Emperor Augustus in embryo, every word and twitch of muscle etching a portrait in bronze'.[1] If the Quayle–Langham revival stands almost alone in having conveyed a sense of the tragic dimension and heroism inherent in Shakespeare's play, it was surpassed in one respect by that of Glen Byam Shaw seven years later. Shaw and his actors grasped the essence of 'Caesarism', so often drowned in over-emphasis on the titular hero's bombastic and self-confident speeches, and presented the picture of a great leader whose weaknesses did not prove detrimental to his high standing but simply made him human and mortal; the danger of a powerful but statue-like and ultimately unconvincing and unmoving Caesar was thus admirably averted. His spirit was ever-present, and after the assassination this aspect was effectively stressed by the appearance of a blazing star at crucial moments. John Schlesinger obviously had Shaw in the back of his mind when he set out to revive *Julius Caesar* with the National Theatre Company in 1977. As Caesar he cast John Gielgud, who endowed the titular hero with a great natural authority, and it was clear from the outset that the conspirators would not be able to conquer his spirit. Caesar's ghost haunted the battle scenes and then, 'an astonishing atmospheric close', appeared 'in quadruplicate ... on the plains of Philippi: four mask-faces staring out into the darkness' – Caesar dominating to the end.[2] A Caesar of human stature was an asset of John Wood's revival at the Stratford Festival Canada a year later, but his production was – and remains – remarkable for his experiment of dispensing with the crowd. Although their absence was not much regretted in the first acts – after all, Lindsay Anderson at the Royal Court in 1964 had made it clear that Shakespeare's jokes were no longer funny and could be cut without causing any damage to the play – Act 3 destroyed the illusion that the populace has no essential function in the play. Antony's Forum speech had some response in indistinct noises, but on the whole he delivered it, like Brutus before him, in a vacuum. The entire tension of the third act, that crucial moment when the people assume power and can turn the scales either way, got lost in this interpretation and the audience was presented with 'a power struggle totally confined to the Roman elite'.[3]

There were other ingenious and innovative attempts. In 1972, Jonathan Miller, staging *Julius Caesar* with the Oxford and Cambridge Shakespeare Company, chose to treat the play as a terrifying dream world with actors moving and speaking in somnambulistic slow-motion. Reviewers were unable to find the deeper meaning of this approach and they were again puzzled when Martin Cobin at the 1981 Colorado Shakespeare Festival presented the events following 4.3 as Brutus's dream, a device only recognised as such when Brutus, who had earlier fallen asleep, rose from his bed, ready

[1] *Ibid.*, p. 374.
[2] Trewin, 'Shakespeare in Britain', p. 217.
[3] Ralph Berry, 'Stratford Festival Canada', *SQ* 30 (1979), 170.

14 The death of Brutus, Act 5, Scene 5, from Glen Byam Shaw's production at the Shakespeare Memorial Theatre, Stratford-upon-Avon, 1957. Brutus (lying) was played by Alec Clunes, Antony by Richard Johnson, and Octavius by Clive Revill. Peter Palmer as Strato is kneeling next to the dead Brutus

to meet the fate announced in his nightmare. The play's extensive references to supernatural events, so little congenial to eighteenth-century taste, filled two directors with a sense of awkwardness, prompting widely different solutions. Bekki Jo Schneider in a 1979 Louisville revival opted for rigorous cutting, which resulted in a rather short playing time – 105 minutes – and 'a tragedy of cabals and corporation men, among whom

15 Paul Richard as Julius Caesar in the German production of the Company of the Duke of Saxe-Meiningen, brought to London in 1881

16 Sir John Gielgud as Cassius in the production by Anthony Quayle and Michael Langham at the Shakespeare Memorial Theatre, Stratford-upon-Avon, 1950

17 Marlon Brando as Antony in the film version directed by Joseph L. Mankiewicz, 1953

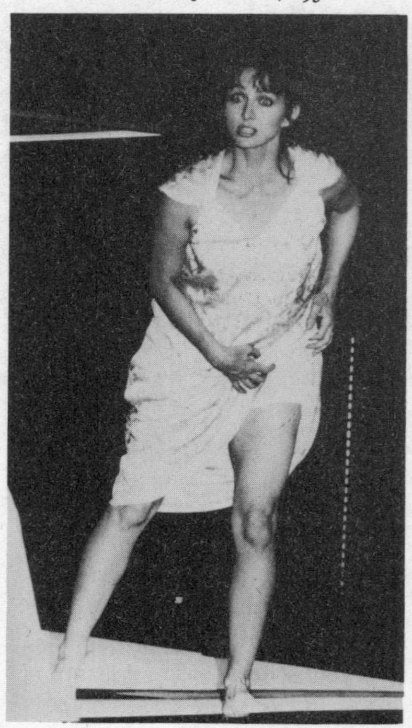

18 'I have made strong proof of my constancy, / Giving myself a voluntary wound / Here, in the thigh.' Christine Kaufmann as Portia (Act 2, Scene 1) in Michael Bogdanov's production at the Deutsches Schauspielhaus, Hamburg, 1986

Caesar seemed the last non-taskforce member'.[1] Ron Daniels at Stratford in 1983, on the other hand, exploited the contrast between the belief in omens and fate, rhetoric and the tragic conception, all firmly rooted in another time, and the political issues – political assassination, democracy versus dictatorship – that lend themselves to comparison with contemporary events. But this attempt at illustrating man's ultimate smallness and perhaps even insignificance in the larger frame of events outside his sphere of influence and his inability to control the forces around him did not yield satisfying results, because the heavily accented contrasts and contradictions overwhelmed the play.

Throughout the four centuries of its stage history, *Julius Caesar* has been subjected to many changes, some of them radical: nationalistic interpretations gave way to idealistic ones, great poses and declamation to realistic stagings, authenticity, and an emphasis on 'Romanness' to neo-Elizabethan approaches and a quest for contemporary parallels. In the twentieth century the obsession with novelty has been reflected in an at times bewildering array of dramatic interpretations and styles. Esther Cloudman Dunn in 1939 concluded her study of *Shakespeare in America* with the words

> Ben Jonson wrote more truly than he knew when he described Shakespeare as 'not for an Age but for all time'. He will survive each separate time, inviolate and indestructible. But he yields, too, to the manipulation, the 'form and pressure' of each succeeding era, and, in the process, turns himself into the most delicate barometer of social and cultural history.[2]

Her judgement has lost nothing of its validity almost fifty years later.

[1] Catherine R. Lewis, 'Shakespeare in Louisville', *SQ* 31 (1980), 228. (By 'non-taskforce member' the reviewer meant 'old-fashioned individual entrepreneur'.)

[2] *Shakespeare in America*, p. 306.

NOTE ON THE TEXT

The copy-text for this edition is the First Folio of 1623 (F), the sole authority. All substantive departures, together with their origin, are recorded in the collation, as are substantive emendations and conjectures which have been adopted in well-known editions or are of textual interest or are plausible orthographic alternatives. Changes involving accidentals, modernisation or normalisation of spelling, metre, or the like have not as a rule been recorded. Obsolete forms have been silently modernised when there is little phonetic or euphonic variation – 'strook', for example, is rendered as 'struck'. Variations in morphology, including inflections, are retained – 'strucken', for example, is not replaced by 'struck'. As for lineation, departures from F are recorded, and other significant alternatives given; in some important instances alternatives are given even when F is retained. Obvious or inevitable combinations of short lines to produce single verse lines, generally following Steevens[3], are not recorded. The placing of stage directions involving a change of one or two lines only is also normally not recorded. Italicised names in entrance directions indicate mutes. Readings from the Folger and Douai MSS., as well as the six quartos, have been supplied by John W. Velz. Also consulted was G. Blakemore Evans, 'Shakespeare's *Julius Caesar* – a seventeenth-century manuscript', *JEGP* 41 (1942), 401–17, and 'The Douai manuscript – six Shakespearean transcripts (1694–95)', *PQ* 41 (1962), 158–72. The dating and description of the quartos – QU1–4, Q (1684), Q (1691) – are based on John W. Velz, '"Pirate Hills" and the quartos of *Julius Caesar*', *PBSA* 63 (1969), 177–93. The uncorrected F readings in the collation are from Charlton Hinman, *The Printing and Proof-reading of the First Folio of Shakespeare*, 2 vols., 1963, I, 300. In the format of the collations the authority for this edition's reading follows immediately after the square bracket enclosing the quotation from the text. Other readings, if any, follow in chronological order. A conjecture not made in an edition is placed in round brackets and is preceded by the first edition to adopt it. The origins of a very select group of unadopted conjectures are also to be found in the List of Abbreviations. Additional information may at times be found in the Commentary, where also asterisks in the lemmas indicate words emended in the text. The punctuation of the text in this edition is considerably lighter than that employed by the compositors of F, about which something is said in the Textual Analysis, pp. 148–53 below.

NOTE ON THE COMMENTARY

The Commentary, which has profited from a long editorial and critical tradition, is designed to assist the reader by providing information rather than interpretation. Semantic information is derived in the main from the *OED*, unless specified otherwise. The dictionary definitions are phrased in a neutral manner in order to avoid the dangers of glosses and paraphrases which dictate a point of view and restrict the linguistic and especially poetic potential of a word or passage (such as the common use of 'atoned' to gloss 'answered' at 3.2.72) or which befuddle by presenting an array of 'meanings' often listed or numbered in no particular sequence. In other words, an attempt is made to remain as close as possible to the literal meaning. When this procedure is not practicable, the literal meaning from which a figurative gloss is derived may be given, as in 'fret' (2.1.104). Grammatical information, essential for the understanding of the Shakespearean idiolect, is normally keyed to Abbott (although it is inferior to the German work of Franz, which is used, however, when Abbott is lacking). Encyclopedic information is taken from the *OCD*, with occasional citations from detailed works like Pauly or Platner/Ashby. References to passages in Plutarch which are not reproduced in the Appendix are to page numbers in Bullough (whose spelling has been modernised) or (in one case) to the 1579 edition of North's Plutarch.

Julius Caesar

LIST OF CHARACTERS

CAESAR	(Caius Julius Caesar)	
OCTAVIUS	(Caius Octavius Caesar)	*Triumvirs after the death of Julius Caesar*
MARK ANTONY	(Marcus Antonius)	
LEPIDUS	(Marcus Aemilius Lepidus)	
CICERO	(Marcus Tullius Cicero)	*Senators*
PUBLIUS	(not clearly identified in Plutarch, possibly Publius Silicius Corona, who spoke up against the persecution of Brutus by Octavius and was proscribed. See 4.1.4–5 n.)	
POPILLIUS LENA	(Caius Popillius Laenas, erroneously Publius Laena and Laenas in Appian)	
BRUTUS	(Marcus Junius Brutus)	*Conspirators against Julius Caesar*
CASSIUS	(Caius Cassius Longinus)	
CASCA	(Publius Servilius Casca Longus)	
TREBONIUS	(Caius Trebonius)	
CAIUS LIGARIUS	(Quintus Ligarius)	
DECIUS BRUTUS	(Decimus Junius Brutus)	
METELLUS CIMBER	(Lucius Tillius Cimber, called Metellus in Plutarch's *Caesar*, Tullius in the *Brutus*)	
CINNA	(Lucius Cornelius Cinna)	
FLAVIUS	(Lucius Caesetius Flavus)	*Tribunes*
MURELLUS	(Caius Epidius Marullus)	
ARTEMIDORUS OF CNIDOS, *a Doctor of Rhetoric*		
SOOTHSAYER	(called Vestritius Spurinna by Suetonius)	
CINNA, *a poet*	(Caius Helvius Cinna, probably the poet and the tribune are one and the same)	
ANOTHER POET	(Marcus Favonius in Plutarch, erroneously Phaonius in North)	
LUCILIUS	no further identification possible	*Friends to Brutus and Cassius*
TITINIUS		
MESSALA	(Marcus Valerius Messala Corvinus)	
YOUNG CATO	(Marcus Porcius Cato)	
VOLUMNIUS	(Publius Volumnius)	
STATILIUS	(non-speaking)	
FLAVIUS	(non-speaking)	*Officers or Servants to Brutus*
LABEO	(non-speaking)	
VARRUS	(Varro)	
CLAUDIO	(Claudius)	
CLITUS	(Cleitus)	
STRATO	(Straton)	
LUCIUS	(not in Plutarch)	
DARDANIUS	(Dardanus)	

PINDARUS, *servant to Cassius*

CALPURNIA, *wife to Caesar*
PORTIA, *wife to Brutus*
CARPENTER, COBBLER, MESSENGER, PLEBEIANS, SENATORS, SERVANTS, SOLDIERS

SCENE: *Rome, near Sardis, fields of Philippi*

Note

As is often the case in Shakespeare there is inaccuracy and confusion in the names of the characters: historical names are garbled or misunderstood, others are invented or ghosts. The perpetrator, intentional or not, may well be Shakespeare or a compositor or an editorial tradition. Thus F's spelling of the name of the tribune Murellus has been changed by almost all editors since Theobald to Marullus, the authentic name and the spelling to be found in North's translation and in Plutarch. F's spelling of the name of the conspirator Decius Brutus is retained in all editions, however, although the authentic name is Decimus Brutus, the spelling to be found in Plutarch, Suetonius, Appian, and in one of the two instances in North's translation (the other has Decius). Similarly, other perversions in F of historical names are retained in all editions: the tribune Flavus is called Flavius, presumably because North and Plutarch spell it so; Brutus's shield-bearer Dardanus is called Dardanius, however, although North and Plutarch employ the former. Varrus and Claudio – F's spellings – are changed by almost all editions to Varro and Claudius, forms which do not appear in Plutarch, North, Suetonius, or Appian but which are presumably held to be Roman rather than Italian.

Under the circumstances it seems best to retain F spellings, followed by the full historical names and remarks about their authenticity. Other information may also be found in the Commentary. Small alterations, usually of only a single letter, designed to bring the name up to the received standard, are made silently: for example Labeo (for Labio), Calpurnia (for Calphurnia); others, for general recognisability, are unchanged: Clitus (for Cleitus), Portia (for Porcia), and Sardis (for Sardes).

JULIUS CAESAR

1.1 *Enter* FLAVIUS, MURELLUS, *and certain* COMMONERS *over the stage*

FLAVIUS Hence! Home, you idle creatures, get you home!
Is this a holiday? What, know you not,
Being mechanical, you ought not walk
Upon a labouring day without the sign
Of your profession? Speak, what trade art thou?
CARPENTER Why, sir, a carpenter.
MURELLUS Where is thy leather apron and thy rule?
What dost thou with thy best apparel on?
You, sir, what trade are you?

COBBLER Truly, sir, in respect of a fine workman, I am but, as you would say, a cobbler.

MURELLUS But what trade art thou? Answer me directly.

COBBLER A trade, sir, that I hope I may use with a safe conscience, which is indeed, sir, a mender of bad soles.

FLAVIUS What trade, thou knave? Thou naughty knave, what trade?

COBBLER Nay, I beseech you, sir, be not out with me; yet if you be out, sir, I can mend you.

Act 1, Scene 1 1.1] *Actus Primus. Scoena Prima.* F Location] *Theobald (after Rowe)* 0 SD MURELLUS] F *(throughout);* Marullus *Theobald (after Plutarch)* 14 soles] Q (1684); soules F 15 SH FLAVIUS] F; *MUR. / Capell (Capell MS.)* 15] *As verse, Johnson; as prose,* F

Act 1, Scene 1

Location Rome. A street. Unless otherwise indicated, the location or place of the action is modern, as supplied by the editors mentioned in the collation.

0 SD *over the stage* 'A conventional phrase indicating that the actors enter and cross the stage before they come to a halt' (Kittredge). Although the persons are named, according to convention, in descending order of rank, it is obvious that the Commoners enter first. Compare F's SD in *Oth.* 2.3.144: *Enter Cassio pursuing Rodorigo.* The stage itself is illustrated by C. Walter Hodges on p. 4.

3 mechanical of the artisan class. In Plutarch, Cassius refers to 'cobblers, tapsters, or suchlike base mechanical people' (p. 164).

5 thou 'Thou' is generally the familiar pronoun but the formal, non-familiar 'you' (as at 9 below) can be found after the appellative 'sir'. See Abbott 232.

11 cobbler one who mends clumsily (with the obvious pun on one who mends soles/souls).

15 SH FLAVIUS Many editors (starting with Capell) assign to Murellus, finding it consistent with his character, a follow-up to his question (12), and connected with his 'me' in 18. But Johnson's argument that Flavius should not 'stand too long unemployed upon the stage' is cogent. Besides, there is no textual evidence to warrant a reassignment.

15 naughty worthless (more pejorative than in modern usage).

16 out at variance.

16 be out i.e. of a normal state of mind (with a play on the soles being in need of repair).

MURELLUS What mean'st thou by that? Mend me, thou saucy fellow?
COBBLER Why, sir, cobble you.
FLAVIUS Thou art a cobbler, art thou?
COBBLER Truly, sir, all that I live by is with the awl. I meddle with no tradesman's matters, nor women's matters; but withal I am indeed, sir, a surgeon to old shoes: when they are in great danger I recover them. As proper men as ever trod upon neat's leather have gone upon my handiwork.
FLAVIUS But wherefore art not in thy shop today?
Why dost thou lead these men about the streets?
COBBLER Truly, sir, to wear out their shoes, to get myself into more work. But indeed, sir, we make holiday to see Caesar and to rejoice in his triumph.
MURELLUS Wherefore rejoice? What conquest brings he home?
What tributaries follow him to Rome
To grace in captive bonds his chariot wheels?
You blocks, you stones, you worse than senseless things!
O you hard hearts, you cruel men of Rome,
Knew you not Pompey? Many a time and oft
Have you climbed up to walls and battlements,
To towers and windows, yea, to chimney tops,

18 SH MURELLUS] *Mur.* F; *Flav. / Theobald* **18**] *As verse, Capell; as prose,* F **22** tradesman's] Tradesmans F; tradesmen's *Warburton (Folger MS.);* man's *Hanmer;* trade, – man's *Steevens*[2] *(conj. Farmer apud Steevens*[2]*);* trades, man's *conj. Staunton* **22** women's] womens F; womans F2 **22** matters; . . . withal] F; matters; . . . with all. *Capell;* matters, . . . with awl. *Jennens (conj. Farmer apud Steevens)* **31**] *Rowe;* Wherefore reioyce? / . . . home? F **36** Pompey? . . . oft] *Rowe*[3] *(Folger MS.); Pompey* . . . oft? F

21 all . . . awl Possibly proverbial (Tilley A406): 'Without awl (all) the cobbler's nobody.'

21 meddle For illustrations of the sexual innuendo, see *OED* sv *v* 5.

22 withal nevertheless. To the glaring pun on 'awl', A. Jonathan Bate ('The cobbler's awl: *Julius Caesar,* I.i.21–24', *SQ* 35 (1984), 461–2) adds the sexual innuendo implicit in *OED*'s definition of the 'small tool, having a slender, cylindrical, tapering, sharp-pointed blade, with which holes may be pierced; a piercer, pricker, bodkin'.

23 recover The inevitable pun on 'repair' and 'save'.

24 As . . . leather Proverbial (Dent M66): 'As good a man as ever trod on shoe (neat's) leather'.

24 proper fine.

24 neat's leather cowhide. 'In order to encourage the home industry, Englishmen were urged to wear neat's leather, and scorn the Spanish product' (Linthicum, p. 239).

30 triumph The entrance of a victorious commander with his army and spoils in solemn procession into Rome. Shakespeare overlaps this occasion – held in October 45 BC in celebration of the victory at Munda (see 50 n.) – with the Feast of Lupercal (see 66 n.).

33 captive bonds i.e. bonds of captives. For the adjective in the passive sense, see Abbott 3.

34 The repetition and rhythm in the line resemble 'like blockes and stockes and senselesse stones' used in Henry Bullinger's popular *Decades* (1577, p. 285) to describe the unnatural numbness resulting from overstringent Stoicism. Proverbial (Dent S866.1): 'As senseless (etc.) as stock(s) and stone(s)'.

34 senseless incapable of sensation or perception.

36 Pompey Cneius Pompeius (106–48 BC), called Magnus after 81, allied with Caesar and Crassus in the First Triumvirate in 60, defeated by Caesar at Pharsalus on 9 August 48, and stabbed to death after flight to Egypt on 28 September 48.

Your infants in your arms, and there have sat
The livelong day, with patient expectation,
To see great Pompey pass the streets of Rome.
And when you saw his chariot but appear
Have you not made an universal shout,
That Tiber trembled underneath her banks
To hear the replication of your sounds
Made in her concave shores?
And do you now put on your best attire?
And do you now cull out a holiday?
And do you now strew flowers in his way,
That comes in triumph over Pompey's blood?
Be gone!
Run to your houses, fall upon your knees,
Pray to the gods to intermit the plague
That needs must light on this ingratitude.

FLAVIUS Go, go, good countrymen, and for this fault
Assemble all the poor men of your sort,
Draw them to Tiber banks, and weep your tears
Into the channel till the lowest stream
Do kiss the most exalted shores of all.

Exeunt all the Commoners

See where their basest metal be not moved:
They vanish tongue-tied in their guiltiness.
Go you down that way towards the Capitol,
This way will I. Disrobe the images
If you do find them decked with ceremonies.

60 where] F; whether *Thomas Johnson* 60 metal] *Theobald*[3]; mettle F

41 pass For the frequent omission of prepositions after verbs of motion, see Abbott 198. Compare 'arrive', 1.2.110.

50 Pompey's The first of numerous orthographic ambiguities. Although the *es* in the old-spelling 'Pompeyes' is most likely the genitive singular, it could as well be the plural. See also 'winter's', 1.2.99; 'praetor's', 1.3.143; 'time's', 2.1.115; *et passim.*

50 blood blood-relations. Meant are Pompey's sons Cneius and Sextus Magnus Pius, who were defeated by Caesar at Munda in Spain in 45 BC.

51 Abbott (512) notes the 'custom of placing ejaculations, appellations, &c. out of the regular verse'. He also cites 2.1.209 and 3.1.281.

60 metal The interchangeable spellings 'metal'/'mettle' lead here to parallel meanings: literally, the basest metal in alchemy is lead, which melts rapidly; figuratively, the basest spirit ('mettle') yields rapidly too. Of the four other instances of the word (always spelt 'mettle' in F), only 1.2.298 is difficult to render unambiguous.

63–4 Disrobe ... ceremonies 'To disrobe the images was to disturb the peace at this time of religious observance. Besides, the "scarfs" ... might also be regarded as decorations for the Lupercalia. On both grounds the action urged ... would be sacrilegious' (Kittredge).

63 images statues.

64 ceremonies External accessories of worship, state, or pomp. See also 2.1.197, 2.2.13.

MURELLUS May we do so?
You know it is the feast of Lupercal.
FLAVIUS It is no matter; let no images
Be hung with Caesar's trophies. I'll about
And drive away the vulgar from the streets;
So do you too, where you perceive them thick.
These growing feathers plucked from Caesar's wing
Will make him fly an ordinary pitch,
Who else would soar above the view of men
And keep us all in servile fearfulness.
Exeunt

1.2 *Enter* CAESAR, ANTONY *for the course*, CALPURNIA, *Portia, Decius, Cicero,* BRUTUS, CASSIUS, CASCA, *a* SOOTHSAYER, [*a great crowd following*]; *after them Murellus and Flavius*

CAESAR Calpurnia.
CASCA Peace ho, Caesar speaks.
CAESAR Calpurnia.
CALPURNIA Here, my lord.
CAESAR Stand you directly in Antonio's way
When he doth run his course. Antonio.
ANTONY Caesar, my lord.

Act 1, Scene 2 1.2] *Pope (after Folger MS.)* Location] *Capell (Capell MS.)* **0** SD *a ... following*] *Capell* 3 Antonio's] F; *Antonius' / Pope* 4, 6 Antonio] F; *Antonius / Pope*

66 feast of Lupercal Roman festival in honour of Lupercus, protector of flocks against wolves and a patron of agriculture, held on 15 February at the Lupercal, a cave below the western corner of the Palatine. Youths – called Luperci – 'naked except for girdles made from the skins of [sacrificial goats] ran about the bounds of the Palatine settlement, striking those whom they met, especially women, with strips of the goat-skins, a form of fertility magic combined with the ritual beating of the bounds and with purificatory rites' (*OCD* Lupercalia). See Plutarch, p. 156.

68 trophies Arms or other spoils taken from the enemy as a memorial of victory (not simply 'ornaments', as commentators often suggest).

69 vulgar Persons belonging to the ordinary or common class in the community.

72 pitch The height to which a falcon or other bird of prey soars before swooping down on its prey.

Act 1, Scene 2

Location Rome. A public place.

0 SD *for the course* The entrance 'for' a particular purpose implies the appropriate dress, as well as other requisites.

0 SD *course* race.

0 SD *Decius* The erroneous spelling 'Decius' is found in Holland's 1606 translation of Suetonius, too late to account for its appearance in Shakespeare. In the second edition of Amyot's translation of Plutarch (Paris, 1565) the 'Table Alphabétique' lists the 'trahison de Decius Brutus contre Iul. Caesar', but the name in the text appears as 'Decimus'.

3 Antonio's Steevens[2] comments on the spellings 'Antonio', 'Octavio', 'Flavio': 'The players were more accustomed to Italian than Roman terminations, on account of the many versions from Italian novels, and the many Italian characters in dramatic pieces formed on the same originals.'

CAESAR Forget not in your speed, Antonio,
To touch Calpurnia, for our elders say
The barren, touchèd in this holy chase,
Shake off their sterile curse.
ANTONY I shall remember:
When Caesar says, 'Do this', it is performed.
CAESAR Set on, and leave no ceremony out.
SOOTHSAYER Caesar!
CAESAR Ha? Who calls?
CASCA Bid every noise be still – peace yet again!
CAESAR Who is it in the press that calls on me?
I hear a tongue shriller than all the music
Cry 'Caesar!' Speak, Caesar is turned to hear.
SOOTHSAYER Beware the Ides of March.
CAESAR What man is that?
BRUTUS A soothsayer bids you beware the Ides of March.
CAESAR Set him before me, let me see his face.
CASSIUS Fellow, come from the throng, look upon Caesar.
CAESAR What say'st thou to me now? Speak once again.
SOOTHSAYER Beware the Ides of March.
CAESAR He is a dreamer, let us leave him. Pass.
Sennet. Exeunt [*all but*] *Brutus and Cassius*
CASSIUS Will you go see the order of the course?
BRUTUS Not I.
CASSIUS I pray you, do.
BRUTUS I am not gamesome: I do lack some part
Of that quick spirit that is in Antony.
Let me not hinder, Cassius, your desires;
I'll leave you.
CASSIUS Brutus, I do observe you now of late:
I have not from your eyes that gentleness

9 curse] F; Course *Rowe*[3] 21 SH CASSIUS] *Cassi.* F; *Casca / Theobald*[4]

9 sterile curse i.e. curse of sterility. For the construction, see 1.1.33 n.

17 turned The view that Caesar turns because he is deaf in one ear is over-ingenious, especially since Shakespeare always uses the verb in the transferred sense of 'bend' or 'direct'.

18 Ides In the old Roman calendar the fifteenth of March (later known as the Day of the Parricide), as well as of May, July, October, but the thirteenth day of the other months.

24 SD *Sennet* A signal call or fanfare on trumpet or cornet to announce entrances and exits of persons of high rank. Compare *Flourish*, 1.2.78 n.

25 order ritualistic proceeding.

28 gamesome Commentary ranges from 'fond of sport' to 'merry' with recent editors characterising the tone as 'contemptuous'.

And show of love as I was wont to have.
You bear too stubborn and too strange a hand
Over your friend that loves you.

BRUTUS Cassius,
Be not deceived. If I have veiled my look
I turn the trouble of my countenance
Merely upon myself. Vexèd I am
Of late with passions of some difference,
Conceptions only proper to myself,
Which give some soil, perhaps, to my behaviours.
But let not therefore my good friends be grieved
(Among which number, Cassius, be you one)
Nor construe any further my neglect
Than that poor Brutus, with himself at war,
Forgets the shows of love to other men.

CASSIUS Then, Brutus, I have much mistook your passion,
By means whereof this breast of mine hath buried
Thoughts of great value, worthy cogitations.
Tell me, good Brutus, can you see your face?

BRUTUS No, Cassius, for the eye sees not itself
But by reflection, by some other things.

CASSIUS 'Tis just,
And it is very much lamented, Brutus,
That you have no such mirrors as will turn
Your hidden worthiness into your eye
That you might see your shadow. I have heard
Where many of the best respect in Rome
(Except immortal Caesar), speaking of Brutus

52–3] *Rowe;* No *Cassius*: / ... reflection, / ... things. F 53 reflection, by] F; reflection from *Pope* 58] *Rowe;* That ... shadow: / ... heard, F

35 bear ... a hand assert yourself in too stubborn and too unfriendly a manner. See *OED* Bear v^1 3e 'maintain or assert to or against (a person)'.

35 strange unfriendly. Most commentators prefer 'unfamiliar', 'distanced'.

39 Merely Entirely.

40 some difference considerable diversity, conflict.

41 proper belonging, peculiar. See Abbott 16.

42 behaviours In Shakespeare both singular (in the main) and plural.

43 grieved vexed.

48 mistook Abbott (343) notes that when the commonly dropped 'en' inflection was in danger of being confused with the infinitive – here 'take' – the past tense was used for the past participle. See also 'took', 2.1.50; 'Stole', 2.1.238; 'chose', 2.1.314; 'spoke', 3.2.53.

52–3 Classified as 'sententious' by Dent (E231a): 'The eye sees not itself but by reflection.'

54 just exact, accurate (of a description).

58 shadow reflected image.

And groaning underneath this age's yoke,
Have wished that noble Brutus had his eyes.

BRUTUS Into what dangers would you lead me, Cassius,
That you would have me seek into myself
For that which is not in me?

CASSIUS Therefore, good Brutus, be prepared to hear.
And since you know you cannot see yourself
So well as by reflection, I, your glass,
Will modestly discover to yourself
That of yourself which you yet know not of.
And be not jealous on me, gentle Brutus,
Were I a common laughter, or did use
To stale with ordinary oaths my love
To every new protester. If you know
That I do fawn on men and hug them hard
And after scandal them, or if you know
That I profess myself in banqueting
To all the rout, then hold me dangerous.

Flourish and shout

BRUTUS What means this shouting? I do fear the people
Choose Caesar for their king.

CASSIUS Ay, do you fear it?
Then must I think you would not have it so.

BRUTUS I would not, Cassius, yet I love him well.
But wherefore do you hold me here so long?
What is it that you would impart to me?
If it be aught toward the general good,

62 his] F; their *conj. Thirlby* 63] *Rowe (Folger MS.);* Into ... you / ... *Cassius?* F 72 laughter] F; Laugher *Rowe;* lover *conj. Herr;* loffer [*obsolete form of* love *and* laugh] *conj. Wilson* 79–80] *Steevens*[3] *(Capell MS.); Bru.* ... Showting? / ... *Caesar* / ... King. F; *Bru.* ... People / ... King. / ... it? *Rowe*

62 his Most commentators find the reference is to Brutus, a few to the 'speaker', and a few to both.

66 Therefore Commentary is equally divided between 'hence' and 'as to that'.

69 modestly without exaggeration, with due measure.

69 discover uncover, expose to view. See also 2.1.75. For *dis-* used for *un-*, see Abbott 439.

71 jealous mistrustful.

71 on 'Used where we use "of" in the sense of "about"' (Abbott 181).

71 gentle well born, noble (the dominant sense in the play). See also 1.2.232, 2.1.171, *et passim.*

72 laughter subject or matter for laughter. Compare 4.3.114.

72–3 did ... stale was in the habit of staling. For the construction 'use' followed by the infinitive, see Franz 620, Anm. 2.

74 protester one who makes a solemn affirmation.

77 profess myself profess friendship or attachment.

78 rout assemblage (often pejorative).

78 SD *Flourish* A fanfare of brass instruments to announce entrances and exits of persons of high rank. See 131 SD n. and 225 n.

Set honour in one eye and death i'th'other
And I will look on both indifferently.
For let the gods so speed me as I love
The name of honour more than I fear death.

CASSIUS I know that virtue to be in you, Brutus,
As well as I do know your outward favour.
Well, honour is the subject of my story:
I cannot tell what you and other men
Think of this life, but for my single self
I had as lief not be as live to be
In awe of such a thing as I myself.
I was born free as Caesar, so were you;
We both have fed as well, and we can both
Endure the winter's cold as well as he.
For once, upon a raw and gusty day,
The troubled Tiber chafing with her shores,
Caesar said to me, 'Dar'st thou, Cassius, now
Leap in with me into this angry flood
And swim to yonder point?' Upon the word,
Accoutred as I was, I plungèd in
And bade him follow; so indeed he did.
The torrent roared, and we did buffet it
With lusty sinews, throwing it aside
And stemming it with hearts of controversy.
But ere we could arrive the point proposed,
Caesar cried, 'Help me, Cassius, or I sink!'
Ay, as Aeneas, our great ancestor,
Did from the flames of Troy upon his shoulder
The old Anchises bear, so from the waves of Tiber

87 both] F; Death *Theobald (conj. Warburton apud Theobald)* 101 chafing] F; chasing F2 105 Accoutred] F; Accounted F2 107–8 it ... sinews,] F; it, ... sinews *Bevington* 112 Ay] *Bevington;* I F

87 indifferently with unconcern (*OED* sv 3 cites this instance). Many commentators prefer 'impartially', however.

88 as For the construction 'so ... as' for modern 'so ... that', see Abbott 133.

88 speed cause to succeed or prosper. See also 2.4.41.

91 favour appearance. See also 1.3.129, 2.1.76.

102–3 An instance of Caesar's leaping into the sea (but demonstrating his courage) is reported by Suetonius, I, 85.

105 Accoutred Dressed.

109 of controversy contentious (as to one's rights). *OED* Controversy 1a cites this instance.

110 arrive See 1.1.41 n.

112 Aeneas ... ancestor Son of Anchises and the goddess Aphrodite whose legendary wanderings and association with the founding of Rome were developed into the great national theme of Virgil's *Aeneid*.

Did I the tired Caesar. And this man
Is now become a god, and Cassius is
A wretched creature and must bend his body
If Caesar carelessly but nod on him.
He had a fever when he was in Spain,
And when the fit was on him I did mark
How he did shake. 'Tis true, this god did shake,
His coward lips did from their colour fly,
And that same eye whose bend doth awe the world
Did lose his lustre. I did hear him groan,
Ay, and that tongue of his that bade the Romans
Mark him and write his speeches in their books,
'Alas', it cried, 'give me some drink, Titinius',
As a sick girl. Ye gods, it doth amaze me
A man of such a feeble temper should
So get the start of the majestic world
And bear the palm alone.

Shout. Flourish

BRUTUS Another general shout!

123 bend] F; beam *conj. Daniel* **125** Ay] *Rowe;* I F **127** 'Alas'] *Quotation marks, Hudson* **131–2**] *As one line, Collier (Capell MS.)* **132** shout!] *Pope;* shout? F

118 carelessly unconcernedly, heedlessly.

119–31 Plutarch, however, reports otherwise: Caesar 'but yet therefore yielded not to the disease of his body, to make it a cloak to cherish him withal, but, contrarily, took the pains of war as a medicine to cure his sick body, fighting always with his disease'. See *Caesar* (Bullough, p. 66).

119–20 'He was ... often subject to headache, and otherwhile to the falling sickness (the which took him the first time ... in Corduba, a city of Spain).' See Plutarch (*Caesar*, Bullough, p. 66, also p. 76). Suetonius (p. 63) reports that Caesar suffered two attacks during his campaigns.

122 The possibility of wordplay – lips white from fever, cowards fleeing their flag – is perhaps weakened by the fact that the noun following 'their' is normally plural in Shakespeare. Still, a similar wordplay is found in *The Rape of Lucrece* 476.

123 bend glance.

124 his The normal genitive of 'it'. See Abbott 228 and also 2.1.251 *et passim*.

125–6 According to Plutarch (*Caesar*, Bullough, p. 60), 'it is reported that Caesar had an excellent natural gift to speak well before the people; and, besides that rare gift, he was excellently well studied, so that doubtless he was counted the second man [to Cicero] for eloquence in his time'. Plutarch also mentions (*Caesar*, Bullough, p. 59) that Caesar, even while prisoner of pirates, 'would write verses and make orations, and call them together to say them before them; and if any of them seemed as though they had not understood him or passed not for them, he called them blockheads and brute beasts, and laughing threatened them that he would hang them up'.

127 'Alas' This is the first of many instances in the play which may be interpreted as either direct or indirect discourse. The presence here of quotation marks indicates that Cassius is quoting Caesar, their absence that the word is his own.

128 amaze stupefy.

130 get the start Nearly all commentators gloss as 'outstrip', although *OED* Start *sb*[2] 6, citing this instance, gives 'priority or position in advance of others in any competitive undertaking'.

131 palm leaf or branch as sign of victory.

131 SD Humphreys reverses the order of the directions, since 'the flourish heralds the offering of the crown and the shout hails Caesar's refusal'. See also 78 SD n. and 225 n.

I do believe that these applauses are
For some new honours that are heaped on Caesar.
CASSIUS Why, man, he doth bestride the narrow world
Like a Colossus, and we petty men
Walk under his huge legs and peep about
To find ourselves dishonourable graves.
Men at some time are masters of their fates:
The fault, dear Brutus, is not in our stars
But in ourselves, that we are underlings.
Brutus and Caesar: what should be in that 'Caesar'?
Why should that name be sounded more than yours?
Write them together, yours is as fair a name;
Sound them, it doth become the mouth as well;
Weigh them, it is as heavy; conjure with 'em,
'Brutus' will start a spirit as soon as 'Caesar'.
Now in the names of all the gods at once,
Upon what meat doth this our Caesar feed
That he is grown so great? Age, thou art shamed!
Rome, thou hast lost the breed of noble bloods!
When went there by an age since the great flood
But it was famed with more than with one man?
When could they say, till now, that talked of Rome,
That her wide walks encompassed but one man?
Now is it Rome indeed and room enough
When there is in it but one only man.
O, you and I have heard our fathers say
There was a Brutus once that would have brooked
Th'eternal devil to keep his state in Rome
As easily as a king.
BRUTUS That you do love me, I am nothing jealous;

155 walks] F; Walls *Rowe*^{2} *(Folger MS.)* **160** eternal] F; infernal *conj. Thirlby*

133 applauses The only use of the plural in Shakespeare, here apparently for metrical reasons.

142, 143 should Blake (p. 96) notes that 'in interrogatives *should* has an emphatic implication which adds a sense of surprise to the question'.

147 start startle so as to raise.

152 great flood Brought about by Zeus to destroy all mankind for the sins of the Bronze Age.

155 walks tracts of land. See *OED* Walk *sb*^{1} 10, which cites *3H6* 5.2.24.

156 room A homophonic pun on 'Rome' earlier in the line. See 3.1.289, or *John* 3.1.80.

159 a Brutus once Lucius Junius Brutus, the traditional founder of the Roman Republic in the sixth century BC. See also 2.1.54 n.

160 eternal 'Used to express extreme abhorrence' (Schmidt).

160 keep . . . state observe the pomp and ceremony befitting a high position.

161 easily comfortably.

162 nothing Often used adverbially. See Abbott 55.

162 jealous doubtful.

What you would work me to, I have some aim.
How I have thought of this, and of these times,
I shall recount hereafter. For this present,
I would not (so with love I might entreat you)
Be any further moved. What you have said
I will consider; what you have to say
I will with patience hear and find a time
Both meet to hear and answer such high things.
Till then, my noble friend, chew upon this:
Brutus had rather be a villager
Than to repute himself a son of Rome
Under these hard conditions as this time
Is like to lay upon us.

CASSIUS I am glad that my weak words
Have struck but thus much show of fire from Brutus.

Enter CAESAR *and his* TRAIN

BRUTUS The games are done and Caesar is returning.

CASSIUS As they pass by, pluck Casca by the sleeve
And he will (after his sour fashion) tell you
What hath proceeded worthy note today.

BRUTUS I will do so. But look you, Cassius,
The angry spot doth glow on Caesar's brow
And all the rest look like a chidden train:
Calpurnia's cheek is pale, and Cicero
Looks with such ferret and such fiery eyes
As we have seen him in the Capitol,
Being crossed in conference by some senators.

CASSIUS Casca will tell us what the matter is.

CAESAR Antonio.

ANTONY Caesar.

166 (so with] *Thomas Johnson;* so (with F **170** Both] F; But *Rowe*[2] **175–7**] F; Is . . . words [*omitting* that *and* weak] / . . . Brutus. *conj. Ritson (apud Steevens*[3]*);* Is . . . words / . . . Brutus. *Collier;* Is . . . glad, / . . . shew / . . . Brutus. *White (conj. Walker)* **178**] *Rowe;* The . . . done, / . . . returning. F **179**] *Rowe;* As . . . by, / . . . Sleeue, F **183** glow] F; *blow* F3 (hlow F2); grow *Folger MS.* **188** senators] F; senator *Dyce*[2] *(conj. Walker)* **190** Antonio] F; *Antonius / Pope*

163 aim conjecture, guess.

170 meet suitable. See also 299 *et passim*.

181 worthy note For the omission of the preposition after some verbs and adjectives that imply 'value' or 'worth', see Abbott 198a.

186 ferret Literally, 'red', but here used attributively, referring to the hunting or worrying of rats by the ferret. Compare *H5* 4.4.29.

186 fiery angry. Eyes are so characterised in *Venus and Adonis* 219 and *3H6* 2.5.131.

188 conference Those who gloss are unanimous for 'debate', a sense not in *OED* as such. Compare 4.2.17.

CAESAR Let me have men about me that are fat,
Sleek-headed men and such as sleep a-nights.
Yond Cassius has a lean and hungry look,
He thinks too much: such men are dangerous.
ANTONY Fear him not, Caesar, he's not dangerous,
He is a noble Roman and well given.
CAESAR Would he were fatter! But I fear him not.
Yet if my name were liable to fear
I do not know the man I should avoid
So soon as that spare Cassius. He reads much,
He is a great observer, and he looks
Quite through the deeds of men. He loves no plays,
As thou dost, Antony, he hears no music;
Seldom he smiles, and smiles in such a sort
As if he mocked himself and scorned his spirit
That could be moved to smile at any thing.
Such men as he be never at heart's ease
Whiles they behold a greater than themselves,
And therefore are they very dangerous.
I rather tell thee what is to be feared
Than what I fear: for always I am Caesar.
Come on my right hand, for this ear is deaf,
And tell me truly what thou think'st of him.

Sennet. Exeunt Caesar and his train

CASCA You pulled me by the cloak, would you speak with me?
BRUTUS Ay, Casca, tell us what hath chanced today
That Caesar looks so sad.
CASCA Why, you were with him, were you not?

215–16] *As prose,* F; *as verse, Pope*[2]

192 Possibly proverbial (Dent F419): 'Fat folks are faithful.'

193 Sleek-headed Agreeable, free of deep thoughts (from 'smooth'). Plutarch reports (*Caesar*, Bullough, p. 61) that Cicero observed 'how finely he [Caesar] combeth his fair bush of hair, and how smooth it lieth' and thus 'should not have so wicked a thought in his head as to overthrow the state of the commonwealth'.

213 ear is deaf Shakespeare's invention, although some critics believe that deafness (especially of the left ear) is associated with epilepsy. An interesting illustration is found in the complaint (of 20 August 1596) against John Clark, who was relieved of his job as 'Waite' in York because, among other things, he was 'diuerse tymes trobled with the falling sicknesse & his hearing vnperfit or almost deaf' (A. F. Johnston and M. Rogerson (eds.), *York* (*Records of Early English Drama*, vol. 1, 1979), p. 469). For medical and other explanations, see Douglas L. Peterson, '"Wisdom consumed in confidence": an examination of Shakespeare's Julius Caesar', *SQ* 16 (1965), 20–2. Peterson himself argues for a figurative use, as in the proverbial locution 'To turn (give) a deaf ear' (Dent E13).

217 sad grave, serious. See also 2.1.308.

BRUTUS I should not then ask, Casca, what had chanced.

CASCA Why, there was a crown offered him, and being offered him he put it by with the back of his hand thus, and then the people fell a-shouting.

BRUTUS What was the second noise for?

CASCA Why, for that too.

CASSIUS They shouted thrice; what was the last cry for?

CASCA Why, for that too.

BRUTUS Was the crown offered him thrice?

CASCA Ay, marry, was't, and he put it by thrice, every time gentler than other; and at every putting-by mine honest neighbours shouted.

CASSIUS Who offered him the crown?

CASCA Why, Antony.

BRUTUS Tell us the manner of it, gentle Casca.

CASCA I can as well be hanged as tell the manner of it. It was mere foolery, I did not mark it. I saw Mark Antony offer him a crown – yet 'twas not a crown neither, 'twas one of these coronets – and, as I told you, he put it by once; but for all that, to my thinking he would fain have had it. Then he offered it to him again; then he put it by again; but to my thinking he was very loath to lay his fingers off it. And then he offered it the third time; he put it the third time by, and still as he refused it, the rabblement hooted, and clapped their chopped hands, and threw up their sweaty nightcaps, and uttered such a deal of stinking breath because Caesar refused the crown that it had, almost, choked Caesar, for he swounded and fell down at it. And for mine own part I durst not

219 ask, Casca,] Q (1691); aske *Caska* F 230–1] F; *as one line, Mason 1919* 240 hooted] howted F; shouted *Hanmer*

219 ask, Casca, See 2.1.255 n.

221 fell began.

225 thrice It is not clear to some commentators why the stage directions mention only two instances (78, 131). Frances Ann Shirley (*Shakespeare's Use of Off-Stage Sounds*, 1963, p. 125) suggests a third *Flourish and shout* before 'And' (115) or, better, after 147 (following Jennens). In Plutarch (p. 157) the crown is offered only twice, followed by two loud shouts by the 'whole people'. In none of the possible sources is it offered three times. Although it is likely that a stage direction is indeed missing, it is at least conceivable that Caesar, preceded by a flourish, could be entering the market-place (off-stage) to the shouts of the crowd at 78 SD; at 131 SD the flourish after the shout may signal his departure, in order for him to reappear on stage at 177 SD. The exit of Caesar (24 SD), the two responses of the crowd, and his re-entry are, interestingly enough, spaced symmetrically.

228 marry Originally the name of the Virgin Mary used as an oath. In the sixteenth century it was a mere interjection; used here to answer a question and imply surprise that it should be asked: = 'why, to be sure'.

228 was't For the transposition of verb and subject after emphatic words (like interjections), see Abbott 425 and 3.2.102 n.

229 mine Unemphatic, often found before words beginning with vowels for the purposes of euphony. See Abbott 237.

239 still as whenever.

240 hooted made a loud inarticulate noise. The sense is not always as disapproving as Casca and modern usage would have it. Plutarch (p. 157) refers to shouts and outcries of 'rejoicing' and 'joy'.

240 chopped chapped.

243 swounded swooned; a later form with excrescent *d*.

laugh for fear of opening my lips and receiving the bad air.

CASSIUS But soft, I pray you; what, did Caesar swound?

CASCA He fell down in the market-place, and foamed at mouth, and was speechless.

BRUTUS 'Tis very like, he hath the falling sickness.

CASSIUS No, Caesar hath it not, but you, and I,
And honest Casca, we have the falling sickness.

CASCA I know not what you mean by that, but I am sure Caesar fell down. If the tag-rag people did not clap him and hiss him according as he pleased and displeased them, as they use to do the players in the theatre, I am no true man.

BRUTUS What said he when he came unto himself?

CASCA Marry, before he fell down, when he perceived the common herd was glad he refused the crown, he plucked me ope his doublet and offered them his throat to cut. And I had been a man of any occupation, if I would not have taken him at a word I would I might go to hell among the rogues. And so he fell. When he came to himself again, he said if he had done or said anything amiss, he desired their worships to think it was his infirmity. Three or four wenches where I stood cried, 'Alas, good soul', and forgave him with all their hearts. But there's no heed to be taken of them: if Caesar had stabbed their mothers they would have done no less.

BRUTUS And after that he came thus sad away?

CASCA Ay.

CASSIUS Did Cicero say anything?

CASCA Ay, he spoke Greek.

248 like,] *Rowe;* like F 266 away?] *Theobald;* away. F

245 **soft** An exclamation with imperative force, either to enjoin silence or deprecate haste. See also 3.1.122.

245 **swound** swoon. See 243 above.

248 **like** likely. The absence of the *-ly* ending may be due to the metre.

248 **falling sickness** See 119–20 n.

252 **tag-rag people** i.e. rabble (from 'dressed in tags and rags').

257 **me** For the use of the dative to call attention to the speaker himself, see Abbott 220.

257 **ope** The only prose instance in Shakespeare, this obsolete adjectival form suits Casca's mocking tone.

258 **And** See 271 n.

259 **occupation** handicraft, trade (*OED* sv 4c). A few prefer 'action'.

266 This is the first of a number of sentences with declarative (or at least ambiguous) word order for which a question mark seems more appropriate than a full stop. See also 3.2.148, 4.3.229, 5.1.35, 109. The reverse is to be found at 4.3.240.

269 Scant comment finds the words appropriate to Cicero's cautious, if not evasive, mode of behaviour or his habit of expressing witticisms in Greek. Both views may have some connection with Plutarch's description (*Life of Cicero*, 1579 edn, p. 914): 'When he came to Rome, at the first he proceeded very warily and discreetly, and did unwillingly seek for any office; and when he did, he was not greatly esteemed, for they commonly called him the Grecian and scholar, which are two words, the which the artificers (and such base mechanical people at Rome) have ever ready at their tongues' end.'

CASSIUS To what effect?

CASCA Nay, and I tell you that, I'll ne'er look you i'th'face again. But those that understood him smiled at one another and shook their heads; but for mine own part it was Greek to me. I could tell you more news too. Murellus and Flavius, for pulling scarves off Caesar's images, are put to silence. Fare you well. There was more foolery yet, if I could remember it.

CASSIUS Will you sup with me tonight, Casca?

CASCA No, I am promised forth.

CASSIUS Will you dine with me tomorrow?

CASCA Ay, if I be alive, and your mind hold, and your dinner worth the eating.

CASSIUS Good, I will expect you.

CASCA Do so. Farewell both. *Exit*

BRUTUS What a blunt fellow is this grown to be!
He was quick mettle when he went to school.

CASSIUS So is he now in execution
Of any bold or noble enterprise,
However he puts on this tardy form.
This rudeness is a sauce to his good wit,
Which gives men stomach to digest his words
With better appetite.

BRUTUS And so it is. For this time I will leave you.
Tomorrow if you please to speak with me,
I will come home to you; or if you will,
Come home to me and I will wait for you.

291–2] *Rowe;* With ... Appetite. / ... is: / ... you: F

270 effect purpose.

271 and I tell Abbott (102) notes that the 'hypothesis, the *if*, is expressed not by the *and*, but by the subjunctive, and that *and* merely means *with the addition of*'.

273 Greek to me The remark is to be taken rhetorically since Casca knew Greek. See Plutarch, pp. 160, 168.

274 scarves Plutarch (pp. 157, 164) refers to diadems; it is Suetonius (p. 103) who mentions the removal from the laurel wreath of a 'ribbon', a white fillet emblematic of royalty.

275 put to silence Plutarch (p. 157) says they were 'deprived ... of their Tribuneships'. Shakespeare's phrase is regarded by some as a cynical euphemism for 'put to death'.

279 dine The main Roman meal, the *prandium*, was taken at midday; although no attempt is made here to apply Roman standards, dinner was the midday meal, supper the evening meal in Shakespeare's time.

285 quick endowed with life, energetic. See 'metal', 1.1.60n.

288 tardy form For a similar application to speech which is not lively or smooth, compare *2H4* 2.3.26: 'speak low and tardily'.

289 rudeness roughness.

289 wit intelligence.

290 gives ... stomach inclines. See also 5.1.66.

CASSIUS I will do so. Till then, think of the world.

Exit Brutus

Well, Brutus, thou art noble; yet I see
Thy honourable metal may be wrought
From that it is disposed. Therefore it is meet
That noble minds keep ever with their likes;
For who so firm that cannot be seduced?
Caesar doth bear me hard, but he loves Brutus.
If I were Brutus now and he were Cassius,
He should not humour me. I will this night,
In several hands, in at his windows throw,
As if they came from several citizens,
Writings, all tending to the great opinion
That Rome holds of his name, wherein obscurely
Caesar's ambition shall be glancèd at.
And after this let Caesar seat him sure,
For we will shake him, or worse days endure. *Exit*

1.3 *Thunder and lightning. Enter [from opposite sides]* CASCA *and* CICERO

CICERO Good even, Casca, brought you Caesar home?
Why are you breathless, and why stare you so?
CASCA Are not you moved when all the sway of earth
Shakes like a thing unfirm? O Cicero,

297 art noble;] F; art: Noble F2 **298** metal] F2; Mettle F **Act 1, Scene 3** **1.3**] *Capell* Location] *Capell (Capell MS.)* **0 SD** *from opposite sides*] *Capell (Capell MS.)*

298 metal See 1.1.60 n.

299 From Away from. See Abbott 158 and 1.3.35, 64, *et passim*.

299 that Abbott (244) notes that the relative – 'to which' – 'is frequently omitted, especially where the antecedent clause is emphatic and evidently incomplete'.

302 bear me hard 'endure [me] with a grudge' (*OED* Bear v^1 16, citing this instance). See also 2.1.215, 3.1.157.

304 humour influence (by complying with the peculiar nature of someone).

305 hands handwritings.

310 him himself (the shortened form often used for metrical reasons). See also 1.3.156.

310 sure The form without the *-ly* ending was most likely chosen because of the metre and the rhyme (with 'endure').

Act 1, Scene 3

Location Rome. A street.

0 SD.1 ***Thunder and lightning*** Thunder was produced by rolling a cannon-ball down a wooden trough, the 'thunder run', by drums or cannon-fire; lightning, by some kind of fireworks.

1 In Elizabethan stage practice the exchange of greetings, farewells, and other information at the beginning or end of a scene implies the use of the two stage doors. See also 2.4.46 SD n. and illustration 3 on p. 7.

3 sway sovereign power or authority (the customary meaning in Shakespeare); 'balanced swing' (Craik) is unlikely.

I have seen tempests when the scolding winds
Have rived the knotty oaks, and I have seen
Th'ambitious ocean swell, and rage, and foam,
To be exalted with the threatening clouds;
But never till tonight, never till now,
Did I go through a tempest dropping fire.
Either there is a civil strife in heaven,
Or else the world, too saucy with the gods,
Incenses them to send destruction.

CICERO Why, saw you anything more wonderful?

CASCA A common slave – you know him well by sight –
Held up his left hand, which did flame and burn
Like twenty torches joined, and yet his hand,
Not sensible of fire, remained unscorched.
Besides – I ha' not since put up my sword –
Against the Capitol I met a lion
Who glazed upon me and went surly by
Without annoying me. And there were drawn
Upon a heap a hundred ghastly women,
Transformèd with their fear, who swore they saw
Men, all in fire, walk up and down the streets.
And yesterday the bird of night did sit
Even at noon-day upon the market-place,
Hooting and shrieking. When these prodigies
Do so conjointly meet let not men say,
'These are their reasons, they are natural',
For I believe they are portentous things

15 know] F; knew *conj. Craik* 21 glazed] F; glar'd *Thomas Johnson;* gaz'd Q (1691) *(Folger MS.);* glased [= glazed *or* glassed] *conj. Nicholson* 30 reasons] F; seasons *Collier*[2] *(Collier MS.)*

8 exalted raised.

12 saucy insolent towards superiors. Used by Shakespeare 'as a term of serious condemnation' (*OED* sv 2b).

14 wonderful such as to excite wonder or astonishment.

18 sensible of liable to be affected by.

20 Against In front of (most commentators prefer 'Opposite').

21 Who 'Often used of animals ... where action is attributed to them' (Abbott 264).

21 glazed stared (*OED* Glaze v^2 cites this instance).

22 annoying harming.

22 drawn assembled.

23 Upon a heap 'In a prostrate mass' (*OED* Heap *sb* 5c).

23 ghastly causing terror (influenced by 'ghost-like', wan). For adjectives with active and passive sense, see Abbott 3.

26 bird of night screech-owl. Pliny (*Naturall Historie*, trans. Philemon Holland, 1601, 10:12, p. 276) notes that this 'verie monster of the night ... betokeneth alwaies some heavie newes, and is most execrable and accursed, and namely, in the presages of public affaires'.

28 prodigies something extraordinary from which omens are drawn. *Prodigia* or *monstra* were believed to be divinely sent. See also 77 n. and 2.1.198.

Unto the climate that they point upon.

CICERO Indeed, it is a strange-disposèd time.
But men may construe things after their fashion
Clean from the purpose of the things themselves.
Comes Caesar to the Capitol tomorrow?

CASCA He doth, for he did bid Antonio
Send word to you he would be there tomorrow.

CICERO Good night then, Casca. This disturbèd sky
Is not to walk in.

CASCA Farewell, Cicero.

Exit Cicero

Enter CASSIUS

CASSIUS Who's there?

CASCA A Roman.

CASSIUS Casca, by your voice.

CASCA Your ear is good. Cassius, what night is this!

CASSIUS A very pleasing night to honest men.

CASCA Who ever knew the heavens menace so?

CASSIUS Those that have known the earth so full of faults.
For my part I have walked about the streets,
Submitting me unto the perilous night,
And, thus unbracèd, Casca, as you see,
Have bared my bosom to the thunderstone;
And when the cross blue lightning seemed to open
The breast of heaven, I did present myself
Even in the aim and very flash of it.

CASCA But wherefore did you so much tempt the heavens?
It is the part of men to fear and tremble
When the most mighty gods by tokens send
Such dreadful heralds to astonish us.

CASSIUS You are dull, Casca, and those sparks of life

37 Antonio] F; *Antonius* / *Pope* **39**] *Rowe;* Good-night . . . *Caska*: / . . . in. F **42**] *Rowe;* Your . . . good. / . . . this? F **42** what] F; what a *Craik* **42** this!] *Johnson;* this? F **57–60**] *Rowe;* You . . . *Caska*: / . . . Roman, / . . . not. / . . . feare, / . . . wonder, F

32 climate region of the earth.

32 point are directed.

35 from away from. See 1.2.299 n.

42 what night For the omission of 'a' after 'what' in the sense of 'what kind of', see Abbott 86.

47 me i.e. myself. See Abbott 223.

48 unbracèd with dress or part of dress unfastened or loosened. See also 2.1.262.

49 thunderstone thunderbolt. A popular belief was that destruction caused by lightning was due to objects hurtled from the sky.

50 cross 'criss-crossing' or, perhaps figuratively, 'adverse'.

53 tempt test. See also 2.1.266, 4.3.36, 4.3.62.

56 astonish terrify.

That should be in a Roman you do want,
Or else you use not. You look pale, and gaze,
And put on fear, and cast yourself in wonder
To see the strange impatience of the heavens.
But if you would consider the true cause
Why all these fires, why all these gliding ghosts,
Why birds and beasts from quality and kind,
Why old men, fools, and children calculate,
Why all these things change from their ordinance,
Their natures, and preformèd faculties,
To monstrous quality – why, you shall find
That heaven hath infused them with these spirits
To make them instruments of fear, and warning
Unto some monstrous state.
Now could I, Casca, name to thee a man
Most like this dreadful night,
That thunders, lightens, opens graves, and roars
As doth the lion in the Capitol –
A man no mightier than thyself, or me,
In personal action, yet prodigious grown
And fearful, as these strange eruptions are.
CASCA 'Tis Caesar that you mean, is it not, Cassius?
CASSIUS Let it be who it is, for Romans now
Have thews and limbs like to their ancestors'.
But, woe the while, our fathers' minds are dead
And we are governed with our mothers' spirits;
Our yoke and sufferance show us womanish.
CASCA Indeed, they say the senators tomorrow
Mean to establish Caesar as a king,

60 cast] F; case *White (conj. Jervis)* **65** men, fools] F; men fools *Steevens*[2] *(Folger MS.)*; men fool *White (conj. Mitford)* **71–3**] F; Unto ... *Casca,* / ... night; *Hanmer (conj. Thirlby)* **74** roars] F; teares F2 **79**] *Rowe;* 'Tis ... meane: / ... *Cassius?* F **81** ancestors'] *This edn;* Ancestors F **85** say] *Blair;* say, F

58 want lack.

64 from away from. See 1.2.299 n.

64 quality and kind Practically synonymous with 'character' or 'nature'. For 'quality', see also 68 and 3.1.41, 61.

65 fools Most likely 'natural' or 'born' fools. See *OED* sv *sb* 4.

65 calculate The gloss 'prophesy' (given by Johnson, and before him by Warburton) is unnecessarily specific, as Craik pointed out, since the customary 'reckon' fits the sense here.

77 prodigious abnormal, ominous. See also 28 n.

78 fearful inducing fear. For the active and passive sense of adjectives ending in *-ful*, see Abbott 3. See also 2.1.98, 3.1.169, 5.1.10.

81 thews sinews (F3's reading).

84 sufferance patient endurance.

And he shall wear his crown by sea and land,
In every place save here in Italy.

CASSIUS I know where I will wear this dagger then:
Cassius from bondage will deliver Cassius.
Therein, ye gods, you make the weak most strong;
Therein, ye gods, you tyrants do defeat.
Nor stony tower, nor walls of beaten brass,
Nor airless dungeon, nor strong links of iron,
Can be retentive to the strength of spirit;
But life, being weary of these worldly bars,
Never lacks power to dismiss itself.
If I know this, know all the world besides,
That part of tyranny that I do bear
I can shake off at pleasure.

Thunder still

CASCA So can I,
So every bondman in his own hand bears
The power to cancel his captivity.

CASSIUS And why should Caesar be a tyrant then?
Poor man, I know he would not be a wolf
But that he sees the Romans are but sheep;
He were no lion, were not Romans hinds.
Those that with haste will make a mighty fire
Begin it with weak straws. What trash is Rome,
What rubbish and what offal, when it serves
For the base matter to illuminate
So vile a thing as Caesar? But, O grief,
Where hast thou led me? I perhaps speak this
Before a willing bondman, then I know
My answer must be made. But I am armed,
And dangers are to me indifferent.

111 Caesar?] F *(question mark after* offal *at 109); Caesar! / Jennens*

87 shall is to. See Abbott 315.

91 ye gods, you Blake (p. 79) notes that the 'ye' before 'gods' is 'understandably unemphatic, but the [emphatic] *you* afterwards is used to stress their power'.

100 SD *still* constantly. See also 3.1.145 *et passim.*

104–5 Proverbial (Dent S300): 'He that makes himself a sheep shall be eaten by the wolf.'

108 trash 'That which is broken, snapped, or lopped off anything in preparing it for use . . . as twigs, splinters, "cuttings from a hedge"' (*OED* sv *sb*[1] 1).

109 offal 'That which falls off or is thrown off, as chips in dressing wood' (*OED* sv 1).

110 illuminate The image calls for the literal meaning 'set alight, light, kindle' (*OED* sv *v* 7).

111 thing Applied to men, with connotations dependent usually on the qualifying words. See also 2.1.29.

CASCA You speak to Casca, and to such a man
That is no fleering tell-tale. Hold, my hand.
Be factious for redress of all these griefs,
And I will set this foot of mine as far
As who goes farthest.
CASSIUS There's a bargain made.
Now know you, Casca, I have moved already
Some certain of the noblest-minded Romans
To undergo with me an enterprise
Of honourable dangerous consequence.
And I do know by this they stay for me
In Pompey's Porch. For now, this fearful night,
There is no stir or walking in the streets,
And the complexion of the element
In favour's like the work we have in hand,
Most bloody, fiery, and most terrible.

Enter CINNA

CASCA Stand close a while, for here comes one in haste.
CASSIUS 'Tis Cinna, I do know him by his gait.
He is a friend. Cinna, where haste you so?
CINNA To find out you. Who's that? Metellus Cimber?
CASSIUS No, it is Casca, one incorporate
To our attempts. Am I not stayed for, Cinna?
CINNA I am glad on't. What a fearful night is this!
There's two or three of us have seen strange sights.

117 Hold,] F; Hold *Theobald* 124 honourable dangerous] F; *hyphen, Capell;* honourable, dangerous *Collier*[3] 125 know by this] F; know, by this *Rowe* 129 In favour's] Q (1691); Is Fauors F; is favorous *Folger MS.;* Is Feav'rous *Rowe;* Is favour'd *Capell (conj. Thirlby);* It favours *Steevens* 130 bloody, fiery] F; *hyphen, Dyce*[2] *(conj. Walker)* 130 SD] F; *at 133 after* friend *Dyce* 131] *As verse,* Q (1684); *as prose,* F 134] *As verse,* Q (1684); *as prose,* F 137] *Rowe;* I ... on't. / ... this? F

117 **fleering** laughing coarsely, sneeringly.

117 **Hold** Here! take it! Used in the imperative when offering or presenting something.

118 **factious** of the faction.

118 **griefs** grievances.

120 **who** i.e. anyone who. See Abbott 257.

124 **honourable dangerous** Many editors insert a hyphen, regarding the construction as a compound adjective, the first word – see Abbott 2 – being a 'kind of adverb qualifying the second'.

126 **Pompey's Porch** *Porticus Pompei*, built in 55 BC by Pompey at the same time as his theatre (see 152) and adjoining its *scaena*. The purpose of the *porticus* was to afford shelter for the spectators in case of rain. It was a rectangular court in which were four parallel rows of columns (Platner/Ashby). In Plutarch it is the scene of the assassination; Shakespeare chooses the Capitol.

128 **complexion** visible aspect, condition.

128 **element** sky.

129 ***favour** appearance; as at 1.2.91.

131 **close** 'so as not to stir' (Schmidt *adv.* 2), 'concealed' (Onions). The latter sense is preferred by most.

135 **incorporate** united in one body.

137 **on't** of it. See 1.2.71 n.

CASSIUS Am I not stayed for? Tell me.
CINNA Yes, you are.
O Cassius, if you could
But win the noble Brutus to our party –
CASSIUS Be you content. Good Cinna, take this paper
And look you lay it in the praetor's chair,
Where Brutus may but find it; and throw this
In at his window; set this up with wax
Upon old Brutus' statue. All this done,
Repair to Pompey's Porch, where you shall find us.
Is Decius Brutus and Trebonius there?
CINNA All but Metellus Cimber, and he's gone
To seek you at your house. Well, I will hie,
And so bestow these papers as you bade me.
CASSIUS That done, repair to Pompey's Theatre.
Exit Cinna
Come, Casca, you and I will yet, ere day,
See Brutus at his house. Three parts of him
Is ours already, and the man entire
Upon the next encounter yields him ours.
CASCA O, he sits high in all the people's hearts,
And that which would appear offence in us
His countenance, like richest alchemy,
Will change to virtue and to worthiness.
CASSIUS Him and his worth and our great need of him

139–41] *Delius*[2], *Singer*[2] *(conj. W. S. Walker); Cassi.* ... me. / ... *Cassius*, / ... Brutus / ... party – F; *Cas.* ... me. / ... are. / ... *Brutus* / ... Party – *Rowe; Cas.* ... me. / ... could / ... party – *Johnson; CAS.* ... me. [*adding* Cinna *after* for,] / ... Yes, / ... win / ... party – *Capell (Capell MS.); Cas.* ... me. / ... Yes, / ... win / ... party – *Steevens; Cas.* ... Cassius! / ... party ... *Keightley;* CASSIUS ... Cassius, / ... Brutus / ... party – *Charney* **144** but] F; best *Hudson*[2] *(conj. Craik)*

142 content satisfied in mind, calm; used in the imperative. See also 4.2.41.

143 praetor Brutus was made *praetor urbanus* by Caesar in 44 BC, a position just below consul.

143 chair Most likely the curule, 'a chair or seat inlaid with ivory and shaped like a camp-stool with curved legs' (*OED* Curule *a* 1).

144 may but cannot but. For the original sense of 'may' = 'can', see Abbott 307. Abbott (128) notes that 'possibly ... *but* may be transposed, and the meaning may be "Brutus only," *i.e.* "Brutus alone"'. Craik wonders, however, whether 'but' may not be a misprint for 'best'.

148 Is .. there Abbott (335) notes that when the plural subject 'is as yet future and ... unsettled, the third person singular might be regarded as the normal inflection'.

152 Pompey's Theatre *Theatrum Pompei*, the first permanent theatre in Rome, built of stone by Pompey in his second consulship in 55 BC and located in the Campus Martius (Platner/Ashby).

155 man entire The not uncommon transposition of the adjective for the purposes of emphasis and metre. See Abbott 419.

156 him himself. See 1.2.310n.

160 to virtue and to worthiness Most likely doublets operating on both the moral and alchemical levels, the latter in reference to the inherent, often magical, power found in precious stones (see *OED* Virtue 9).

You have right well conceited. Let us go,
For it is after midnight, and ere day
We will awake him and be sure of him.

Exeunt

2.1 *Enter* BRUTUS *in his orchard*

BRUTUS What, Lucius, ho!
I cannot by the progress of the stars
Give guess how near to day. Lucius, I say!
I would it were my fault to sleep so soundly.
When, Lucius, when? Awake, I say! What, Lucius!

Enter LUCIUS

LUCIUS Called you, my lord?
BRUTUS Get me a taper in my study, Lucius.
When it is lighted, come and call me here.
LUCIUS I will, my lord. *Exit*
BRUTUS It must be by his death. And for my part
I know no personal cause to spurn at him
But for the general. He would be crowned:
How that might change his nature, there's the question.
It is the bright day that brings forth the adder
And that craves wary walking. Crown him that,
And then I grant we put a sting in him
That at his will he may do danger with.
Th'abuse of greatness is when it disjoins
Remorse from power. And to speak truth of Caesar,
I have not known when his affections swayed

Act 2, Scene 1 **2.1**] *Actus Secundus.* F; ACT II. SCENE I. *Rowe* Location] F *(subst.)*

162 conceited apprehended. See also 3.1.192. Some very recent commentators detect a pun on 'expressed in metaphorical language'.

Act 2, Scene 1

Location Rome. Brutus's garden.

1, 5 What, When Exclamations of impatience.

11 spurn kick.

15 that craves Most likely the demonstrative 'that', although possibly the relative whose antecedent is 'the bright day'.

15 that 'The emphatic *that* appears to be used exactly as *so* often is' (Craik). Most recent editors paraphrase as 'emperor' or 'king'; earlier ones put a dash or similar punctuation before it, as elliptical for 'do that'.

19 Remorse Compassion, scruple.

20 affections emotions.

20 swayed ruled, held sway.

More than his reason. But 'tis a common proof
That lowliness is young ambition's ladder,
Whereto the climber-upward turns his face;
But when he once attains the upmost round
He then unto the ladder turns his back,
Looks in the clouds, scorning the base degrees
By which he did ascend. So Caesar may.
Then lest he may, prevent. And since the quarrel
Will bear no colour for the thing he is,
Fashion it thus: that what he is, augmented,
Would run to these and these extremities.
And therefore think him as a serpent's egg
(Which, hatched, would as his kind grow mischievous)
And kill him in the shell.

Brutus is talking about killing Caesar and how as Caeser climbs the ladder of power he is scorning the people below.

Enter LUCIUS

LUCIUS The taper burneth in your closet, sir.
Searching the window for a flint, I found
This paper, thus sealed up, and I am sure
It did not lie there when I went to bed.

Gives him the letter

BRUTUS Get you to bed again, it is not day.
Is not tomorrow, boy, the Ides of March?
LUCIUS I know not, sir.
BRUTUS Look in the calendar and bring me word.
LUCIUS I will, sir. *Exit*

23 climber-upward] *Hyphen, Warburton* **40** Ides] *Theobald (conj. Warburton apud Theobald)*; first F

21 proof experience (*OED* sv *sb* 5).

23 climber-upward Most editions hyphenate, although Craik, preferring F's omission, quotes *Mac.* 4.2.24–5: 'Things at the worst will cease, or else climb upward / To what they were before.'

24 round rung (of a ladder).

26 degrees rungs (as at 24).

28 prevent use precautionary measures, forestall. See also 160 and 5.1.104, and 'prevention', 85 n. and 3.1.19.

28 quarrel ground or occasion of complaint (a legal term).

29 bear no colour support or endure no specious appearance.

29 thing Applied to a human being; as at 1.3.111.

33 as his kind Commentators are about equally split between 'according to his nature' and 'like the rest of his species'.

33 mischievous harmful (the sense is stronger than in current usage).

35 closet private room. See also 3.2.121.

38 SD *Gives* Stage directions in the present tense are generally thought to be of a literary nature and not infrequently authorial. Compare *knock*, 2.1.59 SD n.

40 *Ides Theobald explains F's 'first' as a misreading of a manuscript contraction I^s, but most believe, following John Hunter, that 'Shakspeare must either have inadvertently quoted from a passage in Plutarch [see p. 164 below] not applicable here, but which refers to Cassius asking Brutus if he intended to be in the senate-house on the first of March ... or else the poet must have meant to represent Brutus as exceedingly oblivious, and even Lucius as rather too unobservant of time's progress.'

BRUTUS The exhalations whizzing in the air
Give so much light that I may read by them.
Opens the letter and reads
'Brutus, thou sleep'st. Awake, and see thyself!
Shall Rome, etc. Speak, strike, redress!'
'Brutus, thou sleep'st. Awake!'
Such instigations have been often dropped
Where I have took them up.
'Shall Rome, etc.' Thus must I piece it out:
Shall Rome stand under one man's awe? What, Rome?
My ancestors did from the streets of Rome
The Tarquin drive when he was called a king.
'Speak, strike, redress!' Am I entreated
To speak and strike? O Rome, I make thee promise,
If the redress will follow, thou receivest
Thy full petition at the hand of Brutus.

Enter LUCIUS

LUCIUS Sir, March is wasted fifteen days.
Knock within
BRUTUS 'Tis good. Go to the gate, somebody knocks.
[*Exit Lucius*]
Since Cassius first did whet me against Caesar
I have not slept.
Between the acting of a dreadful thing
And the first motion, all the interim is
Like a phantasma or a hideous dream.

52 What,] *Rowe;* What F 56 thee] F; the F2 59 fifteen] F; fourteen *Theobald* 60 SD] *Theobald*

44 **exhalations** enkindled vapours, meteors.

48 Editors are split about evenly as to whether this line is part of the letter (first in Q (1691)) or is Brutus's re-reading or quotation of 46 (first in Capell). A few editors, starting with Theobald, even regard 52–4 as a quotation.

50 **took** For the form, see 1.2.48 n.

54 **Tarquin** Tarquinius Superbus (traditionally 534–510 BC), held to be the last king of Rome, is believed to have been expelled by Lucius Junius Brutus, the traditional founder of the Roman Republic. See also 1.2.159 n.

58 **at** from.

59 **fifteen** That it is the morning of the fifteenth day is a more likely explanation than that Lucius is correcting his master's forgetfulness at 40 (due to his absorption in his thoughts) or that Shakespeare had erred in not writing 'fourteen'.

59 SD The imperative is normally thought to be a reminder for the prompter, as is 'within', a theatrical SD which refers to the tiring-house – i.e. the action is off-stage; as at 4.2.24 SD, 4.3.142 SD.2, 5.5.42 SD.

60 **'Tis good** One of the few to comment, John Hunter remarks that 'This expression may be merely a mannerly acknowledgment of the servant's attention; or perhaps the pronoun *it* refers to the fact announced, and Brutus may be here welcoming the near termination of that hideous interim to which he presently refers.'

64 **motion** 'inward prompting or impulse' (*OED* sv *sb* 9).

The genius and the mortal instruments
Are then in council, and the state of a man,
Like to a little kingdom, suffers then
The nature of an insurrection.

Enter LUCIUS

LUCIUS Sir, 'tis your brother Cassius at the door,
Who doth desire to see you.

BRUTUS Is he alone?

LUCIUS No, sir, there are mo with him.

BRUTUS Do you know them?

LUCIUS No, sir, their hats are plucked about their ears
And half their faces buried in their cloaks,
That by no means I may discover them
By any mark of favour.

BRUTUS Let 'em enter.

[*Exit Lucius*]

They are the faction. O conspiracy,
Sham'st thou to show thy dang'rous brow by night,
When evils are most free? O then by day
Where wilt thou find a cavern dark enough
To mask thy monstrous visage? Seek none, conspiracy,
Hide it in smiles and affability,
For if thou path, thy native semblance on,
Not Erebus itself were dim enough
To hide thee from prevention.

67 a] F; *omitted in* F2 **74** cloaks] F; Cloathes F2 **76** of] F; or *Folger MS.* **76** SD] *Rowe* **79** O then] QU1; O then, F; O, then *Globe* **83** path,] path F; hath QU3; march, *Pope;* hadst *conj. White;* put *Dyce*[2] *(Folger MS.);* pass, *Hudson*[2] *(conj. Cartwright);* parle, *conj. Nicholson;* pall [*replacing* on *with* o'er] *conj. Heraud (apud Cam.);* pace, *conj. Anon. (apud Cam.)*

66 genius The tutelary god or attendant spirit allotted to every person at his birth, according to classical pagan belief, to govern his fortunes and determine his character.

66 mortal human.

66 instruments vital organs.

67 in council i.e. are deliberating. Compare 4.1.45 n.

70 brother i.e. brother-in-law. Cassius had married Brutus's sister, Junia Tertia (Tertulla). For a similar usage, compare *Ant.* 2.7.119.

72 mo more. Used only with count nouns in the plural. See also 5.3.101.

73 hats Pope substituted a blank for what he considered an unacceptable anachronism.

75 may am able to. See Abbott 307.

75 discover identify. See 1.2.69 n.

76 favour appearance; as at 1.2.91.

83 path pursue one's course.

83 native natural (the shorter form perhaps for metrical reasons).

84 Erebus Son of Chaos and Darkness, he came to signify the nether world or Darkness itself.

85 prevention 'The action of … securing an advantage over another person by previous action' (*OED* sv 4a). See also 3.1.19 and 'prevent', 28 n.

Enter the conspirators, CASSIUS, CASCA, DECIUS, CINNA, METELLUS, *and* TREBONIUS

CASSIUS I think we are too bold upon your rest.
Good morrow, Brutus, do we trouble you?
BRUTUS I have been up this hour, awake all night.
Know I these men that come along with you?
CASSIUS Yes, every man of them; and no man here
But honours you, and every one doth wish
You had but that opinion of yourself
Which every noble Roman bears of you.
This is Trebonius.
BRUTUS He is welcome hither.
CASSIUS This, Decius Brutus.
BRUTUS He is welcome too.
CASSIUS This, Casca; this, Cinna; and this, Metellus Cimber.
BRUTUS They are all welcome.
What watchful cares do interpose themselves
Betwixt your eyes and night?
CASSIUS Shall I entreat a word?

They whisper

DECIUS Here lies the east, doth not the day break here?
CASCA No.
CINNA O, pardon, sir, it doth, and yon grey lines
That fret the clouds are messengers of day.
CASCA You shall confess that you are both deceived.
Here, as I point my sword, the sun arises,
Which is a great way growing on the south,
Weighing the youthful season of the year.
Some two months hence, up higher toward the north
He first presents his fire, and the high east
Stands, as the Capitol, directly here.

96] *As verse, Thomas Johnson*[2]*; as prose,* F; This ... *Cinna;* / ... *Cimber.* / *Rowe* **99–100]** *As one line, Keightley* **101]** *As verse, Theobald; as prose,* F

98 watchful i.e. causing watchfulness. For the *-ful* suffix, see 1.3.78 n.

100 SD Brutus and Cassius most likely move or turn away from the others. To speculate, as some commentators do, about the subject of their conversation is idle.

104 fret variegate (from fret = 'adorn with interlaced work', *OED v*[2] 1a and b).

106 as 'in proportion as, according as' (Franz 578), not 'where' (Abbott 112). See also 3.2.21.

107 growing advancing.

108 Weighing Considering. For the participle without a noun employed almost as preposition, see Abbott 378.

BRUTUS [*Advancing with Cassius*] Give me your hands all over, one by one.

CASSIUS And let us swear our resolution.

BRUTUS No, not an oath! If not the face of men,
The sufferance of our souls, the time's abuse –
If these be motives weak, break off betimes,
And every man hence to his idle bed;
So let high-sighted tyranny range on,
Till each man drop by lottery. But if these
(As I am sure they do) bear fire enough
To kindle cowards and to steel with valour
The melting spirits of women, then, countrymen,
What need we any spur but our own cause
To prick us to redress? What other bond
Than secret Romans that have spoke the word
And will not palter? And what other oath
Than honesty to honesty engaged
That this shall be or we will fall for it?
Swear priests and cowards and men cautelous,
Old feeble carrions, and such suffering souls
That welcome wrongs: unto bad causes swear
Such creatures as men doubt. But do not stain
The even virtue of our enterprise,
Nor th'insuppressive mettle of our spirits,

112 SD] *Staunton (subst.)* **114** not the face] F; that the face *Theobald;* that the Fate *Warburton (conj. Warburton 1734);* not the faith *conj. Thirlby;* not the faiths *conj. Malone;* not the fate *Singer*[2] **118** high-sighted] F; high-seated *conj. Theobald* **118** range] F; reign *Folger MS.;* rage *Thomas Johnson* **126** palter] F; falter *Thomas Johnson* **132** stain] F; strain *conj. Warburton*

112 all over from all sides, all included.

114 face appearance. See also 5.1.10.

115 sufferance suffering.

116 betimes without delay, speedily.

117 idle Commentators are equally divided between 'unoccupied' and 'in which he is idle'. For the active and passive sense of the adjective, see Abbott 3.

118 high-sighted having the sight directed aloft, supercilious (*OED* High 22b). Some commentators suggest a secondary meaning: in connection with 'range', hawks or eagles flying in search of prey.

119 lottery Steevens was the first commentator to draw attention to the Roman practice of decimation, 'the selection by *lot* of every tenth soldier, in a general mutiny, for punishment'.

125 Than i.e. than that of. For the ellipsis, see Abbott 390.

126 palter shift position (from 'speak indistinctly').

129 Swear i.e. let swear. For the subjunctive used optatively or imperatively, see Abbott 364.

129 cautelous 'cautious, wary' (*OED* sv 2) here, rather than 'deceitful, crafty' (*OED* 1).

130 carrions carcases. Used contemptuously of a living person.

130 suffering patient, all-enduring.

132 as that. For 'as' = 'that' after 'such', see Abbott 109.

133 even impartial, just (from the literal sense 'level').

134 insuppressive i.e. not suppressible. For the passive sense of the adjective and the alternation of the *-ive* and *-ible* suffixes, see Abbott 3.

To think that or our cause or our performance
Did need an oath, when every drop of blood
That every Roman bears, and nobly bears,
Is guilty of a several bastardy
If he do break the smallest particle
Of any promise that hath passed from him.
CASSIUS But what of Cicero? Shall we sound him?
I think he will stand very strong with us.
CASCA Let us not leave him out.
CINNA No, by no means.
METELLUS O, let us have him, for his silver hairs
Will purchase us a good opinion
And buy men's voices to commend our deeds.
It shall be said his judgement ruled our hands;
Our youths and wildness shall no whit appear,
But all be buried in his gravity.
BRUTUS O, name him not, let us not break with him,
For he will never follow anything
That other men begin.
CASSIUS Then leave him out.
CASCA Indeed he is not fit.
DECIUS Shall no man else be touched but only Caesar?
CASSIUS Decius, well urged. I think it is not meet
Mark Antony, so well beloved of Caesar,
Should outlive Caesar. We shall find of him
A shrewd contriver. And, you know, his means,
If he improve them, may well stretch so far
As to annoy us all, which to prevent,
Let Antony and Caesar fall together.
BRUTUS Our course will seem too bloody, Caius Cassius,
To cut the head off and then hack the limbs –
Like wrath in death and envy afterwards –
For Antony is but a limb of Caesar.

152–3] *Steevens*[3]*;* That . . . begin. / . . . out. / . . . fit. F*;* That . . . begin. / . . . fit. *Capell MS.*

135 or our cause either our cause. For the development from 'other . . . other', see Abbott 136, and also 5.4.24, 5.5.3.

138 a several bastardy a separate or distinct act of baseness. See also 3.2.232, 5.5.18.

144 silver Wright notes that 'silver' suggests 'purchase' (145) and 'buy' (146).

150 break with reveal (the plan) to (as in 'to break news').

158 shrewd malicious.

159 improve make good use of.

160 annoy harm; as at 1.3.22.

160 prevent forestall; as at 28.

164 envy malice.

Let's be sacrificers, but not butchers, Caius.
We all stand up against the spirit of Caesar,
And in the spirit of men there is no blood.
O, that we then could come by Caesar's spirit
And not dismember Caesar! But, alas,
Caesar must bleed for it. And, gentle friends,
Let's kill him boldly, but not wrathfully;
Let's carve him as a dish fit for the gods,
Not hew him as a carcass fit for hounds.
And let our hearts, as subtle masters do,
Stir up their servants to an act of rage
And after seem to chide 'em. This shall make
Our purpose necessary, and not envious;
Which so appearing to the common eyes,
We shall be called purgers, not murderers.
And for Mark Antony, think not of him,
For he can do no more than Caesar's arm
When Caesar's head is off.

CASSIUS Yet I fear him,
For in the engrafted love he bears to Caesar –

BRUTUS Alas, good Cassius, do not think of him.
If he love Caesar, all that he can do
Is to himself – take thought and die for Caesar;
And that were much he should, for he is given
To sports, to wildness, and much company.

TREBONIUS There is no fear in him, let him not die,
For he will live and laugh at this hereafter.

Clock strikes

BRUTUS Peace, count the clock.

CASSIUS The clock hath stricken three.

TREBONIUS 'Tis time to part.

CASSIUS But it is doubtful yet
Whether Caesar will come forth today or no,

166 Caius] F; Cassius *Rowe; omitted in Pope* **177** make] F; mark *Collier*[2] *(Collier MS.)* **184** Caesar–] *Rowe; Caesar.* F

175 subtle wickedly cunning.
176 their servants i.e. our passions.
177 make 'make to seem' (Craik).
178 envious malicious. See also 3.2.166.
181 for as for, as regards. See Abbott 149.
187 take thought '*turn* melancholy' (Johnson). Compare *Ant.* 3.13.1: 'Think, and die.'
190 in For the metaphorical use meaning 'in the case of', etc., see Abbott 162.
191 SD Possibly produced by a bell believed to have hung in the huts at the top of the tiring-house.

For he is superstitious grown of late,
Quite from the main opinion he held once
Of fantasy, of dreams, and ceremonies.
It may be these apparent prodigies,
The unaccustomed terror of this night,
And the persuasion of his augurers
May hold him from the Capitol today.

DECIUS Never fear that. If he be so resolved
I can o'ersway him, for he loves to hear
That unicorns may be betrayed with trees,
And bears with glasses, elephants with holes,
Lions with toils, and men with flatterers.
But when I tell him he hates flatterers
He says he does, being then most flatterèd.
Let me work:
For I can give his humour the true bent,
And I will bring him to the Capitol.

CASSIUS Nay, we will all of us be there to fetch him.

BRUTUS By the eighth hour, is that the uttermost?

CINNA Be that the uttermost, and fail not then.

METELLUS Caius Ligarius doth bear Caesar hard,
Who rated him for speaking well of Pompey.
I wonder none of you have thought of him.

BRUTUS Now, good Metellus, go along by him.
He loves me well, and I have given him reasons.
Send him but hither and I'll fashion him.

196 main] F; mean QU4 215 hard] F; Hatred F2 218 by] F; to *Pope*

196 from away from; as at 1.2.299.

197 fantasy delusive imagination. See also 3.3.2.

197 ceremonies portents, omens (or rites of divination?). *OED* Ceremony 5 cites this instance, suggesting that it implies the portents or omens discovered during an act of divination by priest or soothsayer.

198 apparent visible (from 'appearing').

198 prodigies omens. See 1.3.28 n.

204–6 unicorns ... toils 'Unicorns are said to have been taken by one who, running behind a tree, eluded the violent push the animal was making at him, so that his horn spent its force on the trunk, and stuck fast ... *Bears* are reported to have been surprised by means of a *mirror*, which they would gaze on, affording their pursuers an opportunity of taking the surer aim ... *Elephants* were seduced into pitfalls, lightly covered with hurdles and turf, on which a proper bait to tempt them, was exposed' (Steevens).

206 toils nets.

209 For the use of the short line, see 1.1.51 n.

210 humour disposition.

212 there i.e. Caesar's house.

213 uttermost furthest limit (of time).

215 bear ... hard endure with a grudge. See 1.2.302 n.

216 rated reproved vehemently.

218 by to (from the original sense 'near the side'). See Abbott 145.

220 fashion transform (*OED* sv *v* 4 cites this instance).

CASSIUS The morning comes upon's. We'll leave you, Brutus,
And, friends, disperse yourselves, but all remember
What you have said and show yourselves true Romans.

BRUTUS Good gentlemen, look fresh and merrily:
Let not our looks put on our purposes,
But bear it as our Roman actors do,
With untired spirits and formal constancy.
And so good morrow to you every one.

Exeunt [*all but*] *Brutus*

Boy! Lucius! Fast asleep? It is no matter,
Enjoy the honey-heavy dew of slumber.
Thou hast no figures nor no fantasies
Which busy care draws in the brains of men,
Therefore thou sleep'st so sound.

Enter PORTIA

PORTIA Brutus, my lord.

BRUTUS Portia! What mean you? Wherefore rise you now?
It is not for your health thus to commit
Your weak condition to the raw cold morning.

PORTIA Nor for yours neither. Y'have ungently, Brutus,
Stole from my bed; and yesternight at supper
You suddenly arose and walked about,
Musing and sighing, with your arms across,
And when I asked you what the matter was,
You stared upon me with ungentle looks.
I urged you further, then you scratched your head
And too impatiently stamped with your foot.
Yet I insisted, yet you answered not,
But with an angry wafture of your hand
Gave sign for me to leave you. So I did,
Fearing to strengthen that impatience
Which seemed too much enkindled, and withal
Hoping it was but an effect of humour
Which sometime hath his hour with every man.

221] *Rowe;* The … vpon's: / … *Brutus,* F 230 honey-heavy dew] Q (1684); hony-heauy-Dew F; heavy honey-dew *Collier*[2] *(Collier MS.)*

227 formal in outward form or appearance.

227 constancy firmness, resolution. See also 299, 2.4.6; 'constant', 3.1.22, 60, 72, 73; 'constantly', 5.1.91, and see pp. 11–12 above.

231 figures imaginary forms, phantasms.

238 Stole For the form, see 1.2.48 n.

240 across crossed, folded (denoting melancholy).

251 his its.

It will not let you eat nor talk nor sleep;
And could it work so much upon your shape
As it hath much prevailed on your condition,
I should not know you, Brutus. Dear my lord,
Make me acquainted with your cause of grief.

BRUTUS I am not well in health, and that is all.

PORTIA Brutus is wise, and were he not in health
He would embrace the means to come by it.

BRUTUS Why, so I do. Good Portia, go to bed.

PORTIA Is Brutus sick? And is it physical
To walk unbracèd and suck up the humours
Of the dank morning? What, is Brutus sick?
And will he steal out of his wholesome bed
To dare the vile contagion of the night
And tempt the rheumy and unpurgèd air
To add unto his sickness? No, my Brutus,
You have some sick offence within your mind,
Which by the right and virtue of my place
I ought to know of. And upon my knees
I charm you, by my once commended beauty,
By all your vows of love, and that great vow
Which did incorporate and make us one,
That you unfold to me, your self, your half,
Why you are heavy and what men tonight
Have had resort to you, for here have been
Some six or seven who did hide their faces
Even from darkness.

BRUTUS Kneel not, gentle Portia.

255 you,] Q (1684); you F **263** dank] F; darke F2 **267** his] F2; hit F **271** charm] F; charge *Thomas Johnson* **274, 282** your self] F; yourself *Theobald*[4]

253 shape appearance of the body.

254 condition mental disposition.

255 know you, Brutus Many editors omit the comma and interpret as 'recognise you as Brutus', while admitting that 'in the old punctuation a vocative is frequently printed without a separating comma' (Kittredge). Plutarch (p. 164), in one instance, has Cassius ask, 'What, knowest thou not that thou art Brutus?' See also 'ask, Casca,' 1.2.219; 'fall, Caesar', 3.1.77 n.; 'you, Antony,' 3.1.225; and 'Speak hands', 3.1.76.

256 your cause of grief i.e. the cause of your grief. For transpositions of noun clauses containing two nouns connected by 'of', see Abbott 423.

261 physical beneficial to health.

262 humours moisture, vapours.

266 tempt test; as at 1.3.53.

266 unpurgèd not cleansed of baser elements or admixture (vaporous night air was believed to be impure).

268 sick offence 'harmful disorder' (Schmidt, offence 1). For the construction, see 1.1.33 n.

269 virtue power.

271 charm entreat in some potent name. *OED* sv *v*[1] 6 cites this instance.

273 incorporate combine into one body.

278 Kneel not See 2.2.56 n.

PORTIA I should not need if you were gentle Brutus.
Within the bond of marriage, tell me, Brutus,
Is it excepted I should know no secrets
That appertain to you? Am I your self
But, as it were, in sort or limitation,
To keep with you at meals, comfort your bed,
And talk to you sometimes? Dwell I but in the suburbs
Of your good pleasure? If it be no more
Portia is Brutus' harlot, not his wife.

BRUTUS You are my true and honourable wife,
As dear to me as are the ruddy drops
That visit my sad heart.

PORTIA If this were true, then should I know this secret.
I grant I am a woman, but withal
A woman that Lord Brutus took to wife.
I grant I am a woman, but withal
A woman well reputed, Cato's daughter.
Think you I am no stronger than my sex,
Being so fathered and so husbanded?
Tell me your counsels, I will not disclose 'em.
I have made strong proof of my constancy,
Giving myself a voluntary wound
Here, in the thigh. Can I bear that with patience
And not my husband's secrets?

BRUTUS O ye gods,
Render me worthy of this noble wife!

Knock

Hark, hark, one knocks. Portia, go in a while,
And by and by thy bosom shall partake

279 gentle] F; gentle, *Staunton* **284** comfort] F; consort *Theobald (conj. Theobald 1730)* **295** reputed,] reputed: F; reputed *Warburton*

279 gentle Brutus For the punctuation, see 255 n.

283 in sort in some sort or manner. Like 'limitation', this is a legal term; both are perhaps suggested by 'bond' (280), according to Wilson.

284 keep with stay, associate with.

284 comfort give pleasure to. *OED* sv *v* 5 cites this instance.

285 suburbs Frequently regarded as places of 'inferior, debased, and *esp.* licentious habits of life' (*OED* Suburb 4b). Shakespeare is evidently superimposing London on Rome.

289 ruddy drops i.e. blood.

295 well reputed Warburton is almost alone in assuming that 'well reputed' refers to Cato, not to Portia.

295 Cato Marcus Porcius Cato Uticensis (95–46 BC), Republican, who committed suicide to avoid being taken by Caesar. See also 5.1.101.

298 counsels private or secret purposes, designs or opinions. See also 2.4.9 n. and 'in counsel', 4.1.45 n.

299 constancy firmness. See 227 n.

300–1 Giving ... thigh The detail is from Plutarch (p. 166).

The secrets of my heart.
All my engagements I will construe to thee,
All the charactery of my sad brows.
Leave me with haste.

Exit Portia

Lucius, who's that knocks?

Enter LUCIUS *and* LIGARIUS

LUCIUS Here is a sick man that would speak with you.
BRUTUS Caius Ligarius, that Metellus spake of.
Boy, stand aside.

[*Exit Lucius*]

Caius Ligarius, how?
LIGARIUS Vouchsafe good morrow from a feeble tongue.
BRUTUS O, what a time have you chose out, brave Caius,
To wear a kerchief! Would you were not sick!
LIGARIUS I am not sick if Brutus have in hand
Any exploit worthy the name of honour.
BRUTUS Such an exploit have I in hand, Ligarius,
Had you a healthful ear to hear of it.
LIGARIUS By all the gods that Romans bow before,
I here discard my sickness!

[*He pulls off his kerchief*]

Soul of Rome,
Brave son, derived from honourable loins,
Thou, like an exorcist, hast conjured up
My mortifièd spirit. Now bid me run
And I will strive with things impossible,
Yea, get the better of them. What's to do?

309 who's] F; who's there *Pope;* who's that *Capell (conj. Thirlby);* who is *Steevens;* who is't *Rann (conj. Thirlby)* 312 SD] *Capell (Capell MS.)* 313 SH LIGARIUS] *Hanmer; Cai.* F *(throughout)* 321 SD] *Collier[2] (subst.) (Collier MS.)* 326 Yea] F; Yet *Rowe[2]*

307 **engagements** formal agreements, compacts.

307 **construe** Probably 'explain for legal purposes'; like 'engagements', it is a technical term.

308 **charactery** expression of thought by characters or symbols. 'Coined by Dr Timothy Bright as a convenient name for his pioneer shorthand ... it served as the title of his book [1588] and he defined it as "an art of short, swift and secret writing by character"' (W.J. Carlton, 'Charactery', *N&Q* n.s. 15 (1968), 366–7).

308 **sad** grave, serious; as at 1.2.217.

312 **how** 'An exclamation, particularly to express surprise' (Schmidt) is the gloss of earlier commentators; more recent ones prefer 'how are you?'

313 **Vouchsafe** Receive graciously. *OED* sv *v* 3b cites this instance.

314 **chose** For the form, see 1.2.48 n.

314 **brave** worthy, good (a general epithet of admiration or praise; the dominant sense in the play).

315 **kerchief** a head-covering (commonly worn by the sick).

324 **mortifièd** deadened, numbed.

BRUTUS A piece of work that will make sick men whole.
LIGARIUS But are not some whole that we must make sick?
BRUTUS That must we also. What it is, my Caius,
I shall unfold to thee as we are going
To whom it must be done.
LIGARIUS Set on your foot,
And with a heart new fired I follow you
To do I know not what; but it sufficeth
That Brutus leads me on.

Thunder

BRUTUS Follow me then.

Exeunt

2.2 *Thunder and lightning. Enter* JULIUS CAESAR *in his nightgown*

CAESAR Nor heaven nor earth have been at peace tonight.
Thrice hath Calpurnia in her sleep cried out,
'Help ho, they murder Caesar!' Who's within?

Enter a SERVANT

SERVANT My lord?
CAESAR Go bid the priests do present sacrifice
And bring me their opinions of success.
SERVANT I will, my lord. *Exit*

Enter CALPURNIA

CALPURNIA What mean you, Caesar, think you to walk forth?
You shall not stir out of your house today.
CAESAR Caesar shall forth. The things that threatened me
Ne'er looked but on my back; when they shall see
The face of Caesar they are vanishèd.
CALPURNIA Caesar, I never stood on ceremonies,

327] *Rowe;* A ... worke, / ... whole. F 330 going] *Capell;* going, F Act 2, Scene 2 2.2] *Rowe* Location] *Globe (after Rowe)* 1] *Rowe (Folger MS.);* Nor ... Earth, / ... night: F

327 whole hale.

Act 2, Scene 2

Location Rome. Caesar's house.

0 SD *nightgown* dressing-gown. Caesar (and Calpurnia at 7) may well use the curtained central entry.

5 present immediate.

6 success result. See also 5.3.65.

13 ceremonies external accessories of worship. But see 1.1.64 n. and 2.1.197 n.

Yet now they fright me. There is one within,
Besides the things that we have heard and seen,
Recounts most horrid sights seen by the watch.
A lioness hath whelpèd in the streets,
And graves have yawned and yielded up their dead;
Fierce fiery warriors fight upon the clouds
In ranks and squadrons and right form of war,
Which drizzled blood upon the Capitol;
The noise of battle hurtled in the air,
Horses did neigh and dying men did groan,
And ghosts did shriek and squeal about the streets.
O Caesar, these things are beyond all use,
And I do fear them.

CAESAR What can be avoided
Whose end is purposed by the mighty gods?
Yet Caesar shall go forth, for these predictions
Are to the world in general as to Caesar.

CALPURNIA When beggars die there are no comets seen,
The heavens themselves blaze forth the death of princes.

CAESAR Cowards die many times before their deaths,
The valiant never taste of death but once.
Of all the wonders that I yet have heard
It seems to me most strange that men should fear,
Seeing that death, a necessary end,
Will come when it will come.

Enter a SERVANT

What say the augurers?

SERVANT They would not have you to stir forth today.
Plucking the entrails of an offering forth,
They could not find a heart within the beast.

CAESAR The gods do this in shame of cowardice.

19 fight] F; fought *White (conj. Thirlby)* **22** hurtled] F; hurried F2 **23** did] F2; do F **37** augurers] F; augures QUI

20 squadrons soldiers arranged in square formation.

20 right appropriate, regular (from the literal meaning 'straight').

20 form formation.

25 use custom, usual experience.

31 blaze forth proclaim (as with a trumpet); from blaze = 'blow' (*OED* Blaze v^2 2b, citing this instance).

32–3 Proverbial (Dent C774): 'A coward dies many deaths, a brave man but one.'

39–40 A most important form of artificial divination during a long period of time and over a wide geographic range, extispicy (or haruspicy) was based on the observation of the entrails – especially the liver (hepatoscopy) of sacrificial animals.

41 in shame of cowardice to shame cowardice.

Caesar should be a beast without a heart
If he should stay at home today for fear.
No, Caesar shall not. Danger knows full well
That Caesar is more dangerous than he:
We are two lions littered in one day,
And I the elder and more terrible.
And Caesar shall go forth.

CALPURNIA Alas, my lord,
Your wisdom is consumed in confidence.
Do not go forth today. Call it my fear
That keeps you in the house, and not your own.
We'll send Mark Antony to the Senate House
And he shall say you are not well today.
Let me, upon my knee, prevail in this.

CAESAR Mark Antony shall say I am not well,
And for thy humour I will stay at home.

Enter DECIUS

Here's Decius Brutus, he shall tell them so.

DECIUS Caesar, all hail! Good morrow, worthy Caesar,
I come to fetch you to the Senate House.

CAESAR And you are come in very happy time
To bear my greeting to the senators
And tell them that I will not come today.
Cannot is false, and that I dare not, falser:
I will not come today. Tell them so, Decius.

CALPURNIA Say he is sick.

CAESAR Shall Caesar send a lie?
Have I in conquest stretched mine arm so far
To be afeard to tell greybeards the truth?
Decius, go tell them Caesar will not come.

46 We are] *Capell (conj. Thirlby);* We heare F; We heard *Rowe (Folger MS.);* We were *Theobald (conj. Thirlby);* Here are *Sampath Thathachariar (privately)*

46 *are Commentators, seeking to explain the emended homophone 'heare', detect either a complicated error of the copyist (repeating 'he' of line 45 to form 'He are', correcting to 'We are' but failing to delete 'he', or failing to recognise a compressed 'Here') or a fairly improbable Latinate use of 'heare' in the sense of 'prefer to be addressed or called' (*OED* Hear *v* 12b).

56 humour Most commentators gloss as 'whim, caprice', but 'temporary state of mind' or 'mood' (*OED* Humour *sb* 5) would be more in accord with Calpurnia's character, not to mention the omens.

56 Beginning with Collier[2], some commentators add the SD *Raising her* to emphasise the parallel with Brutus and Portia at 2.1.278.

60 happy appropriate, opportune.

67 greybeards Often contemptuously of old men.

DECIUS Most mighty Caesar, let me know some cause,
Lest I be laughed at when I tell them so.
CAESAR The cause is in my will. I will not come:
That is enough to satisfy the Senate.
But for your private satisfaction,
Because I love you, I will let you know:
Calpurnia here, my wife, stays me at home.
She dreamt tonight she saw my statue,
Which like a fountain with an hundred spouts
Did run pure blood, and many lusty Romans
Came smiling and did bathe their hands in it.
And these does she apply for warnings and portents
And evils imminent, and on her knee
Hath begged that I will stay at home today.
DECIUS This dream is all amiss interpreted,
It was a vision fair and fortunate.
Your statue spouting blood in many pipes,
In which so many smiling Romans bathed,
Signifies that from you great Rome shall suck
Reviving blood and that great men shall press
For tinctures, stains, relics, and cognisance.
This by Calpurnia's dream is signified.
CAESAR And this way have you well expounded it.
DECIUS I have, when you have heard what I can say.
And know it now: the Senate have concluded
To give this day a crown to mighty Caesar.
If you shall send them word you will not come,

81 And] F; Of *Hanmer (conj. Thirlby)*

72 'Not ... enough to insure their being satisfied, but enough for me to do towards that end' (Craik).

76 tonight last night (Rowe's emendation).

76 statue The final *e*, probably not of French but of Latin origin (*statua*), is pronounced (see Abbott 487). See also 3.2.179.

80 for as, in the capacity of. See Abbott 148.

89 Johnson was the first to remark on the heraldic terms: 'tinctures' (and the almost synonymous 'stains') referring to colours and 'cognisance' to a device, both identifying retainers of a noble house. While he isolated 'relics' as pertaining to martyrdom, Warburton (as do some other commentators) saw all the terms in that light, from the practice of dipping handkerchiefs in the blood of those who were considered martyrs. This view may be excessive, since 'relics' is not normally associated with martyrdom in Shakespeare; in fact, the other terms are not necessarily associated with heraldry. But the overall interpretation is to be found everywhere, despite Johnson's assertion that the speech is 'somewhat confused'. The more recent connection of 'tinctures' with 'overtones of the alchemical meaning' (Sanders) does not simplify matters.

89 cognisance Considering the other items in the series, this may well be a plural (as in Hanmer's emendation to 'cognisances'), which, as suggested by W. S. Walker (p. 259), could be rendered with an apostrophe after the *e* to avoid an extra syllable.

Their minds may change. Besides, it were a mock
Apt to be rendered for someone to say,
'Break up the Senate till another time,
When Caesar's wife shall meet with better dreams.'
If Caesar hide himself, shall they not whisper,
'Lo, Caesar is afraid'?
Pardon me, Caesar, for my dear dear love
To your proceeding bids me tell you this,
And reason to my love is liable.

CAESAR How foolish do your fears seem now, Calpurnia!
I am ashamèd I did yield to them.
Give me my robe, for I will go.

Enter BRUTUS, *Ligarius, Metellus, Casca,* TREBONIUS, *Cinna, and* PUBLIUS

And look where Publius is come to fetch me.

PUBLIUS Good morrow, Caesar.

CAESAR Welcome, Publius.
What, Brutus, are you stirred so early too?
Good morrow, Casca. Caius Ligarius,
Caesar was ne'er so much your enemy
As that same ague which hath made you lean.
What is't o'clock?

BRUTUS Caesar, 'tis strucken eight.

CAESAR I thank you for your pains and courtesy.

Enter ANTONY

See, Antony, that revels long a-nights,
Is notwithstanding up. Good morrow, Antony.

ANTONY So to most noble Caesar.

103 proceeding] F; proceedings QUI *(Folger MS.)* **107** SD] *Wells and Taylor add Cassius* **117–18]** *Boswell (Capell MS.);* Is … *Antony.* / … *Caesar.* / … within: F; Is … up: – / … Caesar. / … within: – *Steevens*[3]

103 proceeding Most commentators gloss as 'advantage'.

107 SD PUBLIUS Wilson (pp. 95–6), ingeniously but without compelling support, finds the appearance of Publius may be an 'afterthought' of Shakespeare's or the prompter's since 'Ligarius and Cassius were played by the same actor, and therefore could not appear together'. Unconvinced, Humphreys speculates that Cassius's absence was caused by the actor being required for another part at this moment in the play.

112 enemy 'Ligarius, who had taken part in the Civil War on Pompey's side, had recently been pardoned by Caesar and restored to civil rights' (Kittredge).

CAESAR [*To Calpurnia*] Bid them prepare within,
[*Exit Calpurnia*]
I am to blame to be thus waited for.
Now, Cinna, now, Metellus. What, Trebonius,
I have an hour's talk in store for you.
Remember that you call on me today;
Be near me that I may remember you.

TREBONIUS Caesar, I will. [*Aside*] And so near will I be
That your best friends shall wish I had been further.

CAESAR Good friends, go in and taste some wine with me,
And we, like friends, will straightway go together.

BRUTUS [*Aside*] That every like is not the same, O Caesar,
The heart of Brutus earns to think upon.
Exeunt

2.3 *Enter* ARTEMIDORUS [*reading a paper*]

ARTEMIDORUS 'Caesar, beware of Brutus, take heed of Cassius, come not near Casca, have an eye to Cinna, trust not Trebonius, mark well Metellus Cimber, Decius Brutus loves thee not, thou hast wronged Caius Ligarius. There is but one mind in all these men, and it is bent against Caesar. If thou beest not immortal look about you: security gives way to conspiracy. The mighty gods defend thee!

Thy lover,
Artemidorus.'

Here will I stand till Caesar pass along,
And as a suitor will I give him this.
My heart laments that virtue cannot live
Out of the teeth of emulation.

118 SD.1] *Wilson; to an Att*[*endant*] / *Capell (Capell MS.)* 118 SD.2] *Wilson (subst.); at 119, Humphreys* 124 SD] *Rowe (Douai MS.)* 128 SD] *Pope (Douai MS.)* Act 2, Scene 3 2.3] *Rowe* Location] *Rowe* 0 SD *reading a paper*] *Rowe* 1 SH ARTEMIDORUS] *Capell (Capell MS.)*

118 SD.1 Commentators are split as to whether the address is to Calpurnia or to an Attendant.

119 to blame The Elizabethan interchangeability of 'to' and 'too' (F's reading here) is so common that some believe 'blame' may be an adjective, with 'too' meaning 'excessively' (though no edition has 'too' here). See Abbott 73.

128 Proverbial (Dent A167): 'All that is alike is not the same.'

129 earns 'grieves' (*OED* Earn v^3 2) is the interpretation of most editors, but it has occasionally been glossed as 'desires' (*OED* v^3 1) and 'trembles' (*OED* v^3 3).

Act 2, Scene 3

Location Rome. A street.

5 security absence of apprehension, carelessness.

7 lover friend. See also 3.2.13 n.

12 Out of the teeth Away from the direct opposition. Some gloss 'teeth' with 'reach', an anonymous conjecture in Cam.

If thou read this, O Caesar, thou mayst live;
If not, the fates with traitors do contrive. *Exit*

2.4 *Enter* PORTIA *and* LUCIUS

PORTIA I prithee, boy, run to the Senate House.
Stay not to answer me but get thee gone.
Why dost thou stay?
LUCIUS To know my errand, madam.
PORTIA I would have had thee there and here again
Ere I can tell thee what thou shouldst do there.
[*Aside*] O constancy, be strong upon my side,
Set a huge mountain 'tween my heart and tongue!
I have a man's mind, but a woman's might.
How hard it is for women to keep counsel! –
Art thou here yet?
LUCIUS Madam, what should I do?
Run to the Capitol, and nothing else?
And so return to you, and nothing else?
PORTIA Yes, bring me word, boy, if thy lord look well,
For he went sickly forth, and take good note
What Caesar doth, what suitors press to him.
Hark, boy, what noise is that?
LUCIUS I hear none, madam.
PORTIA Prithee listen well:
I heard a bustling rumour, like a fray,
And the wind brings it from the Capitol.
LUCIUS Sooth, madam, I hear nothing.

Enter the SOOTHSAYER

PORTIA Come hither, fellow, which way hast thou been?
SOOTHSAYER At mine own house, good lady.
PORTIA What is't o'clock?

14 SD] F; *he stands aside / Wilson* **Act 2, Scene 4** 2.4] *Capell* Location] *Capell* 3 my] thy *Macmillan (Folger MS.)* 6 SD] *Capell* 16–17] *Steevens*[3] *(Capell MS.)*; Hearke ... that? / ... Madam. / ... well: F; Hark ... Madam. / ... well; *Keightley* **20** SD SOOTHSAYER] F; Artemidorus *Rowe* 20–3] *Delius*[2]; *Luc.* ... nothing. / ... *Soothsayer.* / ... bin? / ... good Lady. / ... clocke? / ... Lady. F; *LUC.* ... fellow: / ... good lady. / ... lady. *Steevens*[3] *(Capell MS.)*; [*at 22–3*] *Art.* At ... clock? *White*

Act 2, Scene 4

Location Rome. Before Brutus's house.

6 constancy firmness. See 2.1.227 n.

9 keep counsel keep a matter secret or confidential. Possibly proverbial (Dent W706.1): 'Women can keep no counsel.' See also 2.1.298 n. and 'in counsel', 4.1.45 n.

18 rumour noise, clamour.

SOOTHSAYER   About the ninth hour, lady.
PORTIA Is Caesar yet gone to the Capitol?
SOOTHSAYER Madam, not yet. I go to take my stand
    To see him pass on to the Capitol.
PORTIA Thou hast some suit to Caesar, hast thou not?
SOOTHSAYER That I have, lady, if it will please Caesar
    To be so good to Caesar as to hear me:
    I shall beseech him to befriend himself.
PORTIA Why, know'st thou any harm's intended towards him?
SOOTHSAYER None that I know will be, much that I fear may chance.
    Good morrow to you. Here the street is narrow:
    The throng that follows Caesar at the heels,
    Of senators, of praetors, common suitors,
    Will crowd a feeble man almost to death.
    I'll get me to a place more void, and there
    Speak to great Caesar as he comes along. *Exit*
PORTIA I must go in. [*Aside*] Ay me, how weak a thing
    The heart of woman is! O Brutus,
    The heavens speed thee in thine enterprise!
    Sure the boy heard me. Brutus hath a suit
    That Caesar will not grant. O, I grow faint. –
    Run, Lucius, and commend me to my lord,
    Say I am merry. Come to me again
    And bring me word what he doth say to thee.
Exeunt [*severally*]

28–9 if ... me:] F; If ... me, *Johnson* **30** befriend] F; defend *Rowe*[2] **31**] *As verse, Theobald; as prose,* F **31** harm's] F; harms QU2; harm *Pope* **32**] *Capell;* None ... be, / ... chance: F; None ... fear, [*omitting* may chance] *Pope* **39**] *Rowe;* I ... in: / ... thing F **39** SD] *Dyce*[2] *(after Rowe)* **46** SD *severally*] *Theobald*

35 **praetors** administrators of justice.

39 SD The vagaries of punctuation, as well as the changes of focus in 39–43, make it difficult to discern the exact extent of the aside. The variation of interpretation seems considerable; some of the less ambiguous instances are to be found in Craik, Dorsch, and Charney. See also 3.1.232 SD n.

44 **commend me** remember me kindly, present my kind regards.

46 SD ***severally*** i.e. at separate doors. See also 3.2.10 n.

3.1 *Flourish. Enter* CAESAR, BRUTUS, CASSIUS, CASCA, DECIUS, METELLUS, TREBONIUS, CINNA, ANTONY, *Lepidus,* ARTEMIDORUS, PUBLIUS, [POPILLIUS, *Ligarius,*] *and the* SOOTHSAYER

CAESAR The Ides of March are come.
SOOTHSAYER Ay, Caesar, but not gone.
ARTEMIDORUS Hail, Caesar! Read this schedule.
DECIUS Trebonius doth desire you to o'er-read
(At your best leisure) this his humble suit.
ARTEMIDORUS O Caesar, read mine first, for mine's a suit
That touches Caesar nearer. Read it, great Caesar.
CAESAR What touches us ourself shall be last served.
ARTEMIDORUS Delay not, Caesar, read it instantly.
CAESAR What, is the fellow mad?
PUBLIUS Sirrah, give place.
CASSIUS What, urge you your petitions in the street?
Come to the Capitol.
[*Caesar enters the Capitol, the rest following*]
POPILLIUS I wish your enterprise today may thrive.
CASSIUS What enterprise, Popillius?
POPILLIUS Fare you well.
[*Leaves him and joins Caesar*]
BRUTUS What said Popillius Lena?
CASSIUS He wished today our enterprise might thrive.
I fear our purpose is discoverèd.
BRUTUS Look how he makes to Caesar, mark him.
CASSIUS Casca, be sudden, for we fear prevention.

Act 3, Scene 1 3.1] *Actus Tertius.* F; ACT III. SCENE I. *Rowe* Location] *Rowe* 0 SD POPILLIUS] F2 0 SD *Ligarius*] *This edn* 8 us ourself] F; us? ourself *Collier*[2] *(Collier MS.)* 12 SD] *Steevens (after Capell)* 14] *Reed (Capell MS.); Cassi.... Popillius? / ...* well. F 14 SD] *Capell (Capell MS.)*

Act 3, Scene 1

Location Rome. The Capitol. The staging of the opening lines of this scene has been much commented on. As the inserted stage direction after 12 indicates, the locus shifts from the street into the Capitol. For a likely staging, see illustration 1, p. 4.

0 SD *Lepidus* Disturbed by the apparent absence of Ligarius and the presence of the mute Lepidus, Ringler (see Textual Analysis, p. 151 below) suggests a compositor's 'misreading "Li" as "Le" ... and so improperly expanding ... to "Lepidus" instead of "Ligarius" which Shakespeare had intended' (p. 116). But mutes are not uncommon in public scenes and Plutarch (p. 160) does mention Lepidus's fleeing the Capitol with Antony after Caesar's assassination (although Appian, p. 22, says Lepidus heard of 'what was done'). It is likely that Ligarius is also present since he is mentioned in Artemidorus's 'paper' (2.3.4).

3 schedule A slip or scroll of parchment or paper containing writing.

18 makes to proceeds towards.

19 sudden swift of action; in this sense, used of persons.

19 prevention being forestalled. See 'prevent', 2.1.28 n.

Brutus, what shall be done? If this be known
Cassius or Caesar never shall turn back,
For I will slay myself.

BRUTUS Cassius, be constant.
Popillius Lena speaks not of our purposes,
For look he smiles, and Caesar doth not change.

CASSIUS Trebonius knows his time, for look you, Brutus,
He draws Mark Antony out of the way.
[*Exeunt Antony and Trebonius*]

DECIUS Where is Metellus Cimber? Let him go
And presently prefer his suit to Caesar.

BRUTUS He is addressed, press near and second him.

CINNA Casca, you are the first that rears your hand.

CAESAR Are we all ready? What is now amiss
That Caesar and his Senate must redress?

METELLUS Most high, most mighty, and most puissant Caesar,
Metellus Cimber throws before thy seat
An humble heart.

CAESAR I must prevent thee, Cimber.
These couchings and these lowly courtesies
Might fire the blood of ordinary men
And turn preordinance and first decree
Into the law of children. Be not fond
To think that Caesar bears such rebel blood
That will be thawed from the true quality

21 or] F; on *Craik (conj. Malone)* **26** SD] *Capell (Capell MS.)* **31** Are ... ready?] *Assigned to Cassius,* QUI; *to Cinna, conj. Ritson (apud Steevens*[3]*); to Casca, Collier*[2] *(conj. Thirlby, reading* We are all ready*)* **36** couchings] F; crouchings *Hanmer (conj. Thirlby)* **38** first] F; fixt *conj. Craik* **39** law] *Malone (conj. Johnson);* lane F; love *conj. Thirlby;* line *conj. Thirlby;* play *Hudson*[2] *(conj. Mason);* lune *conj. Macmillan*

21 or 'Neither' must be understood before 'Cassius'.

21 turn back return.

22 constant See 'constancy', 2.1.227 n.

28 presently immediately. See also 142, 4.1.45, 4.3.197.

28 prefer put forward, present (for acceptance). See also 5.5.62.

29 addressed ready (for the purpose).

30 you ... that rears your Abbott (247) attributes the construction to the 'distance of the relative from the antecedent'.

36 couchings bowings in reverence or subserviency.

36 courtesies curtsies; this is the most likely meaning. Compare 43.

38 preordinance and first decree i.e. 'the natural and immutable laws of the universe that have been preordained and decreed from the beginning of time' (Charney). The doublet is used for emphasis; the almost synonymous terms have legal and ecclesiastical overtones.

39 *law All conjectures have in common the unreliability of children. The meanings are obvious except perhaps for 'lane', which Steevens[2] explains as the 'narrow conceit', and Hulme (p. 210) holds is a variant pronunciation of 'line' in its now obsolete sense 'rule, canon, precept'.

39 fond foolishly credulous.

40–1 blood ... quality For a similar image from alchemy, see 1.2.297–9.

With that which melteth fools – I mean sweet words,
Low-crookèd curtsies, and base spaniel fawning.
Thy brother by decree is banishèd:
If thou dost bend, and pray, and fawn for him,
I spurn thee like a cur out of my way.
Know Caesar doth not wrong, nor without cause
Will he be satisfied.

METELLUS Is there no voice more worthy than my own
To sound more sweetly in great Caesar's ear
For the repealing of my banished brother?

BRUTUS I kiss thy hand, but not in flattery, Caesar,
Desiring thee that Publius Cimber may
Have an immediate freedom of repeal.

CAESAR What, Brutus?

CASSIUS Pardon, Caesar! Caesar, pardon!
As low as to thy foot doth Cassius fall
To beg enfranchisement for Publius Cimber.

CAESAR I could be well moved, if I were as you;
If I could pray to move, prayers would move me.
But I am constant as the northern star,
Of whose true-fixed and resting quality
There is no fellow in the firmament.
The skies are painted with unnumbered sparks,
They are all fire, and every one doth shine;
But there's but one in all doth hold his place.
So in the world: 'tis furnished well with men,
And men are flesh and blood, and apprehensive;
Yet in the number I do know but one

43 Low-crookèd] F; Low-crouched *Collier*[2] 47–8 wrong . . . satisfied] F; wrong, but with just cause, / Nor . . . satisfied. *conj. Pope after* wrong *at 3.2.102; Hudson*[2] *(conj. Tyrwhitt apud Steevens*[2]*)* 61 true-fixed] *Hyphen, Capell (Capell MS.)*; true fixt, F; true, fixt, *Rowe*

42–3 For the association in Shakespeare of fawning dogs with melting sweets and flatterers, see Spurgeon, pp. 195–9. See also 5.1.41.

46 spurn kick; as at 2.1.11.

51 repealing recalling from exile.

53 Publius Cimber Little is known of the brother of the conspirator but it is reasonably certain that he had been a senator who was indeed 'repealed' after the death of Caesar. See Pauly, Tillius 1.

54 freedom of repeal 'Permission to be recalled' is, among editors, the favoured interpretation, with others ranging from 'free, unconditional recall' (Craik) to 'freedom *in consequence* of his recall' (Furness).

57 enfranchisement (restoration of) citizenship. See also 81.

59 pray entreat (others).

60, 72, 73 constant See 'constancy', 2.1.227 n.

61 true sure, secure.

61 resting remaining stationary.

63 unnumbered numberless.

65 his its.

67 apprehensive possessed of intelligence or understanding.

That unassailable holds on his rank,
Unshaked of motion, and that I am he
Let me a little show it, even in this:
That I was constant Cimber should be banished,
And constant do remain to keep him so.

CINNA O Caesar –

CAESAR Hence! Wilt thou lift up Olympus?

DECIUS Great Caesar –

CAESAR Doth not Brutus bootless kneel?

CASCA Speak hands for me!

They stab Caesar

CAESAR *Et tu, Brute?* – Then fall, Caesar! *Dies*

CINNA Liberty! Freedom! Tyranny is dead!
Run hence, proclaim, cry it about the streets.

CASSIUS Some to the common pulpits, and cry out,
'Liberty, freedom, and enfranchisement!'

BRUTUS People and senators, be not affrighted,
Fly not, stand still! Ambition's debt is paid.

CASCA Go to the pulpit, Brutus.

DECIUS And Cassius too.

BRUTUS Where's Publius?

CINNA Here, quite confounded with this mutiny.

METELLUS Stand fast together lest some friend of Caesar's
Should chance –

BRUTUS Talk not of standing. Publius, good cheer,
There is no harm intended to your person,
Nor to no Roman else. So tell them, Publius.

69 rank] F; race [*i.e.* course] *conj. Johnson* 74–5] *Steevens*[3] *(Capell MS.); Cinna. ... Caesar.* / ... Olympus? / ... *Caesar.* / ... kneele? F; *Cin.* ... Olympus? / ... Caesar, – / ... kneel? *Hudson* 75 Doth] F; Do F2 76–7] *As one line, Keightley* 76 Speak hands] F; Speak, hands, *Capell (Capell MS.)* 77 fall,] QU4; fall F 84–5] *Steevens*[3]; *Cask.* ... *Brutus.* / ... too. / ... *Publius?* F; CASCA ... Brutus. / ... Publius? *Bevington*

75 **bootless** uselessly.

76 Plutarch (pp. 160, 168) records that Casca was the first to strike ('but gave him no great wound'). Tradition has it that Brutus was the last.

76 **hands** The ambiguity of construction has led some editors to punctuate 'hands' as a vocative. Compare 2.1.255 n.

77 ***Et tu, Brute*** Suetonius (p. 111) reports that 'when Marcus Brutus rushed at him, [Caesar] said in Greek, "You too, my child?"', an allusion perhaps to the not uncommon belief that Caesar was his father. The non-historical Latin line is to be found in various Renaissance works, most notably in the 'bad' quarto of *3 Henry VI, The True Tragedy of Richard Duke of York* (1595). The *e* in the Latin vocative *Brute* is pronounced, as the accent in F indicates.

77 **Then fall, Caesar** Because Caesar often refers to himself in the third person (see p. 22 above), the temptation is to omit the comma after 'fall', which might then be glossed as 'let fall'. See also 2.1.255 n. and 3.1.76 n.

80 **common** public. See also 3.2.240.

80 **pulpits** Scaffolds, stages or platforms for public representations, speeches, or disputations. Most likely, the *rostra* in the Forum.

81 **enfranchisement** citizenship. Compare 57 n. above.

86 **mutiny** discord.

CASSIUS And leave us, Publius, lest that the people,
Rushing on us, should do your age some mischief.
BRUTUS Do so, and let no man abide this deed
But we the doers.
[*Exeunt all but the conspirators*]

Enter TREBONIUS

CASSIUS Where is Antony?
TREBONIUS Fled to his house amazed.
Men, wives, and children stare, cry out, and run
As it were doomsday.
BRUTUS Fates, we will know your pleasures.
That we shall die we know: 'tis but the time,
And drawing days out, that men stand upon.
CASCA Why, he that cuts off twenty years of life
Cuts off so many years of fearing death.
BRUTUS Grant that, and then is death a benefit.
So are we Caesar's friends, that have abridged
His time of fearing death. Stoop, Romans, stoop,
And let us bathe our hands in Caesar's blood
Up to the elbows and besmear our swords.
Then walk we forth, even to the market-place,
And waving our red weapons o'er our heads
Let's all cry, 'Peace, freedom, and liberty!'
CASSIUS Stoop then and wash. How many ages hence
Shall this our lofty scene be acted over
In states unborn and accents yet unknown!
BRUTUS How many times shall Caesar bleed in sport,
That now on Pompey's basis lies along

95 SD.1] *Capell; at 77, Knight; at 82, Wells and Taylor* 95–6] *Steevens*[3]*;* But . . . Doers. / . . . *Trebonius.* / . . . *Antony?* / . . . amaz'd: F; But . . . Antony? / . . . amaz'd: *Knight* 101 SH CASCA] *Cask.* F; *Cas.* / *Pope* 105–10 Stoop . . . liberty] *Assigned to Brutus,* F; *to Casca, Pope* 113 states] F2; State F 113 accents] F; Nations QU4 114 SH BRUTUS] F; *Casc.* / *Pope* 115 lies] F2; lye F

94 abide Hulme (pp. 312–13) detects a double sense: 'in opposition to "leaue", it has the meaning "stay"; with "this deede" as its object it means "to pay for, meet the consequence of" '. Earlier, Mark Hunter had pointed to the confusion of the former for the latter. See *OED* Abide *v* 17b and 3.2.106 n.

96 amazed stupefied; as at 1.2.128.

99–100 Possibly proverbial (Dent N311): 'Nothing more certain than death and nothing more uncertain than the time of its coming.'

106 The view that Shakespeare is inflecting the ancient custom of drinking human blood in swearing oaths seems far-fetched. More likely is an allusion to the practice of hunters (with whom the conspirators are often compared) dipping their hands in the blood of slain animals.

108 market-place i.e. the Forum.

111 wash Not 'cleanse' but 'immerse' (hands and swords).

115 basis pedestal (as of a statue); the literal meaning.

No worthier than the dust!

CASSIUS So oft as that shall be,
So often shall the knot of us be called
The men that gave their country liberty.

DECIUS What, shall we forth?

CASSIUS Ay, every man away.
Brutus shall lead, and we will grace his heels
With the most boldest and best hearts of Rome.

Enter a SERVANT

BRUTUS Soft, who comes here? A friend of Antony's.

SERVANT Thus, Brutus, did my master bid me kneel,
Thus did Mark Antony bid me fall down,
And, being prostrate, thus he bade me say:
Brutus is noble, wise, valiant, and honest;
Caesar was mighty, bold, royal, and loving.
Say I love Brutus, and I honour him;
Say I feared Caesar, honoured him, and loved him.
If Brutus will vouchsafe that Antony
May safely come to him and be resolved
How Caesar hath deserved to lie in death,
Mark Antony shall not love Caesar dead
So well as Brutus living, but will follow
The fortunes and affairs of noble Brutus
Through the hazards of this untrod state
With all true faith. So says my master Antony.

BRUTUS Thy master is a wise and valiant Roman,
I never thought him worse.
Tell him, so please him come unto this place,
He shall be satisfied and by my honour
Depart untouched.

SERVANT I'll fetch him presently. *Exit Servant*

116 SH CASSIUS] F; *Bru. / Pope* **118** their] F; our *Malone*

121 most boldest The common double superlative used often for emphasis. See Abbott 11 and also 3.2.174.

122 Soft See 1.2.245 n.

126 honest An adjective with a wide spectrum, here most likely meaning 'honourable'.

127 royal noble, generous (*OED* sv *adj.* 9). See also 3.2.234.

131 resolved satisfied, convinced. See also 3.2.170.

136 Through F's 'Thorough', common in Shakespeare, may be used for metrical purposes here. See Abbott 478 and also 5.1.109.

140 so if, provided that. For this use of the subjunctive, see Abbott 133.

142 presently immediately; as at 28.

BRUTUS I know that we shall have him well to friend.
CASSIUS I wish we may. But yet have I a mind
That fears him much, and my misgiving still
Falls shrewdly to the purpose.

Enter ANTONY

BRUTUS But here comes Antony. Welcome, Mark Antony!
ANTONY O mighty Caesar! Dost thou lie so low?
Are all thy conquests, glories, triumphs, spoils
Shrunk to this little measure? Fare thee well!
I know not, gentlemen, what you intend,
Who else must be let blood, who else is rank.
If I myself, there is no hour so fit
As Caesar's death's hour, nor no instrument
Of half that worth as those your swords made rich
With the most noble blood of all this world.
I do beseech ye, if you bear me hard,
Now, whilst your purpled hands do reek and smoke,
Fulfil your pleasure. Live a thousand years,
I shall not find myself so apt to die:
No place will please me so, no mean of death,
As here by Caesar, and by you cut off,
The choice and master spirits of this age.
BRUTUS O Antony, beg not your death of us.
Though now we must appear bloody and cruel,
As by our hands and this our present act
You see we do, yet see you but our hands
And this the bleeding business they have done.
Our hearts you see not, they are pitiful;

147] *Pope (Folger MS.)*; But . . . *Antony*: / . . . *Antony*. F 154 death's] deaths F; death QU2

143 **to** i.e. as a. Abbott (189): '*To*, from meaning "like," came into the meaning of . . . "equivalence," "apposition".'

144 **may** can. See 1.3.144n.

146 **shrewdly** grievously, intensely, seriously (*OED* 5). An adverb of condition qualifying a word or phrase expressive of a painful or adverse condition (*OED* sv *adv.* 6) passing into a mere intensive.

152 **rank** 'Excessively great or large; *esp.* swollen, puffed up, grossly fat' (*OED* sv *adj.* 6); to be understood in connection with the medical connotations of 'shrunk' (150) and 'let blood'.

157 **bear me hard** endure me with a grudge. See 1.2.302n.

158 **purpled** blood-stained (from 'purple', the precious crimson dye used for royal or imperial robes).

158 **reek and smoke** The terms are practically synonymous and are applied to 'blood freshly shed, or [to] things smeared with this' (*OED* Reek *v* 2c).

159 **Live** i.e. if I live (subjunctive).

160 **apt** ready.

161 **mean** means. Shakespeare favoured 'means' over 'mean' by a margin of almost seven to one.

169 **pitiful** full of pity. See 1.3.78n.

And pity to the general wrong of Rome –
As fire drives out fire, so pity pity –
Hath done this deed on Caesar. For your part,
To you our swords have leaden points, Mark Antony;
Our arms in strength of malice, and our hearts
Of brothers' temper, do receive you in
With all kind love, good thoughts, and reverence.

CASSIUS Your voice shall be as strong as any man's
In the disposing of new dignities.

BRUTUS Only be patient till we have appeased
The multitude, beside themselves with fear,
And then we will deliver you the cause
Why I, that did love Caesar when I struck him,
Have thus proceeded.

ANTONY I doubt not of your wisdom.
Let each man render me his bloody hand.
First, Marcus Brutus, will I shake with you;
Next, Caius Cassius, do I take your hand;
Now, Decius Brutus, yours; now yours, Metellus;
Yours, Cinna; and, my valiant Casca, yours;
Though last, not least in love, yours, good Trebonius.
Gentlemen all – alas, what shall I say?
My credit now stands on such slippery ground
That one of two bad ways you must conceit me,
Either a coward or a flatterer.
That I did love thee, Caesar, O, 'tis true.
If then thy spirit look upon us now,
Shall it not grieve thee dearer than thy death
To see thy Antony making his peace,
Shaking the bloody fingers of thy foes –
Most noble – in the presence of thy corse?
Had I as many eyes as thou hast wounds,
Weeping as fast as they stream forth thy blood,
It would become me better than to close
In terms of friendship with thine enemies.

174 in strength of malice] F; no strength of malice *Thomas Johnson;* exempt from malice *Pope;* in strength of welcome *Collier*[2] *(Collier MS.);* in strength of manhood *Collier*[4]; in strength of amity *Hudson*[2] *(conj. Singer apud Hudson*[2]*);* unstrung of malice *Wells and Taylor (after Badham,* unstring their malice*)*

171 Proverbial (Dent F277, P369.1): 'One fire drives out another'; 'Pity destroys pity.'

174 malice power to harm.

192 conceit imagine. *OED v* 2 cites this instance.

202 close come to an agreement.

Pardon me, Julius! Here wast thou bayed, brave hart,
Here didst thou fall, and here thy hunters stand,
Signed in thy spoil and crimsoned in thy Lethe.
O world! Thou wast the forest to this hart,
And this indeed, O world, the heart of thee.
How like a deer strucken by many princes
Dost thou here lie!

CASSIUS Mark Antony –

ANTONY Pardon me, Caius Cassius,
The enemies of Caesar shall say this;
Then, in a friend, it is cold modesty.

CASSIUS I blame you not for praising Caesar so,
But what compact mean you to have with us?
Will you be pricked in number of our friends,
Or shall we on and not depend on you?

ANTONY Therefore I took your hands, but was indeed
Swayed from the point by looking down on Caesar.
Friends am I with you all, and love you all,
Upon this hope, that you shall give me reasons
Why and wherein Caesar was dangerous.

BRUTUS Or else were this a savage spectacle.
Our reasons are so full of good regard
That were you, Antony, the son of Caesar
You should be satisfied.

ANTONY That's all I seek,
And am, moreover, suitor that I may
Produce his body to the market-place,
And in the pulpit, as becomes a friend,
Speak in the order of his funeral.

BRUTUS You shall, Mark Antony.

CASSIUS Brutus, a word with you.

204 hart] F; Heart F2 **206** Lethe] F; death *Pope* **208** heart] *Theobald;* Hart F **225** you,] Q (1691); you F

204 bayed brought to bay; this is the dominant interpretation, but 'bayed' may also imply 'enclosed, cornered' and 'barked at'.

206 thy spoil slaughter of thee; 'spoil' in hunting = the capture of the quarry and the division of rewards.

206 Lethe The river in Hades whose waters, when drunk, caused forgetfulness of the past. It is equated here with Caesar's life-blood and in general with oblivion and death.

208 thee For the use of the pronoun ('thee') instead of the pronominal adjective ('thine'), see Abbott 225. It is used here perhaps for antithesis.

213 modesty moderation.

216 pricked marked (by a 'prick' or tick).

225 you, Antony, See 2.1.255n.

230 order prescribed form of ceremony or rite. See also 'ordered', 5.5.79.

[*Aside to Brutus*] You know not what you do. Do not consent
That Antony speak in his funeral.
Know you how much the people may be moved
By that which he will utter?

BRUTUS [*Aside to Cassius*] By your pardon,
I will myself into the pulpit first
And show the reason of our Caesar's death.
What Antony shall speak, I will protest
He speaks by leave and by permission,
And that we are contented Caesar shall
Have all true rites and lawful ceremonies.
It shall advantage more than do us wrong.

CASSIUS [*Aside to Brutus*] I know not what may fall, I like it not.

BRUTUS Mark Antony, here take you Caesar's body.
You shall not in your funeral speech blame us,
But speak all good you can devise of Caesar
And say you do't by our permission,
Else shall you not have any hand at all
About his funeral. And you shall speak
In the same pulpit whereto I am going,
After my speech is ended.

ANTONY Be it so,
I do desire no more.

BRUTUS Prepare the body then and follow us.

Exeunt [*all but*] *Antony*

ANTONY O, pardon me, thou bleeding piece of earth,
That I am meek and gentle with these butchers!
Thou art the ruins of the noblest man
That ever livèd in the tide of times.
Woe to the hand that shed this costly blood!
Over thy wounds now do I prophesy –
Which like dumb mouths do ope their ruby lips

232 SD] *Rowe* **235** utter?] Q (1684); vtter. F **235** SD] *Capell* **241** true] F; due *Pope* **241** ceremonies.] *Rowe (subst.)*; Ceremonies, F **243** SD] *Capell* **244** here] F; here, Q (1691) **251–2**] *Steevens*[3] *(Capell MS.)*; After . . . ended. / . . . so: / . . . more. F **254** SH ANTONY] Q (1691) **254** bleeding piece of] F; piece of bleeding *Reed* **258** hand] F; hands *White (conj. Thirlby)*

232 SD The exact limits of the aside are, as at 2.4.39 SD, difficult to ascertain. Fairly clear alternatives are offered by Capell, Keightley, and Wilson.

238 What . . . shall Whatever Antony may. 'With verbs of seeing, thinking and finding, *shall* was commonly found in the sense of "may" or "will"' (Blake, p. 94).

238 protest assert publicly.

243 fall befall, happen. See also 5.1.104.

259 prophesy 'Very important [in divination] is prophecy, in which the *vates* acts as the medium or mouthpiece of a divine or demonic power possessing him' (*OCD* divination).

To beg the voice and utterance of my tongue –
A curse shall light upon the limbs of men:
Domestic fury and fierce civil strife
Shall cumber all the parts of Italy;
Blood and destruction shall be so in use
And dreadful objects so familiar
That mothers shall but smile when they behold
Their infants quartered with the hands of war,
All pity choked with custom of fell deeds;
And Caesar's spirit, ranging for revenge,
With Ate by his side come hot from hell,
Shall in these confines with a monarch's voice
Cry havoc and let slip the dogs of war,
That this foul deed shall smell above the earth
With carrion men groaning for burial.

Enter Octavio's SERVANT

You serve Octavius Caesar, do you not?
SERVANT I do, Mark Antony.
ANTONY Caesar did write for him to come to Rome.
SERVANT He did receive his letters, and is coming,
And bid me say to you by word of mouth –
[*Seeing the body*]
O Caesar!
ANTONY Thy heart is big, get thee apart and weep.
Passion, I see, is catching, for mine eyes,
Seeing those beads of sorrow stand in thine,
Began to water. Is thy master coming?
SERVANT He lies tonight within seven leagues of Rome.

262 limbs] F; kind *Hanmer;* ne *Warburton;* lymms *conj. Johnson;* loines *Collier*[2] *(Collier MS.);* lives *Dyce (conj. Johnson);* tombs *conj. Staunton;* sonnes *conj. White;* heads *conj. John Hunter;* minds *Dyce*[2] *(conj. Jervis);* times *conj. Walker* **275** SD *Octavio's*] F; Octavius's QU3 **280** SD] *Rowe* **283** catching, for] F2; catching from F **285** Began] F; Begin QU1

262 limbs F's reading is preferable to the numerous conjectures (see collation) in both the literal and metaphorical sense of the 'body politic'.

264 cumber All commentators gloss as 'burden' or 'harass' or both, but *OED* sv *v* 1 'overwhelm' seems more appropriate.

268 with 'Often used to express the juxtaposition of cause and effect' (Abbott 193).

269 fell fierce, cruel.

271 Daughter of Strife and sister of Lawlessness, Ate is the symbol of infatuation or moral blindness. In Homer she is banished by Zeus to the lower world; in Aeschylus she (like Nemesis) avenges evil deeds. Shakespeare equates her with discord, as in *John* 2.1.63.

273 havoc destruction; originally, to give an army the order 'Havoc!' was the signal for the seizure of spoil.

273 let slip unleash. A slip is a leash so contrived that the dog can be readily released.

281 For the use of the short line, see 1.1.51 n.

ANTONY Post back with speed and tell him what hath chanced.
Here is a mourning Rome, a dangerous Rome,
No Rome of safety for Octavius yet:
Hie hence and tell him so. Yet stay awhile,
Thou shalt not back till I have borne this corse
Into the market-place. There shall I try
In my oration how the people take
The cruel issue of these bloody men,
According to the which thou shalt discourse
To young Octavius of the state of things.
Lend me your hand.

Exeunt [*with Caesar's body*]

3.2 *Enter* BRUTUS *and Cassius with the* PLEBEIANS

ALL We will be satisfied! Let us be satisfied!
BRUTUS Then follow me and give me audience, friends.
Cassius, go you into the other street
And part the numbers.
Those that will hear me speak, let 'em stay here;
Those that will follow Cassius, go with him;
And public reasons shall be renderèd
Of Caesar's death.
1 PLEBEIAN I will hear Brutus speak.
2 PLEBEIAN I will hear Cassius and compare their reasons
When severally we hear them renderèd.

[*Exit Cassius with some of the Plebeians*]

[*Brutus goes into the pulpit*]

3 PLEBEIAN The noble Brutus is ascended, silence!
BRUTUS Be patient till the last.

287] *Rowe;* Post ... speede, / ... chanc'd: F **291** corse] Coarse F3; course F **297** SD *with Caesar's body*] *Rowe* **Act 3, Scene 2** 3.2] *Rowe* Location] *Rowe* **10** SD.1 *Exit ... Plebeians*] *Capell* **10** SD.2 *Brutus ... pulpit*] F *(at o SD)*

289 Rome Upton's conjecture 'room' (p. 246) points up the possible wordplay, as at 1.2.156.

291 corse corpse.

292 try attempt to find out, test. See also 4.3.214, 5.3.110.

294 cruel issue outcome of the cruelty. For the construction, see 1.1.33 n.

Act 3, Scene 2

Location Rome. The Forum.

7 public Commentary is divided: 'concerning the public' or 'given in public' or both. See Abbott 3.

10 severally separately, each in turn. See also 2.4.46 SD.

10 SD.2 *pulpit* For a possible rendition of this structure, see illustration 2, p. 6.

Romans, countrymen, and lovers, hear me for my cause, and be silent that you may hear. Believe me for mine honour, and have respect to mine honour that you may believe. Censure me in your wisdom, and awake your senses that you may the better judge. If there be any in this assembly, any dear friend of Caesar's, to him I say that Brutus' love to Caesar was no less than his. If then that friend demand why Brutus rose against Caesar, this is my answer: not that I loved Caesar less, but that I loved Rome more. Had you rather Caesar were living, and die all slaves, than that Caesar were dead, to live all freemen? As Caesar loved me, I weep for him; as he was fortunate, I rejoice at it; as he was valiant, I honour him; but, as he was ambitious, I slew him. There is tears for his love, joy for his fortune, honour for his valour, and death for his ambition. Who is here so base that would be a bondman? If any, speak, for him have I offended. Who is here so rude that would not be a Roman? If any, speak, for him have I offended. Who is here so vile that will not love his country? If any, speak, for him have I offended. I pause for a reply.

ALL None, Brutus, none.

BRUTUS Then none have I offended. I have done no more to Caesar than you shall do to Brutus. The question of his death is enrolled in the Capitol, his glory not extenuated wherein he was worthy, nor his offences enforced for which he suffered death.

Enter MARK ANTONY [*and others*] *with Caesar's body*

Here comes his body, mourned by Mark Antony, who, though he had no hand in his death, shall receive the benefit of his dying, a place in the commonwealth, as which of you shall not? With this I depart: that, as I slew my best lover for the good of Rome, I have the same dagger for myself when it shall please my country to need my death.

[*Comes down*]

ALL Live, Brutus, live, live!

1 PLEBEIAN Bring him with triumph home unto his house.

21 freemen] Q (1691); Free-men F; free men F2 34 SD *and others*] *Malone (after Capell)* 39 SD] *Capell*

13 **lovers** friends (Pope's emendation), well-wishers.

14 **have respect to** consider, heed. See also 4.3.69.

15 **Censure** Judge (not necessarily negative in connotation).

16 **senses** Normally plural: 'mental faculties … one's "reason" or "wits"' (*OED* Sense *sb* 10).

21 **As** In proportion as. See 2.1.106n.

26 **rude** Apparently synonymous with 'base' (25) and 'vile' (28).

32 **enrolled** written upon a roll or parchment.

34 **enforced** put forward (too) strongly, emphasised. Compare 4.3.112n.

2 PLEBEIAN Give him a statue with his ancestors.
3 PLEBEIAN Let him be Caesar.
4 PLEBEIAN Caesar's better parts
Shall be crowned in Brutus.
1 PLEBEIAN We'll bring him to his house
With shouts and clamours.
BRUTUS My countrymen –
2 PLEBEIAN Peace, silence, Brutus speaks!
1 PLEBEIAN Peace ho!
BRUTUS Good countrymen, let me depart alone,
And, for my sake, stay here with Antony.
Do grace to Caesar's corpse, and grace his speech
Tending to Caesar's glories, which Mark Antony
(By our permission) is allowed to make.
I do entreat you, not a man depart,
Save I alone, till Antony have spoke. *Exit*
1 PLEBEIAN Stay ho, and let us hear Mark Antony.
3 PLEBEIAN Let him go up into the public chair,
We'll hear him. Noble Antony, go up.
ANTONY For Brutus' sake, I am beholding to you.
[*Goes into the pulpit*]
4 PLEBEIAN What does he say of Brutus?
3 PLEBEIAN He says for Brutus' sake
He finds himself beholding to us all.
4 PLEBEIAN 'Twere best he speak no harm of Brutus here!
1 PLEBEIAN This Caesar was a tyrant.
3 PLEBEIAN Nay, that's certain:
We are blest that Rome is rid of him.
2 PLEBEIAN Peace, let us hear what Antony can say.
ANTONY You gentle Romans –
ALL Peace ho, let us hear him.

42, 43 SH 2 PLEBEIAN ... 4 PLEBEIAN] F; *on the assumption that the 'actual' Second Plebeian has left at 9 to hear Cassius, Humphreys substitutes* FOURTH *for* SECOND *and* FIFTH *for* FOURTH *throughout the rest of the scene. In 3.3, however, he reverts to* F*'s four Plebeians. Bevington retains the 'arbitrary' numbering but notes, 'Not the same person who exited at l. 10'* 42 ancestors] F; ancestor's *conj. Velz (privately)* 43–6] *Globe;* 3. ... *Caesar.* / ... parts, / ... *Brutus.* / ... House, / ... Clamors. / ... Country-men. / ... speakes. / ... ho. F; *3 Pleb.* ... *Caesar.* / ... Parts / ... *Brutus.* / ... clamours. QU4; 3. CIT. ... parts / ... Brutus. / ... clamours. / ... speaks. / ... ho! *Steevens*[3] 57 SD] *Globe (after Capell / goes up)* 62 blest] F; glad F2 64 SH ALL] F; SECOND PLEBEIAN *Sanders*

42 ancestors John W. Velz (privately) suggests the possessive singular, noting Plutarch's reference (p. 164) to a statue of Junius Brutus in the Capitol. But his citing of Brutus's reference to his ancestors (2.1.53) would seem to diminish the attractiveness of his effort to remove ambiguity.

50 Tending Relating, referring.

53 spoke For the form, see 1.2.48 n.

57, 59 beholding Common for modern 'beholden', the form may derive from a confusion of 'beholden to' and 'holding to' (Abbott 372, Franz 169).

ANTONY Friends, Romans, countrymen, lend me your ears!
I come to bury Caesar, not to praise him.
The evil that men do lives after them,
The good is oft interrèd with their bones:
So let it be with Caesar. The noble Brutus
Hath told you Caesar was ambitious;
If it were so, it was a grievous fault,
And grievously hath Caesar answered it.
Here, under leave of Brutus and the rest –
For Brutus is an honourable man,
So are they all, all honourable men –
Come I to speak in Caesar's funeral.
He was my friend, faithful and just to me,
But Brutus says he was ambitious,
And Brutus is an honourable man.
He hath brought many captives home to Rome,
Whose ransoms did the general coffers fill;
Did this in Caesar seem ambitious?
When that the poor have cried, Caesar hath wept:
Ambition should be made of sterner stuff;
Yet Brutus says he was ambitious,
And Brutus is an honourable man.
You all did see that on the Lupercal
I thrice presented him a kingly crown,
Which he did thrice refuse. Was this ambition?
Yet Brutus says he was ambitious,
And sure he is an honourable man.
I speak not to disprove what Brutus spoke,
But here I am to speak what I do know.
You all did love him once, not without cause;
What cause withholds you then to mourn for him?
O judgement, thou art fled to brutish beasts,
And men have lost their reason! Bear with me,
My heart is in the coffin there with Caesar,
And I must pause till it come back to me.

1 PLEBEIAN Methinks there is much reason in his sayings.

96 art] F2; are F **96** beasts] F; Breasts QU4

96 brutish Possibly a pun on Latin 'brutus' (= 'dull', 'without reason') and the name 'Brutus'. See Plutarch, p. 157.

2 PLEBEIAN If thou consider rightly of the matter,
Caesar has had great wrong.
3 PLEBEIAN Has he, masters!
I fear there will a worse come in his place.
4 PLEBEIAN Marked ye his words? He would not take the crown,
Therefore 'tis certain he was not ambitious.
1 PLEBEIAN If it be found so, some will dear abide it.
2 PLEBEIAN Poor soul, his eyes are red as fire with weeping.
3 PLEBEIAN There's not a nobler man in Rome than Antony.
4 PLEBEIAN Now mark him, he begins again to speak.
ANTONY But yesterday the word of Caesar might
Have stood against the world; now lies he there,
And none so poor to do him reverence.
O masters, if I were disposed to stir
Your hearts and minds to mutiny and rage,
I should do Brutus wrong and Cassius wrong,
Who (you all know) are honourable men.
I will not do them wrong; I rather choose
To wrong the dead, to wrong myself and you,
Than I will wrong such honourable men.
But here's a parchment with the seal of Caesar,
I found it in his closet, 'tis his will.
Let but the commons hear this testament –
Which, pardon me, I do not mean to read –
And they would go and kiss dead Caesar's wounds
And dip their napkins in his sacred blood,
Yea, beg a hair of him for memory,
And, dying, mention it within their wills,
Bequeathing it as a rich legacy
Unto their issue.
4 PLEBEIAN We'll hear the will. Read it, Mark Antony.
ALL The will, the will, we will hear Caesar's will!
ANTONY Have patience, gentle friends, I must not read it.

102 Has he] Ha's hee F; Has he my *Capell (conj. Thirlby)*; Has he not *Craik*; That has he *Mark Hunter (conj. Morley apud Mark Hunter)*; Ha! has he *conj. Anon. (apud Cam.)* **102–3**] *As verse, Steevens*[3] *(Capell MS.); as prose (turnover),* F **126** Yea] F; Nay *Capell*

102 Has he, masters! Most likely an assertion (as the conjectures indicate) rather than a question. For a similar inversion, see 1.2.228.

106 abide pay for ('through confusion of form with *abye*': *OED* Abide *v* 17b). See also 3.1.94n.

112 none so poor 'The meanest man is now too high' (Johnson).

125 napkins handkerchiefs.

It is not meet you know how Caesar loved you:
You are not wood, you are not stones, but men,
And, being men, hearing the will of Caesar,
It will inflame you, it will make you mad.
'Tis good you know not that you are his heirs,
For if you should, O, what would come of it?

4 PLEBEIAN Read the will, we'll hear it, Antony.
You shall read us the will, Caesar's will!

ANTONY Will you be patient? Will you stay awhile?
I have o'ershot myself to tell you of it.
I fear I wrong the honourable men
Whose daggers have stabbed Caesar, I do fear it.

4 PLEBEIAN They were traitors. Honourable men!

ALL The will! The testament!

2 PLEBEIAN They were villains, murderers! The will, read the will!

ANTONY You will compel me then to read the will?
Then make a ring about the corpse of Caesar
And let me show you him that made the will.
Shall I descend? And will you give me leave?

ALL Come down.

2 PLEBEIAN Descend.

3 PLEBEIAN You shall have leave.

[*Antony comes down from the pulpit*]

4 PLEBEIAN A ring, stand round.

1 PLEBEIAN Stand from the hearse, stand from the body.

2 PLEBEIAN Room for Antony, most noble Antony.

ANTONY Nay, press not so upon me, stand far off.

ALL Stand back! Room, bear back!

ANTONY If you have tears, prepare to shed them now.
You all do know this mantle. I remember
The first time ever Caesar put it on,
'Twas on a summer's evening, in his tent,
That day he overcame the Nervii.
Look, in this place ran Cassius' dagger through;

145–6] F; *as one verse line, Keightley* 146–7] F; ALL ... villains, / ... Read the will! *S. F. Johnson*[2] 147] *As prose,* F; *as verse, splitting after* murderers, *Irving; as one verse line, Craig* 148 will?] *Pope;* Will: F 152–5] F; *Cit.* ... ring; / ... round. *Keightley (conj. Thirlby)* 154 SD] *Rowe (after 161)*

156 **hearse** bier.

158 **far** F's 'farre' suggests the comparative 'farther'. See Franz 220 and 5.3.11.

164 **Nervii** A mixed Celto-German tribe, occupying parts of Hainault and Flanders and called by Plutarch 'the stoutest warriors of all the Belgae', they were defeated by Caesar in 57 BC.

See what a rent the envious Casca made;
Through this the well-belovèd Brutus stabbed,
And as he plucked his cursèd steel away,
Mark how the blood of Caesar followed it,
As rushing out of doors to be resolved
If Brutus so unkindly knocked or no,
For Brutus, as you know, was Caesar's angel.
Judge, O you gods, how dearly Caesar loved him!
This was the most unkindest cut of all.
For when the noble Caesar saw him stab,
Ingratitude, more strong than traitors' arms,
Quite vanquished him. Then burst his mighty heart,
And, in his mantle muffling up his face,
Even at the base of Pompey's statue
(Which all the while ran blood) great Caesar fell.
O, what a fall was there, my countrymen!
Then I, and you, and all of us fell down,
Whilst bloody treason flourished over us.
O, now you weep, and I perceive you feel
The dint of pity. These are gracious drops.
Kind souls, what weep you when you but behold
Our Caesar's vesture wounded? Look you here,
Here is himself, marred as you see with traitors.

1 PLEBEIAN O piteous spectacle!
2 PLEBEIAN O noble Caesar!
3 PLEBEIAN O woeful day!
4 PLEBEIAN O traitors, villains!
1 PLEBEIAN O most bloody sight!

174 cut] F; act *Folger MS.* **186** what] F; what, *Pope* **189–98**] F; *1 Cit.* ... Caesar! / ... sight! / ... burn, – / ... live. / ... Antony. *Keightley. There are numerous attempts to make verse of all or some of these lines*

166 envious malicious; as at 2.1.178.

170 resolved satisfied, convinced; as at 3.1.131.

171 unkindly unnaturally (with, as often in Shakespeare, a possible play on the sense 'cruelly').

172 angel Most take this to mean 'best beloved, darling' rather than 'guardian angel' or 'genius'.

174 most unkindest The double superlative is used for emphasis, as at 3.1.121. E. L. Dachslager ('"The most unkindest cut": a note on *Julius Caesar* 3.2.187', *ELN* 11 (1973–4), 258–9) detects the possibility of an 'oblique' reference to a detail from Plutarch (p. 160) which Shakespeare omits: that in the assassination of Caesar 'Brutus himself gave him one wound about his privities'.

177 Quite Completely.

177 burst Citing contemporary works of physiology, Alan R. Smith (*Explicator* 42:4 (1984), 9–10) finds 'Antony's use of *burst* a panegyric, for it suggests to the mob that Caesar, despite his loss of blood from the dozens of wounds, yet had enough blood to "burst his mighty heart" when grief overcomes him at the sight of Brutus among the conspirators'.

179 statue The final *e* is pronounced. See 2.2.76 n.

183 flourished Most recent interpretations extend 'thrived' to 'exulted, triumphed' and combine with a sword image.

185 dint blow; especially one given with a weapon.

2 PLEBEIAN We will be revenged!
ALL Revenge! About! Seek! Burn! Fire! Kill!
Slay! Let not a traitor live!
ANTONY Stay, countrymen.
1 PLEBEIAN Peace there, hear the noble Antony.
2 PLEBEIAN We'll hear him, we'll follow him, we'll die with him.
ANTONY Good friends, sweet friends, let me not stir you up
To such a sudden flood of mutiny.
They that have done this deed are honourable.
What private griefs they have, alas, I know not,
That made them do it. They are wise and honourable,
And will no doubt with reasons answer you.
I come not, friends, to steal away your hearts.
I am no orator, as Brutus is,
But – as you know me all – a plain blunt man
That love my friend, and that they know full well
That gave me public leave to speak of him.
For I have neither wit, nor words, nor worth,
Action, nor utterance, nor the power of speech
To stir men's blood. I only speak right on.
I tell you that which you yourselves do know,
Show you sweet Caesar's wounds, poor, poor, dumb mouths,
And bid them speak for me. But were I Brutus,
And Brutus Antony, there were an Antony
Would ruffle up your spirits and put a tongue
In every wound of Caesar, that should move
The stones of Rome to rise and mutiny.
ALL We'll mutiny.

194–6] *As prose, Pope; as verse,* We . . . Reuenge / . . . slay, / . . . liue. F **195** SH ALL] *Collier[2] (Collier MS.)* **199**] F; *as verse, Johnson[2]* **205** reasons] F; Reason QU4 **210** gave] F; give F2 **211** wit] F2; writ F

195 About Get to work, bestir yourself (Onions); an imperative use.

203 griefs grievances; as at 1.3.118.

211–13 wit . . . blood Renaissance rhetoric, as exemplified by Thomas Wilson (*The Arte of Rhetorique*, 1553), would equate 'wit' with 'invention' (fol. 3[v]), 'words' with 'elocution' ('an applying of apte wordes and sentences to the matter', fol. 4), and would consider 'Action' as an aspect of 'utterance' ('a framyng of the voyce, countenaunce, and gesture, after a comely maner', fol. 4). Kittredge's neat explanation is popular: 'A complete list of the qualities of a good orator: (1) intellectual cleverness (*wit*); (2) fluency (*words*); (3) *auctoritas*, the weight that comes from character or standing (*worth*); (4) gesture and bearing (*action*); (5) skilful elocution, good delivery (*utterance*) – and finally (6) *the power of speech to stir men's blood*, without which all other accomplishments avail but little'. His terminology may be somewhat misleading, however.

211 *wit F's 'writ', conceivable but doubtful in the semantics and alliteration of the line, is possibly a misprint stemming from the proximity of the final *r* in 'neither', if not the *w* and *r* presence in 'words' and 'worth'.

218 ruffle up stir up to indignation or rage (more intense than in modern usage).

1 PLEBEIAN We'll burn the house of Brutus.
3 PLEBEIAN Away then, come, seek the conspirators.
ANTONY Yet hear me, countrymen, yet hear me speak.
ALL Peace ho, hear Antony, most noble Antony!
ANTONY Why, friends, you go to do you know not what.
Wherein hath Caesar thus deserved your loves?
Alas, you know not! I must tell you then:
You have forgot the will I told you of.
ALL Most true. The will, let's stay and hear the will!
ANTONY Here is the will, and under Caesar's seal:
To every Roman citizen he gives,
To every several man, seventy-five drachmaes.
2 PLEBEIAN Most noble Caesar, we'll revenge his death!
3 PLEBEIAN O royal Caesar!
ANTONY Hear me with patience.
ALL Peace ho!
ANTONY Moreover, he hath left you all his walks,
His private arbours and new-planted orchards,
On this side Tiber; he hath left them you,
And to your heirs for ever – common pleasures,
To walk abroad and recreate yourselves.
Here was a Caesar! When comes such another?
1 PLEBEIAN Never, never! Come, away, away!
We'll burn his body in the holy place
And with the brands fire the traitors' houses.
Take up the body.
2 PLEBEIAN Go fetch fire!
3 PLEBEIAN Pluck down benches!
4 PLEBEIAN Pluck down forms, windows, anything!
Exeunt Plebeians [*with the body*]
ANTONY Now let it work. Mischief, thou art afoot,
Take thou what course thou wilt!

234–6] F; *as one line, Keightley;* O . . . patience. / . . . ho! *Bevington* **239** this] F; that *Theobald (after Plutarch)* **245** fire] F; fire all F2 **246–9**] F; *as* F, *adding* The *before* benches *as separate line, Capell;* Take . . . benches. / . . . thing. *Keightley* **249** SD *with the body*] *Rowe* **251** Take thou] F; Take now *conj. Craik;* Take then *conj. Anon. (apud Cam.)*

232 several separate, individual; as at 2.1.138.

232 drachmaes silver coins. F's spelling may indicate a double plural.

234 royal noble, generous; as at 3.1.127.

239 On this side 'A prepositional phrase is condensed into a preposition' (Abbott 202). According to Plutarch's description it should be on 'that' side. The error is North's (from Amyot).

240 common public; as at 3.1.80.

240 pleasures pleasure grounds (the dominant interpretation).

249 forms Probably synonymous with 'benches' (see *OED* Form *sb* 17), although *OED* (19a) records 'window frames' as well.

Enter SERVANT

How now, fellow?

SERVANT Sir, Octavius is already come to Rome.
ANTONY Where is he?
SERVANT He and Lepidus are at Caesar's house.
ANTONY And thither will I straight to visit him.
He comes upon a wish. Fortune is merry,
And in this mood will give us anything.
SERVANT I heard him say Brutus and Cassius
Are rid like madmen through the gates of Rome.
ANTONY Belike they had some notice of the people,
How I had moved them. Bring me to Octavius.

Exeunt

3.3 *Enter* CINNA THE POET, *and after him the* PLEBEIANS

CINNA THE POET I dreamt tonight that I did feast with Caesar,
And things unluckily charge my fantasy.
I have no will to wander forth of doors,
Yet something leads me forth.
1 PLEBEIAN What is your name?
2 PLEBEIAN Whither are you going?
3 PLEBEIAN Where do you dwell?
4 PLEBEIAN Are you a married man or a bachelor?
2 PLEBEIAN Answer every man directly.
1 PLEBEIAN Ay, and briefly.
4 PLEBEIAN Ay, and wisely.
3 PLEBEIAN Ay, and truly, you were best.
CINNA THE POET What is my name? Whither am I going? Where do I

258 him] F; them *Capell* Act 3, Scene 3 3.3] *Capell* Location] *Capell (Capell MS.)* 2 unluckily] F; unluckey *Warburton (Folger MS.)*; unlikely *Collier*^{2} *(Collier MS.)* 5–12] F; *1 Cit.* ... dwell? / ... bachelor? / ... briefly. / ... best. *Keightley*

256 upon a wish 'according to one's wish' (*OED* Wish *sb*^{1} 1c).

259 Are rid For the use of 'be' with intransitive verbs, mostly of motion, see Abbott 295.

Act 3, Scene 3

Location Rome. A street.

2 unluckily inauspiciously, with ill omen.

2 charge place a load on, burden.

2 fantasy imagination. Compare 2.1.197 n.

3 of out of.

12 you were best 'The old idiom ... where *you* may represent either nominative or dative, but was almost certainly used by Shakespeare as nominative' (Abbott 230).

dwell? Am I a married man or a bachelor? Then to answer every man directly and briefly, wisely and truly. Wisely I say I am a bachelor.

2 PLEBEIAN That's as much as to say they are fools that marry. You'll bear me a bang for that, I fear. Proceed directly.

CINNA THE POET Directly I am going to Caesar's funeral.

1 PLEBEIAN As a friend or an enemy?

CINNA THE POET As a friend.

2 PLEBEIAN That matter is answered directly.

4 PLEBEIAN For your dwelling – briefly.

CINNA THE POET Briefly, I dwell by the Capitol.

3 PLEBEIAN Your name, sir, truly.

CINNA THE POET Truly, my name is Cinna.

1 PLEBEIAN Tear him to pieces, he's a conspirator.

CINNA THE POET I am Cinna the poet, I am Cinna the poet.

4 PLEBEIAN Tear him for his bad verses, tear him for his bad verses.

CINNA THE POET I am not Cinna the conspirator.

4 PLEBEIAN It is no matter, his name's Cinna. Pluck but his name out of his heart and turn him going.

3 PLEBEIAN Tear him, tear him! Come, brands ho, firebrands! To Brutus', to Cassius', burn all! Some to Decius' house, and some to Casca's, some to Ligarius'! Away, go!

Exeunt all the Plebeians [forcing out Cinna]

out for blood

4.1 *Enter* ANTONY, OCTAVIUS, *and* LEPIDUS

ANTONY These many then shall die, their names are pricked.
OCTAVIUS Your brother too must die; consent you, Lepidus?

15 Wisely I say] *Hudson;* wisely I say, F; Wisely, I say – *Rowe;* wisely, I say *Collier*[3] 28] F; *as one verse line, Staunton (Capell MS.)* 33 Brutus' ... Cassius'] *Apostrophes, Capell* 33 Decius'] *Apostrophe,* F4 34 Ligarius'] *Apostrophe, Capell* 34 SD *forcing out Cinna*] *Collier*[2] Act 4, Scene 1 4.1] *Actus Quartus.* F; ACT IV. SCENE I. *Rowe* Location] *Rowe, Capell*

14–15 Then ... bachelor 'The Plebeians intend that each of Cinna's answers should be given in all of the four adverbial ways; Cinna makes fun of them by choosing to interpret their ritual catalogue as a set of pairs: one adverbial mode for each answer. The comedy is enhanced when the Plebeians fall into his mocking pattern' (John W. Velz, privately).

15 Wisely The word is placed so 'that it may express either the wisdom of the answer or the wisdom of being a bachelor' (Macmillan).

17 me i.e. from me. Abbott (220) calls it the 'old dative'.

18 Directly Like 'wisely' at 15, 'Directly' is 'purposely made ambiguous ... It may express either the straightforwardness of the answer or that Cinna is going straight to Caesar's funeral' (Macmillan).

31 turn him going drive him off.

Act 4, Scene 1

Location Rome. Antony's house. Although the scene is traditionally placed in Rome, the triumvirs in reality met on a small island in the river Lavinius near Bononia.

2 brother Mentioned in Plutarch (*Antony*, Bul-

LEPIDUS I do consent.
OCTAVIUS Prick him down, Antony.
LEPIDUS Upon condition Publius shall not live,
Who is your sister's son, Mark Antony.
ANTONY He shall not live – look, with a spot I damn him.
But, Lepidus, go you to Caesar's house,
Fetch the will hither, and we shall determine
How to cut off some charge in legacies.
LEPIDUS What, shall I find you here?
OCTAVIUS Or here or at the Capitol.

Exit Lepidus

ANTONY This is a slight, unmeritable man,
Meet to be sent on errands; is it fit,
The threefold world divided, he should stand
One of the three to share it?
OCTAVIUS So you thought him
And took his voice who should be pricked to die
In our black sentence and proscription.
ANTONY Octavius, I have seen more days than you,
And though we lay these honours on this man
To ease ourselves of divers slanderous loads,
He shall but bear them as the ass bears gold,
To groan and sweat under the business,
Either led or driven, as we point the way;
And having brought our treasure where we will,
Then take we down his load and turn him off
(Like to the empty ass) to shake his ears

10–11] F; *LEP.* ... at / ... Capitol. *Steevens*[3] *(Capell MS.)* **23** point] F; print F2

lough, pp. 268–9), Lucius Aemilius Paullus, elder brother of Lepidus, was named in the proscriptions but allowed to escape.

4–5 Publius ... sister's son Plutarch (*Antony*, Bullough, p. 268) mentions Antony's offering his uncle, Lucius Julius Caesar, the brother of his mother. For a Publius who was also proscribed, see List of Characters. J. and S. Velz ('Publius, Mark Anthony's sister's son', *SQ* 26 (1975), 69–74) attribute the substitution to Shakespeare's 'remembering imperfectly ... [Plutarch's] vivid account ... [of the proscription of] Publius Silicius' (p. 71) and to 'Plutarch or a folk tradition (or both) ... [for] the presence of a "sister's son"' (p. 70).

6 spot mark or stigma. See also 4.3.2 n.

6 damn condemn as guilty (from Latin *damnare*).

9 charge expense, cost.

11 Or Either. For 'or ... or', see Abbott 136.

14 threefold world A reference to the trine structure of the world, consisting of Europe, Asia, and Africa; the Roman world, consisting of the East and West provinces and Africa was divided among the triumvirate: Antony received Cisalpine and Transalpine Gaul, Lepidus Old Gaul and all Spain, and Octavius Africa, Sicily, and Sardinia.

16 voice vote (this sense is more frequent in Shakespeare than 'opinion').

20 slanderous giving cause for slander. For the passive sense of adjectives ending in '-ous', see Abbott 3.

26–7 shake ... graze The movement of the ears which accompanies grazing is at least as fitting as the common figurative interpretation: 'act uselessly or aimlessly'.

And graze in commons.
OCTAVIUS You may do your will,
But he's a tried and valiant soldier.
ANTONY So is my horse, Octavius, and for that
I do appoint him store of provender.
It is a creature that I teach to fight,
To wind, to stop, to run directly on,
His corporal motion governed by my spirit.
And, in some taste, is Lepidus but so:
He must be taught and trained and bid go forth,
A barren-spirited fellow, one that feeds
On objects, arts, and imitations,
Which, out of use and staled by other men,
Begin his fashion. Do not talk of him
But as a property. And now, Octavius,
Listen great things. Brutus and Cassius
Are levying powers; we must straight make head.
Therefore let our alliance be combined,
Our best friends made, our means stretched,
And let us presently go sit in counsel,
How covert matters may be best disclosed
And open perils surest answerèd.
OCTAVIUS Let us do so, for we are at the stake
And bayed about with many enemies,

37 objects, arts] F; abject Orts *Theobald;* abject arts *conj. Becket;* abjects, orts *Staunton;* objects, orts *White*^{2} 38 staled] F; stall'd F4 44 our means stretched] F; and our best meanes stretcht out F2; our best means stretch'd out QU4; our best means stretcht *Johnson (Capell MS.);* our meinies [*i.e.* followers] stretched *Wells and Taylor (conj. J.D.)* 45 counsel] *This edn;* Councell F; Council F3 47 surest] F; soonest *Folger MS.*

27 commons lands belonging to the community.

28 soldier Final *-ier* is most likely disyllabic for metrical reasons, as also in 4.3.51. See Abbott 479.

30 appoint decree formally.

32 wind turn.

34 taste degree.

37 objects, arts, and imitations Most commentators, especially in this century, interpret as 'curiosities, artifices, and followings of fashions', whereas some earlier commentators are more neutral, glossing the first term as 'whatever is presented to the eye' (Malone apud Steevens^3) and the second as '*mechanic operations*' (Steevens).

38 staled out of date, uninteresting (*OED* *v*^{2} 2, citing this instance); many commentators prefer 'made common or cheap'.

39 fashion custom.

40 property means to an end, instrument.

41 Listen i.e. listen to. 'The preposition is ... sometimes omitted before the *thing* heard after verbs of hearing' (Abbott 199).

42 make head 'raise a force' is preferred by most commentators although *OED* (Head *sb* 52a) has 'advance, press forward', distinguishing it from '*make a head*' (52b).

45 presently immediately; as at 3.1.28.

45 in counsel in private. All commentators prefer 'in council' (as at 2.1.67), but see *OED* Counsel *sb* 5c, and 'covert', 46, 2.1.298 n., 2.4.9 n.

48 at the stake i.e. like a bear tied to a post (in the Elizabethan sport of bear-baiting).

49 bayed held at bay (and surrounded by hostile – some say barking – dogs).

And some that smile have in their hearts, I fear,
Millions of mischiefs.
Exeunt

4.2 *Drum. Enter* BRUTUS, LUCILIUS, [*Lucius,*] *and the army. Titinius and* PINDARUS *meet them*

BRUTUS Stand ho!
LUCILIUS Give the word ho, and stand!
BRUTUS What now, Lucilius, is Cassius near?
LUCILIUS He is at hand, and Pindarus is come
To do you salutation from his master.
BRUTUS He greets me well. Your master, Pindarus,
In his own change or by ill officers,
Hath given me some worthy cause to wish
Things done undone, but if he be at hand
I shall be satisfied.
PINDARUS I do not doubt
But that my noble master will appear
Such as he is, full of regard and honour.
BRUTUS He is not doubted.
[*Brutus and Lucilius draw apart*]
A word, Lucilius,
How he received you; let me be resolved.
LUCILIUS With courtesy and with respect enough,

Act 4, Scene 2 **4.2**] *Rowe* Location] *Rowe* **0** SD *Lucius*] *Capell* **1–2**] F; *as one line, Keightley* **2** SH] *The speech heading / Luc. / here and following, in all editions from* F2 *to Singer²*, *may have contributed to the confusion of Lucilius and Lucius in this scene* **7** change] F; charge QU3 **13** SD] *Continues to 30, Sanders (after Capell)* **13–14** Lucilius, ... you;] F *(subst.); Lucilius, — / ... you, Rowe (Folger MS.)*

51 mischiefs harms (stronger than in modern usage).

Act 4, Scene 2

Location Camp near Sardis. Before Brutus's tent.

0 SD The staging of the opening of the scene and of some later movements has caused discussion. Ever since Jennens's explicit comment, F's stage direction and the subsequent dialogue have generally been understood to mean that Brutus, having already arrived and perhaps accompanied by Lucius, meets Lucilius, who brings with him Pindarus and Titinius (some are of the opinion that Pindarus and Titinius enter at the other door and Wilson holds that the latter enters with Cassius at 30). For the staging and the transition to Scene 3, see illustration 3, p. 7.

0 SD.1 *Drum* The usual accompaniment for troops on the march. It is nearly interchangeable with *march* (24).

5 do The transitive use with objective noun. See Abbott 303.

6 He ... well Most editors do not accept Capell's suggestion that Pindarus presents a letter from Cassius but rather that Brutus finds him a worthy ambassador.

8 worthy justifiable (Onions 3); however, many commentators prefer 'considerable', 'substantial'.

14 resolved informed.

But not with such familiar instances,
Nor with such free and friendly conference,
As he hath used of old.

BRUTUS Thou hast described
A hot friend cooling. Ever note, Lucilius,
When love begins to sicken and decay
It useth an enforcèd ceremony.
There are no tricks in plain and simple faith,
But hollow men, like horses hot at hand,
Make gallant show and promise of their mettle.

Low march within

But when they should endure the bloody spur
They fall their crests, and like deceitful jades
Sink in the trial. Comes his army on?

LUCILIUS They mean this night in Sardis to be quartered.
The greater part, the horse in general,
Are come with Cassius.

Enter CASSIUS *and his powers*

BRUTUS Hark, he is arrived.
March gently on to meet him.

CASSIUS Stand ho!

BRUTUS Stand ho, speak the word along!

1 SOLDIER Stand!

2 SOLDIER Stand!

3 SOLDIER Stand!

CASSIUS Most noble brother, you have done me wrong.

BRUTUS Judge me, you gods! Wrong I mine enemies?
And if not so, how should I wrong a brother?

CASSIUS Brutus, this sober form of yours hides wrongs,

24 SD] F; *placed after 30, Capell* 34, 35, 36 SH 1 SOLDIER, 2 SOLDIER, 3 SOLDIER] *Globe (after Capell,* 1. O[fficer], *etc.)*

16 instances evidences, tokens.

17 free frank. See *OED* sv *adj.* 23.

17 conference conversation (not necessarily on important or serious subjects).

21 enforcèd forced, constrained.

23 at hand at the start.

24 SD Considered by Wilson a marginal prompter's note anticipating the response to the drums at 30. He also cites (p. 92) 5.3.96 SD and 5.5.23 SD among the 'noises off' which suggest prompt-book origin since 'they sometimes duplicate directions in the centre of the page'.

28 Sardis The chief city of Lydia, made by the Romans the capital of a *conventus* (administrative division) of the province Asia. See also 5.1.79.

29 in general in a body, collectively.

31 March gently on Since Cassius has already arrived, Brutus's words imply not necessarily movement but a military command (see *OED* March v^2 1e) that Cassius is to be met 'gently' – i.e. not (as most editions gloss) 'slowly' or 'quietly' but in response to the *Low march within* (24 SD) perhaps with dignity, with noble bearing. See 5.3.96 SD n.

And when you do them –
BRUTUS Cassius, be content,
Speak your griefs softly, I do know you well.
Before the eyes of both our armies here –
Which should perceive nothing but love from us –
Let us not wrangle. Bid them move away.
Then in my tent, Cassius, enlarge your griefs
And I will give you audience.
CASSIUS Pindarus,
Bid our commanders lead their charges off
A little from this ground.
BRUTUS Lucius, do you the like, and let no man
Come to our tent till we have done our conference.
Let Lucilius and Titinius guard our door.
Exeunt [*all but*] *Brutus and Cassius*

4.3

CASSIUS That you have wronged me doth appear in this:
You have condemned and noted Lucius Pella
For taking bribes here of the Sardians,
Wherein my letters, praying on his side,
Because I knew the man, was slighted off.
BRUTUS You wronged yourself to write in such a case.
CASSIUS In such a time as this it is not meet
That every nice offence should bear his comment.
BRUTUS Let me tell you, Cassius, you yourself
Are much condemned to have an itching palm,
To sell and mart your offices for gold

50, 52 Lucius ... Lucilius] *Craik (omitting* Let *at 52); Lucillius ... Lucius* F **Act 4, Scene 3** **4.3**] *Pope; although, as the / Mane*[*n*]*t / in* F *indicates, the scene obviously continues, the tradition since Pope (with very few exceptions) has been to observe the scene break* Location] *Theobald* **4** Wherein] F*;* Whereas *Hudson*[2] **4–5** letters ... was] F*;* Letter ... was F2*;* letters ... were *Malone* **5** man,] F2*;* man F **5** off] F*;* of *Rowe*[3] *(Folger MS.)* **6** case] F*;* cause *conj. Thirlby*

41 content satisfied in mind. See 1.3.142 n.
42, 46 griefs grievances; as at 1.3.118.
46 enlarge give free vent to.

Act 4, Scene 3

Location Camp near Sardis. Brutus's tent.
2 noted stigmatised. See 4.1.6 n.
4 praying entreating.
5 was The apparent lack of concord – a singular verb with a plural subject, 'letters' – may be attributed to confusion caused by the proximity of 'man'. See Abbott 412. Or it may be that 'letters' is plural with a singular meaning like Latin *litterae* (*OED* Letter *sb*[1] 4b).
8 nice slight, trivial.
8 his its.
10 to have of having. For the gerundial use of the infinitive, see Abbott 356.

To undeservers.

CASSIUS I, an itching palm?
You know that you are Brutus that speaks this,
Or, by the gods, this speech were else your last.

BRUTUS The name of Cassius honours this corruption,
And chastisement doth therefore hide his head.

CASSIUS Chastisement?

BRUTUS Remember March, the Ides of March remember:
Did not great Julius bleed for justice' sake?
What villain touched his body, that did stab
And not for justice? What, shall one of us,
That struck the foremost man of all this world,
But for supporting robbers, shall we now
Contaminate our fingers with base bribes
And sell the mighty space of our large honours
For so much trash as may be graspèd thus?
I had rather be a dog and bay the moon
Than such a Roman.

CASSIUS Brutus, bait not me,
I'll not endure it. You forget yourself
To hedge me in. I am a soldier, I,
Older in practice, abler than yourself
To make conditions.

BRUTUS Go to, you are not, Cassius!

CASSIUS I am.

BRUTUS I say you are not.

CASSIUS Urge me no more, I shall forget myself.
Have mind upon your health, tempt me no farther!

BRUTUS Away, slight man!

CASSIUS Is't possible?

BRUTUS Hear me, for I will speak.
Must I give way and room to your rash choler?
Shall I be frighted when a madman stares?

12 I] F; Ay *Rowe* 13 speaks] F; speak *Pope* 27 bay] F; baite F2 28 bait] F; bay *Theobald* 30 soldier, I] F; soldier; ay *Steevens* 32 not,] QU4; not F 32–4] *Steevens*[3]; To ... Conditions. / ... *Cassius.* / ... am. / ... not. F; To ... Cassius. / ... not. *Wordsworth (Capell MS.)*; To ... conditions. / ... am. / ... not. *Humphreys*

26 trash 'Contemptuously applied to money' (*OED* sv *sb*[1] 3d).

28 bait Cassius plays on the dog image in 'bay' by extending it to apply to attacks by dogs on chained animals.

32 conditions agreements, treaties.

36 tempt test; as at 1.3.53.

CASSIUS O ye gods, ye gods, must I endure all this?
BRUTUS All this? Ay, more. Fret till your proud heart break.
Go show your slaves how choleric you are,
And make your bondmen tremble. Must I budge?
Must I observe you? Must I stand and crouch
Under your testy humour? By the gods,
You shall digest the venom of your spleen
Though it do split you. For, from this day forth,
I'll use you for my mirth, yea, for my laughter,
When you are waspish.
CASSIUS Is it come to this?
BRUTUS You say you are a better soldier:
Let it appear so, make your vaunting true
And it shall please me well. For mine own part
I shall be glad to learn of noble men.
CASSIUS You wrong me every way, you wrong me, Brutus.
I said an elder soldier, not a better.
Did I say 'better'?
BRUTUS If you did, I care not.
CASSIUS When Caesar lived, he durst not thus have moved me.
BRUTUS Peace, peace, you durst not so have tempted him.
CASSIUS I durst not?
BRUTUS No.
CASSIUS What? Durst not tempt him?
BRUTUS For your life you durst not.
CASSIUS Do not presume too much upon my love,
I may do that I shall be sorry for.
BRUTUS You have done that you should be sorry for.
There is no terror, Cassius, in your threats,
For I am armed so strong in honesty
That they pass by me as the idle wind,
Which I respect not. I did send to you
For certain sums of gold, which you denied me,
For I can raise no money by vile means.

54 noble] F; abler *Collier*[2] *(Collier MS.)*; able *conj. Singer (apud Cam.)*; better *conj. Cartwright*; nobler *conj. Nicholson* 60 not?] Q (1684); not. F

44 **budge** wince, flinch.

45 **observe** show respectful or courteous attention to.

47 **spleen** The seat of the sudden emotions and passions.

62 **tempt** test.

64, 65 **that** For the omission of the relative 'that', perhaps because of the identity of the demonstrative and the relative, see Abbott 244.

69 **respect** heed; as at 3.2.14.

By heaven, I had rather coin my heart
And drop my blood for drachmaes than to wring
From the hard hands of peasants their vile trash
By any indirection. I did send
To you for gold to pay my legions,
Which you denied me. Was that done like Cassius?
Should I have answered Caius Cassius so?
When Marcus Brutus grows so covetous
To lock such rascal counters from his friends,
Be ready, gods, with all your thunderbolts,
Dash him to pieces!

CASSIUS I denied you not.

BRUTUS You did.

CASSIUS I did not. He was but a fool that brought
My answer back. Brutus hath rived my heart.
A friend should bear his friend's infirmities,
But Brutus makes mine greater than they are.

BRUTUS I do not, till you practise them on me.

CASSIUS You love me not.

BRUTUS I do not like your faults.

CASSIUS A friendly eye could never see such faults.

BRUTUS A flatterer's would not, though they do appear
As huge as high Olympus.

CASSIUS Come, Antony, and young Octavius, come,
Revenge yourselves alone on Cassius,
For Cassius is a-weary of the world:
Hated by one he loves, braved by his brother,
Checked like a bondman, all his faults observed,
Set in a notebook, learned, and conned by rote,
To cast into my teeth. O, I could weep
My spirit from mine eyes! There is my dagger
And here my naked breast: within, a heart
Dearer than Pluto's mine, richer than gold.

81 thunderbolts,] F; thunderbolts *Collier* 83–5] *Dyce; Bru.* ... did. / ... Foole / ... hart: F; *BRU.* ... fool. / ... heart: *Steevens*[3] *(Capell MS.)* 88 not, till] F; not: will *Hanmer;* not. Still *Warburton (conj. Warburton apud Theobald)* **102** Pluto's] F; *Plutus' / Pope*

75 **indirection** deviousness.

80 **rascal** common, wretched.

80 **counters** counterfeit coins (applied to debased coin, and contemptuously to money generally).

96 **braved** defied. Compare 5.1.10.

97 **Checked** Rebuked.

99 **To ... teeth** To be reproached, upbraided. For the infinitive used passively, see Abbott 359.

102 **Dearer** More precious.

102 **Pluto** Plutus, son of Demeter and Iasion, who symbolises wealth. He is closely connected – in the Renaissance perhaps confused – in idea with Pluton

If that thou beest a Roman take it forth,
I that denied thee gold will give my heart:
Strike as thou didst at Caesar. For I know
When thou didst hate him worst thou loved'st him better
Than ever thou loved'st Cassius.

BRUTUS Sheathe your dagger.
Be angry when you will, it shall have scope;
Do what you will, dishonour shall be humour.
O Cassius, you are yokèd with a lamb
That carries anger as the flint bears fire,
Who, much enforcèd, shows a hasty spark
And straight is cold again.

CASSIUS Hath Cassius lived
To be but mirth and laughter to his Brutus
When grief and blood ill-tempered vexeth him?

BRUTUS When I spoke that, I was ill-tempered too.

CASSIUS Do you confess so much? Give me your hand.

BRUTUS And my heart too.

CASSIUS O Brutus!

BRUTUS What's the matter?

CASSIUS Have not you love enough to bear with me
When that rash humour which my mother gave me
Makes me forgetful?

BRUTUS Yes, Cassius, and from henceforth
When you are over-earnest with your Brutus,
He'll think your mother chides, and leave you so.

Enter a POET, [LUCILIUS *and Titinius*]

POET Let me go in to see the generals.
There is some grudge between 'em, 'tis not meet
They be alone.

109 humour] F; honour *conj. Craik* **110** lamb] F; man *Pope* **123** SD LUCILIUS . . . TITINIUS] *Rowe; followed by Lucilius, Titinius, and Lucius / Globe; entrance placed after 128, Theobald* **126–7**] F; *as one line, Sisson (Capell MS.)*

(the Rich One), lord of the lower world. Some consider 'Pluto' the Italian form of 'Plutus'.

109 humour mental disposition.

112 Who Strictly speaking, the antecedent is 'flint'. For the use of 'who' with 'irrational antecedents', often animals (here, 'lamb'), see Abbott 264.

112 enforcèd used force upon (*OED* sv 8b). Compare 3.2.34 n.

115, 116 ill-tempered Wordplay on 'badly mixed' (applied to the humours) and the modern 'bad-humoured'.

120 rash humour The reference is to choler, one of the four humours or temperaments. Earlier in the scene Brutus has mentioned Cassius's 'rash choler' (39) and his being 'choleric' (43).

124–8 Some editors, beginning with Theobald, have these lines spoken 'within', the characters entering thereafter.

LUCILIUS You shall not come to them.
POET Nothing but death shall stay me.
CASSIUS How now, what's the matter?
POET For shame, you generals, what do you mean?
Love and be friends, as two such men should be,
For I have seen more years, I'm sure, than ye.
CASSIUS Ha, ha, how vildly doth this cynic rhyme!
BRUTUS Get you hence, sirrah; saucy fellow, hence!
CASSIUS Bear with him, Brutus, 'tis his fashion.
BRUTUS I'll know his humour when he knows his time.
What should the wars do with these jigging fools?
Companion, hence!
CASSIUS Away, away, be gone!

Exit Poet

BRUTUS Lucilius and Titinius, bid the commanders
Prepare to lodge their companies tonight.
CASSIUS And come yourselves, and bring Messala with you
Immediately to us.

[*Exeunt Lucilius and Titinius*]

BRUTUS [*To Lucius within*] Lucius, a bowl of wine!
CASSIUS I did not think you could have been so angry.
BRUTUS O Cassius, I am sick of many griefs.
CASSIUS Of your philosophy you make no use
If you give place to accidental evils.
BRUTUS No man bears sorrow better. Portia is dead.
CASSIUS Ha? Portia?
BRUTUS She is dead.

137 jigging] F; jingling *Pope* 142 SD.1 *Exeunt … Titinius*] *Rowe* 142 SD.2 *To Lucius within*] *Evans*

132 ye Often interchangeable with 'you' (see Abbott 236), 'ye' may be preferred here because of the rhyme.

133 vildly Most likely not a variant of 'vile' with an excrescent *d* but derived from the past participle of 'avile'. See Franz 60.

133 cynic One of the school of philosophy which advocated extreme asceticism, hence a rough, sneering railer. In Plutarch it is Marcus Favonius (erroneously Phaonius or Faonius in North (p. 173 below)).

134 sirrah A term of address expressing contempt or reprimand.

136 'I will admit his right to be eccentric when he chooses a proper occasion to exhibit his eccentricity' (Kittredge). There is also a pun on 'time' in connection with poetic metre.

137 jigging Another reference to the nature of his verse. Compare the opening of Marlowe's *Tamburlaine*: 'From jigging veins of rhyming mother wits'.

138 Companion A term of familiarity or contempt. Here 'fellow, a bad sense' (Schmidt 4).

144 of as a result of. See Abbott 168.

145 your philosophy A reference to Stoic philosophy, especially the influence of Panaetius, one of the chief representatives of the Middle Stoa, who tried to adapt Stoic ethics to the needs of active statesmen and soldiers. See also 5.1.100 n.

146 accidental caused by chance.

CASSIUS How scaped I killing when I crossed you so?
O insupportable and touching loss!
Upon what sickness?

BRUTUS Impatient of my absence,
And grief that young Octavius with Mark Antony
Have made themselves so strong – for with her death
That tidings came. With this she fell distract
And, her attendants absent, swallowed fire.

CASSIUS And died so?

BRUTUS Even so.

CASSIUS O ye immortal gods!

Enter BOY [LUCIUS] *with wine and tapers*

BRUTUS Speak no more of her. Give me a bowl of wine.
In this I bury all unkindness, Cassius. *Drinks*

CASSIUS My heart is thirsty for that noble pledge.
Fill, Lucius, till the wine o'erswell the cup,
I cannot drink too much of Brutus' love. [*Drinks*]
[*Exit Lucius*]

Enter TITINIUS *and* MESSALA

BRUTUS Come in, Titinius; welcome, good Messala.
Now sit we close about this taper here
And call in question our necessities.

CASSIUS Portia, art thou gone?

BRUTUS No more, I pray you.
Messala, I have here receivèd letters
That young Octavius and Mark Antony
Come down upon us with a mighty power,
Bending their expedition toward Philippi.

157] *Dyce (Capell MS.); Cas.* ... so? / ... so. / ... Gods! F 157 SD LUCIUS] *Hanmer (omitting* BOY*)* 162 SD.1 *Drinks*] *Capell (Folger MS.)* 162 SD.2 *Exit Lucius*] *Globe* 163] *Rowe;* Come ... *Titinius*: / ... *Messala*: F

150 killing i.e. being killed. For the passive sense of participles, see Abbott 374.

152 Impatient of 'Unable or unwilling to endure' (*OED* sv *adj.* 1b).

155 That tidings Always spelt with an *-s* ending, the form is used for the singular or the plural.

155 fell distract became (esp. suddenly) anxious, perplexed. Shakespeare prefers the form 'distract' to 'distraught' (which implies madness) and to 'distracted' (which normally precedes a noun).

156 swallowed fire Plutarch relates (p. 183) that she 'took hot burning coals and cast them into her mouth, and kept her mouth so close that she choked herself'. That she committed suicide because Brutus neglected her is a theory which is not substantiated.

165 call in question 'summon for trial or examination' (*OED* Call *v* 18).

170 expedition speedy journey (though 'warlike enterprise' is also a possible meaning).

MESSALA Myself have letters of the selfsame tenor.
BRUTUS With what addition?
MESSALA That by proscription and bills of outlawry
Octavius, Antony, and Lepidus
Have put to death an hundred senators.
BRUTUS Therein our letters do not well agree:
Mine speak of seventy senators that died
By their proscriptions, Cicero being one.
CASSIUS Cicero one?
MESSALA Cicero is dead,
And by that order of proscription.
Had you your letters from your wife, my lord?
BRUTUS No, Messala.
MESSALA Nor nothing in your letters writ of her?
BRUTUS Nothing, Messala.
MESSALA That, methinks, is strange.
BRUTUS Why ask you? Hear you aught of her in yours?
MESSALA No, my lord.
BRUTUS Now as you are a Roman tell me true.
MESSALA Then like a Roman bear the truth I tell,
For certain she is dead, and by strange manner.
BRUTUS Why, farewell, Portia. We must die, Messala.
With meditating that she must die once,
I have the patience to endure it now.
MESSALA Even so, great men great losses should endure.
CASSIUS I have as much of this in art as you,
But yet my nature could not bear it so.
BRUTUS Well, to our work alive. What do you think
Of marching to Philippi presently?
CASSIUS I do not think it good.

179–80] *Thomas Johnson*[2] *(adding* yes *before* Cicero is*); Cicero* one? / . . . proscription F 181–95] *First version of report of Portia's death; final version at 143–58, 166* 185] *Rowe;* Why . . . you? / . . . yours? F 193 so,] *This edn;* so F

173 proscription . . . bills of outlawry The *proscriptio* was a list of Roman citizens who were declared outlaws and whose goods were confiscated. The procedure was employed by Antony, Lepidus, and Octavius (43–42 BC) to get rid of personal and political opponents and to obtain funds. See Plutarch (*Antony*, Bullough, pp. 268–9), and also 'proscription', 4.1.17.

181–95 See p. 149 below.

191 once in any case (*OED* sv *adv.* 2b). The customary gloss 'at some time or other' seems inexact since Portia is already dead.

193 Even so 'Used to answer in the affirmative, = indeed, yes' (Schmidt, even 4).

194 in art as an acquired faculty (as opposed to 'nature').

196 alive in full force or vigour (*OED* sv *adv.* 3); however, most commentators gloss as 'with the living', and some as 'of present concern'.

197 presently immediately; as at 3.1.28.

BRUTUS Your reason?
CASSIUS This it is:
'Tis better that the enemy seek us,
So shall he waste his means, weary his soldiers,
Doing himself offence, whilst we, lying still,
Are full of rest, defence, and nimbleness.
BRUTUS Good reasons must of force give place to better:
The people 'twixt Philippi and this ground
Do stand but in a forced affection,
For they have grudged us contribution.
The enemy, marching along by them,
By them shall make a fuller number up,
Come on refreshed, new added, and encouraged,
From which advantage shall we cut him off
If at Philippi we do face him there,
These people at our back.
CASSIUS Hear me, good brother.
BRUTUS Under your pardon. You must note beside
That we have tried the utmost of our friends,
Our legions are brimful, our cause is ripe;
The enemy increaseth every day,
We, at the height, are ready to decline.
There is a tide in the affairs of men
Which, taken at the flood, leads on to fortune;
Omitted, all the voyage of their life
Is bound in shallows and in miseries.
On such a full sea are we now afloat,
And we must take the current when it serves
Or lose our ventures.
CASSIUS Then with your will go on,
We'll along ourselves and meet them at Philippi.
BRUTUS The deep of night is crept upon our talk,
And nature must obey necessity,
Which we will niggard with a little rest.

209 new added] F; new-hearted *Collier*[2] *(Collier MS.)*; new aided *Singer*[2] *(after Hall apud Thirlby)* **224–5**] *Capell;* Or ... Ventures. / ... along / ... *Philippi.* F

203 of force perforce, of necessity.

205 affection Final *-ion* is most likely disyllabic for metrical reasons, as also in 'contribution' (206), 'apparition' (277), *et passim.* See Abbott 479.

214 tried proved by a test. See 3.1.292 n.

224 ventures 'A figure from seafaring. The amount invested in a ship or cargo was regularly spoken of as a man's *venture*; and persons who took risks of this kind were called *adventurers*' (Kittredge).

There is no more to say?
CASSIUS No more. Good night.
Early tomorrow will we rise and hence.
BRUTUS Lucius!

Enter LUCIUS

My gown.

[*Exit Lucius*]

Farewell, good Messala.
Good night, Titinius. Noble, noble Cassius,
Good night and good repose.
CASSIUS O my dear brother!
This was an ill beginning of the night.
Never come such division 'tween our souls!
Let it not, Brutus.

Enter LUCIUS *with the gown*

BRUTUS Everything is well.
CASSIUS Good night, my lord.
BRUTUS Good night, good brother.
TITINIUS AND MESSALA Good night, Lord Brutus.
BRUTUS Farewell every one.

Exeunt [*Cassius, Titinius, Messala*]

Give me the gown. Where is thy instrument?
LUCIUS Here in the tent.
BRUTUS What, thou speak'st drowsily.
Poor knave, I blame thee not, thou art o'erwatched.
Call Claudio and some other of my men,
I'll have them sleep on cushions in my tent.
LUCIUS Varrus and Claudio!

Enter VARRUS *and* CLAUDIO

VARRUS Calls my lord?
BRUTUS I pray you, sirs, lie in my tent and sleep,
It may be I shall raise you by and by
On business to my brother Cassius.

229 say?] *Capell;* say. F **231** SD.2 *Exit Lucius*] Q (1691) **236** SD] F; *placed after 239, Capell* **238** SD *Cassius ... Messala*] Q (1691) **239** thy] F; my QU4 **240** drowsily.] *This edn (after Keightley);* drowsily? F **242** Claudio] F; Claudius *Rowe* **244** Varrus and Claudio] F; *Varro* and *Claudius / Rowe* **244–5**] F; *as one line, Wells and Taylor* **244** SD] F; Varro *and* Claudius *Rowe*

241 o'erwatched wearied with too much watching. **247 raise** rouse.

VARRUS So please you, we will stand and watch your pleasure.
BRUTUS I will not have it so. Lie down, good sirs,
It may be I shall otherwise bethink me.
[*Varrus and Claudio lie down*]
Look, Lucius, here's the book I sought for so,
I put it in the pocket of my gown.
LUCIUS I was sure your lordship did not give it me.
BRUTUS Bear with me, good boy, I am much forgetful.
Canst thou hold up thy heavy eyes awhile
And touch thy instrument a strain or two?
LUCIUS Ay, my lord, an't please you.
BRUTUS It does, my boy.
I trouble thee too much, but thou art willing.
LUCIUS It is my duty, sir.
BRUTUS I should not urge thy duty past thy might,
I know young bloods look for a time of rest.
LUCIUS I have slept, my lord, already.
BRUTUS It was well done and thou shalt sleep again,
I will not hold thee long. If I do live
I will be good to thee.
Music, and a song
This is a sleepy tune. O murd'rous slumber,
Layest thou thy leaden mace upon my boy,
That plays thee music? Gentle knave, good night,
I will not do thee so much wrong to wake thee.
If thou dost nod thou break'st thy instrument.
I'll take it from thee and, good boy, good night.
Let me see, let me see, is not the leaf turned down
Where I left reading? Here it is, I think.

Enter the GHOST OF CAESAR

How ill this taper burns! Ha, who comes here?
I think it is the weakness of mine eyes
That shapes this monstrous apparition.
It comes upon me. Art thou any thing?

249] *Rowe;* So . . . stand, / . . . pleasure. F **250 will**] F2*;* will it F **251** SD] *Capell (subst.)*

249 stand i.e. stand watch.
249 watch wait for, look out for.
258 an't if it; see 1.2.271 n.
261 should ought. See Abbott 323.

268 'The metaphor is from the bailiff touching persons on the shoulder with his mace or staff in token of arrest' (Mark Hunter).

Art thou some god, some angel, or some devil,
That mak'st my blood cold and my hair to stare?
Speak to me what thou art.

GHOST Thy evil spirit, Brutus.

BRUTUS Why com'st thou?

GHOST To tell thee thou shalt see me at Philippi.

BRUTUS Well, then I shall see thee again?

GHOST Ay, at Philippi.

BRUTUS Why, I will see thee at Philippi then.

[*Exit Ghost*]

Now I have taken heart thou vanishest.
Ill spirit, I would hold more talk with thee.
Boy, Lucius! Varrus! Claudio! Sirs, awake!
Claudio!

LUCIUS The strings, my lord, are false.

BRUTUS He thinks he still is at his instrument.
Lucius, awake!

LUCIUS My lord?

BRUTUS Didst thou dream, Lucius, that thou so cried'st out?

LUCIUS My lord, I do not know that I did cry.

BRUTUS Yes, that thou didst. Didst thou see anything?

LUCIUS Nothing, my lord.

BRUTUS Sleep again, Lucius. Sirrah Claudio!
[*To Varrus*] Fellow, thou, awake!

VARRUS My lord?

CLAUDIO My lord?

BRUTUS Why did you so cry out, sirs, in your sleep?

BOTH Did we, my lord?

BRUTUS Ay. Saw you anything?

VARRUS No, my lord, I saw nothing.

CLAUDIO Nor I, my lord.

BRUTUS Go and commend me to my brother Cassius.
Bid him set on his powers betimes before,

284–5] F; Well; / . . . Philippi. *Steevens*[3] **286** SD] *Rowe (after 285); placed as in Dyce* **287–8** vanishest. Ill spirit,] F; vanishest, Ill Spirit; *Rowe* **289–90** Varrus! Claudio . . . Claudio] F; *Varro! Claudius . . . Claudius / Rowe* **290–1**] F; *as one line, Bevington* **295**] *As verse, Theobald; as prose,* F **299** Claudio] F; *Claudius / Rowe* **299–302**] *Capell; Bru.* . . . Fellow, / . . . Awake. / . . . Lord. / . . . Lord. F; *Bru.* . . . Claudius! / . . . lord . . . lord? *Dorsch (Capell MS.)* **300** SD] *Globe (conj. Warburton)*

280 stare stand on end.

291 strings . . . false i.e. the strings are badly woven and produce an uncertain and untrue tone.

307 betimes Not so much 'without delay' (as 2.1.116) as 'early in the morning'.

And we will follow.

OTH It shall be done, my lord.

Exeunt

5.1 *Enter* OCTAVIUS, ANTONY, *and their army*

OCTAVIUS Now, Antony, our hopes are answerèd.
You said the enemy would not come down
But keep the hills and upper regions.
It proves not so: their battles are at hand,
They mean to warn us at Philippi here,
Answering before we do demand of them.

ANTONY Tut, I am in their bosoms, and I know
Wherefore they do it. They could be content
To visit other places and come down
With fearful bravery, thinking by this face
To fasten in our thoughts that they have courage.
But 'tis not so.

Enter a MESSENGER

MESSENGER Prepare you, generals,
The enemy comes on in gallant show,
Their bloody sign of battle is hung out,
And something to be done immediately.

Talking about the battle

ANTONY Octavius, lead your battle softly on
Upon the left hand of the even field.

OCTAVIUS Upon the right hand I, keep thou the left.

ANTONY Why do you cross me in this exigent?

Act 5, Scene 1 **5.1**] *Actus Quintus.* F; ACT V. SCENE I. *Rowe* Location] *Capell (after Rowe)* **5** warn] F; wage *Hanmer;* wait *conj. Mason* **12** Prepare you,] Q (1691); Prepare you F; Prepare, you *Jennens*

Act 5, Scene 1

Location The plains of Philippi.

4 battles troops in battle array, usually the main force.

5 warn Not 'summon' (the customary gloss) but 'resist' (*OED* Warn v^2).

7 bosoms Considered to be the repository of secret thoughts and counsels.

9 come down attack (by surprise). See also 5.2.6.

10 fearful Commentators are split between the active sense ('inducing fear') and the passive ('full of fear'). Most recent ones give both. See also 1.3.78 n.

10 bravery defiance. Compare 4.3.96.

10 face appearance; as at 2.1.114.

14 bloody sign of battle Plutarch (pp. 176–7) refers to the 'signal of battle ... an arming scarlet coat'. Coat-armour (*OED* sv 1) was a 'vest of rich material embroidered with heraldic devices'.

16 softly slowly (*OED* sv 3).

19 exigent critical occasion.

OCTAVIUS I do not cross you, but I will do so.

March

Drum. Enter BRUTUS, CASSIUS, *and their army;* [LUCILIUS, *Titinius,* MESSALA, *and others*]

BRUTUS They stand and would have parley.
CASSIUS Stand fast, Titinius, we must out and talk.
OCTAVIUS Mark Antony, shall we give sign of battle?
ANTONY No, Caesar, we will answer on their charge.
Make forth, the generals would have some words.
OCTAVIUS Stir not until the signal.
BRUTUS Words before blows; is it so, countrymen?
OCTAVIUS Not that we love words better, as you do.
BRUTUS Good words are better than bad strokes, Octavius.
ANTONY In your bad strokes, Brutus, you give good words.
Witness the hole you made in Caesar's heart,
Crying, 'Long live, hail, Caesar!'
CASSIUS Antony,
The posture of your blows are yet unknown;
But for your words, they rob the Hybla bees
And leave them honeyless.
ANTONY Not stingless too?
BRUTUS O yes, and soundless too,
For you have stolen their buzzing, Antony,
And very wisely threat before you sting.
ANTONY Villains! You did not so when your vile daggers
Hacked one another in the sides of Caesar.
You showed your teeth like apes and fawned like hounds,
And bowed like bondmen, kissing Caesar's feet,
Whilst damnèd Casca, like a cur, behind
Struck Caesar on the neck. O you flatterers!

20 SD.2 LUCILIUS ... *others*] *Capell* **33** posture] F; puncture *conj. Singer 1858;* portents *conj. Bulloch* **35** too?] *Macmillan (conj. Thirlby);* too. F **35–6**] *Steevens[3];* And ... Hony-lesse. / ... too. / ... soundlesse too: F; And ... honeyless. / ... soundless too. *Bevington (Capell MS.)* **41**] *Rowe;* You ... Apes, / ... Hounds, F **41** teeth] F3; teethes F

20 SD.1 *March* See 4.2.0 SD.1 n.

20 SD.2 *Drum* See 4.2.0 SD.1 n.

33 posture position (of a weapon in warfare). See *OED* sv *sb* 2b.

33 are A plural verb with a singular subject is frequent in Shakespeare owing to 'confusion of proximity' (Abbott 412) – i.e. because 'blows' directly precedes 'are'.

34 Hybla Town in Sicily famous for the honey produced in the surrounding hills.

41 showed ... teeth Most commentators gloss as 'grinned insincerely', although *OED* (Tooth *sb* 8f) has 'show[ed] hostility'. Shakespeare's customary treatment of apes would support the former view.

41 fawned like hounds See 3.1.42–3 n.

CASSIUS Flatterers? Now, Brutus, thank yourself.
This tongue had not offended so today
If Cassius might have ruled.
OCTAVIUS Come, come, the cause. If arguing make us sweat,
The proof of it will turn to redder drops.
Look,
I draw a sword against conspirators;
When think you that the sword goes up again?
Never, till Caesar's three and thirty wounds
Be well avenged, or till another Caesar
Have added slaughter to the sword of traitors.
BRUTUS Caesar, thou canst not die by traitors' hands
Unless thou bring'st them with thee.
OCTAVIUS So I hope.
I was not born to die on Brutus' sword.
BRUTUS O, if thou wert the noblest of thy strain,
Young man, thou couldst not die more honourable.
CASSIUS A peevish schoolboy, worthless of such honour,
Joined with a masker and a reveller!
ANTONY Old Cassius still!
OCTAVIUS Come, Antony, away!
Defiance, traitors, hurl we in your teeth.
If you dare fight today, come to the field;
If not, when you have stomachs.
Exeunt Octavius, Antony, and army
CASSIUS Why now blow wind, swell billow, and swim bark!
The storm is up, and all is on the hazard.
BRUTUS Ho, Lucilius, hark, a word with you.
Lucilius and Messala stand forth
LUCILIUS My lord.

50–1] *Steevens*[3]; Looke . . . Conspirators, F 53 thirty] F; twenty *Theobald (after Plutarch)* 55 sword] F; word *Collier*[2] *(Collier MS.)* 57 So I hope.] So I hope: F; So I hope QUI; So; I hope *Collier*[4] 67] *Rowe;* Why . . . Billow, / . . . Barke: F

49 proof i.e. the use of the sword.

53 thirty In Plutarch (p. 160), Appian (p. 21), and Suetonius (p. 111), twenty. 'Such mistakes in copying and in printing were very common on account of the practice of using Roman numerals' (Kittredge).

60 honourable Probably the adjective used as adverb (Abbott 1) rather than a pronounced final *e*.

61 peevish silly, foolish.

61 worthless unworthy. *OED* sv *adj.* 3 cites this instance, the only such usage in Shakespeare.

62 masker one who takes part in a masque or masquerade (used pejoratively). Earlier, Caesar had praised Antony for loving plays (1.2.203–4).

63 Come . . . away F's colon after 'Antony' has led some commentators to the belief that Octavius addresses 'away' not to Antony but to the troops.

66 have stomachs incline; as at 1.2.290.

[*Brutus speaks apart to Lucilius*]

CASSIUS Messala!
MESSALA What says my general?
CASSIUS Messala,
This is my birthday, as this very day
Was Cassius born. Give me thy hand, Messala.
Be thou my witness that against my will
(As Pompey was) am I compelled to set
Upon one battle all our liberties.
You know that I held Epicurus strong
And his opinion. Now I change my mind
And partly credit things that do presage.
Coming from Sardis, on our former ensign
Two mighty eagles fell, and there they perched,
Gorging and feeding from our soldiers' hands,
Who to Philippi here consorted us.
This morning are they fled away and gone,
And in their steads do ravens, crows, and kites
Fly o'er our heads and downward look on us
As we were sickly prey. Their shadows seem
A canopy most fatal under which
Our army lies, ready to give up the ghost.
MESSALA Believe not so.
CASSIUS I but believe it partly,
For I am fresh of spirit and resolved
To meet all perils very constantly.
BRUTUS Even so, Lucilius. [*Advancing*]
CASSIUS Now, most noble Brutus,
The gods today stand friendly that we may,
Lovers in peace, lead on our days to age!

69 SD.2 *Brutus . . . Lucilius*] *Rowe* 70–1] *Pope; Cassi Messala.* / . . . Generall? / . . . day F 79 former] F; foremost *Rowe;* forward *Collier*[2] *(Collier MS.)* 79 ensign] F; ensigns *Humphreys (conj. Lettsom)* 92 SD] *Staunton* 94 Lovers in peace,] F; Lovers, in peace, *Capell;* Lovers, in peace *conj. Furness*

71 **as** i.e. as I may say. See Abbott 114 for this redundant use with definitions of time.

76 **Epicurus** Moral and natural philosopher (341–270 BC), whose main doctrine, that 'pleasure is the beginning and end of living happily', entailed a distrust of the supernatural. Plutarch twice mentions Cassius's aberration: before the murder of Caesar (p. 159) and before the battle at Philippi (p. 176).

79 **Coming** i.e. as we came. For the participle with pronoun implied, see Abbott 379.

79 **Sardis** See 4.2.28 n.

79 **former** foremost (Plutarch's adjective, see p. 175).

79 **ensign** banner, standard.

87 **fatal** 'foreboding . . . ominous' (*OED* sv *adj.* 4c).

89 **I . . . partly** I but partly believe it. For the common transposition of the adverb, see Abbott 420.

91 **constantly** resolutely. See 'constancy', 2.1.227 n.

93 **The gods . . . stand** May the gods stand. The optative subjunctive, with 'may'. See Abbott 365.

But since the affairs of men rests still incertain,
Let's reason with the worst that may befall.
If we do lose this battle, then is this
The very last time we shall speak together.
What are you then determinèd to do?

BRUTUS Even by the rule of that philosophy
By which I did blame Cato for the death
Which he did give himself – I know not how,
But I do find it cowardly and vile,
For fear of what might fall, so to prevent
The time of life – arming myself with patience
To stay the providence of some high powers
That govern us below.

CASSIUS Then if we lose this battle,
You are contented to be led in triumph
Through the streets of Rome?

BRUTUS No, Cassius, no. Think not, thou noble Roman,
That ever Brutus will go bound to Rome:
He bears too great a mind. But this same day
Must end that work the Ides of March begun.
And whether we shall meet again I know not,
Therefore our everlasting farewell take:
For ever and for ever, farewell, Cassius!
If we do meet again, why, we shall smile;
If not, why then this parting was well made.

CASSIUS For ever and for ever, farewell, Brutus!
If we do meet again, we'll smile indeed;
If not, 'tis true this parting was well made.

BRUTUS Why then, lead on. O, that a man might know

105 time] F; turn [of death] *conj. Thirlby;* term *Capell* **106** some] F; those *Collier*[2] **109** Rome?] Q (1691); Rome. F **110**] *Rowe;* No ... no: / ... Romane, F

95 rests Most probably, the third-person plural in *-s*. See Abbott 333.

95 incertain Shakespeare usually prefers the *un-* prefix with negations whereas early-seventeenth-century usage favours *in-*.

100 that philosophy According to almost all commentators, this alludes to Stoicism, whose main tenet is explained in 103–7. See also 4.3.145 n. But J. C. Maxwell ('Brutus's philosophy', *N&Q* n.s. 17 (1970), 128) finds describing Brutus as a Stoic 'harmless, perhaps, if it is meant as a description of temperament, but quite wrong if applied to doctrine. As so often, M. W. MacCallum had got it right long ago, quoting Plutarch on Brutus's preference for "Platoes sect", and citing the *Phaedo* (*Shakespeare's Roman Plays and their Background* (1910), p. 237, n. 1).'

101 Cato See 2.1.295 n.

104 fall befall; as at 3.1.243.

104 prevent forestall; see 2.1.28 n.

106 stay await, stay for.

109 Through For an explanation of F's 'Thorow', see 3.1.136 n.

The end of this day's business ere it come!
But it sufficeth that the day will end,
And then the end is known. Come ho, away!

Exeunt

5.2 *Alarum. Enter* BRUTUS *and Messala*

BRUTUS Ride, ride, Messala, ride, and give these bills
Unto the legions on the other side.

Loud alarum

Let them set on at once, for I perceive
But cold demeanour in Octavio's wing,
And sudden push gives them the overthrow.
Ride, ride, Messala, let them all come down.

Exeunt

5.3 *Alarums. Enter* CASSIUS *and* TITINIUS

CASSIUS O, look, Titinius, look, the villains fly!
Myself have to mine own turned enemy.
This ensign here of mine was turning back;
I slew the coward and did take it from him.

TITINIUS O Cassius, Brutus gave the word too early,
Who, having some advantage on Octavius,
Took it too eagerly. His soldiers fell to spoil
Whilst we by Antony are all enclosed.

Enter PINDARUS

Act 5, Scene 2 5.2] *Capell* Location] *Capell* 4 Octavio's] F; *Octavius' / Thomas Johnson*[2] 5 And] F; One *Hanmer (Folger MS.);* A *Warburton* **Act 5, Scene 3** 5.3] *Capell* Location] *Capell*

Act 5, Scene 2

Location The field of battle.

0 SD *Alarum* Originally a call to arms (from Italian *all'arme*), later accompanied by a signal produced by a musical instrument.

1 bills written orders.

4 cold In contemporary physiology 'cold' (in association with dry or moist) was applied to the elements, complexions, humours, etc. (see 5.5.73 n.) and conveyed, among other things, 'Smallnesse of courage', if cold and moist, or the 'Tymerous and fearefull', if cold and dry (Sir Thomas Elyot, *The Castel of Helthe* (1541), fols. 2b, 3).

6 come down attack (by surprise); as at 5.1.9.

Act 5, Scene 3

Location Another part of the field.

3 ensign standard-bearer; formerly 'officer of the lowest grade in the infantry'; the reference may also be to the standard itself (as in 4, 'it'), although Plutarch (p. 179) mentions the soldier.

PINDARUS Fly further off, my lord, fly further off!
Mark Antony is in your tents, my lord,
Fly therefore, noble Cassius, fly far off.
CASSIUS This hill is far enough. Look, look, Titinius,
Are those my tents where I perceive the fire?
TITINIUS They are, my lord.
CASSIUS Titinius, if thou lovest me,
Mount thou my horse and hide thy spurs in him
Till he have brought thee up to yonder troops
And here again that I may rest assured
Whether yond troops are friend or enemy.
TITINIUS I will be here again even with a thought. *Exit*
CASSIUS Go, Pindarus, get higher on that hill,
My sight was ever thick: regard Titinius
And tell me what thou not'st about the field.
[*Pindarus goes up*]
This day I breathèd first, time is come round
And where I did begin there shall I end:
My life is run his compass. Sirrah, what news?
PINDARUS (*Above*) O my lord!
CASSIUS What news?
PINDARUS Titinius is enclosèd round about
With horsemen that make to him on the spur,
Yet he spurs on. Now they are almost on him.
Now Titinius – Now some light; O, he lights too.
He's ta'en.
(*Shout*)
And hark, they shout for joy.
CASSIUS Come down, behold no more.
O, coward that I am to live so long

20 higher] F; thither F2 **22** SD] *Dyce (after Hanmer / Exit Pin.)* **28–33**] *As Pope (not omitting* Now *before* Titinius *at 31); Pind.* ... about / ... Spurre, / ... him: / ... too. / ... *Showt.* / ... ioy. / ... more: F; *Pin.* ... is / ... that / ... on. – / ... Titinius! – / ... hark! / ... joy. / ... more. – *Malone; as Malone, except 32–3:* They ... more. – *Steevens³; as Pope, except 31–3:* Now ... ta'en; – / And ... more. – *Boswell; as Pope, except 32–3:* He's ... more. – *Singer²; as Pope, except 31–3:* Now, Titinius! – / ... too: – / ... hark! / ... joy. / ... more. *Craik; as Pope, except 31–3:* Now ... Now, / ... hark! / ... more. – *Wordsworth; as Pope, except 31–3:* Now, Titinius! – / ... hark! / ... more. – *Dyce²; as Pope, except 31–2:* Now ... he / ... joy. *Bevington (conj. Nicholson, who adds* now *after* Now*)* **31** Titinius –] *Jennens; Titinius.* F

11 far farther (usually indicated by F spelling 'farre'). Compare 9; see also 3.2.158n.

19 even ... thought as swift as thought, in an instant.

21 thick misty, dim. Compare 'thick-ey'd', *1H4* 2.3.46.

22 SD Pindarus most likely uses the same structure that served as the pulpit in 3.2. See illustration 2 on p. 6.

31 light alight.

To see my best friend ta'en before my face.
Pindarus [*descends*]
Come hither, sirrah.
In Parthia did I take thee prisoner,
And then I swore thee, saving of thy life,
That whatsoever I did bid thee do
Thou shouldst attempt it. Come now, keep thine oath.
Now be a freeman, and with this good sword,
That ran through Caesar's bowels, search this bosom.
Stand not to answer; here, take thou the hilts
And when my face is covered, as 'tis now,
Guide thou the sword.
[*Pindarus stabs him*]
Caesar, thou art revenged
Even with the sword that killed thee. [*Dies*]

PINDARUS So I am free, yet would not so have been
Durst I have done my will. O Cassius,
Far from this country Pindarus shall run,
Where never Roman shall take note of him. [*Exit*]

Enter TITINIUS *and* MESSALA

MESSALA It is but change, Titinius, for Octavius
Is overthrown by noble Brutus' power,
As Cassius' legions are by Antony.
TITINIUS These tidings will well comfort Cassius.
MESSALA Where did you leave him?
TITINIUS All disconsolate,
With Pindarus his bondman, on this hill.
MESSALA Is not that he that lies upon the ground?
TITINIUS He lies not like the living. O my heart!
MESSALA Is not that he?
TITINIUS No, this was he, Messala,
But Cassius is no more. O setting sun,
As in thy red rays thou dost sink to night,

35 SD] *Dyce (Douai MS.); Enter Pindarus* F 36–7] *Pope;* Come ... Prisoner, F 41 freeman] F3; Free-man F; free man *Humphreys* 45 SD] *Globe (Douai MS.)* 46 SD] *Capell (Folger MS.); Kills him* F2; *Kills himself / Rowe*[2] 47] *Rowe;* So ... free, / ... beene F 50 SD.1 *Exit*] *Rowe (Folger MS.)* 61 to night] F; to-night *Thomas Johnson*

37 'Cassius held a command under Crassus in the disastrous expedition against the Parthians 53 BC, and it was at the battle of Carrhae ... that he captured Pindarus' (Mark Hunter).

43 **hilts** Found as a singular on three occasions in Shakespeare and as a plural six times. See also 5.5.28.

51 **change** exchange.

So in his red blood Cassius' day is set.
The sun of Rome is set. Our day is gone,
Clouds, dews, and dangers come. Our deeds are done.
Mistrust of my success hath done this deed.

MESSALA Mistrust of good success hath done this deed.
O hateful error, melancholy's child,
Why dost thou show to the apt thoughts of men
The things that are not? O error, soon conceived,
Thou never com'st unto a happy birth
But kill'st the mother that engendered thee.

TITINIUS What, Pindarus? Where art thou, Pindarus?

MESSALA Seek him, Titinius, whilst I go to meet
The noble Brutus, thrusting this report
Into his ears. I may say 'thrusting' it,
For piercing steel and darts envenomèd
Shall be as welcome to the ears of Brutus
As tidings of this sight.

TITINIUS Hie you, Messala,
And I will seek for Pindarus the while.

[*Exit Messala*]

Why didst thou send me forth, brave Cassius?
Did I not meet thy friends? And did not they
Put on my brows this wreath of victory
And bid me give it thee? Didst thou not hear their shouts?
Alas, thou hast misconstrued everything.
But hold thee, take this garland on thy brow;
Thy Brutus bid me give it thee, and I
Will do his bidding. Brutus, come apace,
And see how I regarded Caius Cassius.
By your leave, gods! – This is a Roman's part.
Come, Cassius' sword, and find Titinius' heart. *Dies*

Alarum. Enter BRUTUS, MESSALA, YOUNG CATO, *Strato, Volumnius, and Lucilius,* [*Labeo, and Flavius*]

BRUTUS Where, where, Messala, doth his body lie?

MESSALA Lo yonder, and Titinius mourning it.

62 is] F; it F2 **63** sun] F; Sonne F2; Son F3 **79** SD] Q (1691) **90** SD.2 *Labeo, and Flavius*] *Wilson*

65 success result; as at 2.2.6. **68 apt** susceptible to impressions.

BRUTUS Titinius' face is upward.
CATO He is slain.
BRUTUS O Julius Caesar, thou art mighty yet,
Thy spirit walks abroad and turns our swords
In our own proper entrails.
Low alarums
CATO Brave Titinius!
Look whe'er he have not crowned dead Cassius.
BRUTUS Are yet two Romans living such as these?
The last of all the Romans, fare thee well!
It is impossible that ever Rome
Should breed thy fellow. Friends, I owe mo tears
To this dead man than you shall see me pay.
I shall find time, Cassius, I shall find time.
Come therefore and to Thasos send his body;
His funerals shall not be in our camp
Lest it discomfort us. Lucilius, come,
And come, young Cato, let us to the field.
Labeo and Flavio, set our battles on.
'Tis three o'clock, and, Romans, yet ere night
We shall try fortune in a second fight.
Exeunt

95 walks] F; wa'kes F2; wakes *Folger MS.* **97** whe'er] whe'r *Capell;* where F **97** not] F; *omitted in* F *(uncorrected)* **99** The] F; Thou *Rowe* **101** owe mo] F; owe no F *(uncorrected);* own mo Q (1684)*;* own my QU3*;* own more Q (1691)*;* owe more *Rowe (Folger MS.)* **104** Thasos] Thassos *Theobald (after Plutarch); Tharsus* F **108** Flavio] F; *Flavius* F2 *(after Plutarch)* **108** Flavio,] F4; *Flavio* F **109** and, Romans, yet] *Rowe;* and Romans yet F; and, Romans yet, *conj. this edn*

96 own proper Pleonastic, often for emphasis. See 1.2.41 n.

96 SD *Low* 'Of or in reference to musical sounds: Produced or characterised by relatively slow vibrations; grave' (*OED* sv *adj.* 10a). Probably misunderstood in uncorrected F's *Loud*, which is possibly a compositorial misreading of a final *e* as *d.* See also 5.5.23 SD for the same sound in connection with the sad end of a battle, as well as *Loud*, 5.2.2 SD, signalling the beginning of an attack. See also *Low march within*, 4.2.24 SD.

101 mo more; see 2.1.72 n.

104 *Thasos An island in the north Aegean Sea, not far from Philippi.

105 funerals Although mainly singular in Shakespeare (24 instances), the plural is to be found also in *Tit.* 1.1.381, *MND* 1.1.14, and Plutarch (pp. 161, 170, 171).

106 discomfort dishearten.

108 Flavio, The majority of editions follow F4 in adding a comma, thus creating a vocative and making Labeo and Flavius mutes. This seems preferable, especially since the context would call for the present perfect of the following verb (i.e. 'have set') and not a simple past.

108 battles troops in battle array, usually the main force; as at 5.1.4.

110 try test; see 3.1.292 n.

110 second fight Shakespeare merges the two battles, although they actually took place some twenty days apart.

4 *Alarum. Enter* BRUTUS, *Messala,* [YOUNG] CATO, LUCILIUS, *and*
lavius, [*Labeo*]

RUTUS Yet, countrymen, O, yet hold up your heads!
[*Exit with Messala, Flavius, and Labeo*]
ATO What bastard doth not? Who will go with me?
I will proclaim my name about the field.
I am the son of Marcus Cato, ho!
A foe to tyrants, and my country's friend.
I am the son of Marcus Cato, ho!

Enter SOLDIERS *and fight*

UCILIUS And I am Brutus, Marcus Brutus, I,
Brutus, my country's friend. Know me for Brutus!
[*Young Cato is slain*]
O young and noble Cato, art thou down?
Why, now thou diest as bravely as Titinius
And mayst be honoured, being Cato's son.
1 SOLDIER Yield, or thou diest.
LUCILIUS Only I yield to die.
There is so much that thou wilt kill me straight.
Kill Brutus and be honoured in his death.
1 SOLDIER We must not. A noble prisoner!

Enter ANTONY

2 SOLDIER Room ho! Tell Antony, Brutus is ta'en.
1 SOLDIER I'll tell the news. Here comes the general.
Brutus is ta'en, Brutus is ta'en, my lord!
ANTONY Where is he?
LUCILIUS Safe, Antony, Brutus is safe enough.

Act 5, Scene 4 5.4] *Capell* Location] *Capell* **0** SD YOUNG] *Dyce* **0** SD *Labeo*] *This edn* **1** SD] *Wilson (subst.)* **7** SH LUCILIUS] *Macmillan; Bru. / Rowe* **8** SD] Cato *falls / Capell* **9** O young] *Macmillan; Luc.* O yong F **12, 15** SH 1] *Capell* **17** the news] Q (1684) *(Folger MS.)*; thee newes F

Act 5, Scene 4

Location Another part of the field.

0 SD It is likely that Labeo, who is coupled with Flavius at 5.3.108, also enters here and exits after line 1. Plutarch mentions Brutus's grieving over his friends slain in battle, 'specially when he came to name Labio and Flavius' (p. 182).

4 Marcus Cato See 2.1.295 n.

7 SH Most editors assign to Lucilius, who impersonates Brutus to protect him from harm. The ruse is referred to by Antony at 26. For this action, see Plutarch (p. 181).

12 Only I yield i.e. I yield only. For the construction, see 5.1.89 n.

13 Most interpretations follow Hanmer's stage direction *Giving him money*; some, however, take the line as a reference to the 'announcement in the next line that he is Brutus' (Evans).

I dare assure thee that no enemy
Shall ever take alive the noble Brutus.
The gods defend him from so great a shame!
When you do find him, or alive or dead,
He will be found like Brutus, like himself.
ANTONY This is not Brutus, friend, but, I assure you,
A prize no less in worth. Keep this man safe,
Give him all kindness. I had rather have
Such men my friends than enemies. Go on,
And see whe'er Brutus be alive or dead,
And bring us word unto Octavius' tent
How everything is chanced.

Exeunt

5.5 *Enter* BRUTUS, DARDANIUS, CLITUS, STRATO, *and* VOLUMNIUS

BRUTUS Come, poor remains of friends, rest on this rock.
CLITUS Statilius showed the torchlight but, my lord,
He came not back. He is or ta'en or slain.
BRUTUS Sit thee down, Clitus. Slaying is the word,
It is a deed in fashion. Hark thee, Clitus. [*Whispering*]
CLITUS What, I, my lord? No, not for all the world.
BRUTUS Peace then, no words.
CLITUS I'll rather kill myself.
BRUTUS Hark thee, Dardanius. [*Whispers*]
DARDANIUS Shall I do such a deed?
CLITUS O Dardanius!
DARDANIUS O Clitus!
CLITUS What ill request did Brutus make to thee?
DARDANIUS To kill him, Clitus. Look, he meditates.
CLITUS Now is that noble vessel full of grief,
That it runs over even at his eyes.
BRUTUS Come hither, good Volumnius, list a word.
VOLUMNIUS What says my lord?

30 whe'er] whe'r *Capell (*whether *Folger MS.)*; where F **Act 5, Scene 5** 5.5] *Capell* Location] *Pope* 1] *As verse, Pope*[2]; *as prose,* F 5 SD] *Rowe (Douai MS.)* 8 SD] *Capell (Douai MS.)*

24 or ... or either ... or; see 2.1.135 n.

Act 5, Scene 5

Location Another part of the field.

3 or ... or either ... or; see 2.1.135 n.

14 even Used for emphasis, like modern 'very'. See Franz 438.

BRUTUS Why, this, Volumnius:
The ghost of Caesar hath appeared to me
Two several times by night, at Sardis once
And this last night here in Philippi fields.
I know my hour is come.
VOLUMNIUS Not so, my lord.
BRUTUS Nay, I am sure it is, Volumnius.
Thou seest the world, Volumnius, how it goes:
Our enemies have beat us to the pit.
Low alarums
It is more worthy to leap in ourselves
Than tarry till they push us. Good Volumnius,
Thou know'st that we two went to school together;
Even for that our love of old, I prithee
Hold thou my sword-hilts whilst I run on it.
VOLUMNIUS That's not an office for a friend, my lord.
Alarum still
CLITUS Fly, fly, my lord, there is no tarrying here.
BRUTUS Farewell to you, and you, and you, Volumnius.
Strato, thou hast been all this while asleep:
Farewell to thee too, Strato. Countrymen,
My heart doth joy that yet in all my life
I found no man but he was true to me.
I shall have glory by this losing day
More than Octavius and Mark Antony
By this vile conquest shall attain unto.
So fare you well at once, for Brutus' tongue
Hath almost ended his life's history.
Night hangs upon mine eyes, my bones would rest,
That have but laboured to attain this hour.
Alarum. Cry within, 'Fly, fly, fly!'
CLITUS Fly, my lord, fly!
BRUTUS Hence! I will follow.
[*Exeunt Clitus, Dardanius, and Volumnius*]
I prithee, Strato, stay thou by thy lord.
Thou art a fellow of a good respect,

23 SD *Low*] F; *Loud* F *(uncorrected)* 28 sword-hilts] *Malone;* Sword Hilts F; Swords Hilt QU3; Sword's hilt *Rowe* 33 thee too] *Thomas Johnson;* thee, to F 43 SD] *Capell*

18 several separate; as at 2.1.138.

23 beat ... pit i.e. driven us with blows into a hole (like animals) or the grave.

Thy life hath had some smatch of honour in it.
Hold then my sword and turn away thy face,
While I do run upon it. Wilt thou, Strato?
STRATO Give me your hand first. Fare you well, my lord.
BRUTUS Farewell, good Strato.
[*Runs on his sword*]
Caesar, now be still,
I killed not thee with half so good a will. *Dies*

Alarum. Retreat. Enter ANTONY, OCTAVIUS, MESSALA, LUCILIUS, *and the army*

OCTAVIUS What man is that?
MESSALA My master's man. Strato, where is thy master?
STRATO Free from the bondage you are in, Messala.
The conquerors can but make a fire of him:
For Brutus only overcame himself,
And no man else hath honour by his death.
LUCILIUS So Brutus should be found. I thank thee, Brutus,
That thou hast proved Lucilius' saying true.
OCTAVIUS All that served Brutus I will entertain them.
Fellow, wilt thou bestow thy time with me?
STRATO Ay, if Messala will prefer me to you.
OCTAVIUS Do so, good Messala.
MESSALA How died my master, Strato?
STRATO I held the sword, and he did run on it.
MESSALA Octavius, then take him to follow thee,
That did the latest service to my master.
ANTONY This was the noblest Roman of them all:
All the conspirators, save only he,
Did that they did in envy of great Caesar.
He only, in a general honest thought

50 SD] *Rowe (after 51)* 63–4] F; *as one line, omitting* good, *Steevens*[3] *(Capell MS.); as one line, Singer* 71 He only,] Q (1691); He, onely F 71–2 general . . . And] F; generous . . . Of *Collier*[2] *(Collier MS.)*

46 **smatch** taste, flavour (later supplanted by 'smack', the reading in Steevens (conj. Thirlby)).

51 SD.2 ***Retreat*** 'The recall of a pursuing force' (*OED* sv *sb* 2b), presumably by a trumpet call.

51 SD.2 ***Enter . . . army*** In many editions since Capell it is Octavius who leads the entrance.

55 **make a fire** Burning on a pyre or *rogus* was the general burial practice. Plutarch (p. 161) reports that the people 'plucked up forms, tables, and stools, and laid them all about the body [of Caesar], and setting them afire burnt the corse'.

56 **only** alone. The position of the adjective after the noun may be for emphasis; see Abbott 419.

60 **entertain them** take them into (my) service.

62 **prefer me** recommend me; see 3.1.28 n.

And common good to all, made one of them.
His life was gentle, and the elements
So mixed in him that Nature might stand up
And say to all the world, 'This was a man!'

OCTAVIUS According to his virtue let us use him,
With all respect and rites of burial.
Within my tent his bones tonight shall lie,
Most like a soldier, ordered honourably.
So call the field to rest, and let's away
To part the glories of this happy day.

Exeunt

72 made one of them The few editors who comment refer to Brutus's joining the conspiracy. See Schmidt, make 10. The expression is Plutarch's (p. 164).

73 gentle noble.

73 elements Strictly speaking, the elements are 'those originall thinges vnmyxt and vncompounde, of whose temperance and myxture all other thynges, hauynge corporall substaunce, be compacte . . . Erthe. Water. Ayre and Fyre' (Sir Thomas Elyot, *The Castel of Helthe* (1541), fol. 1b). Here the humours are meant: 'In the body of Man be foure principall humours, whiche contynuinge in the proportion, that nature hath lymytted, the body is free from all syckenesse . . . Bloudde, Fleume, Choler, Melancoly' (Elyot, fol. 8a).

76 virtue *virtus*, inherent worth.

79 ordered dealt with, treated; see also 3.1.230n.

80 field army.

81 part share.

TEXTUAL ANALYSIS

The overwhelming consensus of opinion is that the Folio text of *Julius Caesar*, the only one with authority, is the 'best-printed play'[1] in the whole Folio. It is further held that the textual problems are 'comparatively simple'.[2] The text is described as 'unusually clean'[3] and 'exceptionally tidy' (Dorsch, p. xxiii) on the evidence of relatively few substantive or semi-substantive mistakes, the treatment of accidentals also demonstrating a careful and caring understanding of the play. But, as is the case with many other features of the play – from the date to the two-part structure to the dramatic focus of the tragedy – 'simple' is a term which must be reserved for only the superficial consideration of these features. It is not to be construed as meaning that there are no problems, still less that the problems have been or can be definitively solved.

A measure of the difficulties involved in the appraisal of the text (inseparable from an appraisal of the nature of the play itself) is to be found in the fact that, as E. K. Chambers wrote, 'in no play of the canon have recent critics more persistently sought other hands'.[4] It is not necessary to detail the views of J. M. Robertson, William Wells, and E. H. C. Oliphant,[5] all of whom find a core of Christopher Marlowe with modifications, in one degree or another, by such leading contemporaries as George Chapman, Michael Drayton, Ben Jonson, and Francis Beaumont. These theories have never achieved general acceptance, of course, although it should be noted that Chambers's not untypical rejection of them is based on his blank acceptance of the 'two peaks' action (the death of Caesar at the Capitol and of Brutus at Philippi), while at the same time admitting that this type of structure does not accord with the movement of Shakespeare's tragedies in a 'single curve to a catastrophe in the death of the title-character', and on his equally blunt conviction that Shakespeare is 'deliberately experimenting in a classical manner, with an extreme simplicity both of vocabulary and of phrasing'.[6] In other words, he acknowledges the singularity and finds it Shakespearean, while the others tend to regard the singularity as un-Shakespearean.

Two concerns emerge. The first and overriding one is that the evidence for both positions is speculative. Chambers, for example, uses Jonson's (mis)quoting in *Timber* of 3.1.47, '*Caesar did never wrong, but with just cause*', as 'testimony ... to Shakespeare's authorship';[7] F. G. Fleay uses a slightly altered version of the same line (with the

[1] W. W. Greg, *The Shakespeare First Folio: Its Bibliographical and Textual History*, 1955, p. 289.

[2] T. J. B. Spencer, '*Julius Caesar* and *Antony and Cleopatra*', in Stanley Wells (ed.), *Shakespeare: Select Bibliographical Guides*, 1973, p. 206.

[3] Greg, *First Folio*, p. 289.

[4] E. K. Chambers, *William Shakespeare*, 2 vols., 1930, I, 398.

[5] J. M. Robertson, 'The origination of *Julius Caesar*', in his *The Shakespeare Canon*, 1922, I, 66–154; William Wells, *The Authorship of 'Julius Caesar'*, 1923; E. H. C. Oliphant, *The Plays of Beaumont and Fletcher*, 1927.

[6] Chambers, *Shakespeare*, I, 399.

[7] *Ibid.*, I, 397–8.

prefixing of 'Cry you mercy') in the Induction to Jonson's *Staple of News* to 'imply that Shakespeare did not make the alterations himself'.[1] Obviously, this concern involves an assessment of stylistic features, especially verbal parallels, treated earlier (see p. 11 above). The second is that revision, in one form or another by Shakespeare or whoever, is generally agreed upon. It is one of the more interesting textual features, both in itself and for what it may have to say about the copy for the setting up of the text. The discussion has far exceeded Chambers's laconic acknowledgement of a 'trace of a revision'.[2]

Since at least the middle of the nineteenth century scholars have commented on the double revelation of the death of Portia: the first is Brutus's report of the suicide to Cassius (4.3.147–57), the second is Messala's announcement and Brutus's reaction (4.3.181–95). Warren D. Smith[3] and Thomas Clayton[4] are the main apologists for the non-revisionists. After summarising the 'somewhat tenuous position of either humbly apologizing for Brutus' concealment of Portia's death, especially for his calm acceptance of Messala's praise, or of admitting that, for reasons not forthcoming, the dramatist decided at this point in the play to disparage his protagonist in the eyes of the audience', Smith asserts that 'a consideration of Shakespeare's text with reference to its source, North's translation of Plutarch's *Lives*, demonstrates not only that the Messala–Brutus passage ... is wholly authentic as it stands in the Folio, but also that the dramatist intended it to be unmistakable witness to the unselfishness, fortitude, and able generalship characteristic of Brutus in other parts of the play'.[5]

Expanding Smith's point of view, and perhaps inspired by his remark that 'interpretation could easily be made clear in the acting',[6] Clayton defends the 'duplicate revelation' as being 'variously consonant with both [a worse and a better Brutus]', grounding his view on three kinds of inferential evidence: '(1) histrionic effect consistent with the text, and character as in one way a function of the text; (2) general, dramatic, and contextual casuistry, as "that part of Ethics which resolves cases of conscience, applying the general rules of religion and morality to particular instances which disclose special circumstances, or conflicting duties," as the *SOED* succinctly puts it; and (3) what may be inferred about intentions from sources and other comparable materials in and out of the play'.[7] Coupled with his rejection of bibliographical evidence, Clayton goes so far as to suggest that both versions may have been added after the original writing, for a '*Julius Caesar* without revelations of Portia's death is both tenable and playable'.[8]

The dominant case for the prevailing revision theory has been made by Brents Stirling,[9] whose study of the variant Cassius speech headings leads him to assert that

1 F. G. Fleay, *A Chronicle History of the Life and Work of William Shakespeare: Player, Poet, and Playmaker*, 1886, p. 216.
2 Chambers, *Shakespeare*, I, 396.
3 Warren D. Smith, 'The duplicate revelation of Portia's death', *SQ* 4 (1953), 153–61.
4 Thomas Clayton, '"Should Brutus never taste of Portia's death but once?": text and performance in *Julius Caesar*', *SEL* 23 (1983), 237–55.
5 Smith, 'Duplicate revelation', p. 154.
6 *Ibid.*, p. 155.
7 Clayton, 'Portia's death', p. 246.
8 *Ibid.*, p. 254.
9 Brents Stirling, '*Julius Caesar* in revision', *SQ* 13 (1962), 187–205.

they are 'inconsistent with compositorial responsibility and consistent with copy as a determining factor'.[1] Since *Cassi.* is the normal prefix, and the variants *Cas.* or *Cass.* appear only in the passages in question, Stirling concludes specifically that the revision, not the compositor, accounted for the variants. He goes on to extend this type of examination to 2.1.86–228, which he also finds to have been subject to authorial revision. Agreeing, Fredson Bowers[2] carries the discussion to the relationship between the revisions and the copy for the play. Since two important revisions can be identified as not being 'organic' – 'insertion' is the word most often used[3] – they throw light on the question 'whether a prompt-book that had represented the final stage of the organization of the text for acting would be revised in such a manner by Shakespeare, or whether the revisions were made in an intermediate manuscript used for its own purposes by the company before the inscription of the prompt-book was ordered'.[4] Explicit in Bowers's argument is the whole drift, if not history *in nuce*, of textual transmission over the past hundred years. Most striking are the increasing injections over this period of the findings of compositor analysis, as well as the growing acceptance of large-scale revision as a feature of Shakespeare's craft.

Although the art of compositor analysis is far from satisfactory,[5] the general consensus is that *Julius Caesar* was set by Jaggard's Compositors A and B. More specifically, Charlton Hinman[6] has postulated that A set kk2^{v}–3 and most likely the lower part of ll5b while B set all the rest, kk1, 2^{r}, 4, 5, 6, and ll1–5. The presence of identifiable compositorial characteristics – especially those of B, who was largely responsible for the play, like his fondness for such heavier pointing as colons and commas at the ends of verse lines – as well as the absence of what have been considered Shakespearean spellings, has counteracted the theory that the copy for the 'clean' Folio text of *Julius Caesar* was the author's own manuscript, a position taken by the editors of the

[1] *Ibid.*, p. 190.

[2] Fredson Bowers, 'The copy for Shakespeare's *Julius Caesar*', *South Atlantic Bulletin* 43 (1977–8), 23–36.

[3] See Chambers, *Shakespeare*, I, 397, and Greg, *First Folio*, p. 291.

[4] Bowers, 'The copy', p. 31.

[5] A measure of the difficulty is reflected in the ever-increasing number of compositors postulated on the basis, as the whole is divided into more and more parts, of less and less evidence – not to mention the general caveat that the actual printing-house conditions, the supposed key to the problem, are not only far from having been reconstructed but may never be so, at least with the detail needed to concretise what is still for the most part printing of the mind (to paraphrase D. F. McKenzie). Even interesting attempts to refine data, like John Jowett's recent 'Ligature shortage and speech-prefix variation in *Julius Caesar*' (*The Library* 6:6 (1984), 244–53), whose aim is to prove that the speech heading variants depend on the shortage of *ssi* ligatures rather than on printer's copy, serve in the long run to expose the fragility of the approach. In this particular instance, the bibliographical evidence, in 'suggesting that there may be no secure grounds for considering that either of the episodes concerning Portia's death is a revision' (*ibid.*, p. 253), ironically serves to support the dramatic and theatrical interpretations. For a strong criticism of compositor analysis based on spelling habits, see A. C. Partridge, *Orthography in Shakespeare and Elizabethan Drama*, 1964, pp. 111–15.

[6] Charlton Hinman, *The Printing and Proof-reading of the First Folio of Shakespeare*, 2 vols., 1963, I, 298–9. In his privately printed *A Reassessment of Compositors B and E in the First Folio Tragedies*, 1977, pp. 9–11, T. H. Howard-Hill presents, on the basis of speech headings and non-spaced commas, an admittedly cautious case for E's having set the second column of ll3. A recent analysis, detailing characteristics of Compositors A and B and focussing on distinguishing compositorial work on part-pages, is J. K. Rogers, 'The Folio compositors of *Julius Caesar*: a quantitative analysis', *Analytical and Enumerative Bibliography* 6 (1982), 143–72. It also contains useful references to the continuing discussion of compositorial analysis, as well as to the claims for other compositors (like E).

nineteenth-century Cambridge edition and accepted even by Stirling, whose data 'strongly point to a finished play in fair-copy form antedating the addition [in Act 4]'.[1] The weakness of the position is evidenced in the fact that W. W. Greg used the same characteristics, adding his special favourite, stage directions, to postulate a promptbook with possible annotations as copy,[2] a theory much in favour in the first half of this century. Most recent textual criticism has tended to focus on intermediate copy between an author's manuscript – fair or foul – and a promptbook. In the case of *Julius Caesar*, all are now agreed – on the basis of evidence ranging from orderly speech headings to typical compositorial spellings – that there must have been a 'careful' (Dorsch, p. xxiv) or 'clean'[3] scribal copy or transcript from Shakespeare's 'foul' (Dorsch, p. xxiv) or 'working'[4] papers. More refined explanations – like J. Dover Wilson's arguing that a 'transcript was specially made for the printer', because the 'company was unwilling to part with the promptbook and no foul papers were available' – are lacking in what Greg calls 'compelling' evidence.[5] In fact, it must be admitted that positions of this kind can never be absolutely convincing, much less compelling, being deduced from partial evidence, bits and pieces at best, whose total is far below that required for certainty.

Two other textual features – mutes and short lines – have variously been mentioned in connection with revision, especially as evidence of cuts. Fleay's unsupported assertion that the 'play has been greatly shortened, [as] is shown by the singularly large number of instances in which mute characters are on the stage; which is totally at variance with Shakespeare's usual practice'[6] has made its way into critical discussions without being effectively substantiated or rejected. Of the 22 instances (not counting unnamed characters) twelve mutes are addressed directly and three are at least mentioned.[7] The appearance of the remaining seven is usually explained by either one or both of the following lines of argument: Ringler's 'there is no necessity to assume that Labio and Flavio are present on the stage [in 5.3]'[8] and Greg's 'There is no reason why they [Messala and Flavius in 5.4] should not be present.'[9] Even Greg's larger thesis (in commenting on the mutes Lamprius, Rannius, and Lucillius in 1.2 of *Antony*) that 'Shakespeare has evidently jotted down the names of characters ... that he thought he might use and did not'[10] is a tempting but nevertheless still speculative attempt to

[1] Stirling, '*Julius Caesar*', p. 205.

[2] Greg, *First Folio*, pp. 290–1. In *The Editorial Problem in Shakespeare*, 1942, p. 143, Greg finds the stage directions 'normal enough for prompt copy ... "Enter Boy with wine and tapers" [4.3.157] is in character for the book-keeper, and so are some flourishes and the like – "Low alarums [5.3.96] ... Alarum still [5.5.29]" '. Another example of alteration is put forward by Wilson (pp. 93–4), who contends that 3.1.47 (see above, pp. 148–9) was changed 'in deference to [Jonson's] literary criticism' by a scribe or even by Ben Jonson himself.

[3] Bowers, 'The copy', p. 23.

[4] *Ibid.*

[5] Greg, *First Folio*, p. 289.

[6] Fleay, *Life and Work*, p. 215.

[7] For a complete list, see William A. Ringler, Jr, 'The number of actors in Shakespeare's early plays', in *The Seventeenth-Century Stage*, ed. Gerald Eades Bentley, 1968, pp. 118–19. The inclusion by Ringler of Messala as mute in 4.2 is perhaps questionable; his omission of Flavius is likewise so.

[8] *Ibid.*, p. 116.

[9] Greg, *First Folio*, p. 291. Chambers, *Shakespeare*, I, 231, puts it more convincingly: 'We must of course allow for mutes, especially in court or processional scenes.'

[10] Greg, *First Folio*, p. 401.

describe Shakespeare's work habits. In so 'clean' a text as *Julius Caesar* it is highly unlikely. Even more unlikely is Fleay's finding equal confirmation of his hypothesis about abridgement in the 'large number of incomplete lines in every possible position, even in the middle of speeches'.[1] Chambers's reference to only 'a few abrupt short lines [which] may be evidence of cuts',[2] noted and quoted by Wilson (as if doctrine) as among the 'indications of change in the text' (p. 95) – although neither writer identifies them – is less convincing an explanation than that of compositorial practice.

Symptomatic of the inevitable, if not indispensable, interaction of literary interpretation and textual analysis is likewise the recent and ongoing discussion of short lines. Surprisingly, the matter has been discussed only scantily in editions of the play, although it presents implications for theories of authorship, revision, compositorial analysis, and ultimately transmission. The surmises of Fleay and Chambers just mentioned were followed by only a brief exchange between A. P. Rossiter, who argued against the conversion of short lines into split lines (the practice formalised by Steevens in his edition of 1793) at the expense of a 'perceptible change of tone or sense',[3] and R. B. McKerrow, who countered that 'few of the split lines ... could have been printed as a single line without either a turnover or undue crowding',[4] basing his position on the compositor's dislike of turnovers. A monograph-length article by Fredson Bowers[5] in 1980 and a briefer monograph by Paul Bertram[6] in 1981 have reinforced the arguments of McKerrow and Rossiter respectively, and a very recent article by Carol Sicherman[7] in 1984, without explicit mention of McKerrow, has defended – on dramatic and rhetorical grounds, especially in connection with characterisation – F's use of lineation to reflect deliberate 'metrical and extrametrical pauses'. It is, of course, debatable whether the typographical arrangement of short lines coincides with actual pauses in delivery, still less with a system of elocution, just as it is debatable whether Elizabethan pointing is coherent and systematic. The statistical evidence produced by Bowers is admittedly selective and dependent on an instinctive willingness to equate the sample with the whole; even what is deemed a *donnée* – Bowers's reference to Compositor B's 'habit of breaking in two a pentameter that was too long for his measure'[8] – is not beyond question. But the weight of opinion – however undeniable the growing scepticism towards textual analysis – seems to favour even a few hard facts over keen interpretations of pentameters which are 'dreary' or 'strong' or pauses which are 'daring' or 'silence

[1] Fleay, *Life and Work*, p. 215.

[2] Chambers, *Shakespeare*, I, 397.

[3] A. P. Rossiter, 'Line-division in "Julius Caesar"', *TLS* (23 July 1939), 454. Rossiter was responding to the policy regarding line arrangement in Ronald B. McKerrow, *Prolegomena for the Oxford Shakespeare*, 1939, pp. 44–9.

[4] R. B. McKerrow, 'Line division in "Julius Caesar"', *TLS* (19 August 1939), 492. The effect of faulty casting-off of copy has been touched on only fleetingly and without urgency. For a most recent instance, see Humphreys, p. 74.

[5] Fredson Bowers, 'Establishing Shakespeare's text: notes on short lines and the problem of verse division', *Studies in Bibliography* 33 (1980), 74–130.

[6] Paul Bertram, *White Spaces in Shakespeare: The Development of the Modern Text*, 1981. The impetus comes from G. B. Harrison's Penguin Shakespeare (1937–59), which on closer examination turns out to be little more than a reprint of the Folio.

[7] Carol Marks Sicherman, 'Short lines and interpretation: the case of *Julius Caesar*', *SQ* 35 (1984), 195.

[8] Bowers, 'Shakespeare's text', p. 90.

illed'.[1] Sicherman may be missing the point in basing her essay on Bowers's leaving the nterpretation of short lines to others, since his 57-page article would seem to make it lear that he does not put much store on such interpretation.

Sicherman, 'Short lines', pp. 183–6.

Appendix: Excerpts from Plutarch

The following excerpts are from Sir Thomas North's translation (1579) of Plutarch's lives of Julius Caesar and Marcus Brutus, the two major sources of Shakespeare's play. Longer, continuous sections are given for a better understanding not merely of the characters and events but also of the distinctive art of both Plutarch and Shakespeare. Although the life of Caesar is used mainly for the first half of the play, and of Brutus for the second, there is some overlapping (at times mentioned by Plutarch himself), which in itself contributes to the density of both Plutarch's narrative and Shakespeare's drama. The spelling has been modernised except for a few older forms which are headwords of a full *OED* entry. Occasionally, the spelling of names has been very slightly altered to accord with recognised usage. The punctuation reflects North's, though somewhat modified.

The Life of Julius Caesar

After all these things were ended, he was chosen Consul the fourth time, and went into Spain to make war with the sons of Pompey; who were yet but very young, but had notwithstanding raised a marvellous great army together, and showed to have had manhood and courage worthy to command such an army, insomuch as they put Caesar himself in great danger of his life. The greatest battle that was fought between them in all this war was by the city of Munda. For then Caesar seeing his men sorely distressed, and having their hands full of their enemies, he ran into the press among his men that fought, and cried out unto them: 'What, are ye not ashamed to be beaten and taken prisoners, yielding yourselves with your own hands to these young boys?' And so, with all the force he could make, having with much ado put his enemies to flight, he slew above thirty thousand of them in the field, and lost of his own men a thousand of the best he had. After this battle he went into his tent, and told his friends that he had often before fought for victory, but, this last time now, that he had fought for the safety of his own life. He won this battle on the very feast day of the Bacchanalians, in the which men say that Pompey the Great went out of Rome, about four years before, to begin this civil war. For his sons, the younger scaped from the battle; but, within few days after, Didius brought the head of the elder.

This was the last war that Caesar made. But the Triumph he made into Rome for the same did as much offend the Romans, and more, than anything that ever he had done before; because he had not overcome captains that were strangers, nor barbarous kings, but had destroyed the sons of the noblest man in Rome, whom fortune had overthrown. And, because he had plucked up his race by the roots, men did not think it meet for him to triumph so for the calamities of his country, rejoicing at a thing for the which he had but one excuse to allege in his defence unto the gods and men – that he was compelled to do that he did. And the rather they thought it not meet, because he had never before sent letters nor messengers unto the commonwealth at Rome, for any victory that he had ever won in all the civil wars, but did always for shame refuse the glory of it.

This notwithstanding, the Romans inclining to Caesar's prosperity, and taking the bit in the mouth, supposing that, to be ruled by one man alone, it would be a good mean for them to take breath a little after so many troubles and miseries as they had abidden in these civil wars, they chose him perpetual Dictator. This was a plain tyranny. For to this absolute power of Dictator they added this, never to be afraid to be deposed. Cicero propounded before the Senate that they should give him such honours as were meet for a man. Howbeit others afterwards added to honours beyond all reason. For, men striving who should most honour him, they made him hateful and troublesome to themselves that most favoured him, by reason of the unmeasurable greatness and honours which they gave him. Thereupon, it is reported that even they that most hated him were no less favourers and furtherers of his honours than they that most flattered him, because they might have greater occasions to rise, and that it might appear they had just cause and colour to attempt that they did against him.

And now for himself, after he had ended his civil wars, he did so honourably behave himself that there was no fault to be found in him; and therefore, methinks, amongst other honours they gave him, he rightly deserved this – that they should build him a Temple of Clemency, to thank him for his courtesy he had used unto them in his victory. For he pardoned many of them that had borne arms against him, and, furthermore, did prefer some of them to honour and office in the commonwealth: as, amongst others, Cassius and Brutus, both the which were made Praetors. And, where Pompey's images had been thrown down, he caused them to be set up again. Whereupon Cicero said then that Caesar setting up Pompey's images again he made his own to stand the surer. And when some of his friends did counsel him to have a guard for the safety of his person, and some also did offer themselves to serve him, he would never consent to it, but said it was better to die once than always to be afraid of death.

But to win himself the love and good will of the people, as the honourablest guard and best safety he could have, he made common feasts again and general distribution of corn. Furthermore, to gratify the soldiers also, he replenished many cities again with inhabitants, which before had been destroyed, and placed them there that had no place to repair unto; of the which the noblest and chiefest cities were these two, Carthage and Corinth; and it chanced so that, like as aforetime they had been both taken and destroyed together, even so were they both set afoot again, and replenished with people, at one self time.

And, as for great personages, he won them also, promising some of them to make them Praetors and Consuls in time to come, and unto others honours and preferments, but to all men generally good hope, seeking all the ways he could to make every man contented with his reign ... Furthermore, Caesar being born to attempt all great enterprises and having an ambitious desire besides to covet great honours, the prosperous good success he had of his former conquests bred no desire in him quietly to enjoy the fruits of his labours, but rather gave him hope of things to come, still kindling more and more in him thoughts of greater enterprises and desire of new glory, as if that which he had present were stale and nothing worth. This humour of his was no other but an emulation with himself as with another man, and a certain contention to overcome the things he prepared to attempt...

But the chiefest cause that made him mortally hated was the covetous desire he had to be called king, which first gave the people just cause, and next his secret enemies honest colour, to bear him ill will. This notwithstanding, they that procured him this honour and dignity gave it out among the people that it was written in the Sibylline prophecies how the Romans might overcome the Parthians, if they made war with them and were led by a king, but otherwise that they were unconquerable. And furthermore they were so bold besides that, Caesar returning to Rome from the city of Alba, when they came to salute him, they called him king. But the people being offended, and Caesar also angry, he said he was not called king, but Caesar. Then, every man keeping silence, he went his way heavy and sorrowful.

When they had decreed divers honours for him in the Senate, the Consuls and Praetors accompanied with the whole assembly of the Senate went unto him in the market-place, where he was set by the pulpit for orations, to tell him what honours they had decreed for him in his absence. But he, sitting still in his majesty, disdaining to rise up unto them when they came in, as if they had been private men, answered them that his honours had more need to be cut off than enlarged. This did not only offend the Senate, but the common people also, to see that he should so lightly esteem of the magistrates of the commonwealth; insomuch as every man that might lawfully go his way departed thence very sorrowfully. Thereupon also Caesar rising departed home to his house, and tearing open his doublet collar, making his neck bare, he cried out aloud to his friends that his throat was ready to offer to any man that would come and cut it. Notwithstanding, it is reported that afterwards, to excuse this folly, he imputed it to his disease, saying that their wits are not perfect which have his disease of the falling evil, when standing of their feet they speak to the common people, but are soon troubled with a trembling of their body and a sudden dimness and giddiness. But that was not true. For he would have risen up to the Senate, but Cornelius Balbus one of his friends (but rather a flatterer) would not let him, saying: 'What, do you not remember that you are Caesar, and will you not let them reverence you and do their duties?'

Besides these occasions and offences, there followed also his shame and reproach, abusing the Tribunes of the People in this sort. At that time the feast Lupercalia was celebrated, the which in old time men say was the feast of shepherds or herdmen and is much like unto the feast of the Lycians in Arcadia. But, howsoever it is, that day there are divers noblemen's sons, young men – and some of them magistrates themselves that govern then – which run naked through the city, striking in sport them they meet in their way with leather thongs, hair and all on, to make them give place. And many noblewomen and gentlewomen also go of purpose to stand in their way, and do put forth their hands to be stricken, as scholars hold them out to their schoolmaster to be stricken with the ferula; persuading themselves that, being with child, they shall have good delivery, and also, being barren, that it will make them to conceive with child. Caesar sat to behold that sport upon the pulpit for orations, in a chair of gold, apparelled in triumphing manner. Antonius, who was Consul at that time, was one of them that ran this holy course. So, when he came into the market-place, the people made a lane for him to run at liberty; and he came to Caesar and presented him a diadem wreathed about with laurel. Whereupon there rose a certain cry of rejoicing, not very great, done only by a few appointed for the purpose. But when Caesar refused the diadem, then all the people together made an outcry of joy. Then, Antonius offering it him again, there was a second shout of joy, but yet of a few. But when Caesar refused it again the second time, then all the whole people shouted. Caesar, having made this proof, found that the people did not like of it, and thereupon rose out of his chair, and commanded the crown to be carried unto Jupiter in the Capitol.

After that, there were set up images of Caesar in the city with diadems upon their heads, like kings. Those the two Tribunes, Flavius and Marullus, went and pulled down; and furthermore, meeting with them that first saluted Caesar as king, they committed them to prison. The people followed them rejoicing at it, and called them 'Brutes', because of Brutus, who had in old time driven the kings out of Rome and that brought the kingdom of one person unto the government of the Senate and people. Caesar was so offended withal that he deprived Marullus and Flavius of their Tribuneships, and, accusing them, he spake also against the people, and called them *Bruti* and *Cumani* (to wit, 'beasts' and 'fools').

Hereupon the people went straight unto Marcus Brutus, who from his father came of the first Brutus and by his mother of the house of the Servilians, a noble house as any was in Rome, and was also nephew and son-in-law of Marcus Cato. Notwithstanding, the great honours and favour Caesar showed unto him kept him back, that of himself alone he did not conspire nor consent to depose him of his kingdom. For Caesar did not only save his life after the battle of Pharsalia when Pompey fled, and did at his request also save many more of his friends besides. But, furthermore, he put a marvellous confidence in him. For he had already preferred him to the Praetorship for that year, and furthermore was appointed to be Consul the fourth year after that, having through Caesar's friendship obtained it before Cassius, who likewise made suit for the same. And Caesar also, as it is reported, said in this contention: 'Indeed Cassius hath alleged best reason, but yet shall he not be chosen before Brutus.' Some one day accusing Brutus while he practised this conspiracy, Caesar would not hear of it, but, clapping his hand on his body, told them: 'Brutus will look for this skin' – meaning thereby that Brutus for his virtue deserved to rule after him, but yet that for ambition's sake he would not show himself unthankful nor dishonourable.

Now they that desired change and wished Brutus only their prince and governor above all other, they durst not come to him themselves to tell him what they would have him to do, but in the night did cast sundry papers into the Praetor's seat where he gave audience and the most of them to this effect: 'Thou sleepest, Brutus, and art not Brutus indeed.' Cassius, finding Brutus' ambition stirred up the more by these seditious bills, did prick him forward and egg him on the more for a private quarrel he had conceived against Caesar – the circumstance whereof we have set down more at large in Brutus' *Life.*

Caesar also had Cassius in great jealousy and suspected him much. Whereupon he said on a time to his friends: 'What will Cassius do, think ye? I like not his pale looks.' Another time, when Caesar's friends complained unto him of Antonius and Dolabella, that they pretended some mischief towards him, he answered them again: 'As for those fat men and smooth-combed heads', quoth he, 'I never reckon of them. But these pale-visaged and carrion lean people, I fear them most' – meaning Brutus and Cassius.

Certainly destiny may easier be foreseen than avoided, considering the strange and wonderful signs that were said to be seen before Caesar's death. For, touching the fires in the element and spirits running up and down in the night, and also these solitary birds to be seen at noondays sitting in the great market-place – are not all these signs perhaps worth the noting, in such a wonderful chance as happened? But Strabo the Philosopher writeth that divers men were seen going up and down in fire; and, furthermore, that there was a slave of the soldiers that did cast a marvellous burning flame out of his hand, insomuch as they that saw it thought he had been burnt, but, when the fire was out, it was found he had no hurt. Caesar self also, doing sacrifice unto the gods, found that one of the beasts which was sacrificed had no heart; and that was a strange thing in nature, how a beast could live without a heart.

Furthermore, there was a certain soothsayer that had given Caesar warning long time afore to take heed of the day of the Ides of March (which is the fifteenth of the month), for on that day he should be in great danger. That day being come, Caesar, going unto the Senate-house and speaking merrily unto the soothsayer, told him: 'The Ides of March be come.' 'So be they', softly answered the soothsayer, 'but yet they are not past.' And the very day before, Caesar, supping with Marcus Lepidus, sealed certain letters as he was wont to do at the board; so, talk falling out amongst them, reasoning what death was best, he preventing their opinions cried out aloud: 'Death unlooked for.'

Then going to bed the same night as his manner was and lying with his wife Calpurnia, all the windows and doors of his chamber flying open, the noise awoke him and made him afraid when he saw such light; but more, when he heard his wife Calpurnia, being fast asleep, weep and sigh and put forth many fumbling lamentable speeches. For she dreamed that Caesar was slain, and that she had him in her arms. Others also do deny that she had any such dream; as, amongst other, Titus Livius writeth that it was in this sort: the Senate having set upon the top of Caesar's house, for an ornament and setting forth of the same, a certain pinnacle, Calpurnia dreamed that she saw it broken down and that she thought she lamented and wept for it. Insomuch that, Caesar rising in the morning, she prayed him if it were possible not to go out of the doors that day, but to adjourn the session of the Senate until another day. And if that he made no reckoning of her dream, yet that he would search further of the soothsayers by their sacrifices, to know what should happen him that day. Thereby it seemed that Caesar likewise did fear and suspect somewhat, because his wife Calpurnia until that time was never given to any fear or superstition, and then, for that he saw her so troubled in mind with this dream she had. But much more afterwards, when the soothsayers, having sacrificed many beasts one after another, told him that none did like them; then he determined to send Antonius to adjourn the session of the Senate.

But in the meantime came Decius Brutus, surnamed Albinus, in whom Caesar put such confidence that in his last will and testament he had appointed him to be his next heir, and yet was of the conspiracy with Cassius and Brutus. He, fearing that if Caesar did adjourn the session that day the conspiracy would out, laughed the soothsayers to scorn, and reproved Caesar, saying that he gave the Senate occasion to mislike with him, and that they might think he mocked them, considering that by his commandment they were assembled, and that they were ready willingly to grant him all things, and to proclaim him king of all the provinces of the Empire of Rome out of Italy, and that he should wear his diadem in all other places both by sea and land; and furthermore, that if any man should tell them from him they should depart for that present time, and return again when Calpurnia should have better dreams – what would his enemies and ill-willers say, and how could they like of his friends' words? And who could persuade them otherwise, but that they would think his dominion a slavery unto them, and tyrannical in himself? 'And yet, if it be so', said he, 'that you utterly mislike of this day, it is better that you go yourself in person, and saluting the Senate to dismiss them till another time.'

Therewithal he took Caesar by the hand and brought him out of his house. Caesar was not gone far from his house but a bondman, a stranger, did what he could to speak with him; and, when he saw he was put back by the great press and multitude of people that followed him, he went straight unto his house, and put himself into Calpurnia's hands to be kept till Caesar came back again, telling her that he had great matters to impart unto him. And one Artemidorus also, born in the isle of Cnidos, a doctor of rhetoric in the Greek tongue, who by means of his profession was very familiar with certain of Brutus' confederates and therefore knew the most part of all their practices against Caesar, came and brought him a little bill written with his own hand, of all that he meant to tell him. He, marking how Caesar received all the supplications that were offered him, and that he gave them straight to his men that were about him, pressed nearer to him and said: 'Caesar, read this memorial to yourself, and that quickly, for they be matters of great weight and touch you nearly.' Caesar took it of him, but could never read it, though he many times attempted it, for the number of people that did salute him; but holding it still in his hand, keeping it to himself, went on withal into the Senate-house. Howbeit other are of opinion that it was some man else that gave him that memorial, and not Artemidorus, who did what he could all the way as he went to give it Caesar, but he was always repulsed by the people.

For these things, they may seem to come by chance. But the place where the murder was prepared, and where the Senate were assembled, and where also there stood up an image of Pompey dedicated by himself amongst other ornaments which he gave unto the Theatre – all these were manifest proofs that it was the ordinance of some god that made this treason to be executed specially in that very place. It is also reported that Cassius – though otherwise he did favour the doctrine of Epicurus – beholding the image of Pompey before they entered into the action of their traitorous enterprise, he did softly call upon it to aid him. But the instant danger of the present time, taking away his former reason, did suddenly put him into a furious passion and made him like a man half besides himself. Now Antonius, that was a faithful friend to Caesar and a valiant man besides of his hands, him Decius Brutus Albinus entertained out of the Senate-house, having begun a long tale of set purpose.

So, Caesar coming into the house, all the Senate stood up on their feet to do him honour. Then part of Brutus' company and confederates stood round about Caesar's chair, and part of them also came towards him, as though they made suit with Metellus

Cimber, to call home his brother again from banishment; and thus, prosecuting still their suit, they followed Caesar till he was set in his chair; who denying their petitions and being offended with them one after another, because the more they were denied, the more they pressed upon him and were the earnester with him. Metellus at length, taking his gown with both his hands, pulled it over his neck, which was the sign given the confederates to set upon him. Then Casca behind him strake him in the neck with his sword. Howbeit the wound was not great nor mortal, because, it seemed, the fear of such a devilish attempt did amaze him and take his strength from him, that he killed him not at the first blow. But Caesar, turning straight unto him, caught hold of his sword and held it hard; and they both cried out, Caesar in Latin: 'O vile traitor Casca, what doest thou?' And Casca in Greek to his brother: 'Brother, help me.' At the beginning of this stir, they that were present, not knowing of the conspiracy, were so amazed with the horrible sight they saw that they had no power to fly, neither to help him, not so much as once to make any outcry. They on the other side that had conspired his death compassed him in on every side with their swords drawn in their hands, that Caesar turned him nowhere but he was stricken at by some, and still had naked swords in his face, and was hacked and mangled among them, as a wild beast taken of hunters. For it was agreed among them that every man should give him a wound, because all their parts should be in this murder. And then Brutus himself gave him one wound about his privities. Men report also that Caesar did still defend himself against the rest, running every way with his body. But when he saw Brutus with his sword drawn in his hand, then he pulled his gown over his head and made no more resistance, and was driven, either casually or purposedly by the counsel of the conspirators, against the base whereupon Pompey's image stood, which ran all of a gore-blood till he was slain. Thus it seemed that the image took just revenge of Pompey's enemy, being thrown down on the ground at his feet and yielding up his ghost there for the number of wounds he had upon him. For it is reported that he had three-and-twenty wounds upon his body; and divers of the conspirators did hurt themselves, striking one body with so many blows.

When Caesar was slain, the Senate, though Brutus stood in the midst amongst them as though he would have said somewhat touching this fact, presently ran out of the house, and flying filled all the city with marvellous fear and tumult; insomuch as some did shut-to their doors, others forsook their shops and warehouses, and others ran to the place to see what the matter was; and others also that had seen it ran home to their houses again. But Antonius and Lepidus, which were two of Caesar's chiefest friends, secretly conveying themselves away, fled into other men's houses and forsook their own.

Brutus and his confederates on the other side, being yet hot with this murder they had committed, having their swords drawn in their hands, came all in a troop together out of the Senate, and went into the market-place, not as men that made countenance to fly, but otherwise boldly holding up their heads like men of courage, and called to the people to defend their liberty, and stayed to speak with every great personage whom they met in their way. Of them, some followed this troop and went amongst them as if they had been of the conspiracy, and falsely challenged part of the honour with them. Among them was Caius Octavius and Lentulus Spinther. But both of them were afterwards put to death, for their vain covetousness of honour, by Antonius and Octavius Caesar the younger;

and yet had no part of that honour for the which they were put to death, neither did any man believe that they were any of the confederates or of counsel with them. For they that did put them to death took revenge rather of the will they had to offend than of any fact they had committed.

The next morning Brutus and his confederates came into the market-place to speak unto the people, who gave them such audience that it seemed they neither greatly reproved nor allowed the fact. For by their great silence they showed that they were sorry for Caesar's death, and also that they did reverence Brutus. Now the Senate granted general pardon for all that was past and, to pacify every man, ordained besides that Caesar's funerals should be honoured as a god, and established all things that he had done, and gave certain provinces also and convenient honours unto Brutus and his confederates, whereby every man thought all things were brought to good peace and quietness again. But when they had opened Caesar's testament and found a liberal legacy of money bequeathed unto every citizen of Rome, and that they saw his body (which was brought into the market-place) all bemangled with gashes of swords, then there was no order to keep the multitude and common people quiet. But they plucked up forms, tables, and stools, and laid them all about the body, and setting them afire burnt the corse. Then, when the fire was well kindled, they took the firebrands and went unto their houses that had slain Caesar, to set them afire. Other also ran up and down the city to see if they could meet with any of them to cut them in pieces; howbeit they could meet with never a man of them, because they had locked themselves up safely in their houses.

There was one of Caesar's friends called Cinna, that had a marvellous strange and terrible dream the night before. He dreamed that Caesar bade him to supper, and that he refused, and would not go; then that Caesar took him by the hand, and led him against his will. Now Cinna hearing at that time that they burnt Caesar's body in the market-place, notwithstanding that he feared his dream and had an ague on him besides, he went into the market-place to honour his funerals. When he came thither, one of the mean sort asked what his name was. He was straight called by his name. The first man told it to another, and that other unto another, so that it ran straight through them all that he was one of them that murdered Caesar; for indeed one of the traitors to Caesar was also called Cinna as himself. Wherefore, taking him for Cinna the murderer, they fell upon him with such fury that they presently dispatched him in the market-place.

This stir and fury made Brutus and Cassius more afraid than of all that was past; and therefore, within few days after, they departed out of Rome. And touching their doings afterwards, and what calamity they suffered till their deaths, we have written it at large in the *Life of Brutus*.

Caesar died at six-and-fifty years of age; and Pompey also lived not passing four years more than he. So he reaped no other fruit of all his reign and dominion, which he had so vehemently desired all his life and pursued with such extreme danger, but a vain name only and a superficial glory that procured him the envy and hatred of his country. But his great prosperity and good fortune, that favoured him all his lifetime, did continue afterwards in the revenge of his death, pursuing the murderers both by sea and land, till they had not left a man more to be executed, of all them that were actors or counsellors in the conspiracy of his death. Furthermore, of all the chances that happen unto men upon the earth, that which came to Cassius above all other is most to be wondered at. For he, being overcome in battle at the journey of Philippes, slew himself with the same sword with the which he strake Caesar. Again, of signs in the element, the great comet, which seven nights together was seen very bright after Caesar's death, the eighth night after was never seen more. Also the brightness of the sun was darkened, the which all that year through rose very pale and shined not out, whereby it gave but small heat; therefore the air being very cloudy and dark, by the weakness of the heat that could not come forth, did cause the earth to bring forth but raw and unripe fruit, which rotted before it could ripe.

But, above all, the ghost that appeared unto Brutus showed plainly that the gods were offended with the murder of Caesar. The vision was thus. Brutus, being ready to pass over his army from the city of Abydos to the other coast lying directly against it, slept every night, as his manner was, in his tent; and being yet awake thinking of his affairs – for by report he was as careful a captain and lived with as little sleep as ever man did – he thought he heard a noise at his tent door; and, looking towards the light of the lamp that waxed very dim, he saw a horrible vision of a man, of a wonderful greatness and dreadful look, which at the first made him marvellously afraid. But when he saw that it did him no hurt, but stood by his bedside and said nothing, at length he asked him what he was. The image answered him: 'I am thy ill angel, Brutus, and thou shalt see me by the city of Philippes.' Then Brutus replied again, and said: 'Well, I shall see thee then.' Therewithal the spirit presently vanished from him.

After that time Brutus being in battle near unto the city of Philippes against Antonius and Octavius Caesar, at the first battle he won the victory, and, overthrowing all them that withstood him, he drave them into young Caesar's camp, which he took. The second battle being at hand, this spirit appeared again unto him, but spake never a word. Thereupon Brutus, knowing he should die, did put himself to all hazard in battle, but yet fighting could not be slain. So, seeing his men put to flight and overthrown, he ran unto a little rock not far off; and there setting his sword's point to his breast fell upon it and slew himself, but yet, as it is reported, with the help of his friend that dispatched him.

The Life of Marcus Brutus

Now there were divers sorts of Praetorships at Rome, and it was looked for that Brutus or Cassius would make suit for the chiefest Praetorship, which they called the Praetorship of the City, because he that had that office was as a judge to minister justice unto the citizens. Therefore they strove one against the other, though some say that there was some little grudge betwixt them for other matters before, and that this contention did set them further out, though they were allied together. For Cassius had married Junia, Brutus' sister. Others say, that this contention betwixt them came by Caesar himself, who secretly gave either of them both hope of his favour. So their suit for the Praetorship was so followed and laboured of either party that one of them put another in suit of law. Brutus with his virtue and good name contended against many noble exploits in arms which Cassius had done against the Parthians. So Caesar, after he had heard both their objections, he told his friends with whom he consulted about this matter: 'Cassius' cause is the juster', said he, 'but Brutus must be first preferred.' Thus Brutus had the first

Praetorship, and Cassius the second; who thanked not Caesar so much for the Praetorship he had, as he was angry with him for that he had lost. But Brutus in many other things tasted of the benefit of Caesar's favour in anything he requested. For, if he had listed, he might have been one of Caesar's chiefest friends and of greatest authority and credit about him. Howbeit Cassius' friends did dissuade him from it (for Cassius and he were not yet reconciled together sithence their first contention and strife for the Praetorship) and prayed him to beware of Caesar's sweet enticements and to fly his tyrannical favours; the which they said Caesar gave him, not to honour his virtue but to weaken his constant mind, framing it to the bent of his bow.

Now Caesar on the other side did not trust him overmuch, nor was not without tales brought unto him against him; howbeit he feared his great mind, authority, and friends. Yet, on the other side also, he trusted his good nature and fair conditions. For, intelligence being brought him one day that Antonius and Dolabella did conspire against him, he answered that these fat long-haired men made him not afraid, but the lean and whitely-faced fellows, meaning that by Brutus and Cassius. At another time also when one accused Brutus unto him and bade him beware of him: 'What', said he again, clapping his hand on his breast, 'think ye that Brutus will not tarry till this body die?' – meaning that none but Brutus after him was meet to have such power as he had. And surely, in my opinion, I am persuaded that Brutus might indeed have come to have been the chiefest man of Rome, if he could have contented himself for a time to have been next unto Caesar and to have suffered his glory and authority which he had gotten by his great victories to consume with time.

But Cassius being a choleric man and hating Caesar privately, more than he did the tyranny openly, he incensed Brutus against him. It is also reported that Brutus could evil away with the tyranny, and that Cassius hated the tyrant, making many complaints for the injuries he had done him, and, amongst others, for that he had taken away his lions from him. Cassius had provided them for his sports, when he should be Aedilis, and they were found in the city of Megara when it was won by Calenus, and Caesar kept them. The rumour went that these lions did marvellous great hurt to the Megarians. For, when the city was taken, they brake their cages where they were tied up, and turned them loose, thinking they would have done great mischief to the enemies, and have kept them from setting upon them. But the lions, contrary to expectation, turned upon themselves that fled unarmed, and did so cruelly tear some in pieces that it pitied their enemies to see them. And this was the cause, as some do report, that made Cassius conspire against Caesar. But this holdeth no water. For Cassius even from his cradle could not abide any manner of tyrants, as it appeared when he was but a boy, and went unto the same school that Faustus the son of Sylla did. And Faustus, bragging among other boys, highly boasted of his father's kingdom. Cassius rose up on his feet, and gave him two good wirts on the ear. Faustus' governors would have put this matter in suit against Cassius. But Pompey would not suffer them, but caused the two boys to be brought before him, and asked them how the matter came to pass. Then Cassius, as it is written of him, said unto the other: 'Go to, Faustus, speak again, and thou darest, before this nobleman here, the same words that made me angry with thee, that my fists may walk once again about thine ears.' Such was Cassius' hot stirring nature.

But for Brutus, his friends and countrymen, both by divers procurements and sundry rumours of the city and by many bills also, did openly call and procure him to do that he did. For, under the image of his ancestor Junius Brutus, that drave the kings out of Rome, they wrote: 'O, that it pleased the gods thou wert now alive, Brutus.' And again: 'That thou wert here among us now.' His tribunal, or chair, where he gave audience during the time he was Praetor, was full of such bills: 'Brutus, thou art asleep, and art not Brutus indeed.' And of all this, Caesar's flatterers were the cause; who beside many other exceeding and unspeakable honours they daily devised for him, in the night-time they did put diadems upon the heads of his images, supposing thereby to allure the common people to call him King, instead of Dictator. Howbeit it turned to the contrary, as we have written more at large in Julius Caesar's *Life*.

Now when Cassius felt his friends and did stir them up against Caesar, they all agreed and promised to take part with him, so Brutus were the chief of their conspiracy. For they told him that so high an enterprise and attempt as that did not so much require men of manhood and courage to draw their swords, as it stood them upon to have a man of such estimation as Brutus, to make every man boldly think that by his only presence the fact were holy and just. If he took not this course, then that they should go to it with fainter hearts; and when they had done it they should be more fearful, because every man would think that Brutus would not have refused to have made one with them, if the cause had been good and honest. Therefore Cassius, considering this matter with himself, did first of all speak to Brutus since they grew strange together for the suit they had for the Praetorship. So when he was reconciled to him again, and that they had embraced one another, Cassius asked him if he were determined to be in the Senate-house the first day of the month of March, because he heard say that Caesar's friends should move the council that day that Caesar should be called King by the Senate. Brutus answered him, he would not be there. 'But if we be sent for', said Cassius, 'how then?' 'For myself then', said Brutus, 'I mean not to hold my peace, but to withstand it, and rather die than lose my liberty.' Cassius, being bold and taking hold of this word, 'Why', quoth he, 'what Roman is he alive that will suffer thee to die for the liberty? What, knowest thou not that thou art Brutus? Thinkest thou that they be cobblers, tapsters, or suchlike base mechanical people, that write these bills and scrolls which are found daily in thy Praetor's chair, and not the noblest men and best citizens that do it? No, be thou well assured that of other Praetors they look for gifts, common distributions amongst the people, and for common plays, and to see fencers fight at the sharp, to show the people pastime. But at thy hands they specially require, as a due debt unto them, the taking away of the tyranny, being fully bent to suffer any extremity for thy sake, so that thou wilt show thyself to be the man thou art taken for, and that they hope thou art.' Thereupon he kissed Brutus, and embraced him; and so, each taking leave of other, they went both to speak with their friends about it.

Now amongst Pompey's friends there was one called Caius Ligarius, who had been accused unto Caesar for taking part with Pompey, and Caesar discharged him. But Ligarius thanked not Caesar so much for his discharge, as he was offended with him for that he was brought in danger by his tyrannical power. And therefore in his heart he was alway his mortal enemy, and was besides very familiar with Brutus, who went to see him being sick in his bed, and said unto him: 'O Ligarius, in what a time art thou sick!'

Ligarius, rising up in his bed and taking him by the right hand, said unto him: 'Brutus', said he, 'if thou hast any great enterprise in hand worthy of thyself, I am whole.'

After that time they began to feel all their acquaintance whom they trusted, and laid their heads together consulting upon it, and did not only pick out their friends, but all those also whom they thought stout enough to attempt any desperate matter, and that were not afraid to lose their lives. For this cause they durst not acquaint Cicero with their conspiracy, although he was a man whom they loved dearly and trusted best. For they were afraid that he being a coward by nature, and age also having increased his fear, he would quite turn and alter all their purpose, and quench the heat of their enterprise (the which specially required hot and earnest execution), seeking by persuasion to bring all things to such safety as there should be no peril.

Brutus also did let other of his friends alone, as Statilius Epicurean and Fa[v]onius, that made profession to follow Marcus Cato: because that having cast out words afar off, disputing together in philosophy to feel their minds, Fa[v]onius answered that civil war was worse than tyrannical government usurped against the law. And Statilius told him also that it were an unwise part of him to put his life in danger for a sight of ignorant fools and asses. Labeo was present at this talk, and maintained the contrary against them both. But Brutus held his peace, as though it had been a doubtful matter and a hard thing to have decided. But afterwards, being out of their company, he made Labeo privy to his intent, who very readily offered himself to make one. And they thought good also to bring in another Brutus to join with him, surnamed Albinus, who was no man of his hands himself, but because he was able to bring good force of a great number of slaves and fencers at the sharp, whom he kept to show the people pastime with their fighting; besides also that Caesar had some trust in him. Cassius and Labeo told Brutus Albinus of it at the first, but he made them no answer. But when he had spoken with Brutus himself alone, and that Brutus had told him he was the chief ringleader of all this conspiracy, then he willingly promised him the best aid he could. Furthermore the only name and great calling of Brutus did bring on the most of them to give consent to this conspiracy; who having never taken oaths together nor taken or given any caution or assurance, nor binding themselves one to another by any religious oaths, they all kept the matter so secret to themselves and could so cunningly handle it that, notwithstanding the gods did reveal it by manifest signs and tokens from above and by predictions of sacrifices, yet all this would not be believed.

Now Brutus (who knew very well that for his sake all the noblest, valiantest, and most courageous men of Rome did venture their lives) weighing with himself the greatness of the danger, when he was out of his house he did so frame and fashion his countenance and looks that no man could discern he had anything to trouble his mind. But when night came that he was in his own house, then he was clean changed. For, either care did wake him against his will when he would have slept, or else oftentimes of himself he fell into such deep thoughts of this enterprise, casting in his mind all the dangers that might happen, that his wife, lying by him, found that there was some marvellous great matter that troubled his mind, not being wont to be in that taking, and that he could not well determine with himself. His wife Porcia (as we have told you before) was the daughter of Cato, whom Brutus married being his cousin, not a maiden, but a young widow after the death of her first husband Bibulus, by whom she had also a young son called Bibulus, who afterwards wrote a book *Of the Acts and Gests of Brutus*, extant at this present day.

This young lady being excellently well seen in philosophy, loving her husband well, and being of a noble courage, as she was also wise – because she would not ask her husband what he ailed before she had made some proof by her self – she took a little razor such as barbers occupy to pare men's nails, and, causing all her maids and women to go out of her chamber, gave her self a great gash withal in her thigh, that she was straight all of a gore-blood; and, incontinently after, a vehement fever took her, by reason of the pain of her wound. Then, perceiving her husband was marvellously out of quiet and that he could take no rest, even in her greatest pain of all, she spake in this sort unto him: 'I being, O Brutus', said she, 'the daughter of Cato, was married unto thee, not to be thy bedfellow and companion in bed and at board only, like a harlot, but to be partaker also with thee of thy good and evil fortune. Now for thyself, I can find no cause of fault in thee touching our match. But for my part, how may I show my duty towards thee and how much I would do for thy sake, if I cannot constantly bear a secret mischance or grief with thee, which requireth secrecy and fidelity? I confess that a woman's wit commonly is too weak to keep a secret safely. But yet, Brutus, good education and the company of virtuous men have some power to reform the defect of nature. And for myself, I have this benefit moreover: that I am the daughter of Cato and wife of Brutus. This notwithstanding, I did not trust to any of these things before, until that now I have found by experience that no pain nor grief whatsoever can overcome me.' With those words she showed him her wound on her thigh and told him what she had done to prove herself. Brutus was amazed to hear what she said unto him, and, lifting up his hands to heaven, he besought the gods to give him the grace he might bring his enterprise to so good pass, that he might be found a husband worthy of so noble a wife as Porcia. So he then did comfort her the best he could.

Now a day being appointed for the meeting of the Senate, at what time they hoped Caesar would not fail to come, the conspirators determined then to put their enterprise in execution, because they might meet safely at that time without suspicion, and the rather, for that all the noblest and chiefest men of the city would be there; who when they should see such a great matter executed, would every man then set-to their hands, for the defence of their liberty. Furthermore, they thought also that the appointment of the place where the council should be kept was chosen of purpose by divine providence and made all for them. For it was one of the porches about the Theatre, in the which there was a certain place full of seats for men to sit in, where also was set up the image of Pompey which the city had made and consecrated in honour of him, when he did beautify that part of the city with the Theatre he built, with divers porches about it. In this place was the assembly of the Senate appointed to be, just on the fifteenth day of the month of March, which the Romans call *Idus Martias*. So that it seemed some god of purpose had brought Caesar thither to be slain, for revenge of Pompey's death.

So, when the day was come, Brutus went out of his house with a dagger by his side under his long gown, that nobody saw nor knew, but his wife only. The other conspirators were all assembled at Cassius' house, to bring his son into the market-place, who on that day did put on the man's gown, called *toga virilis*; and from thence they came all in a troop together unto Pompey's porch, looking that Caesar would straight come thither. But here is to be noted the wonderful assured constancy of these conspirators in so dangerous and weighty an enterprise as they had undertaken. For many of them being Praetors, by reason of their office, whose duty is to minister justice to everybody, they did not only with great quietness and courtesy hear them that spake unto them or that pleaded matters before them, and gave them attentive ear as if they had had no other matter in their heads; but moreover they gave just sentence and carefully dispatched the causes before them. So there was one among them who, being condemned in a certain sum of money, refused to pay it and cried out that he did appeal unto Caesar. Then Brutus, casting his eyes upon the conspirators, said: 'Caesar shall not let me to see the law executed.'

Notwithstanding this, by chance there fell out many misfortunes unto them which was enough to have marred the enterprise. The first and chiefest was Caesar's long tarrying, who came very late to the Senate. For, because the signs of the sacrifices appeared unlucky, his wife Calpurnia kept him at home, and the soothsayers bade him beware he went not abroad. The second cause was when one came unto Casca being a conspirator, and, taking him by the hand, said unto him: 'O Casca, thou keptest it close from me, but Brutus hath told me all.' Casca being amazed at it, the other went on with his tale and said: 'Why, how now, how cometh it to pass thou art thus rich, that thou dost sue to be Aedilis?' Thus Casca being deceived by the other's doubtful words, he told them it was a thousand to one he blabbed not out all the conspiracy. Another Senator, called Popilius Laena, after he had saluted Brutus and Cassius more friendly than he was wont to do, he rounded softly in their ears and told them: 'I pray the gods you may go through with that you have taken in hand. But withal, dispatch I rede you, for your enterprise is bewrayed.' When he had said, he presently departed from them, and left them both afraid that their conspiracy would out.

Now in the meantime there came one of Brutus' men post-haste unto him and told him his wife was a-dying. For Porcia being very careful and pensive for that which was to come and being too weak to away with so great and inward grief of mind, she could hardly keep within, but was frighted with every little noise and cry she heard, as those that are taken and possessed with the fury of the Bacchants, asking every man that came from the market-place what Brutus did, and still sent messenger after messenger to know what news. At length, Caesar's coming being prolonged as you have heard, Porcia's weakness was not able to hold out any lenger, and thereupon she suddenly swounded, that she had no leisure to go to her chamber, but was taken in the midst of her house, where her speech and senses failed her. Howbeit she soon came to herself again, and so was laid in her bed and tended by her women. When Brutus heard these news, it grieved him, as it is to be presupposed. Yet he left not off the care of his country and commonwealth, neither went home to his house for any news he heard.

Now it was reported that Caesar was coming in his litter; for he determined not to stay in the Senate all that day, because he was afraid of the unlucky signs of the sacrifices, but to adjourn matters of importance unto the next session and council holden, feigning himself not to be well at ease. When Caesar came out of his litter, Popilius Laena, that had talked before with Brutus and Cassius and had prayed the gods they might bring this enterprise to pass, went unto Caesar and kept him a long time with a talk. Caesar gave good ear unto him. Wherefore the conspirators (if so they should be called), not hearing what he said to Caesar, but conjecturing, by that he had told them a little before, that his talk was none other but the very discovery of their conspiracy, they were afraid every man of them; and, one looking in another's face, it was easy to see that they all were of a mind that it was no tarrying for them till they were apprehended, but rather that they should kill themselves with their own hands. And when Cassius and certain other clapped their hands on their swords under their gowns to draw them, Brutus marking the countenance and gesture of Laena, and considering that he did use himself rather like an humble and earnest suitor than like an accuser, he said nothing to his companion (because there were many amongst them that were not of the conspiracy), but with a pleasant countenance encouraged Cassius. And immediately after, Laena went from Caesar and kissed his hand; which showed plainly that it was for some matter concerning himself that he had held him so long in talk.

Now all the Senators being entered first into this place or chapter house where the council should be kept, all the other conspirators straight stood about Caesar's chair, as if they had had something to have said unto him. And some say that Cassius, casting his eyes upon Pompey's image, made his prayer unto it, as if it had been alive. Trebonius, on the other side, drew Antonius at one side as he came into the house where the Senate sat, and held him with a long talk without.

When Caesar was come into the house, all the Senate rose to honour him at his coming in. So, when he was set, the conspirators flocked about him, and amongst them they presented one Tullius Cimber, who made humble suit for the calling home again of his brother that was banished. They all made as though they were intercessors for him, and took him by the hands and kissed his head and breast. Caesar at the first simply refused their kindness and entreaties. But afterwards, perceiving they still pressed on him, he violently thrust them from him. Then Cimber with both his hands plucked Caesar's gown over his shoulders; and Casca that stood behind him drew his dagger first, and strake Caesar upon the shoulder, but gave him no great wound. Caesar, feeling himself hurt, took him straight by the hand he held his dagger in, and cried out in Latin: 'O traitor, Casca, what doest thou?' Casca on the other side cried in Greek and called his brother to help him. So divers running on a heap together to fly upon Caesar, he looking about him to have fled, saw Brutus with a sword drawn in his hand ready to strike at him. Then he let Casca's hand go, and, casting his gown over his face, suffered every man to strike at him that would. Then the conspirators thronging one upon another because every man was desirous to have a cut at him, so many swords and daggers lighting upon one body, one of them hurt another; and among them Brutus caught a blow on his hand, because he would make one in murdering of him, and all the rest also were every man of them bloodied.

Caesar being slain in this manner, Brutus, standing in the midst of the house, would have spoken, and stayed the other Senators that were not of the conspiracy, to have told them the reason why they had done this fact. But they, as men both afraid and amazed, fled one upon another's neck in haste to get out at the door; and no man followed them. For it was set down and agreed between them that they should kill no man but Caesar only, and should entreat all the rest to look to defend their liberty. All the conspirators but Brutus, determining upon this matter, thought it good also to kill Antonius, because he was a wicked man and that in nature favoured tyranny; besides also, for that he was in great estimation with soldiers, having been conversant of long time amongst them; and specially, having a mind bent to great enterprises, he was also of great authority at that time, being Consul with Caesar. But Brutus would not agree to it. First, for that he said it was not honest; secondly, because he told them there was hope of change in him. For he did not mistrust but that Antonius, being a noble-minded and courageous man, when he should know that Caesar was dead, would willingly help his country to recover her liberty, having them an example unto him, to follow their courage and virtue. So Brutus by this means saved Antonius' life, who at that present time disguised himself and stale away.

But Brutus and his consorts, having their swords bloody in their hands, went straight to the Capitol, persuading the Romans, as they went, to take their liberty again. Now at the first time, when the murder was newly done, there were sudden outcries of people that ran up and down the city, the which indeed did the more increase the fear and tumult. But when they saw they slew no man, neither did spoil or make havoc of anything, then certain of the Senators and many of the people, emboldening themselves, went to the Capitol unto them. There a great number of men being assembled together one after another, Brutus made an oration unto them to win the favour of the people and to justify that they had done. All those that were by said they had done well, and cried unto them that they should boldly come down from the Capitol. Whereupon Brutus and his companions came boldly down into the market-place. The rest followed in troop; but Brutus went foremost, very honourably compassed in round about with the noblest men of the city, which brought him from the Capitol, through the market-place, to the pulpit for orations.

When the people saw him in the pulpit, although they were a multitude of rakehells of all sorts and had a good will to make some stir, yet, being ashamed to do it for the reverence they bare unto Brutus, they kept silence, to hear what he would say. When Brutus began to speak, they gave him quiet audience. Howbeit, immediately after, they showed that they were not all contented with the murder. For when another called Cinna would have spoken and began to accuse Caesar, they fell into a great uproar among them and marvellously reviled him. Insomuch that the conspirators returned again into the Capitol. There Brutus, being afraid to be besieged, sent back again the noblemen that came thither with him, thinking it no reason that they, which were no partakers of the murder, should be partakers of the danger.

Then the next morning the Senate being assembled and holden within the Temple of the goddess Tellus (to wit, 'the Earth'), and Antonius, Plancus, and Cicero having made a motion to the Senate in that assembly that they should take an order to pardon and forget all that was past and to stablish friendship and peace again, it was decreed that they should not only be pardoned, but also that the Consuls should refer it to the Senate what honours should be appointed unto them. This being agreed upon, the Senate brake up, and Antonius the Consul, to put them in heart that were in the Capitol, sent them his son for a pledge. Upon this assurance, Brutus and his companions came down from the

Capitol, where every man saluted and embraced each other; among the which Antonius himself did bid Cassius to supper to him, and Lepidus also bade Brutus, and so one bade another, as they had friendship and acquaintance together.

The next day following, the Senate being called again to council did first of all commend Antonius, for that he had wisely stayed and quenched the beginning of a civil war. Then they also gave Brutus and his consorts great praises; and lastly they appointed them several governments of provinces. For unto Brutus they appointed Creta, Afric unto Cassius, Asia unto Trebonius, Bithynia unto Cimber, and unto the other Decius Brutus Albinus, Gaul on this side the Alps. When this was done, they came to talk of Caesar's will and testament, and of his funerals and tomb. Then Antonius thinking good his testament should be read openly, and also that his body should be honourably buried and not in hugger-mugger, lest the people might thereby take occasion to be worse offended if they did otherwise, Cassius stoutly spake against it. But Brutus went with the motion, and agreed unto it; wherein it seemeth he committed a second fault. For the first fault he did was when he would not consent to his fellow conspirators that Antonius should be slain; and therefore he was justly accused that thereby he had saved and strengthened a strong and grievous enemy of their conspiracy. The second fault was when he agreed that Caesar's funerals should be as Antonius would have them, the which indeed marred all. For first of all, when Caesar's testament was openly read among them, whereby it appeared that he bequeathed unto every citizen of Rome seventy-five drachmas a man, and that he left his gardens and arbours unto the people, which he had on this side of the river of Tiber (in the place where now the Temple of Fortune is built), the people then loved him and were marvellous sorry for him.

Afterwards, when Caesar's body was brought into the market-place, Antonius making his funeral oration in praise of the dead, according to the ancient custom of Rome, and perceiving that his words moved the common people to compassion, he framed his eloquence to make their hearts yearn the more; and, taking Caesar's gown all bloody in his hand, he laid it open to the sight of them all, showing what a number of cuts and holes it had upon it. Therewithal the people fell presently into such a rage and mutiny that there was no more order kept amongst the common people. For some of them cried out: 'Kill the murderers.' Others plucked up forms, tables, and stalls about the market-place, as they had done before at the funerals of Clodius; and, having laid them all on a heap together, they set them on fire, and thereupon did put the body of Caesar, and burnt it in the middest of the most holy places. And furthermore, when the fire was thoroughly kindled, some here, some there, took burning fire-brands, and ran with them to the murderers' houses that had killed him, to set them a-fire. Howbeit the conspirators, foreseeing the danger before, had wisely provided for themselves, and fled.

But there was a poet called Cinna, who had been no partaker of the conspiracy but was alway one of Caesar's chiefest friends. He dreamed, the night before, that Caesar bade him to supper with him and that, he refusing to go, Caesar was very importunate with him and compelled him, so that at length he led him by the hand into a great dark place, where, being marvellously afraid, he was driven to follow him in spite of his heart. This dream put him all night into a fever. And yet, notwithstanding, the next morning when he heard that they carried Caesar's body to burial, being ashamed not to accompany his funerals, he went out of his house, and thrust himself into the press of the common people that were in a great uproar. And because some one called him by his name, Cinna, the people thinking he had been that Cinna who in an oration he made had spoken very evil of Caesar, they falling upon him in their rage slew him outright in the market-place.

This made Brutus and his companions more afraid than any other thing, next unto the change of Antonius. Wherefore they got them out of Rome, and kept at the first in the city of Antium, hoping to return again to Rome when the fury of the people were a little assuaged; the which they hoped would be quickly, considering that they had to deal with a fickle and unconstant multitude, easy to be carried, and that the Senate stood for them; who notwithstanding made no inquiry of them that had torn poor Cinna the poet in pieces, but caused them to be sought for and apprehended that went with fire-brands to set fire of the conspirators' houses...

After that, these three, Octavius Caesar, Antonius, and Lepidus, made an agreement between themselves, and by those articles divided the provinces belonging to the Empire of Rome among themselves, and did set up bills of proscription and outlawry, condemning two hundred of the noblest men of Rome to suffer death; and among that number Cicero was one. News being brought thereof into Macedon, Brutus, being then enforced to it, wrote unto Hortensius that he should put Caius Antonius to death, to be revenged of the death of Cicero and of the other Brutus, of the which the one was his friend and the other his kinsman. For this cause therefore, Antonius afterwards taking Hortensius at the battle of Philippes, he made him to be slain upon his brother's tomb. But then Brutus said that he was more ashamed of the cause for the which Cicero was slain than he was otherwise sorry for his death; and that he could not but greatly reprove his friends he had at Rome who were slaves more through their own fault than through their valiantness or manhood which usurped the tyranny, considering that they were so cowardly and faint-hearted as to suffer the sight of those things before their eyes, the report whereof should only have grieved them to the heart.

Now when Brutus had passed over his army (that was very great) into Asia, he gave order for the gathering of a great number of ships together, as well in the coast of Bithynia, as also in the city of Cyzicum, because he would have an army by sea; and himself in the meantime went unto the cities, taking order for all things and giving audience unto princes and noblemen of the country that had to do with him. Afterwards he sent unto Cassius in Syria, to turn him from his journey into Egypt, telling him that it was not for the conquest of any kingdom for themselves that they wandered up and down in that sort, but, contrarily, that it was to restore their country again to their liberty; and that the multitude of soldiers they gathered together was to subdue the tyrants that would keep them in slavery and subjection. Wherefore, regarding their chief purpose and intent, they should not be far from Italy, as near as they could possible, but should rather make all the haste they could to help their countrymen. Cassius believed him and returned. Brutus went to meet him; and they both met at the city of Smyrna, which was the first time that they saw together since they took leave of each other at the haven of Piraea in Athens, the one going into Syria and the other into Macedon. So they were marvellous joyful, and no less courageous when they saw the great armies together which they had both levied; considering that they departing out of Italy like naked and poor banished men, without armour and money, nor having any ship ready, nor soldier about them, nor any one town at their commandment; yet, notwithstanding, in a short time after they were now met together, having ships, money, and soldiers enow, both footmen and horsemen, to fight for the Empire of Rome.

Now Cassius would have done Brutus as much honour as Brutus did unto him. But Brutus most commonly prevented him and went first unto him, both because he was the elder man, as also for that he was sickly of body. And men reputed him commonly to be very skilful in wars, but otherwise marvellous choleric and cruel, who sought to rule men by fear rather than with lenity; and on the other side he was too familiar with his friends and would jest too broadly with them. But Brutus in contrary manner, for his virtue and valiantness was well-beloved of the people and his own, esteemed of noblemen, and hated of no man, not so much as of his enemies; because he was a marvellous lowly and gentle person, noble minded, and would never be in any rage, nor carried away with pleasure and covetousness, but had ever an upright mind with him, and would never yield to any wrong or injustice, the which was the chiefest cause of his fame, of his rising, and of the good will that every man bare him; for they were all persuaded that his intent was good. For they did not certainly believe that if Pompey himself had overcome Caesar he would have resigned his authority to the law; but rather they were of opinion that he would still keep the sovereignty and absolute government in his hands, taking only, to please the people, the title of Consul or Dictator, or of some other more civil office. And as for Cassius, a hot, choleric, and cruel man, that would oftentimes be carried away from justice for gain, it was certainly thought that he made war, and put himself into sundry dangers, more to have absolute power and authority than to defend the liberty of his country. For they that will also consider others that were elder men than they – as Cinna, Marius, and Carbo: it is out of doubt that the end and hope of their victory was to be lords of their country; and in manner they did all confess that they fought for the tyranny and to be lords of the Empire of Rome. And in contrary manner, his enemies themselves did never reprove Brutus for any such change or desire. For it was said that Antonius spake it openly divers times that he thought that of all them that had slain Caesar there was none but Brutus only that was moved to do it as thinking the act commendable of itself; but that all the other conspirators did conspire his death for some private malice or envy that they otherwise did bear unto him.

Hereby it appeareth that Brutus did not trust so much to the power of his army as he did to his own virtue, as is to be seen by his writings. For, approaching near to the instant danger, he wrote unto Pomponius Atticus that his affairs had the best hap that could be. 'For', said he, 'either I will set my country at liberty by battle, or by honourable death rid me of this bondage.' And furthermore, that, they being certain and assured of all things else, this one thing only was doubtful to them: whether they should live or die with liberty. He wrote also that Antonius had his due payment for his folly. For, where he might have been a partner equally of the glory of Brutus, Cassius, and Cato, and have made one with them, he liked better to choose to be joined with Octavius Caesar alone, 'with whom, though now he be not overcome by us, yet shall he shortly after also have war with him'. And truly he proved a true prophet, for so came it indeed to pass.

Now, whilst Brutus and Cassius were together in the city of Smyrna, Brutus prayed

Cassius to let him have some part of his money, whereof he had great store, because all that he could rap and rend of his side he had bestowed it in making so great a number of ships, that by means of them they should keep all the sea at their commandment. Cassius' friends hindered this request and earnestly dissuaded him from it, persuading him that it was no reason that Brutus should have the money which Cassius hath gotten together by sparing and levied with great evil will of the people their subjects, for him to bestow liberally upon his soldiers and by this means to win their good wills by Cassius' charge. This notwithstanding, Cassius gave him the third part of his total sum...

About that time Brutus sent to pray Cassius to come to the city of Sardis; and so he did. Brutus, understanding of his coming, went to meet him with all his friends. There, both their armies being armed, they called them both emperors. Now, as it commonly happeneth in great affairs between two persons, both of them having many friends and so many captains under them, there ran tales and complaints betwixt them. Therefore before they fell in hand with any other matter, they went into a little chamber together, and bade every man avoid, and did shut the doors to them. Then they began to pour out their complaints one to the other, and grew hot and loud, earnestly accusing one another, and at length fell both a-weeping. Their friends that were without the chamber hearing them loud within and angry between themselves, they were both amazed and afraid also lest it would grow to further matter. But yet they were commanded that no man should come to them. Notwithstanding, one Marcus Fa[v]onius, that had been a friend and follower of Cato while he lived, and took upon him to counterfeit a philosopher, not with wisdom and discretion but with a certain bedlam and frantic motion, he would needs come into the chamber, though the men offered to keep him out. But it was no boot to let Fa[v]onius, when a mad mood or toy took him in the head, for he was a hot hasty man and sudden in all his doings, and cared for never a senator of them all. Now though he used this bold manner of speech after the profession of the Cynic philosophers (as who would say, 'dogs'), yet this boldness did no hurt many times, because they did but laugh at him to see him so mad. This Fa[v]onius at that time, in despite of the doorkeepers, came into the chamber, and, with a certain scoffing and mocking gesture which he counterfeited of purpose, he rehearsed the verses which old Nestor said in Homer:

My lords, I pray you hearken both to me,
For I have seen mo years than suchye three.

Cassius fell a-laughing at him. But Brutus thrust him out of the chamber, and called him dog and counterfeit Cynic. Howbeit his coming in brake their strife at that time, and so they left each other.

The self-same night Cassius prepared his supper in his chamber, and Brutus brought his friends with him. So when they were set at supper, Fa[v]onius came to sit down after he had washed. Brutus told him aloud, no man sent for him; and bade them set him at the upper end, meaning indeed at the lower end of the bed. Fa[v]onius made no ceremony, but thrust in amongst the midst of them, and made all the company laugh at him. So they were merry all supper-time and full of their philosophy. The next day after, Brutus, upon complaint of the Sardians, did condemn and noted Lucius Pella for a defamed person, that had been a Praetor of the Romans and whom Brutus had given charge unto; for that he was accused and convicted of robbery and pilfery in his office. This judgement much misliked Cassius, because he himself had secretly, not many days before, warned two of his friends, attainted and convicted of the like offences, and openly had cleared them; but yet he did not therefore leave to employ them in any manner of service as he did before. And therefore he greatly reproved Brutus for that he would show himself so strait and severe in such a time as was meeter to bear a little than to take things at the worst. Brutus in contrary manner answered that he should remember the Ides of March, at which time they slew Julius Caesar; who neither pilled nor polled the country, but only was a favourer and suborner of all them that did rob and spoil by his countenance and authority. And, if there were any occasion whereby they might honestly set aside justice and equity, they should have had more reason to have suffered Caesar's friends to have robbed and done what wrong and injury they had would, than to bear with their own men. For then, said he, they could but have said they had been cowards, 'And now they may accuse us of injustice, beside the pains we take, and the danger we put ourselves into.' And thus may we see what Brutus' intent and purpose was.

But, as they both prepared to pass over again out of Asia into Europe, there went a rumour that there appeared a wonderful sign unto him. Brutus was a careful man and slept very little, both for that his diet was moderate, as also because he was continually occupied. He never slept in the day time, and in the night no lenger than the time he was driven to be alone, and when everybody else took their rest. But now whilst he was in war and his head ever busily occupied to think of his affairs, and what would happen, after he had slumbered a little after supper, he spent all the rest of the night in dispatching of his weightiest causes; and after he had taken order for them, if he had any leisure left him, he would read some book till the third watch of the night, at what time the captains, petty-captains, and colonels did use to come unto him.

So, being ready to go into Europe, one night very late, when all the camp took quiet rest, as he was in his tent with a little light, thinking of weighty matters, he thought he heard one come in to him and, casting his eye towards the door of his tent, that he saw a wonderful strange and monstruous shape of a body coming towards him, and said never a word. So Brutus boldly asked what he was, a god or a man, and what cause brought him thither. The spirit answered him: 'I am thy evil spirit, Brutus; and thou shalt see me by the city of Philippes.' Brutus, being no otherwise afraid, replied again unto it: 'Well, then I shall see thee again.' The spirit presently vanished away; and Brutus called his men unto him, who told him that they heard no noise, nor saw anything at all. Thereupon Brutus returned again to think on his matters as he did before. And when the day brake he went unto Cassius to tell him what vision had appeared unto him in the night. Cassius being in opinion an Epicurean, and reasoning thereon with Brutus, spake to him touching the vision thus: 'In our sect, Brutus, we have an opinion that we do not always feel or see that which we suppose we do both see and feel; but that our senses being credulous, and therefore easily abused, when they are idle and unoccupied in their own objects, are induced to imagine they see and conjecture that which they in truth do not. For our mind is quick and cunning to work, without either cause or matter, anything in the imagination whatsoever. And therefore the imagination is resembled to clay, and the mind to the potter, who, without any other cause than his fancy and pleasure, changeth it into what fashion and form he will. And this doth the diversity of our dreams show unto us. For our imagination doth upon a small fancy grow from conceit to conceit, altering both in passions and forms of things imagined. For the mind of man is ever occupied, and that continual moving is nothing but an imagination. But yet there is a further cause of this in you. For, you being by nature given to melancholic discoursing, and of late continually occupied, your wits and senses having been overlaboured do easilier yield to such imaginations. For, to say that there are spirits or angels, and, if there were, that they had the shape of men, or such voices, or any power at all to come unto us, it is a mockery. And for mine own part I would there were such, because that we should not only have soldiers, horses, and ships, but also the aid of the gods, to guide and further our honest and honourable attempts.' With these words Cassius did somewhat comfort and quiet Brutus.

When they raised their camp, there came two eagles that, flying with a marvellous force, lighted upon two of the foremost ensigns, and always followed the soldiers, which gave them meat, and fed them, until they came near to the city of Philippes; and there, one day only before the battle, they both flew away.

Now Brutus had conquered the most part of all the people and nations of that country. But if there were any other city or captain to overcome, then they made all clear before them, and so drew towards the coasts of Thasos. There Norbanus lying in camp in a certain place called the Straits, by another place called Symbolon (which is a port of the sea), Cassius and Brutus compassed him in in such sort that he was driven to forsake the place, which was of great strength for him, and he was also in danger beside to have lost all his army. For Octavius Caesar could not follow him because of his sickness, and therefore stayed behind. Whereupon they had taken his army, had not Antonius' aid been, which made such wonderful speed that Brutus could scant believe it. So Caesar came not thither of ten days after; and Antonius camped against Cassius, and Brutus on the other side against Caesar.

The Romans called the valley between both camps, the Philippian fields; and there were never seen two so great armies of the Romans, one before the other, ready to fight. In truth, Brutus' army was inferior to Octavius Caesar's in number of men. But, for bravery and rich furniture, Brutus' army far excelled Caesar's. For the most part of their armours were silver and gilt, which Brutus had bountifully given them, although in all other things he taught his captains to live in order without excess. But, for the bravery of armour and weapon which soldiers should carry in their hands or otherwise wear upon their backs, he thought that it was an encouragement unto them that by nature are greedy of honour, and that it maketh them also fight like devils, that love to get and be afraid to lose; because they fight to keep their armour and weapon, as also their goods and lands.

Now when they came to muster their armies, Octavius Caesar took the muster of his army within the trenches of his camp, and gave his men only a little corn, and five silver drachmas to every man to sacrifice to the gods and to pray for victory. But Brutus, scorning this misery and niggardliness, first of all mustered his army and did purify it in the fields, according to the manner of the Romans. And then he gave unto every band a number of wethers to sacrifice, and fifty silver drachmas to every soldier. So that Brutus' and Cassius' soldiers were better pleased, and more courageously bent to fight at the day of battle, than their enemies' soldiers were.

Notwithstanding, being busily occupied about the ceremonies of this purification, it is reported that there chanced certain unlucky signs unto Cassius. For one of his sergeants that carried the rods before him brought him the garland of flowers turned backwards, the which he should have worn on his head in the time of sacrificing. Moreover it is reported also that at another time before, in certain sports and triumph where they carried an image of Cassius' victory of clean gold, it fell by chance, the man stumbling that carried it. And yet further, there were seen a marvellous number of fowls of prey, that feed upon dead carcases. And beehives also were found, where bees were gathered together in a certain place within the trenches of the camp; the which place the soothsayers thought good to shut out of the precinct of the camp, for to take away the superstitious fear and mistrust men would have of it. The which began somewhat to alter Cassius' mind from Epicurus' opinions, and had put the soldiers also in a marvellous fear. Thereupon Cassius was of opinion not to try this war at one battle, but rather to delay time and to draw it out in length, considering that they were the stronger in money and the weaker in men and armours. But Brutus in contrary manner did alway before, and at that time also, desire nothing more than to put all to the hazard of battle, as soon as might be possible, to the end he might either quickly restore his country to her former liberty, or rid him forthwith of this miserable world, being still troubled in following and maintaining of such great armies together. But perceiving that in the daily skirmishes and bickerings they made his men were alway the stronger and ever had the better, that yet quickened his spirits again, and did put him in better heart. And furthermore, because that some of their own men had already yielded themselves to their enemies, and that it was suspected moreover divers others would do the like, that made many of Cassius' friends which were of his mind before (when it came to be debated in council whether the battle should be fought or not) that they were then of Brutus' mind. But yet was there one of Brutus' friends called Atilius, that was against it, and was of opinion that they should tarry the next winter. Brutus asked him what he should get by tarrying a year lenger? 'If I get nought else', quoth Atilius again, 'yet have I lived so much lenger.' Cassius was very angry with this answer; and Atilius was maliced and esteemed the worse for it of all men. Thereupon it was presently determined they should fight battle the next day.

So Brutus all supper time looked with a cheerful countenance, like a man that had good hope, and talked very wisely of philosophy, and after supper went to bed. But touching Cassius, Messala reporteth that he supped by himself in his tent with a few of his friends, and that all supper time he looked very sadly, and was full of thoughts, although it was against his nature; and that after supper he took him by the hand, and holding him fast, in token of kindness as his manner was, told him in Greek: 'Messala, I protest unto thee, and make thee my witness, that I am compelled against my mind and will, as Pompey the Great was, to jeopard the liberty of our country to the hazard of a battle. And yet we must be lively and of good courage, considering our good fortune, whom we should wrong too much to mistrust her, although we follow evil counsel.' Messala writeth that Cassius having spoken these last words unto him, he bade him farewell and willed him to come to supper to him the next night following, because it was his birthday.

The next morning, by break of day, the signal of battle was set out in Brutus' and

Cassius' camp, which was an arming scarlet coat; and both the chieftains spake together in the midst of their armies. There Cassius began to speak first, and said: 'The gods grant us, O Brutus, that this day we may win the field and ever after to live all the rest of our life quietly one with another. But sith the gods have so ordained it that the greatest and chiefest things amongst men are most uncertain, and that, if the battle fall out otherwise today than we wish or look for, we shall hardly meet again, what art thou then determined to do – to fly, or die?' Brutus answered him: 'Being yet but a young man and not over greatly experienced in the world, I trust (I know not how) a certain rule of philosophy by the which I did greatly blame and reprove Cato for killing of himself, as being no lawful nor godly act, touching the gods, nor, concerning men, valiant; not to give place and yield to divine providence, and not constantly and patiently to take whatsoever it pleaseth him to send us, but to draw back and fly. But being now in the midst of the danger, I am of a contrary mind. For, if it be not the will of God that this battle fall out fortunate for us, I will look no more for hope, neither seek to make any new supply for war again, but will rid me of this miserable world, and content me with my fortune. For I gave up my life for my country in the Ides of March, for the which I shall live in another more glorious world.' Cassius fell a-laughing to hear what he said, and embracing him, 'Come on then', said he, 'let us go and charge our enemies with this mind. For either we shall conquer, or we shall not need to fear the conquerors.'

After this talk, they fell to consultation among their friends for the ordering of the battle. Then Brutus prayed Cassius he might have the leading of the right wing, the which men thought was far meeter for Cassius, both because he was the elder man, and also for that he had the better experience. But yet Cassius gave it him, and willed that Messala, who had charge of one of the warlikest legions they had, should be also in that wing with Brutus. So Brutus presently sent out his horsemen, who were excellently well appointed; and his footmen also were as willing and ready to give charge.

Now Antonius' men did cast a trench from the marsh by the which they lay, to cut off Cassius' way to come to the sea; and Caesar, at the least, his army stirred not. As for Octavius Caesar himself, he was not in his camp, because he was sick. And for his people, they little thought the enemies would have given them battle, but only have made some light skirmishes to hinder them that wrought in the trench, and with their darts and slings to have kept them from finishing of their work. But they, taking no heed to them that came full upon them to give them battle, marvelled much at the great noise they heard, that came from the place where they were casting their trench. In the meantime Brutus, that led the right wing, sent little bills to the colonels and captains of private bands, in the which he wrote the word of the battle; and he himself, riding a-horseback by all the troops, did speak to them and encouraged them to stick to it like men. So by this means very few of them understood what was the word of the battle, and, besides, the most part of them never tarried to have it told them, but ran with great fury to assail the enemies; whereby, through this disorder, the legions were marvellously scattered and dispersed one from the other.

For first of all, Messala's legion, and then the next unto them, went beyond the left wing of the enemies, and did nothing, but glancing by them overthrew some as they went; and so going on further fell right upon Caesar's camp, out of the which (as himself writeth in his *Commentaries*) he had been conveyed away a little before, through the counsel and advice of one of his friends called Marcus Artorius; who, dreaming in the night, had a vision appeared unto him, that commanded Octavius Caesar should be carried out of his camp, insomuch as it was thought he was slain, because his litter, which had nothing in it, was thrust through and through with pikes and darts. There was great slaughter in this camp. For amongst others there were slain two thousand Lacedaemonians, who were arrived but even a little before, coming to aid Caesar. The other also that had not glanced by, but had given a charge full upon Caesar's battle; they easily made them fly, because they were greatly troubled for the loss of their camp, and of them there were slain by hand three legions. Then, being very earnest to follow the chase of them that fled, they ran in amongst them hand over head into their camp, and Brutus among them.

But that which the conquerors thought not of, occasion showed it unto them that were overcome; and that was the left wing of their enemies left naked and unguarded of them of the right wing, who were strayed too far off, in following of them that were overthrown. So they gave a hot charge upon them. But notwithstanding all the force they made, they could not break into the midst of their battle, where they found men that received them and valiantly made head against them. Howbeit they brake and overthrew the left wing where Cassius was, by reason of the great disorder among them, and also because they had no intelligence how the right wing had sped. So they chased them, beating them into their camp, the which they spoiled, none of both the chieftains being present there. For Antonius, as it is reported, to fly the fury of the first charge, was gotten into the next marsh; and no man could tell what became of Octavius Caesar after he was carried out of his camp; insomuch that there were certain soldiers that showed their swords bloodied, and said that they had slain him, and did describe his face and showed what age he was of. Furthermore, the vaward and the midst of Brutus' battle had already put all their enemies to flight that withstood them, with great slaughter; so that Brutus had conquered all of his side, and Cassius had lost all on the other side. For nothing undid them but that Brutus went not to help Cassius, thinking he had overcome them, as himself had done; and Cassius on the other side tarried not for Brutus, thinking he had been overthrown, as himself was. And, to prove that the victory fell on Brutus' side, Messala confirmeth it, that they won three eagles and divers other ensigns of their enemies, and their enemies won never a one of theirs.

Now Brutus returning from the chase after he had slain and sacked Caesar's men, he wondered much that he could not see Cassius' tent standing up high as it was wont, neither the other tents of his camp standing as they were before, because all the whole camp had been spoiled and the tents thrown down, at the first coming in of the enemies. But they that were about Brutus, whose sight served them better, told him that they saw a great glistering of harness and a number of silvered targets, that went and came into Cassius' camp and were not, as they took it, the armours nor the number of men that they had left there to guard the camp; and yet that they saw not such a number of dead bodies, and great overthrow, as there should have been if so many legions had been slain.

This made Brutus at the first mistrust that which had happened. So he appointed a number of men to keep the camp of his enemy which he had taken, and caused his men to be sent for that yet followed the chase, and gathered them together, thinking to lead them to aid Cassius, who was in this state as you shall hear. First of all he was marvellous angry to see how Brutus' men ran to give charge upon their enemies and tarried not for the word of the battle nor commandment to give charge; and it grieved him beside that, after he had overcome them, his men fell straight to spoil and were not careful to compass in the rest of the enemies behind. But with tarrying too long also, more than through the valiantness or foresight of the captains his enemies, Cassius found himself compassed in with the right wing of his enemies' army. Whereupon his horsemen brake immediately, and fled for life towards the sea. Furthermore, perceiving his footmen to give ground, he did what he could to keep them from flying, and took an ensign from one of the ensign-bearers that fled, and stuck it fast at his feet, although with much ado he could scant keep his own guard together. So Cassius himself was at length compelled to fly, with a few about him, unto a little hill from whence they might easily see what was done in all the plain; howbeit Cassius himself saw nothing, for his sight was very bad, saving that he saw, and yet with much ado, how the enemies spoiled his camp before his eyes. He saw also a great troop of horsemen whom Brutus sent to aid him, and thought that they were his enemies that followed him. But yet he sent Titinius, one of them that was with him, to go and know what they were. Brutus' horsemen saw him coming afar off, whom when they knew that he was one of Cassius' chiefest friends, they shouted out for joy; and they that were familiarly acquainted with him lighted from their horses, and went and embraced him. The rest compassed him in round about a-horseback, with songs of victory and great rushing of their harness, so that they made all the field ring again for joy.

But this marred all. For Cassius thinking indeed that Titinius was taken of the enemies, he then spake these words: 'Desiring too much to live, I have lived to see one of my best friends taken, for my sake, before my face.' After that, he got into a tent where nobody was, and took Pindarus with him, one of his freed bondmen, whom he reserved ever for such a pinch, since the cursed battle of the Parthians where Crassus was slain, though he notwithstanding scaped from that overthrow. But then casting his cloak over his head and holding out his bare neck unto Pindarus, he gave him his head to be stricken off. So the head was found severed from the body. But after that time Pindarus was never seen more. Whereupon some took occasion to say that he had slain his master without his commandment.

By and by they knew the horsemen that came towards them, and might see Titinius crowned with a garland of triumph, who came before with great speed unto Cassius. But when he perceived, by the cries and tears of his friends which tormented themselves, the misfortune that had chanced to his captain Cassius by mistaking, he drew out his sword, cursing himself a thousand times that he had tarried so long, and so slew himself presently in the field. Brutus in the meantime came forward still, and understood also that Cassius had been overthrown. But he knew nothing of his death, till he came very near to his camp. So when he was come thither, after he had lamented the death of Cassius, calling him the last of all the Romans, being unpossible that Rome should ever breed again so noble and valiant a man as he, he caused his body to be buried and sent it to the city of Thasos, fearing lest his funerals within the camp should cause great disorder.

Then he called his soldiers together and did encourage them again. And when he saw that they had lost all their carriage, which they could not brook well, he promised every man of them two thousand drachmas in recompense. After his soldiers had heard his oration, they were all of them prettily cheered again, wondering much at his great liberality, and waited upon him with great cries when he went his way, praising him for that he only of the four chieftains was not overcome in battle. And, to speak the truth, his deeds showed that he hoped not in vain to be conqueror. For with few legions he had slain and driven all them away that made head against him. And yet if all his people had fought, and that the most of them had not out-gone their enemies to run to spoil their goods, surely it was like enough he had slain them all and had left never a man of them alive . . .

The self-same night, it is reported that the monstruous spirit, which had appeared before unto Brutus in the city of Sardis, did now appear again unto him in the self-same shape and form, and so vanished away, and said never a word. Now Publius Volumnius, a grave and wise philosopher, that had been with Brutus from the beginning of this war, he doth make [no] mention of this spirit; but saith that the greatest eagle and ensign was covered over with a swarm of bees, and that there was one of the captains whose arm suddenly fell a-sweating, that it dropped oil of roses from him, and that they oftentimes went about to dry him, but all would do no good. And that, before the battle was fought, there were two eagles fought between both armies, and all the time they fought there was a marvellous great silence all the valley over, both the armies, being one before the other, marking this fight between them; and that in the end the eagle towards Brutus gave over and flew away. But this is certain, and a true tale: that, when the gate of the camp was open, the first man the standard-bearer met that carried the eagle was an Ethiopian, whom the soldiers for ill-luck mangled with their swords.

Now after that Brutus had brought his army into the field and had set them in battle ray, directly against the vaward of his enemy, he paused a long time before he gave the signal of battle. For Brutus riding up and down to view the bands and companies, it came in his head to mistrust some of them, besides that some came to tell him so much as he thought. Moreover, he saw his horsemen set forward but faintly, and did not go lustily to give charge, but still stayed to see what the footmen would do. Then suddenly one of the chiefest knights he had in all his army, called Camulatius [the Celt Camulatus], and that was alway marvellously esteemed of for his valiantness until that time, he came hard by Brutus a-horseback and rode before his face to yield himself unto his enemies. Brutus was marvellous sorry for it, wherefore, partly for anger and partly for fear of greater treason and rebellion, he suddenly caused his army to march, being past three of the clock in the afternoon. So, in that place where he himself fought in person he had the better and brake into the left wing of his enemies, which gave him way, through the help of his horsemen that gave charge with his footmen, when they saw the enemies in a maze and afraid. Howbeit the other also on the right wing, when the captains would have had them to have marched, they were afraid to have been compassed in behind, because they were fewer in number than their enemies; and therefore did spread themselves and leave the midst of their battle. Whereby they having weakened themselves, they could not withstand the force of their enemies, but turned tail straight and fled. And those that had put them to flight came in straight upon it to compass Brutus behind, who in the midst of the conflict did all that was possible for a skilful captain and valiant soldier, both for his wisdom as also for his hardiness, for the obtaining of victory. But that which won him the victory at the first battle did now lose it him at the second. For at the first time the enemies that were broken and fled were straight cut in pieces; but at the second battle, of Cassius' men that were put to flight, there were few slain; and they that saved themselves by speed, being afraid because they had been overcome, did discourage the rest of the army when they came to join with them and filled all the army with fear and disorder.

There was the son of M. Cato slain, valiantly fighting amongst the lusty youths. For, notwithstanding that he was very weary and overharried, yet would he not therefore fly, but manfully fighting and laying about him, telling aloud his name and also his father's name, at length he was beaten down amongst many other dead bodies of his enemies which he had slain round about him. So there were slain in the field all the chiefest gentlemen and nobility that were in his army, who valiantly ran into any danger to save Brutus' life.

Amongst them there was one of Brutus' friends called Lucilius, who seeing a troop of barbarous men making no reckoning of all men else they met in their way, but going all together right against Brutus, he determined to stay them with the hazard of his life, and, being left behind, told them that he was Brutus; and, because they should believe him, he prayed them to bring him to Antonius, for he said he was afraid of Caesar, and that he did trust Antonius better. These barbarous men being very glad of this good hap, and thinking themselves happy men, they carried him in the night, and sent some before unto Antonius to tell him of their coming. He was marvellous glad of it, and went out to meet them that brought him. Others also understanding of it that they had brought Brutus prisoner, they came out of all parts of the camp to see him, some pitying his hard fortune and others saying that it was not done like himself, so cowardly to be taken alive of the barbarous people for fear of death. When they came near together, Antonius stayed awhile bethinking himself how he should use Brutus. In the meantime Lucilius was brought to him, who stoutly with a bold countenance said: 'Antonius, I dare assure thee that no enemy hath taken nor shall take Marcus Brutus alive; and I beseech God keep him from that fortune. For wheresoever he be found, alive or dead, he will be found like himself. And now for myself, I am come unto thee, having deceived these men of arms here, bearing them down that I was Brutus; and do not refuse to suffer any torment thou wilt put me to.' Lucilius' words made them all amazed that heard him. Antonius on the other side, looking upon all them that had brought him, said unto them: 'My companions, I think ye are sorry you have failed of your purpose, and that you think this man hath done you great wrong. But, I do assure you, you have taken a better booty than that you followed. For, instead of an enemy, you have brought me a friend; and for my part, if you had brought me Brutus alive, truly I cannot tell what I should have done to him. For I had rather have such men my friends as this man here, than enemies.' Then he embraced Lucilius and at that time delivered him to one of his friends in custody; and Lucilius ever after served him faithfully, even to his death.

Now Brutus having passed a little river walled in on either side with high rocks and shadowed with great trees, being then dark night he went no further, but stayed at the foot of a rock with certain of his captains and friends that followed him. And looking up to the firmament that was full of stars, sighing, he rehearsed two verses, of the which Volumnius wrote the one, to this effect:

Let not the wight from whom this mischief went,
O Jove, escape without due punishment.

And saith that he had forgotten the other. Within a little while after, naming his friends that he had seen slain in battle before his eyes, he fetched a greater sigh than before; specially when he came to name Labio and Flavius, of the which the one was his lieutenant and the other captain of the pioneers of his camp.

In the meantime, one of the company being a-thirst and seeing Brutus a-thirst also, he ran to the river for water and brought it in his sallet. At the self-same time they heard a noise on the other side of the river. Whereupon Volumnius took Dardanus, Brutus' servant, with him to see what it was; and, returning straight again, asked if there were any water left. Brutus, smiling, gently told them all was drunk; 'but they shall bring you some more'. Thereupon he sent him again that went for water before, who was in great danger of being taken by the enemies, and hardly scaped, being sore hurt. Furthermore, Brutus thought that there was no great number of men slain in battle; and, to know the truth of it, there was one called Statilius that promised to go through his enemies, for otherwise it was impossible to go see their camp, and from thence, if all were well, that he would lift up a torch-light in the air, and then return again with speed to him. The torch-light was lift up as he had promised, for Statilius went thither. Now Brutus seeing Statilius tarry long after that, and that he came not again, he said: 'If Statilius be alive, he will come again.' But his evil fortune was such that as he came back he lighted in his enemies' hands and was slain.

Now, the night being far spent, Brutus as he sat bowed towards Clitus, one of his men, and told him somewhat in his ear, the other answered him not, but fell a-weeping. Thereupon he proved Dardanus, and said somewhat also to him. At length he came to Volumnius himself, and, speaking to him in Greek, prayed him, for the study's sake which brought them acquainted together, that he would help him to put his hand to his sword, to thrust it in him to kill him. Volumnius denied his request, and so did many others. And, amongst the rest, one of them said, there was no tarrying for them there, but that they must needs fly. Then Brutus rising up: 'We must fly indeed', said he, 'but it must be with our hands not with our feet.' Then, taking every man by the hand, he said these words unto them with a cheerful countenance: 'It rejoiceth my heart that not one of my friends hath failed me at my need, and I do not complain of my fortune, but only for my country's sake. For, as for me, I think myself happier than they that have overcome, considering that I leave a perpetual fame of our courage and manhood, the which our enemies the conquerors shall never attain unto by force nor money, neither can let their posterity to say that they, being naughty and unjust men, have slain good men, to usurp tyrannical power not pertaining to them.'

Having said so, he prayed every man to shift for themselves. And then he went a little aside with two or three only, among the which Strato was one, with whom he came first acquainted by the study of rhetoric. He came as near to him as he could, and, taking his sword by the hilts with both his hands and falling down upon the point of it, ran himself through. Others say that not he, but Strato, at his request, held the sword in his hand, and turned his head aside, and that Brutus fell down upon it; and so ran himself through, and died presently.

Messala, that had been Brutus' great friend, became afterwards Octavius Caesar's friend. So, shortly after, Caesar being at good leisure, he brought Strato, Brutus' friend, unto him and weeping said: 'Caesar, behold, here is he that did the last service to my Brutus.' Caesar welcomed him at that time, and afterwards he did him as faithful service in all his affairs as any Grecian else he had about him, until the battle of Actium. It is reported also that this Messala himself answered Caesar one day, when he gave him great praise before his face that he had fought valiantly and with great affection for him at the battle of Actium (notwithstanding that he had been his cruel enemy before, at the battle of Philippes, for Brutus' sake): 'I ever loved', said he, 'to take the best and justest part.'

Now, Antonius having found Brutus' body, he caused it to be wrapped up in one of the richest coat-armours he had. Afterwards also, Antonius understanding that this coat-armour was stolen, he put the thief to death that had stolen it, and sent the ashes of his body unto Servilia his mother. And for Porcia, Brutus' wife, Nicolaus the philosopher and Valerius Maximus do write that she, determining to kill herself (her parents and friends carefully looking to her to keep her from it), took hot burning coals and cast them into her mouth, and kept her mouth so close that she choked herself. There was a letter of Brutus found written to his friends, complaining of their negligence, that, his wife being sick, they would not help her but suffered her to kill herself, choosing to die rather than to languish in pain. Thus it appeareth that Nicolaus knew not well that time, sith the letter (at the least if it were Brutus' letter) doth plainly declare the disease and love of this lady and also the manner of her death.

READING LIST

This list contains some of the more important books referred to in the Introduction, together with a few additional items of interest, and may serve as a guide for those who wish to undertake further study of the play.

Bayley, John. *Shakespeare and Tragedy*, 1981
Blits, Jan H. *The End of the Ancient Republic: Essays on 'Julius Caesar'*, 1982
Bonjour, Adrien. *The Structure of 'Julius Caesar'*, 1958
Brooke, Nicholas. *Shakespeare's Early Tragedies*, 1968
Brown, John Russell. *Shakespeare's Dramatic Style*, 1970
Cantor, Paul A. *Shakespeare's Rome: Republic and Empire*, 1976
Charlton, H. B. *Shakespearian Tragedy*, 1948
Charney, Maurice. *Shakespeare's Roman Plays: The Function of Imagery in the Drama*, 1961
Danson, Lawrence. *Tragic Alphabet: Shakespeare's Drama of Language*, 1974
Evans, Bertrand. *Shakespeare's Tragic Practice*, 1979
Granville-Barker, Harley. 'Julius Caesar' in his *Prefaces to Shakespeare*, 1928
Honigmann, E. A. J. *Shakespeare: Seven Tragedies*, 1976
Knight, G. Wilson. *The Imperial Theme: Further Interpretations of Shakespeare's Tragedies Including the Roman Plays*, 1931
Knights, L. C. *Further Explorations*, 1965
MacCallum, M. W. *Shakespeare's Roman Plays and their Background*, 1910
Maxwell, J. C. 'Shakespeare's Roman plays: 1900–1956', *S.Sur.* 10 (1957), 1–11
Mehl, Dieter. *Shakespeare's Tragedies: An Introduction*, 1986
Miola, Robert S. *Shakespeare's Rome*, 1983
Nevo, Ruth. *Tragic Form in Shakespeare*, 1972
Palmer, John. *Political Characters of Shakespeare*, 1945
Phillips, James Emerson, Jr. *The State in Shakespeare's Greek and Roman Plays*, 1940
Proser, Matthew N. *The Heroic Image in Five Shakespearean Tragedies*, 1965
Rabkin, Norman. *Shakespeare and the Common Understanding*, 1967
Schanzer, Ernest. *The Problem Plays of Shakespeare*, 1963
Shackford, Martha Hale. *Plutarch in Renaissance England*, 1929
Simmons, J. L. *Shakespeare's Pagan World: The Roman Tragedies*, 1974
Spencer, T. J. B. 'Shakespeare and the Elizabethan Romans', *S.Sur.* 10 (1957), 27–38
Stewart, J. I. M. *Character and Motive in Shakespeare*, 1949
Stirling, Brents. *The Populace in Shakespeare*, 1949
Taylor, Gary. *Moment by Moment by Shakespeare*, 1985
Traversi, Derek. *Shakespeare: The Roman Plays*, 1963
Velz, John W. *Shakespeare and the Classical Tradition*, 1968
'Clemency, will, and just cause in "Julius Caesar"', *S.Sur.* 22 (1969), 109–18
Walker, Roy. 'The northern star: an essay on the Roman plays', *SQ* 2 (1951), 287–93
Whitaker, Virgil K. *The Mirror up to Nature: The Technique of Shakespeare's Tragedies*, 1965
Wilson, Harold S. *On the Design of Shakespearian Tragedy*, 1957

REGENTS RESTORATION DRAMA SERIES

General Editor: John Loftis

THE WAY OF THE WORLD

WILLIAM CONGREVE

The Way of the World

Edited by

Kathleen M. Lynch

UNIVERSITY OF NEBRASKA PRESS
LINCOLN • LONDON

Library of Congress Catalog Card Number: 65–10543
International Standard Book Number 0–8032–0354–3
International Standard Book Number 0–8032–5354–0 pbk

First Bison Book Printing November 1965
Most recent printing shown by first digit below:

10

MANUFACTURED IN THE UNITED STATES OF AMERICA

Regents Restoration Drama Series

The Regents Restoration Drama Series, similar in objectives and format to the Regents Renaissance Drama Series, will provide soundly edited texts, in modern spelling, of the more significant English plays of the late seventeenth and early eighteenth centuries. The word "Restoration" is here used ambiguously and must be explained. If to the historian it refers to the period between 1660 and 1685 (or 1688), it has long been used by the student of drama in default of a more precise word to refer to plays belonging to the dramatic tradition established in the 1660's, weakening after 1700, and displaced in the 1730's. It is in this extended sense—imprecise though justified by academic custom—that the word is used in this series, which will include plays first produced between 1660 and 1737. Although these limiting dates are determined by political events, the return of Charles II (and the removal of prohibitions against the operation of theaters) and the passage of Walpole's Stage Licensing Act, they enclose a period of dramatic history having a coherence of its own in the establishment, development, and disintegration of a tradition.

Each text in the series is based on a fresh collation of the seventeenth- and eighteenth-century editions that might be presumed to have authority. The textual notes, which appear above the rule at the bottom of each page, record all substantive departures from the edition used as the copy-text. Variant substantive readings among contemporary editions are listed there as well. Editions later than the eighteenth century are referred to in the textual notes only when an emendation originating in some one of them is received into the text. Variants of accidentals (spelling, punctuation, capitalization) are not recorded in the notes. Contracted forms of characters' names are silently expanded in speech prefixes and stage directions, and, in the case of speech prefixes, are regularized. Additions to the stage directions of the copy-text are enclosed in brackets. Stage directions such as "within" or "aside" are enclosed in parentheses when they occur in the copy-text.

Spelling has been modernized along consciously conservative lines, but within the limits of a modernized text the linguistic quality of the original has been carefully preserved. Punctuation has been brought into accord with modern practices. The objective has been to achieve a balance between the generally light pointing of the old editions, and a system of punctuation which, without overloading the text with exclamation marks, semicolons, and dashes, will make the often loosely flowing verse and prose of the original syntactically intelligible to the modern reader. Dashes are regularly used only to indicate interrupted speeches, or shifts of address within a single speech.

Explanatory notes, chiefly concerned with glossing obsolete words and phrases, are printed below the textual notes at the bottom of each page. References to stage directions in the notes follow the admirable system of the Revels editions, whereby stage directions are keyed, decimally, to the line of the text before or after which they occur. Thus, a note on 0.2 has reference to the second line of the stage direction at the beginning of the scene in question. A note on 115.1 has reference to the first line of the stage direction following line 115 of the text of the relevant scene. Speech prefixes, and any stage directions attached to them, are keyed to the first line of accompanying dialogue.

JOHN LOFTIS

Stanford University

Contents

Introduction

The present edition of *The Way of the World* is based on the first quarto (Q1), published in 1700. The second quarto (Q2), published in 1706, was set from the first quarto and does not substantially differ from it. There are some minor improvements, as well as minor errors, in spelling and punctuation in Q2; but in Q2 the regularizing of Mincing's illiterate language must be deplored, and phrases which are by no means redundant are carelessly omitted. In the 1710 edition of Congreve's collected works (W1) the text of *The Way of the World* was set from Q2, repeats its omissions and some of its unjustified changes, and corrects certain errors. In W1 new scenes are indicated within the acts for the first time, following the French convention, at the entrance or exit of characters. The textual notes of the present edition give variants from Q1 which appear in Q2 and in W1.

The Way of the World was somewhat coolly received when it was first acted at Lincoln's Inn Fields Theatre, probably in the first week of March, 1700. Dryden wrote to Mrs. Steward on March 12: "Congreve's new play has had but moderate success, though it deserves much better."[1] On the same day Lady Marow wrote to an acquaintance in the country that "Congreve's new play doth not answer expectation, there being no plot in it but many witty things to ridicule the Chocolate House, and the fantastical part of the world."[2] Downes attributed the fact that the play "had not the success the company expected" to the fact that it was "too keen a satire."[3] Congreve himself acknowledged in his *Dedication* that he had scarcely expected the play to succeed, "for but little of it was prepared for that general taste which seems now to be predominant in the palates of an audience." He resolved to "commit his quiet and his fame

[1] John Dryden, *Letters*, ed. Charles E. Ward (Durham, North Carolina, 1942), p. 134.

[2] Historical MSS. Commission, *Dartmouth*, III, 145.

[3] John Downes, *Roscius Anglicanus*, ed. Montague Summers (London, n.d.), p. 45.

no more to the caprices of an audience"[4] and retired from the stage at the early age of thirty. Had Dryden not died in May of that year, it is possible that, as Congreve's "true lover," he might have dissuaded his brilliant disciple from so drastic a decision.

For its première *The Way of the World* had an excellent cast. Anne Bracegirdle, for whom, as for his other heroines, Congreve had created the role of leading lady, "performing her part so exactly and just, gained the applause of court and city."[5] She presumably again played Millamant (although the cast is not known) in the 1705 revival of the play. Cibber recorded that when she acted Millamant "all the faults, follies, and affectations of that agreeable tyrant were venially melted down into so many charms and attractions of a conscious beauty."[6] Mrs. Bracegirdle was well matched with John Verbruggen as Mirabell. When the pair acted in Aphra Behn's *The Rover*, audiences were enchanted by his "untaught airs" and her "smiling repartees" and "were afraid they were going off the stage every moment."[7] Thomas Betterton, nearing retirement, must have played Fainall with the flamboyant vigor which always distinguished his acting. The original cast included Elizabeth Barry as Marwood, effectively drawling out her words, William Bowen, "an actor of spirit," as Witwoud, and Cave Underhill, who had been D'Avenant's best comedian, as corpulent and awkward Sir Wilfull.

The Way of the World was only sporadically revived for some years and continued to be surpassed in popularity by two of Congreve's other plays, *The Old Bachelor* and *Love for Love*. Slowly, however, "the most intellectually accomplished of English comedies" gained an honorable place in the repertories of the London theaters. Such able actresses as Anne Oldfield, Christiana Horton, Hannah Pritchard, Peg Woffington, and Frances Abington graced the role of Millamant and often chose *The Way of the World* for their benefit performances. Robert Wilks, debonair and genteel, excelled as Mirabell, Colley Cibber as Witwoud, Richard Yates as Sir Wilfull. After 1777 none of Congreve's plays held the stage with success, and

[4] Samuel Johnson, *Lives of the English Poets*, ed. George Birkbeck Hill (Oxford, 1905), II, 224.

[5] Downes, p. 45.

[6] Colley Cibber, *An Apology for the Life of Mr. Colley Cibber*, ed. Robert W. Lowe (London, 1889), I, 173.

[7] [John Genest], *Some Account of the English Stage* (Bath, 1833), II, 380–381.

their performance became infrequent.[8] Two of the plays, *Love for Love* and *The Way of the World,* have fared better in the twentieth century than for many years previously, with notable revivals in both England and America. In the late autumn of 1924 *The Way of the World* had its longest run—one hundred and twenty performances—at the Cherry Lane Theater in New York.

In varying aspects Congreve's drama is always richly reminiscent of earlier drama. In *The Way of the World* the influence of Elizabethan tradition is considerably more diluted than in *Love for Love,* and the influence of Molière is less marked than in *The Double Dealer.* Although certain specific borrowings are made from both sources, *The Way of the World* remains essentially the superlative expression of the courtly mode initiated in pre-Restoration court drama and sustained and enhanced by Congreve's precursors in Restoration comedy.

In a subplot which has important bearings on the main action, *The Way of the World* revives a phase of the intrigue in Ben Jonson's *The Devil is an Ass* (1616). Fitzdottrel and Fainall both treat their wives unfairly and are disposed to desert them for other women. Both wives have lovers who champion their interests and who reduce the husbands to a state of financial dependence on these abused mates. In Jonson's comedy Wittipol secures Fitzdottrel's estate for Frances by causing the unsuspecting Fitzdottrel to convey it in trust to Manly, Wittipol's good friend. In *The Way of the World* Mrs. Fainall had the foresight to give her estate in trust to Mirabell before her marriage with Fainall. Toward the close of each play the husband is suddenly informed of the financial authority with which the signing of the deed has invested his wife, and the wife's security in this matter brings about the husband's surrender and effects a *modus vivendi* for all parties. The Elizabethan influence is also conspicuous in the portrait of Sir Wilfull Witwoud, the boorish country rustic, representing a type that throughout the Restoration period continued to offset the elegance of the city gallant.

In a general way certain characters and certain scenes in *The Way of the World* owe a debt to Molière. The role of Waitwell resembles

[8] For an illuminating account of the stage history thus briefly outlined see Emmett L. Avery, *Congreve's Plays on the Eighteenth-Century Stage* (New York, 1951).

that of Mascarille in *Les Précieuses Ridicules*, although Waitwell's courtship of Lady Wishfort is much more condensed than Mascarille's similar exploit. Lady Wishfort's pert maid Foible is in the tradition of Molière's saucy soubrettes, and there is a parallel between the relations of lumpish Peg and her mistress and those of Andrée and the Countess in *La Comtesse d'Escarbagnas*.

Comparisons are often made between *The Way of the World* and *Le Misanthrope*, in which masterpiece Molière is more preoccupied than elsewhere with the tyranny of fashionable society and offers no remedy for its encroachments. Célimène and Millamant have no equals in all the arts of coquetry. In the quarrels of Millamant and Marwood and Célimène and Arsinoé the two younger women deprecate with similar irony their unassailable advantages of youthful charm. It is true that in *Le Misanthrope* Molière permits "the way of the world" to pose a more serious threat to sensible living than in any of his other plays. Yet Célimène, heartless at twenty, seems likely to remain so; Alceste's indignant strictures against the beau monde cannot be laughed away; and the compliant and urbane Philinte cuts a rather sorry figure.

Common sense, so violated in *Le Misanthrope*, remains Molière's comic standard of judgment. By its terms he defines folly and gives wisdom its due. He exposes folly and wishes, whenever possible, to cure it; whereas Congreve, also exposing folly, has not the slightest corrective intention. Congreve's laughter at fools is good-natured; he enjoys them. They are ridiculous because they play the social game unintelligently or extravagantly. They mean well and are usually harmless people in a world where good taste, rather than good sense, is the mark of a disciplined life. With Molière all affectation is folly. Congreve reserves a milder laughter for the intelligent, sensitive, but still affected gentlemen and ladies who constitute his ideal of social excellence, who play the social game with perfect dexterity, with complete grace, but at the expense of their humanity. For the art of being civilized is, after all, a delicious fiction, an amazing make-believe, denying those normal human emotions which sooner or later must intrude and must be reckoned with. Like the Restoration dramatists who preceded him and unlike Molière, Congreve limited his world to an artificial society, the vagaries of which he pretty thoroughly explored.

Declining to adapt himself to the sentimental vogue in comedy which Colley Cibber was popularizing, Congreve chose to follow the literary conventions which had been initiated at the court of Charles I and which, in brighter patterns, had delighted the court of Charles II. The *précieuse* code of etiquette, introduced from France to please the French tastes of Queen Henrietta Maria, had for many years determined the basic requirements of English comedies of manners.[9]

By the rules of that code, briefly stated, a courtship which finally terminates in marriage must be hampered by the hero's lingering relations with other women, which may not be abruptly and rudely broken off. Thus in *The Way of the World* Mirabell must divert Lady Wishfort with the amorous attentions of Sir Rowland, thwart Marwood's jealous scheming, and reconcile the Fainalls before he can win the hand of Millamant. Mirabell's good taste, as he achieves these objectives, is opposed by the extravagant bad taste of Witwoud and Petulant, the rustic gaucherie of Sir Wilfull, and the ill-bred widow-wooing of Waitwell, the servant masquerading as courtier.

Such false wits as Witwoud and Petulant are familiar figures in Restoration comedy. Like Cutter and Worm in Cowley's *The Cutter of Coleman Street* (1661) they are "detracting fops," each disparaging his friend in a burst of confidence to a third party. Cutter privately assures Lucia that Worm is "a good ingenious fellow, that's the truth on't, and a pleasant droll when h'as got a cup o' wine in his pate" but is not to be trusted in serious matters. In a similar confession, Worm explains to Lucia that Cutter is an unreliable fellow, only "he has some wit (to give the devil his due) and that 'tis makes us endure him." In the same spirit, Witwoud confides to Mirabell that Petulant has "a pretty deal of an odd sort of a small wit . . . and if he had but any judgment in the world, he would not be altogether contemptible." And Petulant pays Witwoud back in his own coin by describing him to Mirabell as "soft, you know . . . he's what you call a—what-d'ye-call-'em, a fine gentleman, but he's silly withal." In spite of mutual reservations, Witwoud and Petulant enjoy a congenial camaraderie. They conform to a literary tradition which prescribes their agility in witty raillery.

Mrs. Fainall, loyal to Mirabell, is the least conventional of the "other" women in Mirabell's life. Mrs. Marwood is doomed to failure in her attempts to reclaim a young lover, like Loveit in Etherege's *The Man of Mode* (1676), numerous affected older women

[9] For a detailed study of the influence of the *précieuse* code see the present editor's *The Social Mode of Restoration Comedy* (New York, 1926).

in the comedies of Thomas Shadwell, and Congreve's own Lady Touchwood in *The Double Dealer*. Lady Wishfort is the old coquette par excellence. Her name and tastes recall Loveit in *The Man of Mode* and Lady Loveyouth in Shadwell's *The Humourists* (1670). Shadwell had created a whole gallery of such portraits. When Lady Wishfort represses her fastidiousness and encourages the grotesque wooing of Sir Rowland, her behavior resembles Beliza's treatment of the vulgar Bernado in Shadwell's *The Amorous Bigot* (1690). Lady Wishfort's pride in the refined education of her daughter, who, however, sadly shames her, parallels Lady Fantast's satisfaction in her ridiculous training of a similar daughter in Shadwell's *Bury Fair* (1689). But Lady Wishfort's characterization is more rounded than that of persons resembling her in earlier comedy. With his usual good humor and perceptiveness, Congreve softens her conventional follies.

In the courtship scenes of *The Way of the World* Congreve followed well-established conventions for railing lovers. Mirabell and Millamant had been presaged by Benedick and Beatrice in Shakespeare's *Much Ado about Nothing* (1599), by Fairfield and Carol in Shirley's *Hyde Park* (1632), and by various lesser lights in Jacobean comedies. Sex duels, often culminating in "proviso" scenes, had long been popular with Restoration dramatists.

The formal proviso scene, in which two lovers frame an argument, item by item, safeguarding with legal precision the freedom of each, had been invented by Honoré D'Urfé in his celebrated codebook of *précieuse* gallantry, *L'Astrée* (1607–1627). D'Urfé's Hylas and Stelle draw up, in the presence of witnesses, a proviso contract insuring their mutual rights of inconstancy. They agree to banish jealousy, respect each other's liberty of speech and action, and abolish in their discourse all terms of endearment. Struck by the comic possibilities of such ostensibly reluctant love-making, Dryden incorporated lively proviso contracts in four of his comedies, *The Wild Gallant* (1663), *Secret Love, or The Maiden Queen* (1667), *Marriage à la Mode* (1672), and *Amphitryon* (1690). Celadon and Florimel in *Secret Love* are so fearful of conjugal boredom that they agree to be married by the "agreeable names" of mistress and gallant, since "the names of husband and wife hold forth nothing, but clashing and cloying, and dullness and faintness in their signification." Proviso scenes took a more farcical turn in James Howard's *All Mistaken, or The Mad Couple* (1667) and Edward Ravenscroft's *The Careless Lovers* (1673) and *The Canterbury Guests* (1694).

In the famous proviso contract of Mirabell and Millamant in the fourth act of *The Way of the World*, Congreve preserved many details of the earlier proviso scenes. Millamant insures her "dear liberty" in carefully detailed provisos. Like Melantha in *Marriage à la Mode* she requests: "Let us never visit together, nor go to a play together." Like Isabelle in *The Wild Gallant*, she describes most of her articles as mere "trifles." She does not, like Florimel, threaten inconstancy, although she insists on the privilege of paying and receiving visits at her pleasure and of writing and receiving letters "without interrogatories or wry faces" on Mirabell's part. Terms of conjugal affection she condemns as emphatically as Celadon and Florimel. She declares that she abhors such names as "wife, spouse, my dear, joy, jewel, love, sweetheart, and the rest of that nauseous cant, in which men and their wives are so fulsomely familiar." Mirabell, like Isabelle's lover, finds her first terms reasonable enough but her later "bill of fare" somewhat alarming.

Mirabell's own provisos, although fairly original, are expressed with all the formality displayed in corresponding scenes in *Secret Love* and in *Amphitryon*. The conventional *imprimis* or *item* introduces each of his articles. In conclusion he concedes: "These provisos admitted, in other things I may prove a tractable and complying husband." With due ceremony he begs leave to kiss Millamant's hand upon the contract. At this moment Mrs. Fainall enters, and Mirabell claims her, as Hillaria in *The Careless Lovers* had claimed her uncle, as a witness to the sealing of the deed. To the end Millamant remains in control of the situation. Quite appropriately she departs from established custom in having her own very characteristic last word:

> Well, you ridiculous thing you, I'll have you—I won't be kissed, nor I won't be thanked—here, kiss my hand though.—So, hold your tongue now, and don't say a word.

Congreve had borrowed much, but he improved on what he had borrowed. He achieved the finest of all the proviso scenes in Restoration comedy. The prose of that scene has a poetic luminosity; and the graceful evasiveness of the lovers, sustained with the proper touch of well-bred nonchalance, yields with equal grace to their desired capitulation.

To Jeremy Collier's contemporary invectives against the "immorality and profaneness" of Restoration comedy Congreve somewhat frivolously replied in his *Amendments of Mr. Collier's False and Imperfect Citations* (1698). Collier's attacks seem not to have affected Congreve's literary reputation in that circle of famous men of letters to which he belonged and in which he was highly esteemed. Among his contemporaries perhaps only a few Puritan critics and Congreve himself took exception to Dryden's claim that Heaven had endowed Shakespeare and Congreve equally.[10]

Pope considered Congreve "one of the most valuable men, as well as finest writers of my age and century."[11] Addison ranked "harmonious Congreve"[12] as Dryden's successor. Steele considered that Congreve excelled in "every way of writing."[13] He devoted a whole *Spectator* paper[14] to condemning the corrupt morals of Etherege in *The Man of Mode*, but seems never to have thought of Congreve as belonging to Etherege's school. Dennis, who attacked in venomous fashion most of the men of letters of the day, expressed only unbounded admiration for Congreve. Dennis observed aptly, "most persons" thought, that Congreve "left the stage early, and comedy has quitted it with him."[15]

Nevertheless, the taste of theatergoers had changed, and sophisticated comedy of manners was increasingly subjected to charges of heartlessness and immorality. It is not surprising that Samuel Johnson, the great moral arbiter of his age, felt compelled to decree, as he summed up Congreve's achievement, that "the general tenour and tendency of his plays must always be condemned. It is acknowledged with universal conviction that the perusal of his works will make no man better; and that their ultimate effect is to represent pleasure in alliance with vice, and to relax those obligations by which life ought to be regulated."[16] Yet even Johnson reflected: "Among all the efforts of early genius which literary history records, I doubt whether any one can be produced that more surpasses the common limits of nature than the plays of Congreve."[17] And "one

[10] See Dryden's verses prefixed to *The Double Dealer* (London, 1694).

[11] *The Iliad of Homer Translated by Alexander Pope, Esq.* (London, 1750), Vol. VI, Dedication.

[12] Joseph Addison, *Works* (London, 1721), I, 40.

[13] See Steele's Commendatory Verses "To Mr. Congreve, occasioned by his Comedy called *The Way of the World*."

[14] *The Spectator*, No. 65.

[15] [Giles Jacob], *The Poetical Register* (London, 1719), p. 46.

[16] Johnson, *Lives*, II, 222.

[17] *Ibid.*, p. 219

of the best" of Johnson's "little *Lives*" concludes with the tribute: "While comedy or while tragedy is regarded Congreve's plays are likely to be read."[18]

The romantic critics of the nineteenth century took a cautious delight in Restoration comedy, which they found curiously remote from the life of their own era. Lamb chose to envisage the world of Restoration society as released from all laws of time and space, "a speculative scene of things, which has no reference whatever to the world that is," a fairy country "beyond the diocese of the strict conscience."[19] Hazlitt was more aware of the historical importance of dramatists who commemorated "a gala day of wit and pleasure,"[20] among whom he regarded Congreve as by far the wittiest and most elegant. Leigh Hunt urged that intelligent comprehension of the manners of an earlier period should stimulate, rather than dismay, all minds "candidly and healthily trained."[21]

Victorian moral earnestness supplanted this more gracious approach to Restoration comedy. Macaulay eloquently disparaged the "exceedingly bad" morality of a beau monde that he found "a great deal too real" in "everything ridiculous and degrading."[22] George Meredith, in the very act of assailing the unlovely English propensity for moralistic judgments, heartily decried the "so-called comedy of manners" as "comedy of the manners of South-sea islanders under city veneer; and, as to comic idea, vacuous as the mask without the face behind it."[23] *The Way of the World*, indeed, Meredith praised as an exceptional achievement, refusing to recognize that play as a very perfect example of the mode which he condemned.

In the twentieth century there has been a vigorous revival of interest in Restoration comedy. Critics have taken a fresh look at the Restoration tradition, and Congreve has had his rightful share in that reappraisal. In his admirable and definitive biography,

18 *Ibid.*, p. 234.

19 Charles Lamb, *Works*, ed. E. V. Lucas (London, 1903–1905), IV, 142–143.

20 William Hazlitt, *Works*, ed. A. R. Waller and Arnold Glover (London, 1902–1904), VIII, 70.

21 *The Dramatic Works of Wycherley, Congreve, Vanbrugh, and Farquhar*, ed. Leigh Hunt (London and New York, 1866), Preface, p. lxiii.

22 Thomas Babington Macaulay, *Critical and Historical Essays*, ed. F. C. Montague (London, 1903), III, 11–12.

23 George Meredith, *An Essay on Comedy and the Uses of the Comic Spirit*, ed. Lane Cooper (New York, Chicago, Boston [1918]), p. 83.

William Congreve, the Man (1941), John Hodges demolished Gosse's dull image of Congreve as a man who went through life "as if in felt slippers"[24] and Voltaire's distorted image of Congreve as an elegant trifler. No longer encumbered by moral blinkers, a fair number of modern scholars have dedicated themselves to the rewarding task, initiated by John Palmer, of exploring "a mood of the human spirit which is in every age, though in this particular age it was more conspicuous."[25] Foremost among these scholars has been the humane and gifted English critic Bonamy Dobrée, whose essays on Restoration comedy have been distinguished by a brilliance of style worthy of the subject.

Congreve's plots have been the despair of his admirers, and the plot of *The Way of the World* is no exception. In fact, the ramifications of the intrigues in *The Way of the World* are considerably more difficult to follow than those in *Love for Love* and only a little less confusing than those in *The Double Dealer*. The salient facts of the predicaments that must be resolved in *The Way of the World* are dropped allusively, almost casually, here and there; and when the play is read, a hawk's eye is required to detect them and keep them in order. The close family relationships of the characters and their developing schemes are not easily remembered; and when all threads have been untangled, it appears that nothing is really concluded. It is unlikely that the Fainalls will cease wrangling. Lady Wishfort will continue to hanker for a young lover. Mirabell and Millamant are apprehensive that the constancy for which they long may not be realized.

There is some justice in the complaint that *The Way of the World* is "a series of still-life pictures." Of physical action the play offers only occasional outbursts. Mrs. Marwood turns from Fainall with the threat: "Break my hands, do! I'd leave 'em to get loose." Millamant is on one occasion so "nettled" that she tears her fan. Sir Wilfull, noisily and joyously drunk, shatters throughout a single scene the decorous atmosphere of the drawing room. Lady Wishfort paces the stage in a furious passion and faints with calculated vehemence. But the usual tone of the play is "a harmony of agreeable voices." Despite these handicaps *The Way of the World* acts well.[26] Agreeable voices

[24] Edmund Gosse, *Life of William Congreve* (London, 1888), p. 175.

[25] John Palmer, *The Comedy of Manners* (London, 1913), p. 293.

[26] The present editor has had a share in sponsoring three highly successful undergraduate revivals at Mount Holyoke College.

have never been more enchanting, and the gestures that emphasize those flawless cadences make up in precision for what they lack in force.

Toward the end of his life, Congreve remarked that he refrained from "wondering at the world's new wicked ways," and added

> Believe it, men have ever been the same,
> And all the Golden Age is but a dream.[27]

It is ironic that so tolerant an observer of the persistent follies of humanity should have been accused of having created "nothing but a set of heartless fine ladies and gentlemen, coming in and out, saying witty things at each other, and buzzing in some maze of intrigue."[28] Congreve's characters are rounded portraits. The numerous fools have very human qualities, and the thoughtful few have a warmth of feeling which is inconvenient in the beau monde in which they live.

Witwoud and Petulant are eagerly complaisant fops who when united make "one man." Although each delights in using the other as a target for raillery, they "agree in the main, like treble and bass." To "smoke" Sir Wilfull, and especially to "smoke" his boots, gives them a double pleasure because it is a pleasure shared.

Sir Wilfull cannot adorn a London drawing room, but he speaks some homely truths there. In his native Shropshire his hearty manners must have commended him to his friends "round the Wrekin." Baffled by the conventions of polite society, he enjoys, "when a little in disguise," a brief, refreshing respite from its exactions. He is too good-natured to resent Millamant's snubs, offers himself as Mirabell's "fellow traveler," makes a contract with his cousin to help his aunt, and breaks it to make the young lovers happy.

Painted in darker colors, Fainall and Mrs. Marwood are less convincing characters. Mrs. Marwood's bitterness and Fainall's angry resentment seem out of place in an artificial milieu, and the punishment of the two sinners can scarcely be taken seriously. Mrs. Fainall, on the contrary, if only sketched, is one of Congreve's most sympathetic characters. If she had had less stamina, she might have been wrecked by her bad education and hateful marriage; but she

27 *The Mourning Bride, Poems & Miscellanies by William Congreve*, ed. Bonamy Dobrée, World's Classics (Oxford and London [1928]), "Letter, to Viscount Cobham," p. 402.

28 Leigh Hunt in *The Dramatic Works of Wycherley*, etc., Preface, p. xxx.

remains unembittered, quietly dignified, and a faithful friend to her former lover.

Lady Wishfort is a full-length portrait of the old coquette. We observe her various moods: her spirited encounters with her maids; her indulgence of her nephew; her languishing reception of Sir Rowland; her romantic friendship with Mrs. Marwood; her selfish affection for her daughter; and her plaintive surrender of Mirabell, who "rakes the embers" of a smothered fire in her breast. The contradictions in Lady Wishfort's character are the secret of her extraordinary vitality. Congreve endowed her with a gift of shrewd, cutting irony and a keen sense of humor, which extends to a perception of her own decayed charms, her "arrant ash-color" complexion and her painted face, cracked "like an old peeled wall." "Female frailty!" comments Mrs. Fainall, "we must all come to it, if we live to be old."

Millamant is Congreve's greatest triumph. Her lover, "sententious" Mirabell, is a paler figure than Etherege's Dorimant; but Millamant is the wisest, wittiest, most mature of Restoration coquettes. Other characters in Restoration comedy, even Etherege's Dorimant, have elusive personalities. Although it is apparent that many of these people have warm hearts and generous sympathies, the social mask conceals their best impulses. But through all her subterfuges we know intimately the real Millamant, or at least we boldly fancy so.

Millamant's personality is not exhibited solely through sparkling rejoinders, inspired, from moment to moment, by the wit of her associates. She has a gift for interpreting a situation as a whole and molds her caprices to suit the temper of the occasion. She has an advantage over Mirabell in being able to laugh at his "love-sick face" and mild admonitions, and she gaily exposes the weak spots in his lover's self-conceit. She begs of him in merry concern: "Ha! ha! ha! What would you give that you could help loving me?" And poor Mirabell can only reply: "I would give something that you did not know I could not help it."

Millamant has reflected about marriage. To marry is to relinquish not just one's "dear liberty" but one's separate and individual self. It is to stake all for love—for a love the continuance of which would be a miracle. Where in the circle of her acquaintance has she seen a lasting love? Yet it is in vain that she demurs. Although she maintains her wit and coquetry to the end, her tender, generous, and whole-hearted love for Mirabell is never really obscured in her gay and graceful evasions. She confesses to Mrs. Fainall: "Well, if Mirabell should not make a good husband, I am a lost thing."

Congreve's characters are best revealed in the vivacity of their language. Even the fools contribute to the conquest of dullness. It has been objected that the false wits "are permitted to stumble on too many brilliants."[29] Witwoud's head would be empty if it were not well stocked with similitudes. He is almost breathless in his haste to get them out and is never in better form than when others consent to play the similitude game with him. His flow of similitudes suits his character, as Petulant's snappishness suits his. Lady Wishfort's "boudoir Billingsgate" is a superb invention. Even the servants have their special accents. Foible sweetens impudence with flattery, and Mincing struggles to be genteel.

Millamant's whimsical manner of speech is always unmistakably hers and hers alone. Her very flippancies are charged with meaning. It is plain that her excessive gaiety is forced. She talks very fast and is afraid of pauses, fearful lest the realities of love may somehow rudely intrude upon the pretty decorum of the beau monde. In those inarticulate silences, charged with warmth and color, that check now and again the flashing current of her raillery, Millamant seems wistfully pleading with Mirabell to accept her love without the shame of a confession and to permit her to remain in appearance imperious, brilliant, heartless, the finest of fine ladies.

There has always been unanimity of opinion regarding Congreve's style and particularly regarding its excellence in *The Way of the World*. Hazlitt considered that Congreve attained "the highest model of comic dialogue" and that "there is a peculiar flavour in his very words, which is to be found in hardly any other writer."[30] Dobrée has noted that the melody occasionally heard in *The Double Dealer* and more often in *Love for Love* is pervasive in *The Way of the World*. In Congreve's last comedy a way of life is recorded in matchless prose, with never a false note to mar the interpretation.

KATHLEEN M. LYNCH

Funchal, Madeira

[29] George Henry Nettleton, *English Drama of the Restoration and Eighteenth Century* (New York, 1914), p. 130.

[30] Hazlitt, *Works*, VIII, 71.

Bibliography

Twentieth-Century Studies

AVERY, EMMETT L. *Congreve's Plays on the Eighteenth-Century Stage.* New York, 1951.

DOBRÉE, BONAMY. *Restoration Comedy, 1660–1720.* Oxford, 1924.

FUJIMURA, THOMAS H. *Restoration Comedy of Wit.* Princeton, 1952.

GOSSE, EDMUND. *Life of William Congreve.* London, 1924.

HODGES, JOHN C. *William Congreve, the Man.* New York, 1941.

———, ed. *William Congreve: Letters and Documents.* New York, 1964.

HOLLAND, NORMAN N. *The First Modern Comedies.* Cambridge, Mass., 1959.

KRUTCH, JOSEPH WOOD. *Comedy and Conscience after the Restoration.* New York, 1949.

LOFTIS, JOHN. *Comedy and Society from Congreve to Fielding.* Stanford, 1959.

LYNCH, KATHLEEN M. *The Social Mode of Restoration Comedy.* New York, 1926.

———. *A Congreve Gallery.* Cambridge, Mass., 1951.

MUESCHKE, PAUL and MIRIAM. *A New View of Congreve's Way of the World.* Ann Arbor, Mich., 1958.

NICOLL, ALLARDYCE. *A History of Restoration Drama, 1660–1700.* Fourth edn. Cambridge, 1952.

PALMER, JOHN. *The Comedy of Manners.* London, 1913.

———. *Comedy.* London [1914].

PERRY, HENRY TEN EYCK. *The Comic Spirit in Restoration Drama.* New Haven, 1925.

SMITH, JOHN HARRINGTON. *The Gay Couple in Restoration Comedy.* Cambridge, Mass., 1948.

TAYLOR, D. CRANE. *William Congreve.* London, 1931.

THE WAY OF THE WORLD

COMMENDATORY VERSES

To Mr. Congreve, occasioned by his Comedy called "The Way of the World."

When pleasure's falling to the low delight,
In the vain joys of the uncertain sight;
No sense of wit when rude spectators know,
But in distorted gesture, farce and show;
How could, great author, your aspiring mind
Dare to write only to the few refined?
Yet though that nice ambition you pursue,
'Tis not in Congreve's power to please but few.
Implicitly devoted to his fame,
Well-dressed barbarians know his awful name;
Though senseless they're of mirth, but when they laugh,
As they feel wine, but when, till drunk, they quaff.
  On you from fate a lavish portion fell
In every way of writing to excel.
Your muse applause to Arabella brings,
In notes as sweet as Arabella sings.
Whene'er you draw an undissembled woe,
With sweet distress your rural numbers flow;
Pastora's the complaint of every swain,
Pastora still the echo of the plain!
Or if your muse describe, with warming force,
The wounded Frenchman falling from his horse;
And her own William glorious in the strife,
Bestowing on the prostrate foe his life;
You the great act as generously rehearse,
And all the English fury's in your verse.
By your selected scenes and handsome choice,
Ennobled Comedy exalts her voice;

0.1. These verses first appeared in W1.

---

15. *Arabella*] a reference to Congreve's *Ode on Mrs. Arabella Hunt, Singing.*
19. *Pastora*] a reference to Congreve's *The Mourning Muse of Alexis*, in which, under the name of Pastora, Congreve laments the death of Queen Mary.
23. *William*] William III, eulogized by Congreve in *Pindarique Ode to the King, On His taking Namur.*

You check unjust esteem and fond desire,
And teach to scorn what else we should admire;
The just impression taught by you we bear,
The player acts the world, the world the player,
Whom still that world unjustly disesteems,
Though he alone professes what he seems.
But when your muse assumes her tragic part,
She conquers and she reigns in every heart;
To mourn with her men cheat their private woe,
And generous pity's all the grief they know.
The widow, who, impatient of delay,
From the town joys must mask it to the play,
Joins with your Mourning Bride's resistless moan,
And weeps a loss she slighted, when her own;
You give us torment, and you give us ease,
And vary our afflictions as you please,
Is not a heart so kind as yours in pain,
To load your friends with cares you only feign;
Your friends in grief, composed yourself, to leave?
But 'tis the only way you'll e'er deceive.
Then still, great sir, your moving power employ,
To lull our sorrow, and correct our joy.

R. STEELE

41. *Mourning Bride*] Congreve's sole tragedy, *The Mourning Bride* (1697).
51. *R. Steele*] Sir Richard Steele (1672–1729), essayist and dramatist.

TO THE RIGHT HONORABLE RALPH, EARL OF MONTAGUE, &c.

My Lord,

Whether the world will arraign me of vanity or not, that I have presumed to dedicate this comedy to your Lordship, I am yet in doubt, though it may be it is some degree of vanity even to doubt of it. One who has at any time had the honor of your Lordship's conversation, cannot be supposed to think very meanly of that which he would prefer to your perusal; yet it were to incur the imputation of too much sufficiency, to pretend to such a merit as might abide the test of your Lordship's censure.

Whatever value may be wanting to this play while yet it is mine, will be sufficiently made up to it when it is once become your Lordship's; and it is my security that I cannot have overrated it more by my dedication than your Lordship will dignify it by your patronage.

That it succeeded on the stage was almost beyond my expectation; for but little of it was prepared for that general taste which seems now to be predominant in the palates of our audience.

Those characters which are meant to be ridiculous in most of our comedies are of fools so gross that, in my humble opinion, they should rather disturb than divert the well-natured and reflecting part of an audience; they are rather objects of charity than contempt; and instead of moving our mirth, they ought very often to excite our compassion.

This reflection moved me to design some characters which should appear ridiculous, not so much through a natural folly (which is incorrigible, and therefore not proper for the stage) as through an affected wit; a wit, which, at the same time that it is affected, is also false. As there is some difficulty in the formation of a character of this nature, so

20. ridiculous] *Q1;* ridiculed *Q2, W1.*

0.1. *Ralph, Earl of Montague*] Ralph Montagu (1638?–1709), created Earl of Montagu in 1689 and Duke of Montagu in 1705.

7. *prefer*] offer.

there is some hazard which attends the progress of its success upon the stage; for many come to a play so over-charged with criticism that they very often let fly their censure, when through their rashness they have mistaken their aim. This I had occasion lately to observe; for this play had been acted two or three days before some of these hasty judges could find the leisure to distinguish betwixt the character of a Witwoud and a Truewit.

I must beg your Lordship's pardon for this digression from the true course of this epistle; but that it may not seem altogether impertinent, I beg that I may plead the occasion of it, in part of that excuse of which I stand in need, for recommending this comedy to your protection. It is only by the countenance of your Lordship, and the *few* so qualified, that such who write with care and pains can hope to be distinguished; for the prostituted name of *poet* promiscuously levels all that bear it.

Terence, the most correct writer in the world, had a Scipio and a Laelius, if not to assist him, at least to support him in his reputation; and notwithstanding his extraordinary merit, it may be their countenance was not more than necessary.

The purity of his style, the delicacy of his turns, and the justness of his characters were all of them beauties which the greater part of his audience were incapable of tasting; some of the coarsest strokes of Plautus, so severely censured by Horace, were more likely to affect the multitude, such who come with expectation to laugh out the last act of a play, and are better entertained with two or three unseasonable jests than with the artful solution of the *fable*.

As Terence excelled in his performances, so had he great advantages to encourage his undertakings, for he built most on the foundations of Menander; his plots were generally

---

39. *a Witwoud and a Truewit*] the would-be wit, Witwoud, in *The Way of the World* and the genuinely witty Truewit in Jonson's *Epicoene; or The Silent Woman* (1609).

49–50. *a Scipio and a Laelius*] Scipio Africanus and Caius Laelius, patrons of the Roman comic dramatist Terence.

61. *fable*] plot. 64. *Menander*] Greek writer of New Comedy.

modeled, and his characters ready drawn to his hand. He copied Menander, and Menander had no less light in the formation of his characters from the observations of Theophrastus, of whom he was a disciple; and Theophrastus, it is known, was not only the disciple, but the immediate successor of Aristotle, the first and greatest judge of poetry. These were great models to design by; and the further advantage which Terence possessed, towards giving his plays the due ornaments of purity of style and justness of manners, was not less considerable from the freedom of conversation which was permitted him with Laelius and Scipio, two of the greatest and most polite men of his age. And indeed the privilege of such a conversation is the only certain means of attaining to the perfection of dialogue.

If it has happened in any part of this comedy that I have gained a turn of style or expression more correct, or at least more corrigible, than in those which I have formerly written, I must, with equal pride and gratitude, ascribe it to the honor of your Lordship's admitting me into your conversation, and that of a society where everybody else was so well worthy of you, in your retirement last summer from the town; for it was immediately after that this comedy was written. If I have failed in my performance, it is only to be regretted, where there were so many not inferior either to a Scipio or a Laelius, that there should be one wanting equal to the capacity of a Terence.

If I am not mistaken, poetry is almost the only art which has not yet laid claim to your Lordship's patronage. Architecture and painting, to the great honor of our country, have flourished under your influence and protection. In the meantime, poetry, the eldest sister of all arts, and parent of most, seems to have resigned her birthright, by having neglected to pay her duty to your Lordship, and by permitting others of a later extraction to prepossess that place in your esteem to which none can pretend a better title. Poetry,

90. to the capacity of] *Q1;* in capacity to *W1.*

67–68. *Theophrastus*] Greek author, whose *Characters* had a marked influence on the "character writing" of the seventeenth century.

in its nature, is sacred to the good and great; the relation between them is reciprocal, and they are ever propitious to it. It is the privilege of poetry to address to them, and it is their prerogative alone to give it protection.

This received maxim is a general apology for all writers who consecrate their labors to great men; but I could wish at this time that this address were exempted from the common pretense of all dedications; and that, as I can distinguish your Lordship even among the most deserving, so this offering might become remarkable by some particular instance of respect, which should assure your Lordship that I am, with all due sense of your extreme worthiness and humanity,

My Lord,
Your Lordship's most obedient
and most obliged humble servant
WILL. CONGREVE

PROLOGUE

Spoken by Mr. Betterton

Of those few fools, who with ill stars are cursed,
Sure scribbling fools, called poets, fare the worst;
For they're a sort of fools which Fortune makes,
And after she has made 'em fools, forsakes.
With Nature's oafs 'tis quite a different case,
For Fortune favors all her idiot race;
In her own nest the cuckoo eggs we find,
O'er which she broods to hatch the changeling kind.
No portion for her own she has to spare,
So much she dotes on her adopted care.
  Poets are bubbles, by the town drawn in,
Suffered at first some trifling stakes to win;
But what unequal hazards do they run!
Each time they write they venture all they've won;
The squire that's buttered still is sure to be undone.
This author, heretofore, has found your favor,
But pleads no merit from his past behavior.
To build on that might prove a vain presumption,
Should grants to poets made admit resumption;
And in Parnassus he must lose his seat
If that be found a forfeited estate.
  He owns, with toil he wrote the following scenes,
But if they're naught ne'er spare him for his pains.
Damn him the more; have no commiseration
For dullness on mature deliberation.
He swears he'll not resent one hissed-off scene,
Nor, like those peevish wits, his play maintain,
Who, to assert their sense, your taste arraign.
Some plot we think he has, and some new thought,
Some humor too, no farce—but that's a fault.
Satire, he thinks, you ought not to expect;

---

5. *Nature's oafs*] Nature's stupid children.

7. *cuckoo eggs*] referring to the habit of cuckoos of laying eggs in the nests of other birds.

11. *bubbles*] dupes. 15. *buttered*] flattered.

For so reformed a town who dares correct?
To please this time has been his sole pretense;
He'll not instruct, lest it should give offense.
Should he by chance a knave or fool expose
That hurts none here; sure here are none of those.
In short, our play shall (with your leave to show it)
Give you one instance of a passive poet,
Who to your judgments yields all resignation;
So save or damn, after your own discretion.

DRAMATIS PERSONAE

Men

Character	Actor
FAINALL, in love with MRS. MARWOOD	*Mr. Betterton*
MIRABELL, in love with MRS. MILLAMANT	*Mr. Verbruggen*
WITWOUD, } Followers of MRS. MILLAMANT	*Mr. Bowen*
PETULANT, } Followers of MRS. MILLAMANT	*Mr. Bowman*
SIR WILFULL WITWOUD, Half-brother to WITWOUD, and Nephew to LADY WISHFORT	*Mr. Underhill*
WAITWELL, Servant to MIRABELL	*Mr. Bright*

Women

Character	Actor
LADY WISHFORT, Enemy to MIRABELL, for having falsely pretended love to her	*Mrs. Leigh*
MRS. MILLAMANT, A fine Lady, Niece to LADY WISHFORT, and loves MIRABELL	*Mrs. Bracegirdle*
MRS. MARWOOD, Friend to MR. FAINALL, and likes MIRABELL	*Mrs. Barry*
MRS. FAINALL, Daughter to LADY WISHFORT, and Wife to FAINALL, formerly Friend to MIRABELL	*Mrs. Bowman*
FOIBLE, Woman to LADY WISHFORT	*Mrs. Willis*
MINCING, Woman to MRS. MILLAMANT	*Mrs. Prince*

Dancers, Footmen, and Attendants

SCENE—LONDON

The time equal to that of the presentation.

The Way of the World
A Comedy

[I] *A Chocolate-house.*

Mirabell *and* Fainall, *rising from cards;* Betty *waiting.*

MIRABELL.

You are a fortunate man, Mr. Fainall.

FAINALL.

Have we done?

MIRABELL.

What you please. I'll play on to entertain you.

FAINALL.

No, I'll give you your revenge another time, when you are not so indifferent; you are thinking of something else now, and play too negligently. The coldness of a losing gamester lessens the pleasure of the winner. I'd no more play with a man that slighted his ill fortune than I'd make love to a woman who undervalued the loss of her reputation.

MIRABELL.

You have a taste extremely delicate and are for refining on your pleasures.

FAINALL.

Prithee, why so reserved? Something has put you out of humor.

MIRABELL.

Not at all; I happen to be grave today, and you are gay; that's all.

FAINALL.

Confess, Millamant and you quarreled last night, after I left you; my fair cousin has some humors that would tempt

17. *humors*] moods.

the patience of a stoic. What, some coxcomb came in, and was well received by her, while you were by.

MIRABELL.

Witwoud and Petulant, and what was worse, her aunt, your wife's mother, my evil genius; or to sum up all in her own name, my old Lady Wishfort came in.

FAINALL.

Oh, there it is then! She has a lasting passion for you, and with reason. What, then my wife was there?

MIRABELL.

Yes, and Mrs. Marwood and three or four more, whom I never saw before. Seeing me, they all put on their grave faces, whispered one another; then complained aloud of the vapors, and after fell into a profound silence.

FAINALL.

They had a mind to be rid of you.

MIRABELL.

For which reason I resolved not to stir. At last the good old lady broke through her painful taciturnity, with an invective against long visits. I would not have understood her, but Millamant joining in the argument, I rose and with a constrained smile told her, I thought nothing was so easy as to know when a visit began to be troublesome. She reddened and I withdrew, without expecting her reply.

FAINALL.

You were to blame to resent what she spoke only in compliance with her aunt.

MIRABELL.

She is more mistress of herself than to be under the necessity of such a resignation.

FAINALL.

What? though half her fortune depends upon her marrying with my lady's approbation?

MIRABELL.

I was then in such a humor, that I should have been better pleased if she had been less discreet.

---

28. *vapors*] a fashionable disorder indicating a depressed nervous condition.

FAINALL.

Now I remember, I wonder not they were weary of you. Last night was one of their cabal-nights; they have 'em three times a week, and meet by turns, at one another's apartments, where they come together like the coroner's inquest, to sit upon the murdered reputations of the week. You and I are excluded; and it was once proposed that all the male sex should be excepted; but somebody moved that, to avoid scandal, there might be one man of the community; upon which motion Witwoud and Petulant were enrolled members.

MIRABELL.

And who may have been the foundress of this sect? My Lady Wishfort, I warrant, who publishes her detestation of mankind, and full of the vigor of fifty-five, declares for a friend and ratafia; and let posterity shift for itself, she'll breed no more.

FAINALL.

The discovery of your sham addresses to her, to conceal your love to her niece, has provoked this separation. Had you dissembled better, things might have continued in the state of nature.

MIRABELL.

I did as much as man could, with any reasonable conscience. I proceeded to the very last act of flattery with her, and was guilty of a song in her commendation. Nay, I got a friend to put her into a lampoon, and compliment her with the imputation of an affair with a young fellow, which I carried so far, that I told her the malicious town took notice that she was grown fat of a sudden; and when she lay in of a dropsy, persuaded her she was reported to be in labor. The devil's in't, if an old woman is to be flattered further, unless a man should endeavor downright personally to debauch her; and that my virtue forbade me. But for the discovery of that amour, I am indebted to your friend, or your wife's friend, Mrs. Marwood.

75. that amour] *Q1;* this amour *Q2, W1.*

46. *cabal-nights*] private evening parties of a small group of intriguers.
58. *ratafia*] a cordial flavored with certain fruits.

FAINALL.

What should provoke her to be your enemy, unless she has made you advances, which you have slighted? Women do not easily forgive omissions of that nature.

MIRABELL.

She was always civil to me, till of late. I confess I am not one of those coxcombs who are apt to interpret a woman's good manners to her prejudice, and think that she who does not refuse 'em everything can refuse 'em nothing.

FAINALL.

You are a gallant man, Mirabell; and though you may have cruelty enough not to satisfy a lady's longing, you have too much generosity not to be tender of her honor. Yet you speak with an indifference which seems to be affected, and confesses you are conscious of a negligence.

MIRABELL.

You pursue the argument with a distrust that seems to be unaffected, and confesses you are conscious of a concern for which the lady is more indebted to you than your wife.

FAINALL.

Fie, fie, friend! If you grow censorious, I must leave you. I'll look upon the gamesters in the next room.

MIRABELL.

Who are they?

FAINALL.

Petulant and Witwoud. [*To Betty.*] Bring me some chocolate. *Exit.*

MIRABELL.

Betty, what says your clock?

BETTY.

Turned of the last canonical hour, sir. *Exit.*

MIRABELL.

How pertinently the jade answers me! (*Looking on his watch.*) Ha? almost one o'clock! Oh, y'are come!

77. unless] *W1*; without *Q1–2*.

99. answers me] *Q1, W1;* answers we *Q2*.

98. *last canonical hour*] twelve o'clock (noon). At this date the canonical hours, when marriages might be legally performed, were from eight to twelve in the morning.

Enter a Servant.

Well, is the grand affair over? You have been something tedious.

SERVANT.

Sir, there's such coupling at Pancras, that they stand behind one another, as 'twere in a country dance. Ours was the last couple to lead up; and no hopes appearing of dispatch, besides the parson growing hoarse, we were afraid his lungs would have failed before it came to our turn; so we drove round to Duke's Place, and there they were riveted in a trice.

MIRABELL.

So, so, you are sure they are married.

SERVANT.

Married and bedded, sir; I am witness.

MIRABELL.

Have you the certificate?

SERVANT.

Here it is, sir.

MIRABELL.

Has the tailor brought Waitwell's clothes home, and the new liveries?

SERVANT.

Yes, sir.

MIRABELL.

That's well. Do you go home again, d'ye hear, and adjourn the consummation till farther order; bid Waitwell shake his ears, and Dame Partlet rustle up her feathers, and meet me at one o'clock by Rosamond's Pond, that I may see her before

117. d'ye hear] *Q2, W1;* d'ee *Q1. The* d'ye *of Q2 and W1 has been followed throughout the text.*

---

103. *Pancras*] St. Pancras Church, where couples might marry without licenses.

108. *Duke's Place*] St. James' Church in Aldgate, where marriages, sometimes referred to as Fleet weddings, could also be performed without licenses.

119. *Partlet*] Pertelote, wife of Chauntecleer in Chaucer's *The Nun's Priest's Tale.*

120. *Rosamond's Pond*] a little lake in the southwest corner of St. James's Park, around which Charles II planted groves, a resort of lovers.

she returns to her lady; and as you tender your ears, be secret.

Exit Servant.

Re-enter Fainall [*and* Betty].

FAINALL.

Joy of your success, Mirabell; you look pleased.

MIRABELL.

Aye, I have been engaged in a matter of some sort of mirth, which is not yet ripe for discovery. I am glad this is not a cabal-night. I wonder, Fainall, that you who are married, and of consequence should be discreet, will suffer your wife to be of such a party.

FAINALL.

Faith, I am not jealous. Besides, most who are engaged are women and relations; and for the men, they are of a kind too contemptible to give scandal.

MIRABELL.

I am of another opinion. The greater the coxcomb, always the more scandal; for a woman who is not a fool can have but one reason for associating with a man that is.

FAINALL.

Are you jealous as often as you see Witwoud entertained by Millamant?

MIRABELL.

Of her understanding I am, if not of her person.

FAINALL.

You do her wrong; for, to give her her due, she has wit.

MIRABELL.

She has beauty enough to make any man think so, and complaisance enough not to contradict him who shall tell her so.

FAINALL.

For a passionate lover, methinks you are a man somewhat too discerning in the failings of your mistress.

MIRABELL.

And for a discerning man, somewhat too passionate a lover; for I like her with all her faults; nay, like her for her faults. Her follies are so natural, or so artful, that they become her;

121. *tender*] have regard for.

and those affectations which in another woman would be odious, serve but to make her more agreeable. I'll tell thee, Fainall, she once used me with that insolence, that in revenge I took her to pieces; sifted her and separated her failings; I studied 'em, and got 'em by rote. The catalogue was so large that I was not without hopes one day or other to hate her heartily: to which end I so used myself to think of 'em that at length, contrary to my design and expectation, they gave me every hour less and less disturbance; till in a few days it became habitual to me to remember 'em without being displeased. They are now grown as familiar to me as my own frailties; and in all probability, in a little time longer I shall like 'em as well.

FAINALL.

Marry her, marry her! Be half as well acquainted with her charms as you are with her defects, and my life on't, you are your own man again.

MIRABELL.

Say you so?

FAINALL.

Aye, aye, I have experience: I have a wife, and so forth.

Enter Messenger.

MESSENGER.

Is one Squire Witwoud here?

BETTY.

Yes; what's your business?

MESSENGER.

I have a letter for him, from his brother Sir Wilfull, which I am charged to deliver into his own hands.

BETTY.

He's in the next room, friend; that way. *Exit* Messenger.

MIRABELL.

What, is the chief of that noble family in town, Sir Wilfull Witwoud?

FAINALL.

He is expected today. Do you know him?

---

149. *sifted*] examined very closely.
152. *used*] accustomed.

MIRABELL.

I have seen him. He promises to be an extraordinary person; I think you have the honor to be related to him.

FAINALL.

Yes, he is half brother to this Witwoud by a former wife, who was sister to my Lady Wishfort, my wife's mother. If you marry Millamant, you must call cousins too.

MIRABELL.

I had rather be his relation than his acquaintance.

FAINALL.

He comes to town in order to equip himself for travel.

MIRABELL.

For travel! Why the man I mean is above forty.

FAINALL.

No matter for that; 'tis for the honor of England that all Europe should know we have blockheads of all ages.

MIRABELL.

I wonder there is not an act of parliament to save the credit of the nation, and prohibit the exportation of fools.

FAINALL.

By no means; 'tis better as 'tis. 'Tis better to trade with a little loss, than to be quite eaten up with being overstocked.

MIRABELL.

Pray, are the follies of this knight-errant and those of the squire his brother anything related?

FAINALL.

Not at all; Witwoud grows by the knight, like a medlar grafted on a crab. One will melt in your mouth, and t'other set your teeth on edge; one is all pulp, and the other all core.

MIRABELL.

So one will be rotten before he be ripe, and the other will be rotten without ever being ripe at all.

FAINALL.

Sir Wilfull is an odd mixture of bashfulness and obstinacy.

189–190. *a medlar grafted on a crab*] a soft pulpy fruit grafted on a crab-apple.

But when he's drunk, he's as loving as the monster in *The Tempest*, and much after the same manner. To give t'other his due, he has something of good nature and does not always want wit.

MIRABELL.

Not always; but as often as his memory fails him, and his commonplace of comparisons. He is a fool with a good memory and some few scraps of other folks' wit. He is one whose conversation can never be approved, yet it is now and then to be endured. He has indeed one good quality, he is not exceptious; for he so passionately affects the reputation of understanding raillery, that he will construe an affront into a jest, and call downright rudeness and ill language satire and fire.

FAINALL.

If you have a mind to finish his picture, you have an opportunity to do it at full length. Behold the original!

Enter Witwoud.

WITWOUD.

Afford me your compassion, my dears! Pity me, Fainall! Mirabell, pity me!

MIRABELL.

I do from my soul.

FAINALL.

Why, what's the matter?

WITWOUD.

No letters for me, Betty?

BETTY.

Did not the messenger bring you one but now, sir?

196. t'other] *W1;* the t'other *Q1.*

215. the messenger] *Q1;* a messenger *W1.*

195–196. *the monster in The Tempest*] In Dryden and D'Avenant's *The Tempest* (1667), Trincalo says of Caliban: "The poor monster is loving in his drink." In the same play Sycorax, Caliban's sister, is also a loving monster, but without the incentive of wine.

198. *want*] lack.

200. *commonplace of comparisons*] commonplace, or memorandum, book in which he records clever remarks which he has heard or read.

204. *is not exceptious*] does not contradict.

WITWOUD.

Aye, but no other?

BETTY.

No, sir.

WITWOUD.

That's hard, that's very hard. A messenger, a mule, a beast of burden! He has brought me a letter from the fool my brother, as heavy as a panegyric in a funeral sermon, or a copy of commendatory verses from one poet to another. And what's worse, 'tis as sure a forerunner of the author as an epistle dedicatory.

MIRABELL.

A fool, and your brother Witwoud!

WITWOUD.

Aye, aye, my half brother. My half brother he is, no nearer upon honor.

MIRABELL.

Then 'tis possible he may be but half a fool.

WITWOUD.

Good, good, Mirabell, *le drôle!* Good, good; hang him, don't let's talk of him. Fainall, how does your lady? Gad, I say anything in the world to get this fellow out of my head. I beg pardon that I should ask a man of pleasure, and the town, a question at once so foreign and domestic. But I talk like an old maid at a marriage, I don't know what I say; but she's the best woman in the world.

FAINALL.

'Tis well you don't know what you say, or else your commendation would go near to make me either vain or jealous.

WITWOUD.

No man in town lives well with a wife but Fainall. Your judgment, Mirabell.

MIRABELL.

You had better step and ask his wife, if you would be credibly informed.

WITWOUD.

Mirabell.

---

228. *le drôle*] the amusing fellow.

MIRABELL.

Aye.

WITWOUD.

My dear, I ask ten thousand pardons. Gad, I have forgot what I was going to say to you!

MIRABELL.

I thank you heartily, heartily.

WITWOUD.

No, but prithee excuse me: my memory is such a memory.

MIRABELL.

Have a care of such apologies, Witwoud; for I never knew a fool but he affected to complain, either of the spleen or his memory.

FAINALL.

What have you done with Petulant?

WITWOUD.

He's reckoning his money, my money it was. I have no luck today.

FAINALL.

You may allow him to win of you at play, for you are sure to be too hard for him at repartee; since you monopolize the wit that is between you, the fortune must be his of course.

MIRABELL.

I don't find that Petulant confesses the superiority of wit to be your talent, Witwoud.

WITWOUD.

Come, come, you are malicious now, and would breed debates. Petulant's my friend, and a very honest fellow, and a very pretty fellow, and has a smattering—faith and troth, a pretty deal of an odd sort of a small wit: nay, I'll do him justice. I'm his friend, I won't wrong him neither. And if he had but any judgment in the world, he would not be altogether contemptible. Come, come, don't detract from the merits of my friend.

FAINALL.

You don't take your friend to be over-nicely bred?

263. neither] *Q1; omitted in W1.* 264. but] *Q1; omitted in W1.*

249. *spleen*] low spirits believed to result from a diseased condition of that organ.

WITWOUD.

No, no, hang him, the rogue has no manners at all, that I must own. No more breeding than a bum-baily, that I grant you. 'Tis pity, faith; the fellow has fire and life.

MIRABELL.

What, courage?

WITWOUD.

Hum, faith, I don't know as to that, I can't say as to that. Yes, faith, in a controversy he'll contradict anybody.

MIRABELL.

Though 'twere a man whom he feared, or a woman whom he loved.

WITWOUD.

Well, well, he does not always think before he speaks; we have all our failings. You're too hard upon him, you are, faith. Let me excuse him. I can defend most of his faults, except one or two. One he has, that's the truth on't; if he were my brother, I could not acquit him. That, indeed, I could wish were otherwise.

MIRABELL.

Aye, marry, what's that, Witwoud?

WITWOUD.

Oh, pardon me! Expose the infirmities of my friend! No, my dear, excuse me there.

FAINALL.

What, I warrant he's unsincere, or 'tis some such trifle.

WITWOUD.

No, no, what if he be? 'Tis no matter for that, his wit will excuse that. A wit should no more be sincere than a woman constant; one argues a decay of parts, as t'other of beauty.

MIRABELL.

Maybe you think him too positive?

WITWOUD.

No, no, his being positive is an incentive to argument, and keeps up conversation.

---

269. *bum-baily*] a low type of bailiff or sheriff's officer.
288. *parts*] talents.

FAINALL.

Too illiterate?

WITWOUD.

That! that's his happiness; his want of learning gives him the more opportunities to show his natural parts.

MIRABELL.

He wants words?

WITWOUD.

Aye, but I like him for that now; for his want of words gives me the pleasure very often to explain his meaning.

FAINALL.

He's impudent?

WITWOUD.

No, that's not it.

MIRABELL.

Vain?

WITWOUD.

No.

MIRABELL.

What! he speaks unseasonable truths sometimes, because he has not wit enough to invent an evasion?

WITWOUD.

Truths! ha! ha! ha! No, no, since you will have it, I mean he never speaks truth at all, that's all. He will lie like a chambermaid, or a woman of quality's porter. Now that is a fault.

Enter Coachman.

COACHMAN.

Is Master Petulant here, mistress?

BETTY.

Yes.

COACHMAN.

Three gentlewomen in the coach would speak with him.

FAINALL.

Oh brave Petulant! Three!

BETTY.

I'll tell him.

310. the coach] *Q1;* a coach *W1.*

COACHMAN.

You must bring two dishes of chocolate and a glass of cinnamon-water. [*Exeunt* Betty *and* Coachman.]

WITWOUD.

That should be for two fasting strumpets, and a bawd troubled with wind. Now you may know what the three are.

MIRABELL.

You are very free with your friend's acquaintance.

WITWOUD.

Aye, aye, friendship without freedom is as dull as love without enjoyment, or wine without toasting; but to tell you a secret, these are trulls that he allows coach-hire, and something more, by the week, to call on him once a day at public places.

MIRABELL.

How!

WITWOUD.

You shall see he won't go to 'em because there's no more company here to take notice of him. Why, this is nothing to what he used to do: before he found out this way, I have known him call for himself.

FAINALL.

Call for himself? What dost thou mean?

WITWOUD.

Mean! Why, he would slip you out of this chocolate-house, just when you had been talking to him. As soon as your back was turned, whip, he was gone! Then trip to his lodging, clap on a hood and scarf, and mask, slap into a hackney-coach, and drive hither to the door again in a trice, where he would send in for himself; that I mean, call for himself, wait for himself; nay, and what's more, not finding himself, sometimes leave a letter for himself.

MIRABELL.

I confess this is something extraordinary. I believe he waits for himself now, he is so long a-coming. Oh! I ask his pardon.

---

314. *cinnamon-water*] a drink composed of sugar, spirits, powdered cinnamon, and hot water, considered an aid to digestion.

321. *trulls*] prostitutes.

Enter Petulant [*and* Betty].

BETTY.

Sir, the coach stays.

PETULANT.

Well, well; I come. 'Sbud, a man had as good be a professed midwife as a professed whoremaster, at this rate! To be knocked up and raised at all hours, and in all places! Pox on 'em, I won't come! D'ye hear, tell 'em I won't come. Let 'em snivel and cry their hearts out.

FAINALL.

You are very cruel, Petulant.

PETULANT.

All's one, let it pass. I have a humor to be cruel.

MIRABELL.

I hope they are not persons of condition that you use at this rate.

PETULANT.

Condition! Condition's a dried fig, if I am not in humor! By this hand, if they were your—a—a—your what-d'ye-call-'ems themselves, they must wait or rub off, if I want appetite.

MIRABELL.

What-d'ye-call-'ems! What are they, Witwoud?

WITWOUD.

Empresses, my dear; by your what-d'ye-call-'ems he means sultana queens.

PETULANT.

Aye, Roxolanas.

MIRABELL.

Cry you mercy.

FAINALL.

Witwoud says they are—

PETULANT.

What does he say th'are?

---

341. *'Sbud*] a contraction of the oath *God's blood.*

352. *rub off*] clear out.

357. *Roxolanas*] Roxolana is the wife of Solyman the Magnificent in D'Avenant's *The Siege of Rhodes* (Part I, 1656, Part II, 1661).

WITWOUD.

I? Fine ladies, I say.

PETULANT.

Pass on, Witwoud. Harkee, by this light his relations: two co-heiresses his cousins, and an old aunt, that loves caterwauling better than a conventicle.

WITWOUD.

Ha! ha! ha! I had a mind to see how the rogue would come off. Ha! ha! ha! Gad, I can't be angry with him, if he had said they were my mother and my sisters.

MIRABELL.

No!

WITWOUD.

No; the rogue's wit and readiness of invention charm me. Dear Petulant!

BETTY.

They are gone, sir, in great anger.

PETULANT.

Enough, let 'em trundle. Anger helps complexion, saves paint.

FAINALL.

This continence is all dissembled; this is in order to have something to brag of the next time he makes court to Millamant, and swear he has abandoned the whole sex for her sake.

MIRABELL.

Have you not left off your impudent pretensions there yet? I shall cut your throat some time or other, Petulant, about that business.

PETULANT.

Aye, aye, let that pass. There are other throats to be cut.

MIRABELL.

Meaning mine, sir?

PETULANT.

Not I. I mean nobody; I know nothing. But there are uncles and nephews in the world, and they may be rivals. What then? All's one for that.

---

362. *Harkee*] a corruption of *hark ye*.
364. *conventicle*] meetinghouse of a nonconformist sect.
372. *trundle*] roll along.

MIRABELL.

How! Harkee Petulant, come hither. Explain, or I shall call your interpreter.

PETULANT.

Explain! I know nothing. Why, you have an uncle, have you not, lately come to town, and lodges by my Lady Wishfort's?

MIRABELL.

True.

PETULANT.

Why, that's enough. You and he are not friends; and if he should marry and have a child, you may be disinherited, ha?

MIRABELL.

Where hast thou stumbled upon all this truth?

PETULANT.

All's one for that; why, then say I know something.

MIRABELL.

Come, thou art an honest fellow, Petulant, and shalt make love to my mistress, thou sha't, faith. What hast thou heard of my uncle?

PETULANT.

I? Nothing I. If throats are to be cut, let swords clash! Snug's the word; I shrug and am silent.

MIRABELL.

Oh, raillery, raillery! Come, I know thou art in the women's secrets. What, you're a cabalist; I know you stayed at Millamant's last night, after I went. Was there any mention made of my uncle or me? Tell me. If thou hadst but good nature equal to thy wit, Petulant, Tony Witwoud, who is now thy competitor in fame, would show as dim by thee as a dead whiting's eye by a pearl of orient; he would no more be seen by thee than Mercury is by the sun. Come, I'm sure thou wo't tell me.

---

387. *your interpreter*] Witwoud (?).
400. *Snug's the word*] Secrecy's the watchword.
402. *cabalist*] secret intriguer.
408. *by thee*] beside thee.

PETULANT.

If I do, will you grant me common sense then for the future?

MIRABELL.

Faith, I'll do what I can for thee; and I'll pray that Heaven may grant it thee in the meantime.

PETULANT.

Well, harkee. [Mirabell *and* Petulant *talk apart.*]

FAINALL.

Petulant and you both will find Mirabell as warm a rival as a lover.

WITWOUD.

Pshaw! pshaw! That she laughs at Petulant is plain. And for my part, but that it is almost a fashion to admire her, I should—harkee, to tell you a secret, but let it go no further; between friends, I shall never break my heart for her.

FAINALL.

How!

WITWOUD.

She's handsome; but she's a sort of an uncertain woman.

FAINALL.

I thought you had died for her.

WITWOUD.

Umh—no—

FAINALL.

She has wit.

WITWOUD.

'Tis what she will hardly allow anybody else. Now, demme, I should hate that, if she were as handsome as Cleopatra. Mirabell is not so sure of her as he thinks for.

FAINALL.

Why do you think so?

WITWOUD.

We stayed pretty late there last night, and heard something of an uncle to Mirabell, who is lately come to town, and is between him and the best part of his estate. Mirabell and he are at some distance, as my Lady Wishfort has been told;

426. *demme*] damn me.

and you know she hates Mirabell worse than a Quaker hates a parrot, or than a fishmonger hates a hard frost. Whether this uncle has seen Mrs. Millamant or not, I cannot say; but there were items of such a treaty being in embryo, and if it should come to life, poor Mirabell would be in some sort unfortunately fobbed, i'faith.

FAINALL.

'Tis impossible Millamant should hearken to it.

WITWOUD.

Faith, my dear, I can't tell; she's a woman and a kind of a humorist.

MIRABELL.

And is this the sum of what you could collect last night?

PETULANT.

The quintessence. Maybe Witwoud knows more; he stayed longer. Besides, they never mind him; they say anything before him.

MIRABELL.

I thought you had been the greatest favorite.

PETULANT.

Aye, *tête à tête*, but not in public, because I make remarks.

MIRABELL.

You do?

PETULANT.

Aye, aye, pox, I'm malicious, man! Now he's soft, you know, they are not in awe of him. The fellow's well-bred, he's what you call a—what-d'ye-call-'em, a fine gentleman, but he's silly withal.

MIRABELL.

I thank you. I know as much as my curiosity requires. Fainall, are you for the Mall?

448. *tête à tête*] *Spelled tete a tete W1; teste a teste Q1–2.*

434–435. *worse than a Quaker hates a parrot*] i.e., because the parrot is so talkative.

435. *or than a fishmonger hates a hard frost*] i.e., because cold weather makes his work difficult.

439. *fobbed*] tricked. 442. *humorist*] one given to whims.

455. *the Mall*] a fashionable promenade adjoining St. James's Park, now the street known as Pall Mall.

FAINALL.
Aye, I'll take a turn before dinner.

WITWOUD.
Aye, we'll all walk in the park; the ladies talked of being there.

MIRABELL.
I thought you were obliged to watch for your brother Sir Wilfull's arrival.

WITWOUD.
No, no, he comes to his aunt's, my Lady Wishfort. Pox on him! I shall be troubled with him too; what shall I do with the fool?

PETULANT.
Beg him for his estate, that I may beg you afterwards; and so have but one trouble with you both.

WITWOUD.
Oh, rare Petulant! Thou art as quick as a fire in a frosty morning; thou shalt to the Mall with us, and we'll be very severe.

PETULANT.
Enough, I'm in a humor to be severe.

MIRABELL.
Are you? Pray then walk by yourselves. Let not us be accessory to your putting the ladies out of countenance with your senseless ribaldry, which you roar out aloud as often as they pass by you; and when you have made a handsome woman blush, then you think you have been severe.

PETULANT.
What, what? Then let 'em show their innocence by not understanding what they hear, or else show their discretion by not hearing what they would not be thought to understand.

MIRABELL.
But hast not thou then sense enough to know that thou ought'st to be most ashamed thyself, when thou hast put another out of countenance?

PETULANT.
Not I, by this hand! I always take blushing either for a sign of guilt or ill-breeding.

MIRABELL.

I confess you ought to think so. You are in the right, that you may plead the error of your judgment in defense of your practice.

Where modesty's ill manners, 'tis but fit
That impudence and malice pass for wit. *Exeunt.*

[II]

St. James's Park.

Enter Mrs. Fainall *and* Mrs. Marwood.

MRS. FAINALL.

Aye, aye, dear Marwood, if we will be happy, we must find the means in ourselves, and among ourselves. Men are ever in extremes, either doting or averse. While they are lovers, if they have fire and sense, their jealousies are insupportable. And when they cease to love (we ought to think at least) they loathe; they look upon us with horror and distaste; they meet us like the ghosts of what we were, and as such, fly from us.

MRS. MARWOOD.

True, 'tis an unhappy circumstance of life, that love should ever die before us; and that the man so often should outlive the lover. But say what you will, 'tis better to be left than never to have been loved. To pass our youth in dull indifference, to refuse the sweets of life because they once must leave us, is as preposterous as to wish to have been born old, because we one day must be old. For my part, my youth may wear and waste, but it shall never rust in my possession.

MRS. FAINALL.

Then it seems you dissemble an aversion to mankind, only in compliance with my mother's humor.

MRS. MARWOOD.

Certainly. To be free, I have no taste of those insipid dry discourses with which our sex of force must entertain themselves, apart from men. We may affect endearments to each other, profess eternal friendships, and seem to dote like

18. compliance with] *Q1;* compliance to *W1.*

---

19. *free*] frank.

lovers; but 'tis not in our natures long to persevere. Love will resume his empire in our breasts; and every heart, or soon or late, receive and readmit him as its lawful tyrant.

MRS. FAINALL.

Bless me, how have I been deceived! Why you profess a libertine!

MRS. MARWOOD.

You see my friendship by my freedom. Come, be as sincere, acknowledge that your sentiments agree with mine.

MRS. FAINALL.

Never!

MRS. MARWOOD.

You hate mankind?

MRS. FAINALL.

Heartily, inveterately.

MRS. MARWOOD.

Your husband?

MRS. FAINALL.

Most transcendently; aye, though I say it, meritoriously.

MRS. MARWOOD.

Give me your hand upon it.

MRS. FAINALL.

There.

MRS. MARWOOD.

I join with you; what I have said has been to try you.

MRS. FAINALL.

Is it possible? Dost thou hate those vipers, men?

MRS. MARWOOD.

I have done hating 'em, and am now come to despise 'em; the next thing I have to do, is eternally to forget 'em.

MRS. FAINALL.

There spoke the spirit of an Amazon, a Penthesilea.

MRS. MARWOOD.

And yet I am thinking sometimes to carry my aversion further.

---

34. *transcendently*] supremely.

41. *Penthesilea*] famous Queen of the Amazons, a race of female warriors.

MRS. FAINALL.
How?

MRS. MARWOOD.
Faith, by marrying; if I could but find one that loved me very well and would be thoroughly sensible of ill usage, I think I should do myself the violence of undergoing the ceremony.

MRS. FAINALL.
You would not make him a cuckold?

MRS. MARWOOD.
No, but I'd make him believe I did, and that's as bad.

MRS. FAINALL.
Why had not you as good do it?

MRS. MARWOOD.
Oh, if he should ever discover it, he would then know the worst, and be out of his pain; but I would have him ever to continue upon the rack of fear and jealousy.

MRS. FAINALL.
Ingenious mischief! Would thou wert married to Mirabell.

MRS. MARWOOD.
Would I were!

MRS. FAINALL.
You change color.

MRS. MARWOOD.
Because I hate him.

MRS. FAINALL.
So do I; but I can hear him named. But what reason have you to hate him in particular?

MRS. MARWOOD.
I never loved him; he is, and always was, insufferably proud.

MRS. FAINALL.
By the reason you give for your aversion, one would think it dissembled; for you have laid a fault to his charge of which his enemies must acquit him.

MRS. MARWOOD.
Oh, then it seems you are one of his favorable enemies! Methinks you look a little pale, and now you flush again.

MRS. FAINALL.
Do I? I think I am a little sick o' the sudden.

MRS. MARWOOD.

What ails you?

MRS. FAINALL.

My husband. Don't you see him? He turned short upon me unawares, and has almost overcome me.

Enter Fainall *and* Mirabell.

MRS. MARWOOD.

Ha! ha! ha! He comes opportunely for you.

MRS. FAINALL.

For you, for he has brought Mirabell with him.

FAINALL.

My dear!

MRS. FAINALL.

My soul!

FAINALL.

You don't look well today, child.

MRS. FAINALL.

D'ye think so?

MIRABELL.

He is the only man that does, madam.

MRS. FAINALL.

The only man that would tell me so at least; and the only man from whom I could hear it without mortification.

FAINALL.

Oh my dear, I am satisfied of your tenderness; I know you cannot resent anything from me, especially what is an effect of my concern.

MRS. FAINALL.

Mr. Mirabell, my mother interrupted you in a pleasant relation last night; I would fain hear it out.

MIRABELL.

The persons concerned in that affair have yet a tolerable reputation. I am afraid Mr. Fainall will be censorious.

MRS. FAINALL.

He has a humor more prevailing than his curiosity, and will willingly dispense with the hearing of one scandalous story, to avoid giving an occasion to make another by being seen to walk with his wife. This way, Mr. Mirabell, and I dare promise you will oblige us both.

Exeunt Mrs. Fainall *and* Mirabell.

FAINALL.
Excellent creature! Well, sure if I should live to be rid of my wife, I should be a miserable man.

MRS. MARWOOD.
Aye!

FAINALL.
For having only that one hope, the accomplishment of it, of consequence must put an end to all my hopes; and what a wretch is he who must survive his hopes! Nothing remains when that day comes, but to sit down and weep like Alexander, when he wanted other worlds to conquer.

MRS. MARWOOD.
Will you not follow 'em?

FAINALL.
Faith, I think not.

MRS. MARWOOD.
Pray let us; I have a reason.

FAINALL.
You are not jealous?

MRS. MARWOOD.
Of whom?

FAINALL.
Of Mirabell.

MRS. MARWOOD.
If I am, is it inconsistent with my love to you that I am tender of your honor?

FAINALL.
You would intimate then, as if there were a fellow-feeling between my wife and him.

MRS. MARWOOD.
I think she does not hate him to that degree she would be thought.

FAINALL.
But he, I fear, is too insensible.

MRS. MARWOOD.
It may be you are deceived.

99–100. *Alexander*] Alexander the Great, King of Macedon.

FAINALL.

It may be so. I do now begin to apprehend it.

MRS. MARWOOD.

What?

FAINALL.

That I have been deceived, madam, and you are false.

MRS. MARWOOD.

That I am false! What mean you?

FAINALL.

To let you know I see through all your little arts. Come, you both love him; and both have equally dissembled your aversion. Your mutual jealousies of one another have made you clash till you have both struck fire. I have seen the warm confession reddening on your cheeks, and sparkling from your eyes.

MRS. MARWOOD.

You do me wrong.

FAINALL.

I do not. 'Twas for my ease to oversee and wilfully neglect the gross advances made him by my wife; that by permitting her to be engaged, I might continue unsuspected in my pleasures, and take you oftener to my arms in full security. But could you think, because the nodding husband would not wake, that e'er the watchful lover slept?

MRS. MARWOOD.

And wherewithal can you reproach me?

FAINALL.

With infidelity, with loving of another, with love of Mirabell.

MRS. MARWOOD.

'Tis false. I challenge you to show an instance that can confirm your groundless accusation. I hate him.

FAINALL.

And wherefore do you hate him? He is insensible, and your resentment follows his neglect. An instance? The injuries you have done him are a proof, your interposing in his love. What cause had you to make discoveries of his pretended

115. I do now] *Q1;* I do not now *Q2, W1.*

---

126. *oversee*] overlook.

passion? To undeceive the credulous aunt, and be the officious obstacle of his match with Millamant?

MRS. MARWOOD.

My obligations to my lady urged me; I had professed a friendship to her, and could not see her easy nature so abused by that dissembler.

FAINALL.

What, was it conscience then? Professed a friendship! Oh, the pious friendships of the female sex!

MRS. MARWOOD.

More tender, more sincere, and more enduring, than all the vain and empty vows of men, whether professing love to us, or mutual faith to one another.

FAINALL.

Ha! ha! ha! you are my wife's friend too.

MRS. MARWOOD.

Shame and ingratitude! Do you reproach me? You, you upbraid me! Have I been false to her, through strict fidelity to you, and sacrificed my friendship to keep my love inviolate? And have you the baseness to charge me with the guilt, unmindful of the merit! To you it should be meritorious, that I have been vicious; and do you reflect that guilt upon me, which should lie buried in your bosom?

FAINALL.

You misinterpret my reproof. I meant but to remind you of the slight account you once could make of strictest ties, when set in comparison with your love to me.

MRS. MARWOOD.

'Tis false; you urged it with deliberate malice! 'Twas spoke in scorn, and I never will forgive it.

FAINALL.

Your guilt, not your resentment, begets your rage. If yet you loved, you could forgive a jealousy; but you are stung to find you are discovered.

MRS. MARWOOD.

It shall be all discovered. You too shall be discovered; be sure you shall. I can but be exposed. If I do it myself, I shall prevent your baseness.

---

168. *prevent*] anticipate.

FAINALL.

Why, what will you do?

MRS. MARWOOD.

Disclose it to your wife; own what has passed between us.

FAINALL.

Frenzy!

MRS. MARWOOD.

By all my wrongs I'll do't! I'll publish to the world the injuries you have done me, both in my fame and fortune! With both I trusted you, you bankrupt in honor, as indigent of wealth.

FAINALL.

Your fame I have preserved. Your fortune has been bestowed as the prodigality of your love would have it, in pleasures which we both have shared. Yet had not you been false, I had ere this repaid it. 'Tis true, had you permitted Mirabell with Millamant to have stolen their marriage, my lady had been incensed beyond all means of reconcilement; Millamant had forfeited the moiety of her fortune, which then would have descended to my wife. And wherefore did I marry, but to make lawful prize of a rich widow's wealth, and squander it on love and you?

MRS. MARWOOD.

Deceit and frivolous pretense!

FAINALL.

Death, am I not married? What's pretense? Am I not imprisoned, fettered? Have I not a wife? Nay a wife that was a widow, a young widow, a handsome widow; and would be again a widow, but that I have a heart of proof, and something of a constitution to bustle through the ways of wedlock and this world. Will you yet be reconciled to truth and me?

MRS. MARWOOD.

Impossible. Truth and you are inconsistent. I hate you, and shall for ever.

FAINALL.

For loving you?

---

182. *moiety*] half.
190. *of proof*] of tested strength.

MRS. MARWOOD.

I loathe the name of love after such usage; and next to the guilt with which you would asperse me, I scorn you most. Farewell!

FAINALL.

Nay, we must not part thus.

MRS. MARWOOD.

Let me go.

FAINALL.

Come, I'm sorry.

MRS. MARWOOD.

I care not, let me go. Break my hands, do! I'd leave 'em to get loose.

FAINALL.

I would not hurt you for the world. Have I no other hold to keep you here?

MRS. MARWOOD.

Well, I have deserved it all.

FAINALL.

You know I love you.

MRS. MARWOOD.

Poor dissembling! Oh, that—Well, it is not yet—

FAINALL.

What? what is it not? What is it not yet? It is not yet too late—

MRS. MARWOOD.

No, it is not yet too late; I have that comfort.

FAINALL.

It is, to love another.

MRS. MARWOOD.

But not to loathe, detest, abhor mankind, myself, and the whole treacherous world.

FAINALL.

Nay, this is extravagance. Come, I ask your pardon. No tears. I was to blame; I could not love you and be easy in my doubts. Pray, forbear. I believe you. I'm convinced I've done you wrong; and any way, every way will make amends. I'll hate my wife yet more, damn her! I'll part with her, rob her of all she's worth, and we'll retire somewhere, anywhere,

221. we'll retire] *W1;* will retire *Q1.*

to another world. I'll marry thee; be pacified. 'Sdeath, they come; hide your face, your tears. You have a mask; wear it a moment. This way, this way. Be persuaded. *Exeunt.*

Enter Mirabell *and* Mrs. Fainall.

MRS. FAINALL.
They are here yet.

MIRABELL.
They are turning into the other walk.

MRS. FAINALL.
While I only hated my husband, I could bear to see him; but since I have despised him, he's too offensive.

MIRABELL.
Oh, you should hate with prudence.

MRS. FAINALL.
Yes, for I have loved with indiscretion.

MIRABELL.
You should have just so much disgust for your husband as may be sufficient to make you relish your lover.

MRS. FAINALL.
You have been the cause that I have loved without bounds, and would you set limits to that aversion of which you have been the occasion? Why did you make me marry this man?

MIRABELL.
Why do we daily commit disagreeable and dangerous actions? To save that idol, reputation. If the familiarities of our loves had produced that consequence of which you were apprehensive, where could you have fixed a father's name with credit, but on a husband? I knew Fainall to be a man lavish of his morals, an interested and professing friend, a false and a designing lover; yet one whose wit and outward fair behavior have gained a reputation with the town enough to make that woman stand excused who has suffered herself to be won by his addresses. A better man ought not to have been sacrificed to the occasion; a worse had not answered to

---

222. *'Sdeath*] a contraction of *God's death*.

223. *mask*] a covering of silk or velvet, with openings for the eyes, concealing the upper part of the face and worn for disguise.

241. *interested and professing*] self-interested and making a pretense (of friendship).

the purpose. When you are weary of him, you know your remedy.

MRS. FAINALL.

I ought to stand in some degree of credit with you, Mirabell.

MIRABELL.

In justice to you, I have made you privy to my whole design, and put it in your power to ruin or advance my fortune.

MRS. FAINALL.

Whom have you instructed to represent your pretended uncle?

MIRABELL.

Waitwell, my servant.

MRS. FAINALL.

He is an humble servant to Foible, my mother's woman, and may win her to your interest.

MIRABELL.

Care is taken for that. She is won and worn by this time. They were married this morning.

MRS. FAINALL.

Who?

MIRABELL.

Waitwell and Foible. I would not tempt my servant to betray me by trusting him too far. If your mother, in hopes to ruin me, should consent to marry my pretended uncle, he might, like Mosca in *The Fox*, stand upon terms; so I made him sure beforehand.

MRS. FAINALL.

So, if my poor mother is caught in a contract, you will discover the imposture betimes, and release her by producing a certificate of her gallant's former marriage.

MIRABELL.

Yes, upon condition she consent to my marriage with her niece, and surrender the moiety of her fortune in her possession.

269. upon condition she] *Q1;* upon condition that she *W1.*

---

251. *privy to*] privately aware of.

264. *like Mosca . . . terms*] In Jonson's *Volpone* (1606) the clever parasite, Mosca, threatens to expose his master if the latter will not give him half of his wealth.

MRS. FAINALL.

She talked last night of endeavoring at a match between Millamant and your uncle.

MIRABELL.

That was by Foible's direction, and my instruction, that she might seem to carry it more privately.

MRS. FAINALL.

Well, I have an opinion of your success, for I believe my lady will do anything to get a husband; and when she has this, which you have provided for her, I suppose she will submit to anything to get rid of him.

MIRABELL.

Yes, I think the good lady would marry anything that resembled a man, though 'twere no more than what a butler could pinch out of a napkin.

MRS. FAINALL.

Female frailty! We must all come to it, if we live to be old and feel the craving of a false appetite when the true is decayed.

MIRABELL.

An old woman's appetite is depraved like that of a girl. 'Tis the green sickness of a second childhood; and like the faint offer of a latter spring, serves but to usher in the fall, and withers in an affected bloom.

MRS. FAINALL.

Here's your mistress.

Enter Mrs. Millamant, Witwoud, *and* Mincing.

MIRABELL.

Here she comes, i'faith, full sail, with her fan spread and her streamers out, and a shoal of fools for tenders. Ha,

291–292. and her streamers] *Q1;* and streamers *W1.*

---

275. *carry it*] carry on the business.

281–282. *what a butler could pinch out of a napkin*] i.e., in a fancy shape for a dinner table.

287. *green sickness*] an anemic disease of young women.

291. *i'faith, full sail*] In Dryden's *An Evening's Love* (1668) Wildblood says of Jacintha, as she approaches: "Yonder she comes, with full sails i'faith!"

292. *streamers*] flags, i.e., the lappets of her headdress.

no, I cry her mercy!

MRS. FAINALL.

I see but one poor empty sculler; and he tows her woman after him.

MIRABELL.

You seem to be unattended, madam. You used to have the beau monde throng after you, and a flock of gay fine perukes hovering round you.

WITWOUD.

Like moths about a candle. I had like to have lost my comparison for want of breath.

MILLAMANT.

Oh, I have denied myself airs today. I have walked as fast through the crowd—

WITWOUD.

As a favorite in disgrace, and with as few followers.

MILLAMANT.

Dear Mr. Witwoud, truce with your similitudes; for I am as sick of 'em—

WITWOUD.

As a physician of a good air. I cannot help it, madam, though 'tis against myself.

MILLAMANT.

Yet again! Mincing, stand between me and his wit.

WITWOUD.

Do, Mrs. Mincing, like a screen before a great fire. I confess I do blaze today; I am too bright.

MRS. FAINALL.

But, dear Millamant, why were you so long?

MILLAMANT.

Long! Lord, have I not made violent haste? I have asked every living thing I met for you; I have inquired after you, as after a new fashion.

WITWOUD.

Madam, truce with your similitudes. No, you met her

303. in disgrace] *Q1;* just disgraced *W1.*

---

294. *sculler*] a single rower of a boat with two sculls, or short oars.
297. *perukes*] wigs. 304. *similitudes*] comparisons.

husband, and did not ask him for her.

MIRABELL.

By your leave, Witwoud, that were like inquiring after an old fashion, to ask a husband for his wife.

WITWOUD.

Hum, a hit! a hit! a palpable hit! I confess it.

MRS. FAINALL.

You were dressed before I came abroad.

MILLAMANT.

Aye, that's true. Oh, but then I had—Mincing, what had I? Why was I so long?

MINCING.

O mem, your la'ship stayed to peruse a pecquet of letters.

MILLAMANT.

Oh, aye, letters; I had letters. I am persecuted with letters. I hate letters. Nobody knows how to write letters; and yet one has 'em, one does not know why. They serve one to pin up one's hair.

WITWOUD.

Is that the way? Pray, madam, do you pin up your hair with all your letters? I find I must keep copies.

MILLAMANT.

Only with those in verse, Mr. Witwoud. I never pin up my hair with prose. I fancy one's hair would not curl if it were pinned up with prose. I think I tried once, Mincing.

MINCING.

O mem, I shall never forget it.

MILLAMANT.

Aye, poor Mincing tift and tift all the morning.

MINCING.

'Till I had the cremp in my fingers, I'll vow, mem. And all to no purpose. But when your la'ship pins it up with poetry, it sits so pleasant the next day as anything, and is so pure and so crips.

323. pecquet] *Q1;* pacquet *Q2, W1.*
331–332. I fancy . . . prose] *Q1; omitted in Q2, W1.*
335. cremp] *Q1;* cramp *Q2, W1.*

319. *a palpable hit*] an easily perceptible, effectively turned phrase.
323. *mem*] contraction of *madam.* 323. *la'ship*] i.e., ladyship.
323. *pecquet*] packet. 334. *tift*] patted and arranged (her hair).
335. *cremp*] cramp. 338. *crips*] a variation of crisp.

WITWOUD.

Indeed, so crips?

MINCING.

You're such a critic, Mr. Witwoud.

MILLAMANT.

Mirabell, did not you take exceptions last night? Oh, aye, and went away. Now I think on't, I'm angry. No, now I think on't, I'm pleased; for I believe I gave you some pain.

MIRABELL.

Does that please you?

MILLAMANT.

Infinitely; I love to give pain.

MIRABELL.

You would affect a cruelty which is not in your nature; your true vanity is in the power of pleasing.

MILLAMANT.

Oh, I ask your pardon for that. One's cruelty is one's power; and when one parts with one's cruelty, one parts with one's power; and when one has parted with that, I fancy one's old and ugly.

MIRABELL.

Aye, aye, suffer your cruelty to ruin the object of your power, to destroy your lover, and then how vain, how lost a thing you'll be! Nay, 'tis true: you are no longer handsome when you've lost your lover; your beauty dies upon the instant. For beauty is the lover's gift; 'tis he bestows your charms, your glass is all a cheat. The ugly and the old, whom the looking glass mortifies, yet after commendation can be flattered by it, and discover beauties in it; for that reflects our praises, rather than your face.

MILLAMANT.

Oh, the vanity of these men! Fainall, d'ye hear him? If they did not commend us, we were not handsome! Now you must know they could not commend one, if one was not handsome. Beauty the lover's gift! Lord, what is a lover, that it can give? Why, one makes lovers as fast as one pleases, and they live as long as one pleases, and they die as soon as one pleases; and then, if one pleases, one makes more.

341. did not] *Q1;* not *omitted in W1.*

WITWOUD.

Very pretty. Why, you make no more of making of lovers, madam, than of making so many card-matches.

MILLAMANT.

One no more owes one's beauty to a lover than one's wit to an echo. They can but reflect what we look and say; vain empty things if we are silent or unseen, and want a being.

MIRABELL.

Yet to those two vain empty things you owe two [of] the greatest pleasures of your life.

MILLAMANT.

How so?

MIRABELL.

To your lover you owe the pleasure of hearing yourselves praised; and to an echo the pleasure of hearing yourselves talk.

WITWOUD.

But I know a lady that loves talking so incessantly, she won't give an echo fair play; she has that everlasting rotation of tongue, that an echo must wait till she dies, before it can catch her last words.

MILLAMANT.

Oh, fiction! Fainall, let us leave these men.

MIRABELL.

Draw off Witwoud. (*Aside to* Mrs. Fainall.)

MRS. FAINALL.

Immediately. I have a word or two for Mr. Witwoud.

Exeunt Witwoud *and* Mrs. Fainall.

MIRABELL.

I would beg a little private audience too. You had the tyranny to deny me last night, though you knew I came to impart a secret to you that concerned my love.

MILLAMANT.

You saw I was engaged.

MIRABELL.

Unkind! You had the leisure to entertain a herd of fools; things who visit you from their excessive idleness, bestowing

---

369. *card-matches*] pieces of cardboard dipped in melted sulphur and used as matches.

on your easiness that time which is the incumbrance of their lives. How can you find delight in such society? It is impossible they should admire you; they are not capable. Or if they were, it should be to you as a mortification, for sure to please a fool is some degree of folly.

MILLAMANT.

I please myself. Besides, sometimes to converse with fools is for my health.

MIRABELL.

Your health! Is there a worse disease than the conversation of fools?

MILLAMANT.

Yes, the vapors; fools are physic for it, next to assafoetida.

MIRABELL.

You are not in a course of fools?

MILLAMANT.

Mirabell, if you persist in this offensive freedom, you'll displease me. I think I must resolve, after all, not to have you; we shan't agree.

MIRABELL.

Not in our physic, it may be.

MILLAMANT.

And yet our distemper, in all likelihood, will be the same; for we shall be sick of one another. I shan't endure to be reprimanded nor instructed; 'tis so dull to act always by advice, and so tedious to be told of one's faults—I can't bear it. Well, I won't have you, Mirabell—I'm resolved—I think—you may go. —Ha! ha! ha! What would you give that you could help loving me?

MIRABELL.

I would give something that you did not know I could not help it.

MILLAMANT.

Come, don't look grave then. Well, what do you say to me?

MIRABELL.

I say that a man may as soon make a friend by his wit, or a

---

392. *easiness*] indulgence.
401. *assafoetida*] a gum resin used in medicine to prevent spasms.
402. *a course of fools*] a cure of fools, in place of medicine, for low spirits.

fortune by his honesty, as win a woman with plain dealing and sincerity.

MILLAMANT.

Sententious Mirabell! Prithee, don't look with that violent and inflexible wise face, like Solomon at the dividing of the child in an old tapestry hanging.

MIRABELL.

You are merry, madam, but I would persuade you for one moment to be serious.

MILLAMANT.

What, with that face? No, if you keep your countenance, 'tis impossible I should hold mine. Well, after all, there is something very moving in a love-sick face. Ha! ha! ha! —Well, I won't laugh, don't be peevish—Heighho! Now I'll be melancholy, as melancholy as a watch-light. Well, Mirabell, if ever you will win me, woo me now. —Nay, if you are so tedious, fare you well. —I see they are walking away.

MIRABELL.

Can you not find in the variety of your disposition one moment—

MILLAMANT.

To hear you tell me Foible's married, and your plot like to speed? —No.

MIRABELL.

But how came you to know it?

MILLAMANT.

Unless by the help of the devil, you can't imagine; unless she should tell me herself. Which of the two it may have been, I will leave you to consider; and when you have done thinking of that, think of me. *Exit* [*with* Mincing].

MIRABELL.

I have something more—Gone! Think of you! To think of a whirlwind, though 'twere in a whirlwind, were a case of more steady contemplation; a very tranquility of mind and mansion. A fellow that lives in a windmill has not a more

430. woo] *Q2, W1;* woe *Q1.*

437. Unless by the help] *Q1;* without the help *W1.*

421–422. *like Solomon . . . child*] cf. I Kings 3:16–28.

429. *watch-light*] night-light, or slow-burning candle.

whimsical dwelling than the heart of a man that is lodged in a woman. There is no point of the compass to which they cannot turn, and by which they are not turned; and by one as well as another, for motion, not method, is their occupation. To know this, and yet continue to be in love, is to be made wise from the dictates of reason, and yet persevere to play the fool by the force of instinct. —Oh, here come my pair of turtles! —What, billing so sweetly! Is not Valentine's Day over with you yet?

Enter Waitwell *and* Foible.

Sirrah, Waitwell, why sure you think you were married for your own recreation, and not for my conveniency.

WAITWELL.

Your pardon, sir. With submission, we have indeed been solacing in lawful delights; but still with an eye to business, sir. I have instructed her as well as I could. If she can take your directions as readily as my instructions, sir, your affairs are in a prosperous way.

MIRABELL.

Give you joy, Mrs. Foible.

FOIBLE.

O las, sir, I'm so ashamed! I'm afraid my lady has been in a thousand inquietudes for me. But I protest, sir, I made as much haste as I could.

WAITWELL.

That she did indeed, sir. It was my fault that she did not make more.

MIRABELL.

That I believe.

FOIBLE.

But I told my lady as you instructed me, sir, that I had a prospect of seeing Sir Rowland, your uncle; and that I would put her ladyship's picture in my pocket to show him, which I'll be sure to say has made him so enamored of her beauty, that he burns with impatience to lie at her ladyship's feet and worship the original.

---

452. *turtles*] turtle doves.
462. *O las*] Alas.

MIRABELL.

Excellent Foible! Matrimony has made you eloquent in love.

WAITWELL.

I think she has profited, sir. I think so.

FOIBLE.

You have seen Madam Millamant, sir?

MIRABELL.

Yes.

FOIBLE.

I told her, sir, because I did not know that you might find an opportunity; she had so much company last night.

MIRABELL.

Your diligence will merit more. In the meantime—

Gives money.

FOIBLE.

O dear sir, your humble servant.

WAITWELL.

Spouse. .

MIRABELL.

Stand off, sir, not a penny! Go on and prosper, Foible; the lease shall be made good and the farm stocked, if we succeed.

FOIBLE.

I don't question your generosity, sir; and you need not doubt of success. If you have no more commands, sir, I'll be gone; I'm sure my lady is at her toilet and can't dress till I come. —Oh dear, I'm sure that (*looking out*) was Mrs. Marwood that went by in a mask; if she has seen me with you I'm sure she'll tell my lady. I'll make haste home and prevent her. Your servant, sir. B'w'y, Waitwell.

Exit.

WAITWELL.

Sir Rowland, if you please. The jade's so pert upon her preferment she forgets herself.

---

483. *Spouse*] Waitwell attempts to take from Foible the money which Mirabell has given her.

493. *B'w'y*] contraction of *God be with you* or *Good-by.*

494. *jade*] hussy.

MIRABELL.

Come, sir, will you endeavor to forget yourself, and transform into Sir Rowland?

WAITWELL.

Why, sir, it will be impossible I should remember myself. Married, knighted, and attended all in one day! 'Tis enough to make any man forget himself. The difficulty will be how to recover my acquaintance and familiarity with my former self, and fall from my transformation to a reformation into Waitwell. Nay, I shan't be quite the same Waitwell neither; for now I remember me, I am married and can't be my own man again.

Aye, there's the grief; that's the sad change of life,
To lose my title, and yet keep my wife. *Exeunt.*

[III] *A Room in* Lady Wishfort's *House.*

Lady Wishfort *at her toilet*, Peg *waiting.*

LADY WISHFORT.

Merciful! no news of Foible yet?

PEG.

No, madam.

LADY WISHFORT.

I have no more patience. If I have not fretted myself till I am pale again, there's no veracity in me! Fetch me the red; the red, do you hear, sweetheart? An arrant ash-color, as I'm a person! Look you how this wench stirs! Why dost thou not fetch me a little red? Didst thou not hear me, mopus?

PEG.

The red ratafia does your ladyship mean, or the cherry brandy?

LADY WISHFORT.

Ratafia, fool! No, fool! Not the ratafia, fool. Grant me patience! I mean the Spanish paper, idiot; complexion,

---

499. *attended*] waited for (with a pun upon *waited on*).

[III]

1. *Merciful!*] Heaven (or God) understood. 5. *arrant*] complete.
6. *a person*] a person of distinction. 8. *mopus*] stupid person.
12. *Spanish paper*] a kind of rouge imported from Spain.

darling. Paint, paint, paint, dost thou understand that, changeling, dangling thy hands like bobbins before thee? Why dost thou not stir, puppet? thou wooden thing upon wires!

PEG.

Lord, madam, your ladyship is so impatient! I cannot come at the paint, madam; Mrs. Foible has locked it up and carried the key with her.

LADY WISHFORT.

A pox take you both! Fetch me the cherry brandy then. (*Exit* Peg.) I'm as pale and as faint, I look like Mrs. Qualmsick, the curate's wife, that's always breeding. Wench, come, come, wench, what art thou doing? sipping? tasting? Save thee, dost thou not know the bottle?

Re-enter Peg *with a bottle and china cup.*

PEG.

Madam, I was looking for a cup.

LADY WISHFORT.

A cup, save thee! and what a cup hast thou brought! Dost thou take me for a fairy, to drink out of an acorn? Why didst thou not bring thy thimble? Hast thou ne'er a brass thimble clinking in thy pocket with a bit of nutmeg? I warrant thee. Come, fill, fill! So; again. (*One knocks.*) See who that is. Set down the bottle first. Here, here, under the table. What, wouldst thou go with the bottle in thy hand, like a tapster? As I'm a person, this wench has lived in an inn upon the road, before she came to me, like Maritornes the Asturian in *Don Quixote!* No Foible yet?

PEG.

No, madam, Mrs. Marwood.

LADY WISHFORT.

Oh, Marwood, let her come in. Come in, good Marwood.

---

14. *changeling*] child secretly exchanged in infancy for a more desirable one, hence an idiot.

14. *bobbins*] small wooden pins with a notch, to wind thread about in weaving or sewing.

29. *brass thimble . . . nutmeg*] as good luck charms.

35. *Maritornes the Asturian*] an ill-favored chambermaid who brings a jug of water to revive Sancho in Cervantes' *Don Quixote*.

Enter Mrs. Marwood.

MRS. MARWOOD.

I'm surprised to find your ladyship in dishabillé at this time of day.

LADY WISHFORT.

Foible's a lost thing; has been abroad since morning, and never heard of since.

MRS. MARWOOD.

I saw her but now, as I came masked through the park, in conference with Mirabell.

LADY WISHFORT.

With Mirabell! You call my blood into my face with mentioning that traitor. She durst not have the confidence! I sent her to negotiate an affair in which, if I'm detected, I'm undone. If that wheedling villain has wrought upon Foible to detect me, I'm ruined. Oh my dear friend, I'm a wretch of wretches if I'm detected.

MRS. MARWOOD.

O madam, you cannot suspect Mrs. Foible's integrity.

LADY WISHFORT.

Oh, he carries poison in his tongue that would corrupt integrity itself! If she has given him an opportunity, she has as good as put her integrity into his hands. Ah, dear Marwood, what's integrity to an opportunity? Hark! I hear her! Go, you thing, and send her in. (*Exit* Peg.) Dear friend, retire into my closet, that I may examine her with more freedom. You'll pardon me, dear friend; I can make bold with you. There are books over the chimney. Quarles and Prynne, and the *Short View of the Stage*, with Bunyan's works, to entertain you. *Exit* Mrs. Marwood.

38. dishabillé] *Q2, W1;* dishabilie *Q1.*

55. *W1 places* Go . . . in! *at the end of this speech.*

---

56. *closet*] small room for privacy.

58. *Quarles*] Francis Quarles, a religious poet, author of *Emblems, Divine and Moral* (1635).

59. *Prynne*] William Prynne, author of *Histrio-Mastix* (1633), a Puritan attack on the stage.

59. *Short View of the Stage*] In *A Short View of the Immorality and Profaneness of the English Stage* (1698) the author, Jeremy Collier, an Anglican clergyman, had included an attack on Congreve's earlier plays.

59–60. *Bunyan's works*] One volume of *The Works of that Eminent Servant of Christ, Mr. John Bunyan*, had been published in 1692.

Enter Foible.

O Foible, where hast thou been? What hast thou been doing?

FOIBLE.

Madam, I have seen the party.

LADY WISHFORT.

But what hast thou done?

FOIBLE.

Nay, 'tis your ladyship has done, and are to do; I have only promised. But a man so enamored, so transported! Well, here it is, all that is left; all that is not kissed away. Well, if worshiping of pictures be a sin, poor Sir Rowland, I say.

LADY WISHFORT.

The miniature has been counted like. But hast thou not betrayed me, Foible? Hast thou not detected me to that faithless Mirabell? What hadst thou to do with him in the Park? Answer me, has he got nothing out of thee?

FOIBLE [*aside*].

So the devil has been beforehand with me. What shall I say? —Alas, madam, could I help it, if I met that confident thing? Was I in fault? If you had heard how he used me, and all upon your ladyship's account, I'm sure you would not suspect my fidelity. Nay, if that had been the worst, I could have borne; but he had a fling at your ladyship too. And then I could not hold; but i'faith I gave him his own.

LADY WISHFORT.

Me? What did the filthy fellow say?

FOIBLE.

O madam! 'tis a shame to say what he said, with his taunts and his fleers, tossing up his nose. Humph! (says he), what, you are a hatching some plot (says he), you are so early abroad, or catering (says he), ferreting for some disbanded officer, I warrant. Half-pay is but thin subsistence (says he). Well, what pension does your lady propose? Let me see

67. Well, here . . . away] *Q1; omitted in Q2, W1.*

---

68. *if worshiping . . . sin*] the worship of religious pictures in Roman Catholic churches.

83. *fleers*] sneers.

(says he), what, she must come down pretty deep now, she's superannuated (says he) and—

LADY WISHFORT.

Ods my life, I'll have him, I'll have him murdered. I'll have him poisoned. Where does he eat? I'll marry a drawer to have him poisoned in his wine. I'll send for Robin from Locket's immediately.

FOIBLE.

Poison him? Poisoning's too good for him. Starve him, madam, starve him; marry Sir Rowland and get him disinherited. Oh, you would bless yourself to hear what he said!

LADY WISHFORT.

A villain! superannuated!

FOIBLE.

Humph! (says he), I hear you are laying designs against me too (says he), and Mrs. Millamant is to marry my uncle (he does not suspect a word of your ladyship); but (says he) I'll fit you for that. I warrant you (says he), I'll hamper you for that (says he), you and your old frippery too (says he), I'll handle you—

LADY WISHFORT.

Audacious villain! Handle me! would he durst! Frippery? old frippery! Was there ever such a foulmouthed fellow? I'll be married tomorrow; I'll be contracted tonight.

FOIBLE.

The sooner the better, madam.

LADY WISHFORT.

Will Sir Rowland be here, say'st thou? When, Foible?

FOIBLE.

Incontinently, madam. No new sheriff's wife expects the return of her husband after knighthood with that impatience in which Sir Rowland burns for the dear hour of kissing your ladyship's hands after dinner.

113. hands] *Q1;* hand *Q2, W1.*

---

90. *Ods*] a contraction of *God's*. 91. *drawer*] waiter.
93. *Locket's*] a fashionable tavern in Charing Cross.
103. *frippery*] cast-off garments.
110. *incontinently*] immediately.

LADY WISHFORT.

Frippery? superannuated frippery! I'll frippery the villain; I'll reduce him to frippery and rags! A tatterdemalion! I hope to see him hung with tatters, like a Long Lane penthouse or a gibbet thief. A slander-mouthed railer! I warrant the spendthrift prodigal's in debt as much as the million lottery, or the whole court upon a birthday. I'll spoil his credit with his tailor. Yes, he shall have my niece with her fortune, he shall!

FOIBLE.

He! I hope to see him lodge in Ludgate first, and angle into Blackfriars for brass farthings with an old mitten.

LADY WISHFORT.

Aye, dear Foible; thank thee for that, dear Foible. He has put me out of all patience. I shall never recompose my features to receive Sir Rowland with any economy of face. This wretch has fretted me that I am absolutely decayed. Look, Foible.

FOIBLE.

Your ladyship has frowned a little too rashly, indeed, madam. There are some cracks discernible in the white varnish.

LADY WISHFORT.

Let me see the glass. Cracks, say'st thou? Why I am arrantly flayed; I look like an old peeled wall. Thou must repair me, Foible, before Sir Rowland comes, or I shall

133. flayed] *Spelled* flea'd *Q1–2, W1.*

---

115. *tatterdemalion*] ragged fellow.

116–117. *Long Lane penthouse*] stall under an overhanging roof in Long Lane, where rags were sold.

118–119. *the million lottery*] a government scheme to raise a million pounds by the sale of lottery tickets.

119. *court . . . birthday*] Courtiers were expected to wear new and expensive clothes on the sovereign's birthday.

122. *Ludgate*] Ludgate Prison in Blackfriars, chiefly used for debtors.

122–123. *angle . . . mitten*] Debtors in Ludgate Prison were in the habit of begging alms of passers-by through a grating. By means of a mitten let down on a string from an upper window contributions could be drawn up.

126. *economy*] orderly arrangement.

never keep up to my picture.

FOIBLE.

I warrant you, madam, a little art once made your picture like you; and now a little of the same art must make you like your picture. Your picture must sit for you, madam.

LADY WISHFORT.

But art thou sure Sir Rowland will not fail to come? Or will he not fail when he does come? Will he be importunate, Foible, and push? For if he should not be importunate, I shall never break decorums. I shall die with confusion, if I am forced to advance. Oh no, I can never advance! I shall swoon if he should expect advances. No, I hope Sir Rowland is better bred than to put a lady to the necessity of breaking her forms. I won't be too coy neither. I won't give him despair; but a little disdain is not amiss, a little scorn is alluring.

FOIBLE.

A little scorn becomes your ladyship.

LADY WISHFORT.

Yes, but tenderness becomes me best, a sort of a dyingness. You see that picture has a sort of a—ha, Foible? a swimmingness in the eyes. Yes, I'll look so. My niece affects it; but she wants features. Is Sir Rowland handsome? Let my toilet be removed. I'll dress above. I'll receive Sir Rowland here. Is he handsome? Don't answer me. I won't know; I'll be surprised, I'll be taken by surprise.

FOIBLE.

By storm, madam. Sir Rowland's a brisk man.

LADY WISHFORT.

Is he! Oh, then he'll importune, if he's a brisk man. I shall save decorums if Sir Rowland importunes. I have a mortal terror at the apprehension of offending against decorums. Nothing but importunity can surmount decorums. Oh, I'm glad he's a brisk man. Let my things be removed, good Foible. *Exit.*

151–152. swimmingness] *Q2, W1;* swimminess *Q1.*

161. Nothing . . . decorums] *Q1; omitted in Q2, W1.*

142. *break decorums*] violate propriety.

153. *wants*] lacks.

Enter Mrs. Fainall.

MRS. FAINALL.

O Foible, I have been in a fright, lest I should come too late! That devil Marwood saw you in the Park with Mirabell, and I'm afraid will discover it to my lady.

FOIBLE.

Discover what, madam?

MRS. FAINALL.

Nay, nay, put not on that strange face. I am privy to the whole design, and know that Waitwell, to whom thou wert this morning married, is to personate Mirabell's uncle, and as such, winning my lady, to involve her in those difficulties from which Mirabell only must release her, by his making his conditions to have my cousin and her fortune left to her own disposal.

FOIBLE.

O dear madam, I beg your pardon. It was not my confidence in your ladyship that was deficient; but I thought the former good correspondence between your ladyship and Mr. Mirabell might have hindered his communicating this secret.

MRS. FAINALL.

Dear Foible, forget that.

FOIBLE.

O dear madam, Mr. Mirabell is such a sweet, winning gentleman, but your ladyship is the pattern of generosity. Sweet lady, to be so good! Mr. Mirabell cannot choose but be grateful. I find your ladyship has his heart still. Now, madam, I can safely tell your ladyship our success. Mrs. Marwood had told my lady; but I warrant I managed myself. I turned it all for the better. I told my lady that Mr. Mirabell railed at her. I laid horrid things to his charge, I'll vow; and my lady is so incensed that she'll be contracted to Sir Rowland tonight, she says. I warrant I worked her up, that he may have her for asking for, as they say of a Welsh maidenhead.

MRS. FAINALL.

O rare Foible!

---

170. *personate*] impersonate.

FOIBLE.

Madam, I beg your ladyship to acquaint Mr. Mirabell of his success. I would be seen as little as possible to speak to him; besides, I believe Madame Marwood watches me. She has a month's mind; but I know Mr. Mirabell can't abide her. (*Enter* Footman.) John, remove my lady's toilet. Madam, your servant. My lady is so impatient, I fear she'll come for me, if I stay.

MRS. FAINALL.

I'll go with you up the backstairs, lest I should meet her.

Exeunt.

Enter Mrs. Marwood.

MRS. MARWOOD.

Indeed, Mrs. Engine, is it thus with you? Are you become a go-between of this importance? Yes, I shall watch you. Why this wench is the *passe-partout*, a very master key to everybody's strongbox. My friend Fainall, have you carried it so swimmingly? I thought there was something in it; but it seems it's over with you. Your loathing is not from a want of appetite then, but from a surfeit. Else you could never be so cool to fall from a principal to be an assistant; to procure for him! A pattern of generosity, that I confess. Well, Mr. Fainall, you have met with your match. O man, man! woman, woman! The devil's an ass; if I were a painter, I would draw him like an idiot, a driveler with a bib and bells. Man should have his head and horns, and woman the rest of him. Poor simple fiend! Madam Marwood has a month's mind, but he can't abide her. 'Twere better for him you had not been his confessor in that affair, without you could have kept his counsel closer. I shall not prove another pattern of generosity and stalk for him, till he takes his stand to aim at a fortune. He has not obliged me to that,

218–219. and stalk . . . fortune] *Q1;* *omitted in W1.*

---

196. *month's mind*] strong inclination.

201. *Mrs. Engine*] Mrs. Trickery.

203. *passe-partout*] key that opens any door.

212. *driveler*] one who talks in a foolish way.

213. *horns*] referring to the horns which were imagined to sprout on the head of a cuckold.

with those excesses of himself; and now I'll have none of him. Here comes the good lady, panting ripe; with a heart full of hope, and a head full of care, like any chemist upon the day of projection.

Enter Lady Wishfort.

LADY WISHFORT.

O dear Marwood, what shall I say, for this rude forgetfulness? But my dear friend is all goodness.

MRS. MARWOOD.

No apologies, dear madam. I have been very well entertained.

LADY WISHFORT.

As I'm a person, I am in a very chaos to think I should so forget myself; but I have such an olio of affairs, really I know not what to do. —(*Calls.*) Foible! —I expect my nephew, Sir Wilfull, every moment too. —Why, Foible! —He means to travel for improvement.

MRS. MARWOOD.

Methinks Sir Wilfull should rather think of marrying than traveling at his years. I hear he is turned of forty.

LADY WISHFORT.

Oh, he's in less danger of being spoiled by his travels. I am against my nephew's marrying too young. It will be time enough when he comes back and has acquired discretion to choose for himself.

MRS. MARWOOD.

Methinks Mrs. Millamant and he would make a very fit match. He may travel afterwards. 'Tis a thing very usual with young gentlemen.

LADY WISHFORT.

I promise you I have thought on't; and since 'tis your judgment, I'll think on't again. I assure you I will; I value your judgment extremely. On my word, I'll propose it.

---

223. *projection*] the final process of alchemy in the attempt to transmute base metal into gold.

228. *chaos*] utter disorder.

229. *olio*] hodgepodge.

Enter Foible.

Come, come, Foible, I had forgot my nephew will be here before dinner. I must make haste.

FOIBLE.

Mr. Witwoud and Mr. Petulant are come to dine with your ladyship.

LADY WISHFORT.

Oh dear, I can't appear till I'm dressed. Dear Marwood, shall I be free with you again, and beg you to entertain 'em? I'll make all imaginable haste. Dear friend, excuse me.

Exeunt Lady Wishfort *and* Foible.

Enter Mrs. Millamant *and* Mincing.

MILLAMANT.

Sure never anything was so unbred as that odious man! Marwood, your servant.

MRS. MARWOOD.

You have a color, what's the matter?

MILLAMANT.

That horrid fellow, Petulant, has provoked me into a flame. I have broke my fan. Mincing, lend me yours; is not all the powder out of my hair?

MRS. MARWOOD.

No, what has he done?

MILLAMANT.

Nay, he has done nothing; he has only talked. Nay, he has said nothing neither; but he has contradicted everything that has been said. For my part, I thought Witwoud and he would have quarreled.

MINCING.

I vow, mem, I thought once they would have fit.

MILLAMANT.

Well, 'tis a lamentable thing, I'll swear, that one has not the liberty of choosing one's acquaintance as one does one's clothes.

264. I'll swear] *Q1;* I swear *Q2, W1.*

---

263. *fit*] fought.

MRS. MARWOOD.

If we had the liberty, we should be as weary of one set of acquaintance, though never so good, as we are of one suit, though never so fine. A fool and a doily stuff would now and then find days of grace, and be worn for variety.

MILLAMANT.

I could consent to wear 'em, if they would wear alike; but fools never wear out—they are such *drap-de-Berry* things without one could give 'em to one's chambermaid after a day or two!

MRS. MARWOOD.

'Twere better so indeed. Or what think you of the playhouse? A fine, gay, glossy fool should be given there, like a new masking habit, after the masquerade is over, and we have done with the disguise. For a fool's visit is always a disguise, and never admitted by a woman of wit, but to blind her affair with a lover of sense. If you would but appear barefaced now, and own Mirabell, you might as easily put off Petulant and Witwoud as your hood and scarf. And indeed 'tis time, for the town has found it; the secret is grown too big for the pretense. 'Tis like Mrs. Primly's great belly; she may lace it down before, but it burnishes on her hips. Indeed, Millamant, you can no more conceal it than my Lady Strammel can her face, that goodly face, which, in defiance of her Rhenish wine tea, will not be comprehended in a mask.

MILLAMANT.

I'll take my death, Marwood, you are more censorious than a decayed beauty, or a discarded toast. Mincing, tell the men they may come up. My aunt is not dressing [here]. —Their folly is less provoking than your malice. (*Exit*

292. dressing here] *W1;* here *omitted in Q1.*

---

269. *doily stuff*] a light, cheap woollen cloth.

272. *drap-de-Berry*] coarse woollen cloth from the province of Berry in France.

288. *Rhenish wine tea*] strong wine instead of tea. White Rhenish wine was believed to reduce corpulence and correct a high color.

290. *I'll take my death*] I hope to die if what I say is untrue.

291. *discarded toast*] person whose health was formerly drunk.

Mincing.) The town has found it! What has it found? That Mirabell loves me is no more a secret than it is a secret that you discovered it to my aunt, or than the reason why you discovered it is a secret.

MRS. MARWOOD.

You are nettled.

MILLAMANT.

You're mistaken. Ridiculous!

MRS. MARWOOD.

Indeed, my dear, you'll tear another fan, if you don't mitigate those violent airs.

MILLAMANT.

O silly! Ha! ha! ha! I could laugh immoderately. Poor Mirabell! His constancy to me has quite destroyed his complaisance for all the world beside. I swear, I never enjoined it him to be so coy. If I had the vanity to think he would obey me, I would command him to show more gallantry. 'Tis hardly well-bred to be so particular on one hand, and so insensible on the other. But I despair to prevail, and so let him follow his own way. Ha! ha! ha! Pardon me, dear creature, I must laugh, ha! ha! ha!—though I grant you 'tis a little barbarous, ha! ha! ha!

MRS. MARWOOD.

What pity 'tis, so much fine raillery, and delivered with so significant gesture, should be so unhappily directed to miscarry.

MILLAMANT.

Ha? Dear creature, I ask your pardon. I swear I did not mind you.

MRS. MARWOOD.

Mr. Mirabell and you both may think it a thing impossible, when I shall tell him by telling you—

MILLAMANT.

Oh dear, what? For it is the same thing, if I hear it, ha! ha! ha!

MRS. MARWOOD.

That I detest him, hate him, madam.

315. Ha] *Spelled* Hae *Q1–2, W1.*

---

316. *mind*] pay attention to.

MILLAMANT.

O madam, why so do I—and yet the creature loves me, ha! ha! ha! How can one forbear laughing to think of it! I am a sybil if I am not amazed to think what he can see in me. I'll take my death, I think you are handsomer—and within a year or two as young. If you could but stay for me, I should overtake you—but that cannot be. —Well, that thought makes me melancholy. —Now I'll be sad.

MRS. MARWOOD.

Your merry note may be changed sooner than you think.

MILLAMANT.

D'ye say so? Then I'm resolved to have a song to keep up my spirits.

Enter Mincing.

MINCING.

The gentlemen stay but to comb, madam, and will wait on you.

MILLAMANT.

Desire Mrs. ——, that is in the next room, to sing the song I would have learned yesterday. You shall hear it, madam, not that there's any great matter in it, but 'tis agreeable to my humor.

Song

Set by Mr. John Eccles *and sung by* Mrs. Hodgson.

I

Love's but the frailty of the mind,
When 'tis not with ambition joined;
A sickly flame, which, if not fed, expires,
And feeding, wastes in self-consuming fires.

II

'Tis not to wound a wanton boy
Or amorous youth, that gives the joy;
But 'tis the glory to have pierced a swain,
For whom inferior beauties sighed in vain.

328. melancholy] *Q1–2;* melancholick *W1.*

337.2 and . . . Hodgson] *Q1; omitted in W1.*

324. *sybil*] prophetess.

332. *comb*] i.e., their wigs.

III

Then I alone the conquest prize,
When I insult a rival's eyes;
If there's delight in love, 'tis when I see
That heart, which others bleed for, bleed for me.

Enter Petulant *and* Witwoud.

MILLAMANT.

Is your animosity composed, gentlemen?

WITWOUD.

Raillery, raillery, madam; we have no animosity. We hit off a little wit now and then, but no animosity. The falling-out of wits is like the falling-out of lovers; we agree in the main, like treble and bass. Ha, Petulant?

PETULANT.

Aye, in the main, but when I have a humor to contradict.

WITWOUD.

Aye, when he has a humor to contradict, then I contradict too. What, I know my cue. Then we contradict one another like two battledores; for contradictions beget one another like Jews.

PETULANT.

If he says black's black, if I have a humor to say 'tis blue, let that pass; all's one for that. If I have a humor to prove it, it must be granted.

WITWOUD.

Not positively must, but it may, it may.

PETULANT.

Yes, it positively must, upon proof positive.

WITWOUD.

Aye, upon proof positive it must; but upon proof presumptive it only may. That's a logical distinction now, madam.

MRS. MARWOOD.

I perceive your debates are of importance and very learnedly handled.

---

353. *in the main*] the mean, the middle or tenor part, with which the other two harmonize; also in the sense of *mainly*.

358. *battledores*] two who play with small rackets, as they strike a shuttlecock to and from each other.

PETULANT.

Importance is one thing, and learning's another; but a debate's a debate, that I assert.

WITWOUD.

Petulant's an enemy to learning; he relies altogether on his parts.

PETULANT.

No, I'm no enemy to learning; it hurts not me.

MRS. MARWOOD.

That's a sign indeed it's no enemy to you.

PETULANT.

No, no, it's no enemy to anybody but them that have it.

MILLAMANT.

Well, an illiterate man's my aversion. I wonder at the impudence of any illiterate man to offer to make love.

WITWOUD.

That I confess I wonder at too.

MILLAMANT.

Ah! to marry an ignorant that can hardly read or write!

PETULANT.

Why should a man be ever the further from being married, though he can't read, any more than he is from being hanged? The ordinary's paid for setting the psalm, and the parish priest for reading the ceremony. And for the rest which is to follow in both cases, a man may do it without book; so all's one for that.

MILLAMANT.

D'ye hear the creature? Lord, here's company, I'll be gone.

Exeunt Millamant *and* Mincing.

WITWOUD.

In the name of Bartlemew and his fair, what have we here?

MRS. MARWOOD.

'Tis your brother, I fancy. Don't you know him?

WITWOUD.

Not I. Yes, I think it is he. I've almost forgot him; I

382. any more] *Q1; omitted in W1.*

---

383. *The ordinary's paid . . . psalm*] A member of the clergy was appointed to minister to condemned criminals.

388. *Bartlemew and his fair*] Bartholomew Fair was a popular fair held annually in Smithfield on August 24, St. Bartholomew's Day.

have not seen him since the Revolution.

Enter Sir Wilfull Witwoud *in a country riding habit, and a* Servant to Lady Wishfort.

SERVANT.

Sir, my lady's dressing. Here's company; if you please to walk in, in the meantime.

SIR WILFULL.

Dressing! What, it's but morning here, I warrant, with you in London; we should count it towards afternoon in our parts, down in Shropshire. Why then, belike my aunt han't dined yet, ha, friend?

SERVANT.

Your aunt, sir?

SIR WILFULL.

My aunt, sir! Yes, my aunt, sir, and your lady, sir; your lady is my aunt, sir. Why, what, dost thou not know me, friend? Why then, send somebody here that does. How long hast thou lived with thy lady, fellow, ha?

SERVANT.

A week, sir; longer than anybody in the house, except my lady's woman.

SIR WILFULL.

Why then, belike thou dost not know thy lady, if thou seest her, ha, friend?

SERVANT.

Why truly, sir, I cannot safely swear to her face in a morning, before she is dressed. 'Tis like I may give a shrewd guess at her by this time.

SIR WILFULL.

Well, prithee try what thou canst do; if thou canst not guess, inquire her out, dost hear, fellow? And tell her, her nephew, Sir Wilfull Witwoud, is in the house.

SERVANT.

I shall, sir.

391.1 Servant] *Q1;* Footman *W1.* *So until Exit.*

---

391. *the Revolution*] the Bloodless Revolution of 1688 which brought William and Mary to the throne.

405. *belike*] probably.

SIR WILFULL.

Hold ye, hear me, friend; a word with you in your ear. Prithee who are these gallants?

SERVANT.

Really, sir, I can't tell; here come so many here, 'tis hard to know 'em all. *Exit* Servant.

SIR WILFULL.

Oons, this fellow knows less than a starling; I don't think a' knows his own name.

MRS. MARWOOD.

Mr. Witwoud, your brother is not behindhand in forgetfulness; I fancy he has forgot you too.

WITWOUD.

I hope so. The devil take him that remembers first, I say.

SIR WILFULL.

Save you, gentlemen and lady!

MRS. MARWOOD.

For shame, Mr. Witwoud; why won't you speak to him? And you, sir.

WITWOUD.

Petulant, speak.

PETULANT.

And you, sir.

SIR WILFULL.

No offense, I hope. *Salutes* Marwood.

MRS. MARWOOD.

No sure, sir.

WITWOUD.

This is a vile dog, I see that already. No offense! Ha! ha! ha! to him; to him, Petulant, smoke him.

PETULANT.

It seems as if you had come a journey, sir; hem, hem.

Surveying him round.

SIR WILFULL.

Very likely, sir, that it may seem so.

---

418. *Oons*] a corruption of *God's wounds*.
418. *starling*] considered a very stupid bird.
431. *smoke him*] make fun of him.

PETULANT.

No offense, I hope, sir.

WITWOUD.

Smoke the boots, the boots; Petulant, the boots, ha! ha! ha!

SIR WILFULL.

May be not, sir; thereafter as 'tis meant, sir.

PETULANT.

Sir, I presume upon the information of your boots.

SIR WILFULL.

Why, 'tis like you may, sir. If you are not satisfied with the information of my boots, sir, if you will step to the stable, you may inquire further of my horse, sir.

PETULANT.

Your horse, sir! Your horse is an ass, sir!

SIR WILFULL.

Do you speak by way of offense, sir?

MRS. MARWOOD.

The gentleman's merry, that's all, sir. —[*Aside.*] 'Slife, we shall have a quarrel betwixt an horse and an ass, before they find one another out. —[*Aloud.*] You must not take anything amiss from your friends, sir. You are among your friends here, though it may be you don't know it. If I am not mistaken, you are Sir Wilfull Witwoud.

SIR WILFULL.

Right, lady; I am Sir Wilfull Witwoud, so I write myself; no offense to anybody, I hope; and nephew to the Lady Wishfort of this mansion.

MRS. MARWOOD.

Don't you know this gentleman, sir?

SIR WILFULL.

Hum! What, sure 'tis not—yea by'r Lady, but 'tis. 'Sheart, I know not whether 'tis or no. Yea, but 'tis, by the Wrekin. Brother Anthony! What, Tony, i'faith! What, dost thou not know me? By'r Lady, nor I thee, thou art so be-cravated

455. Anthony] *Q1;* Antony *W1.*

---

436. *thereafter*] according. 443. *'Slife*] a corruption of *God's life.*

453. *'Sheart*] a corruption of *God's heart.*

454. *Wrekin*] a high hill near the center of Shropshire. "All friends round the Wrekin" is a famous Shropshire toast.

and be-periwigged. 'Sheart, why dost not speak? Art thou o'erjoyed?

WITWOUD.

Odso, brother, is it you? Your servant, brother.

SIR WILLFULL.

Your servant! Why, yours, sir. Your servant again, 'sheart, and your friend and servant to that, and a—(*puff*) and a flapdragon for your service, sir! and a hare's foot, and a hare's scut for your service, sir, an you be so cold and so courtly!

WITWOUD.

No offense, I hope, brother.

SIR WILFULL.

'Sheart, sir, but there is, and much offense! A pox, is this your Inns o' Court breeding, not to know your friends and your relations, your elders and your betters?

WITWOUD.

Why, brother Wilfull of Salop, you may be as short as a Shrewsbury cake, if you please. But I tell you, 'tis not modish to know relations in town. You think you're in the country, where great lubberly brothers slabber and kiss one another when they meet, like a call of serjeants. 'Tis not the fashion here; 'tis not indeed, dear brother.

SIR WILFULL.

The fashion's a fool; and you're a fop, dear brother. 'Sheart, I've suspected this. By'r Lady, I conjectured you were a fop, since you began to change the style of your letters and write in a scrap of paper, gilt round the edges, no broader than a subpoena. I might expect this when you

---

459. *Odso*] a variant of *Godso*, expressing surprise.

462. *flapdragon*] a raisin snatched from burning brandy and extinguished by closing the mouth and swallowing, hence something valueless.

463. *hare's scut*] a term still in country use for a hare's tail.

467. *Inns o' Court*] the societies in London in which lawyers are trained for the bar.

469. *Salop*] Shropshire.

470. *Shrewsbury cake*] a flat, round, biscuit-like cake. Shrewsbury is the county town of Shropshire.

472. *slabber*] slobber.

473. *a call of serjeants*] a group of serjeants-at-law who had been raised to that rank at the same time.

left off Honored Brother, and hoping you are in good health, and so forth—to begin with a Rat me, knight, I'm so sick of a last night's debauch—ods heart, and then tell a familiar tale of a cock and a bull, and a whore and a bottle, and so conclude. You could write news before you were out of your time, when you lived with honest Pumple Nose, the attorney of Furnival's Inn; you could entreat to be remembered then to your friends round the Wrekin. We could have gazettes then, and *Dawks's Letter*, and the *Weekly Bill*, till of late days.

PETULANT.

'Slife, Witwoud, were you ever an attorney's clerk? of the family of the Furnivals? Ha! ha! ha!

WITWOUD.

Aye, aye, but that was for a while, not long, not long. Pshaw! I was not in my own power then; an orphan, and this fellow was my guardian. Aye, aye, I was glad to consent to that man to come to London. He had the disposal of me then. If I had not agreed to that, I might have been bound prentice to a felt-maker in Shrewsbury; this fellow would have bound me to a maker of felts.

SIR WILFULL.

'Sheart, and better than to be bound to a maker of fops, where, I suppose, you have served your time; and now you may set up for yourself.

MRS. MARWOOD.

You intend to travel, sir, as I'm informed.

SIR WILFULL.

Belike I may, madam. I may chance to sail upon the salt

---

481. *Rat me*] an abbreviated form of *May God rot me.*

482. *ods heart*] a contraction of *God's heart.*

484–485. *before you were out of your time*] while you were still indentured to an attorney.

485. *Pumple*] i.e., Pimple.

486. *Furnival's Inn*] a subordinate inn of court attached to Lincoln's Inn.

488. *gazettes*] news sheets.

488. *Dawks's Letter*] a weekly newsletter.

489. *Weekly Bill*] the official publication of deaths occurring in and around London.

497. *bound prentice*] bound as an apprentice.

seas, if my mind hold.

PETULANT.

And the wind serve.

SIR WILFULL.

Serve or not serve, I shan't ask license of you, sir; nor the weathercock your companion. I direct my discourse to the lady, sir. 'Tis like my aunt may have told you, madam. Yes, I have settled my concerns, I may say now, and am minded to see foreign parts. If an how that the peace holds, whereby, that is, taxes abate.

MRS. MARWOOD.

I thought you had designed for France at all adventures.

SIR WILFULL.

I can't tell that; 'tis like I may, and 'tis like I may not. I am somewhat dainty in making a resolution, because when I make it, I keep it. I don't stand shill I, shall I, then; if I say't, I'll do't. But I have thoughts to tarry a small matter in town, to learn somewhat of your lingo first, before I cross the seas. I'd gladly have a spice of your French, as they say, whereby to hold discourse in foreign countries.

MRS. MARWOOD.

Here is an academy in town for that use.

SIR WILFULL.

There is? 'Tis like there may.

MRS. MARWOOD.

No doubt you will return very much improved.

WITWOUD.

Yes, refined, like a Dutch skipper from a whale-fishing.

Enter Lady Wishfort *and* Fainall.

LADY WISHFORT.

Nephew, you are welcome.

SIR WILFULL.

Aunt, your servant.

510–511. *the peace holds*] The Peace of Ryswick (1697), which had temporarily halted the war with France, was broken in 1701, the year after this play was first acted.

512. *at all adventures*] at all costs.

515. *shill I, shall I*] shilly-shally, irresolute.

521. '*Tis like there may*] Very likely there is.

FAINALL.

Sir Wilfull, your most faithful servant.

SIR WILFULL.

Cousin Fainall, give me your hand.

LADY WISHFORT.

Cousin Witwoud, your servant; Mr. Petulant, your servant. Nephew, you are welcome again. Will you drink anything after your journey, nephew, before you eat? Dinner's almost ready.

SIR WILFULL.

I'm very well, I thank you, aunt; however, I thank you for your courteous offer. 'Sheart, I was afraid you would have been in the fashion too, and have remembered to have forgot your relations. Here's your cousin Tony; belike I mayn't call him brother for fear of offense.

LADY WISHFORT.

Oh, he's a rallier, nephew. My cousin's a wit; and your great wits always rally their best friends to choose. When you have been abroad, nephew, you'll understand raillery better.

Fainall *and* Mrs. Marwood *talk apart.*

SIR WILFULL.

Why then, let him hold his tongue in the meantime, and rail when that day comes.

Enter Mincing.

MINCING.

Mem, I come to acquaint your la'ship that dinner is impatient.

SIR WILFULL.

Impatient? Why then, belike it won't stay till I pull off my boots. Sweetheart, can you help me to a pair of slippers? My man's with his horses, I warrant.

LADY WISHFORT.

Fie, fie, nephew, you would not pull off your boots here. Go down into the hall; dinner shall stay for you. My nephew's a little unbred; you'll pardon him, madam. Gentlemen, will you walk? Marwood?

---

537. *rallier*] one who indulges in raillery.

538. *rally their best friends to choose*] make as much fun of them as they like.

MRS. MARWOOD.

I'll follow you, madam, before Sir Wilfull is ready.

Exeunt all but Mrs. Marwood *and* Fainall.

FAINALL.

Why then, Foible's a bawd, an arrant, rank, match-making bawd. And I, it seems, am a husband, a rank husband; and my wife a very arrant, rank wife, all in the way of the world. 'Sdeath, to be an anticipated cuckold, a cuckold in embryo! Sure I was born with budding antlers, like a young satyr, or a citizen's child. 'Sdeath, to be out-witted, to be out-jilted, out-matrimonied! If I had kept my speed like a stag, 'twere somewhat; but to crawl after, with my horns like a snail, and outstripped by my wife, 'tis scurvy wedlock.

MRS. MARWOOD.

Then shake it off. You have often wished for an opportunity to part; and now you have it. But first prevent their plot; the half of Millamant's fortune is too considerable to be parted with, to a foe, to Mirabell.

FAINALL.

Damn him! that had been mine, had you not made that fond discovery. That had been forfeited, had they been married. My wife had added luster to my horns by that increase of fortune; I could have worn 'em tipt with gold, though my forehead had been furnished like a deputy lieutenant's hall.

MRS. MARWOOD.

They may prove a cap of maintenance to you still, if you can away with your wife. And she's no worse than when you had her. I dare swear she had given up her game before she was married.

555. an anticipated cuckold] *Q1;* a cuckold by anticipation *W1.*

560. and outstripped] *Q1;* and be outstripped *Q2, W1.*

557. *citizen's child*] Ciitzens were often cuckolded by fine gentlemen of the town.

561. *scurvy*] contemptible.

567. *fond*] foolish.

570–571. *deputy lieutenant's hall*] i.e., with numerous antlers.

572. *cap of maintenance*] a technical term in heraldry, implying that being cuckolded will help to maintain him financially.

573. *away with*] endure.

FAINALL.

Hum! That may be. She might throw up her cards; but I'll be hanged if she did not put Pam in her pocket.

MRS. MARWOOD.

You married her to keep you; and if you can contrive to have her keep you better than you expected, why should you not keep her longer than you intended?

FAINALL.

The means, the means.

MRS. MARWOOD.

Discover to my lady your wife's conduct; threaten to part with her. My lady loves her, and will come to any composition to save her reputation. Take the opportunity of breaking it, just upon the discovery of this imposture. My lady will be enraged beyond bounds, and sacrifice niece and fortune and all, at that conjuncture. And let me alone to keep her warm; if she should flag in her part, I will not fail to prompt her.

FAINALL.

Faith, this has an appearance.

MRS. MARWOOD.

I'm sorry I hinted to my lady to endeavor a match between Millamant and Sir Wilfull; that may be an obstacle.

FAINALL.

Oh, for that matter leave me to manage him; I'll disable him for that. He will drink like a Dane; after dinner, I'll set his hand in.

MRS. MARWOOD.

Well, how do you stand affected towards your lady?

FAINALL.

Why, faith, I'm thinking of it. Let me see. I am married

576–577. She might . . . pocket] *Q1; omitted in W1.*

---

577. *Pam . . . pocket*] Pam, the jack of clubs, is the highest card in the game of loo. Fainall implies that although his wife might have given up other lovers, she has an "ace" up her sleeve, i.e., Mirabell.

583–584. *composition*] agreement.

590. *appearance*] probability (of succeeding).

594. *drink like a Dane*] drink to excess.

594–595. *set his hand in*] start him.

already, so that's over. My wife has played the jade with me; well, that's over too. I never loved her, or if I had, why that would have been over too by this time. Jealous of her I cannot be, for I am certain; so there's an end of jealousy. Weary of her I am, and shall be. No, there's no end of that; no, no, that were too much to hope. Thus far concerning my repose; now for my reputation. As to my own, I married not for it; so that's out of the question. And as to my part in my wife's, why she had parted with hers before; so bringing none to me, she can take none from me. 'Tis against all rule of play that I should lose to one who has not wherewithal to stake.

MRS. MARWOOD.

Besides, you forget, marriage is honorable.

FAINALL.

Hum! Faith, and that's well thought on. Marriage is honorable, as you say; and if so, wherefore should cuckoldom be a discredit, being derived from so honorable a root?

MRS. MARWOOD.

Nay, I know not; if the root be honorable, why not the branches?

FAINALL.

So, so; why this point's clear. Well, how do we proceed?

MRS. MARWOOD.

I will contrive a letter which shall be delivered to my lady at the time when that rascal who is to act Sir Rowland is with her. It shall come as from an unknown hand, for the less I appear to know of the truth, the better I can play the incendiary. Besides, I would not have Foible provoked if I could help it, because you know she knows some passages. Nay, I expect all will come out; but let the mine be sprung first, and then I care not if I'm discovered.

FAINALL.

If the worst come to the worst, I'll turn my wife to grass. I have already a deed of settlement of the best part of her

598. *played the jade*] acted the part of a hussy.
600. *Jealous*] suspicious.
615. *branches*] i.e., of the cuckold's horns.
625. *turn . . . grass*] turn her out to pasture.

estate, which I have wheedled out of her; and that you shall partake at least.

MRS. MARWOOD.

I hope you are convinced that I hate Mirabell; now you'll be no more jealous.

FAINALL.

Jealous! No, by this kiss. Let husbands be jealous; but let the lover still believe. Or if he doubt, let it be only to endear his pleasure, and prepare the joy that follows, when he proves his mistress true. But let husbands' doubts convert to endless jealousy; or if they have belief, let it corrupt to superstition and blind credulity. I am single, and will herd no more with 'em. True, I wear the badge, but I'll disown the order. And since I take my leave of 'em, I care not if I leave 'em a common motto to their common crest:

All husbands must or pain or shame endure;
The wise too jealous are, fools too secure. *Exeunt.*

[IV] *Scene continues.*

Enter Lady Wishfort *and* Foible.

LADY WISHFORT.

Is Sir Rowland coming, say'st thou, Foible? and are things in order?

FOIBLE.

Yes, madam, I have put wax lights in the sconces, and placed the footmen in a row in the hall, in their best liveries, with the coachman and postilion to fill up the equipage.

LADY WISHFORT.

Have you pulvilled the coachman and postilion that they may not stink of the stable when Sir Rowland comes by?

FOIBLE.

Yes, madam.

LADY WISHFORT.

And are the dancers and the music ready, that he may be entertained in all points with correspondence to his passion?

---

640. *or pain*] either pain.

[IV]

5. *equipage*] retinue.

6. *pulvilled*] sprinkled with perfumed powder.

FOIBLE.

All is ready, madam.

LADY WISHFORT.

And—well—and how do I look, Foible?

FOIBLE.

Most killing well, madam.

LADY WISHFORT.

Well, and how shall I receive him? In what figure shall I give his heart the first impression? There is a great deal in the first impression. Shall I sit? —No, I won't sit—I'll walk—aye, I'll walk from the door upon his entrance; and then turn full upon him. —No, that will be too sudden. I'll lie—aye, I'll lie down—I'll receive him in my little dressing-room; there's a couch—yes, yes, I'll give the first impression on a couch. —I won't lie neither, but loll and lean upon one elbow, with one foot a little dangling off, jogging in a thoughtful way—yes—and then as soon as he appears, start, aye, start and be surprised, and rise to meet him in a pretty disorder—yes—oh, nothing is more alluring than a levee from a couch in some confusion. —It shows the foot to advantage, and furnishes with blushes, and recomposing airs beyond comparison. Hark! There's a coach.

FOIBLE.

'Tis he, madam.

LADY WISHFORT.

Oh dear, has my nephew made his addresses to Millamant? I ordered him.

FOIBLE.

Sir Wilfull is set in to drinking, madam, in the parlor.

LADY WISHFORT.

Ods my life, I'll send him to her. Call her down, Foible; bring her hither. I'll send him as I go. When they are together, then come to me, Foible, that I may not be too long alone with Sir Rowland. *Exit.*

32. in to] *W1;* into *Q1–2.*

---

25. *levee*] rising.
32. *is set in to*] has set to work at.
33. *Ods my life*] a corruption of *God* [*save*] *my life.*

Enter Mrs. Millamant *and* Mrs. Fainall.

FOIBLE.

Madam, I stayed here, to tell your ladyship that Mr. Mirabell has waited this half hour for an opportunity to talk with you, though my lady's orders were to leave you and Sir Wilfull together. Shall I tell Mr. Mirabell that you are at leisure?

MILLAMANT.

No—what would the dear man have? I am thoughtful and would amuse myself—bid him come another time.

There never yet was woman made,
Nor shall, but to be cursed. (*Repeating and walking about.*)

That's hard!

MRS. FAINALL.

You are very fond of Sir John Suckling today, Millamant, and the poets.

MILLAMANT.

He? Aye, and filthy verses; so I am.

FOIBLE.

Sir Wilfull is coming, madam. Shall I send Mr. Mirabell away?

MILLAMANT.

Aye, if you please, Foible, send him away—or send him hither—just as you will, dear Foible. —I think I'll see him—shall I? Aye, let the wretch come. [*Exit* Foible.]

Thyrsis, a youth of the inspired train. (*Repeating.*)

Dear Fainall, entertain Sir Wilfull. Thou hast philosophy to undergo a fool; thou art married and hast patience. I would confer with my own thoughts.

MRS. FAINALL.

I am obliged to you, that you would make me your proxy in this affair; but I have business of my own.

Enter Sir Wilfull.

O Sir Wilfull, you are come at the critical instant. There's your mistress up to the ears in love and contemplation;

44–45. *There never yet . . . cursed*] the first lines of an untitled poem by Sir John Suckling.

55. *Thyrsis, a youth of the inspired train*] the first line of Edmund Waller's *The Story of Phoebus and Daphne, Applied.*

57. *undergo*] endure.

pursue your point, now or never.

SIR WILFULL.

Yes; my aunt would have it so. I would gladly have been encouraged with a bottle or two, because I'm somewhat wary at first, before I am acquainted. (*This while* Millamant *walks about repeating to herself.*) But I hope, after a time, I shall break my mind; that is, upon further acquaintance. So for the present, cousin, I'll take my leave. If so be you'll be so kind to make my excuse, I'll return to my company.

MRS. FAINALL.

Oh, fie, Sir Wilfull! What, you must not be daunted.

SIR WILFULL.

Daunted! No, that's not it. It is not so much for that; for if so be that I set on't, I'll do't. But only for the present; 'tis sufficient till further acquaintance, that's all. Your servant.

MRS. FAINALL.

Nay, I'll swear you shall never lose so favorable an opportunity, if I can help it. I'll leave you together and lock the door. *Exit.*

SIR WILFULL.

Nay, nay, cousin. I have forgot my gloves. What d'ye do? 'Sheart, 'a has locked the door indeed, I think. Nay, Cousin Fainall, open the door! Pshaw, what a vixen trick is this? Nay, now 'a has seen me too. Cousin, I made bold to pass through as it were. I think this door's enchanted!

MILLAMANT (*repeating*).

I prithee spare me, gentle boy,
Press me no more for that slight toy—

SIR WILFULL.

Anan? Cousin, your servant.

MILLAMANT (*repeating*).

That foolish trifle of a heart—
Sir Wilfull!

64. would have] *Q1;* will have *Q2, W1.*

80. *'a*] a countrified abbreviation of *she* (more commonly *he*).

84–85. *I prithee . . . toy*] These two lines and the three which Millamant next repeats constitute the first stanza of an untitled poem by Suckling.

86. *Anan?*] a countrified expression meaning *What?* or *What say?*

SIR WILFULL.

Yes. Your servant. No offense, I hope, cousin.

MILLAMANT (*repeating*).

I swear it will not do its part,
Though thou dost thine, employ'st thy power and art.

Natural, easy Suckling!

SIR WILFULL.

Anan? Suckling? No such suckling neither, cousin, nor stripling; I thank heaven, I'm no minor.

MILLAMANT.

Ah, rustic! ruder than Gothic!

SIR WILFULL.

Well, well, I shall understand your lingo one of these days, cousin; in the meanwhile, I must answer in plain English.

MILLAMANT.

Have you any business with me, Sir Wilfull?

SIR WILFULL.

Not at present, cousin. Yes, I made bold to see, to come and know if that how you were disposed to fetch a walk this evening, if so be that I might not be troublesome, I would have fought a walk with you.

MILLAMANT.

A walk! What then?

SIR WILFULL.

Nay, nothing. Only for the walk's sake, that's all.

MILLAMANT.

I nauseate walking; 'tis a country diversion. I loathe the country and everything that relates to it.

SIR WILFULL.

Indeed! Ha! Look ye, look ye, you do? Nay, 'tis like you may. Here are choice of pastimes here in town, as plays and the like; that must be confessed indeed.

MILLAMANT.

Ah, *l'étourdie!* I hate the town too.

102. fought] *Q1–2;* sought *W1.*

---

95. *Gothic*] barbarian.

102. *fought*] a provincial form of *fetched.*

110. *Ah, l'étourdie!*] Ah, the giddy town! Some editors have emended to *Ah, l'étourdi,* meaning *Ah, the dolt!*

SIR WILFULL.

Dear heart, that's much. Ha! that you should hate 'em both! Ha! 'tis like you may; there are some can't relish the town, and others can't away with the country. 'Tis like you may be one of those, cousin.

MILLAMANT.

Ha! ha! ha! Yes, 'tis like I may. You have nothing further to say to me?

SIR WILFULL.

Not at present, cousin. 'Tis like when I have an opportunity to be more private, I may break my mind in some measure. I conjecture you partly guess. —However, that's as time shall try; but spare to speak and spare to speed, as they say.

MILLAMANT.

If it is of no great importance, Sir Wilfull, you will oblige me to leave me; I have just now a little business—

SIR WILFULL.

Enough, enough, cousin, yes, yes, all a case; when you're disposed, when you're disposed. Now's as well as another time; and another time as well as now. All's one for that. Yes, yes, if your concerns call you, there's no haste; it will keep cold, as they say. Cousin, your servant. I think this door's locked.

MILLAMANT.

You may go this way, sir.

SIR WILFULL.

Your servant; then with your leave I'll return to my company. *Exit.*

MILLAMANT.

Aye, aye; ha! ha! ha!
  Like Phoebus sung the no less amorous boy.

Enter Mirabell.

MIRABELL.

  Like Daphne she, as lovely and as coy.
Do you lock yourself up from me, to make my search more

123. *all a case*] all the same.

133. *Like Phoebus sung the no less amorous boy*] the third line of the poem by Waller previously quoted by Millamant. Mirabell, entering, completes the couplet.

curious? Or is this pretty artifice contrived, to signify that here the chase must end and my pursuit be crowned, for you can fly no further?

MILLAMANT.

Vanity! No. I'll fly and be followed to the last moment. Though I am upon the very verge of matrimony, I expect you should solicit me as much as if I were wavering at the grate of a monastery, with one foot over the threshold. I'll be solicited to the very last, nay and afterwards.

MIRABELL.

What, after the last?

MILLAMANT.

Oh, I should think I was poor and had nothing to bestow, if I were reduced to an inglorious ease and freed from the agreeable fatigues of solicitation.

MIRABELL.

But do not you know that when favors are conferred upon instant and tedious solicitation, that they diminish in their value, and that both the giver loses the grace, and the receiver lessens his pleasure?

MILLAMANT.

It may be in things of common application; but never sure in love. Oh, I hate a lover that can dare to think he draws a moment's air independent on the bounty of his mistress. There is not so impudent a thing in nature as the saucy look of an assured man, confident of success. The pedantic arrogance of a very husband has not so pragmatical an air. Ah! I'll never marry, unless I am first made sure of my will and pleasure.

MIRABELL.

Would you have 'em both before marriage? Or will you be contented with the first now, and stay for the other till after grace?

MILLAMANT.

Ah! don't be impertinent. —My dear liberty, shall I leave

---

136. *curious*] complicated.

152. *things of common application*] affairs of everyday life.

157. *pragmatical*] matter-of-fact.

161–162. *after grace*] referring to the prayer concluding the marriage ceremony.

thee? My faithful solitude, my darling contemplation, must I bid you then adieu? Ay-h adieu—my morning thoughts, agreeable wakings, indolent slumbers, all ye *douceurs*, ye *sommeils du matin*, adieu? —I can't do't, 'tis more than impossible. Positively, Mirabell, I'll lie abed in a morning as long as I please.

MIRABELL.

Then I'll get up in a morning as early as I please.

MILLAMANT.

Ah! Idle creature, get up when you will. —And d'ye hear, I won't be called names after I'm married; positively I won't be called names.

MIRABELL.

Names!

MILLAMANT.

Aye, as wife, spouse, my dear, joy, jewel, love, sweetheart, and the rest of that nauseous cant, in which men and their wives are so fulsomely familiar—I shall never bear that. —Good Mirabell, don't let us be familiar or fond, nor kiss before folks, like my Lady Fadler and Sir Francis; nor go to Hyde Park together the first Sunday in a new chariot, to provoke eyes and whispers; and then never to be seen there together again; as if we were proud of one another the first week, and ashamed of one another ever after. Let us never visit together, nor go to a play together. But let us be very strange and well-bred; let us be as strange as if we had been married a great while, and as well-bred as if we were not married at all.

MIRABELL.

Have you any more conditions to offer? Hitherto your demands are pretty reasonable.

MILLAMANT.

Trifles! —As liberty to pay and receive visits to and from whom I please; to write and receive letters, without interro-

181. never to be] *Q1;* never be *W1.*

183. ever after] *Q2, W1*; for ever after *Q1.*

166. *douceurs*] sweetnesses.

167. *sommeils du matin*] morning slumbers.

179. *Fadler*] To faddle is to fondle.

185. *strange*] reserved.

gatories or wry faces on your part; to wear what I please; and choose conversation with regard only to my own taste; to have no obligation upon me to converse with wits that I don't like, because they are your acquaintance; or to be intimate with fools, because they may be your relations. Come to dinner when I please; dine in my dressing room when I'm out of humor, without giving a reason. To have my closet inviolate; to be sole empress of my tea table, which you must never presume to approach without first asking leave. And lastly, wherever I am, you shall always knock at the door before you come in. These articles subscribed, if I continue to endure you a little longer, I may by degrees dwindle into a wife.

MIRABELL.

Your bill of fare is something advanced in this latter account. Well, have I liberty to offer conditions—that when you are dwindled into a wife, I may not be beyond measure enlarged into a husband?

MILLAMANT.

You have free leave. Propose your utmost; speak and spare not.

MIRABELL.

I thank you. *Imprimis* then, I covenant that your acquaintance be general; that you admit no sworn confidante, or intimate of your own sex; no she-friend to screen her affairs under your countenance, and tempt you to make trial of a mutual secrecy. No decoy-duck to wheedle you a fop, scrambling to the play in a mask; then bring you home in a pretended fright, when you think you shall be found out, and rail at me for missing the play, and disappointing the frolic which you had, to pick me up and prove my constancy.

MILLAMANT.

Detestable *imprimis!* I go to the play in a mask!

MIRABELL.

Item, I article that you continue to like your own face as

---

211. *Imprimis*] In the first place.

215–216. *decoy-duck . . . mask*] a female confidante to coax a fop to hurry you, masked, to the theater.

221. *article*] stipulate.

long as I shall; and while it passes current with me, that you endeavor not to new-coin it. To which end, together with all vizards for the day, I prohibit all masks for the night, made of oiled skins and I know now what—hog's bones, hare's gall, pig-water, and the marrow of a roasted cat. In short, I forbid all commerce with the gentlewoman in What-d'ye-call-it Court. *Item,* I shut my doors against all bawds with baskets, and pennyworths of muslin, china, fans, atlases, etc. —*Item,* when you shall be breeding—

MILLAMANT.

Ah! name it not.

MIRABELL.

Which may be presumed, with a blessing on our endeavors—

MILLAMANT.

Odious endeavors!

MIRABELL.

I denounce against all strait-lacing, squeezing for a shape, till you mold my boy's head like a sugar loaf, and instead of a man-child, make me the father to a crooked billet. Lastly, to the dominion of the tea table I submit, but with proviso, that you exceed not in your province, but restrain yourself to native and simple tea-table drinks, as tea, chocolate, and coffee. As likewise to genuine and authorized tea-table talk—such as mending of fashions, spoiling reputations, railing at absent friends, and so forth; but that on no account you encroach upon the men's prerogative, and presume to drink healths, or toast fellows; for prevention of which, I banish all foreign forces, all auxiliaries to the tea table, as orange brandy, all aniseed, cinnamon, citron, and Barbadoes waters, together with ratafia and the most

227. gentlewoman] *Q1, W1;* gentlewomen *Q2.*

237. me the father] *Q1*; me father *W1.*

---

224. *vizards*] masks.

226. *pig-water*] an ingredient in cosmetics.

227–228. *gentlewoman in What-d'ye-call-it Court*] referring to a seller of cosmetics.

230. *atlases*] a kind of oriental satin.

237. *billet*] small stick.

248. *Barbadoes waters*] brandy flavored with orange and lemon peel.

noble spirit of clary. But for cowslip-wine, poppy-water, and all dormitives, those I allow. These provisos admitted, in other things I may prove a tractable and complying husband.

MILLAMANT.

Oh, horrid provisos! filthy strong waters! I toast fellows, odious men! I hate your odious provisos.

MIRABELL.

Then we're agreed. Shall I kiss your hand upon the contract? And here comes one to be a witness to the sealing of the deed.

Enter Mrs. Fainall.

MILLAMANT.

Fainall, what shall I do? Shall I have him? I think I must have him.

MRS. FAINALL.

Aye, aye, take him, take him, what should you do?

MILLAMANT.

Well then—I'll take my death I'm in a horrid fright—Fainall, I shall never say it—well—I think—I'll endure you.

MRS. FAINALL.

Fie, fie! have him, have him, and tell him so in plain terms; for I am sure you have a mind to him.

MILLAMANT.

Are you? I think I have—and the horrid man looks as if he thought so too. —Well, you ridiculous thing you, I'll have you—I won't be kissed, nor I won't be thanked—here, kiss my hand though. —So, hold your tongue now, and don't say a word.

MRS FAINALL.

Mirabell, there's a necessity for your obedience; you have neither time to talk nor stay. My mother is coming; and in my conscience, if she should see you, would fall into fits and maybe not recover, time enough to return to Sir Rowland,

268. and don't] *Q1;* and *omitted in W1.*

---

249. *clary*] clary water, brandy flavored with clary flowers and various spices.

250. *dormitives*] drinks to promote sleep.

who, as Foible tells me, is in a fair way to succeed. Therefore spare your ecstasies for another occasion, and slip down the backstairs, where Foible waits to consult you.

MILLAMANT.

Aye, go, go. In the meantime I suppose you have said something to please me.

MIRABELL.

I am all obedience. *Exit.*

MRS. FAINALL.

Yonder Sir Wilfull's drunk, and so noisy that my mother has been forced to leave Sir Rowland to appease him; but he answers her only with singing and drinking. What they have done by this time I know not; but Petulant and he were quarreling as I came by.

MILLAMANT.

Well, if Mirabell should not make a good husband, I am a lost thing—for I find I love him violently.

MRS. FAINALL.

So it seems, when you mind not what's said to you. If you doubt him, you had best take up with Sir Wilfull.

MILLAMANT.

How can you name that superannuated lubber? foh!

Enter Witwoud *from drinking.*

MRS. FAINALL.

So, is the fray made up, that you have left 'em?

WITWOUD.

Left 'em? I could stay no longer. I have laughed like ten christenings; I am tipsy with laughing. If I had stayed any longer I should have burst; I must have been let out and pieced in the sides like an unsized camlet. Yes, yes, the fray is composed; my lady came in like a *nolle prosequi* and stopped their proceedings.

282–283. they have] *Q1;* they may have *W1.*
295. *nolle prosequi*] *Spelled noli prosequi* *Q1–2, W1.*
296. their proceedings] *Q1;* the proceedings *W1.*

294. *unsized camlet*] an unstiffened oriental fabric.
295. *nolle prosequi*] a legal term for terminating the prosecution of a lawsuit.

MILLAMANT.

What was the dispute?

WITWOUD.

That's the jest; there was no dispute. They could neither of 'em speak for rage, and so fell a-sputtering at one another like two roasting apples.

Enter Petulant *drunk.*

Now Petulant, all's over, all's well. Gad, my head begins to whim it about. Why dost thou not speak? Thou art both as drunk and as mute as a fish.

PETULANT.

Look you, Mrs. Millamant, if you can love me, dear nymph, say it, and that's the conclusion. Pass on, or pass off; that's all.

WITWOUD.

Thou hast uttered volumes, folios, in less than *decimo sexto,* my dear Lacedemonian. Sirrah Petulant, thou art an epitomizer of words.

PETULANT.

Witwoud, you are an annihilator of sense.

WITWOUD.

Thou art a retailer of phrases and dost deal in remnants of remnants, like a maker of pincushions; thou art in truth (metaphorically speaking) a speaker of shorthand.

PETULANT.

Thou art (without a figure) just one half of an ass, and Baldwin yonder, thy half brother, is the rest. A gemini of asses split would make just four of you.

WITWOUD.

Thou dost bite, my dear mustard seed; kiss me for that.

---

302. *whim it about*] spin.

307. *decimo sexto*] a small-sized book in which each sheet is folded into sixteen leaves.

308. *Lacedemonian*] Spartan. The Spartans were famous for brevity of speech.

308–309. *epitomizer*] one who states briefly the essence of a matter.

315. *Baldwin*] the name of the ass in the beast epic of Reynard the Fox.

315. *gemini*] a pair of twins.

317. *mustard seed*] A paste made from mustard seeds, with the addition of water and vinegar, was a pungent kind of seasoning.

PETULANT.

Stand off! I'll kiss no more males. I have kissed your twin yonder in a humor of reconciliation, till he *(hiccup)* rises upon my stomach like a radish.

MILLAMANT.

Eh! filthy creature! What was the quarrel?

PETULANT.

There was no quarrel; there might have been a quarrel.

WITWOUD.

If there had been words enow between 'em to have expressed provocation, they had gone together by the ears like a pair of castanets.

PETULANT.

You were the quarrel.

MILLAMANT.

Me!

PETULANT.

If I have a humor to quarrel, I can make less matters conclude premises. If you are not handsome, what then, if I have a humor to prove it? If I shall have my reward, say so; if not, fight for your face the next time yourself. I'll go sleep.

WITWOUD.

Do, wrap thyself up like a wood louse, and dream revenge; and hear me, if thou canst learn to write by tomorrow morning, pen me a challenge. I'll carry it for thee.

PETULANT.

Carry your mistress's monkey a spider! Go flea dogs, and read romances! I'll go to bed to my maid. *Exit.*

MRS. FAINALL.

He's horridly drunk. How came you all in this pickle?

WITWOUD.

A plot! a plot! to get rid of the knight. Your husband's advice; but he sneaked off.

---

323. *enow*] enough.

329. *conclude premises*] bring matters to a head.

333. *wood louse*] small insect found in old wood or under stones, capable of rolling itself up in a ball.

336. *flea dogs*] pick fleas from the coats of lap-dogs.

Enter Lady Wishfort, *and* Sir Wilfull *drunk.*

LADY WISHFORT.

Out upon't, out upon't! At years of discretion, and comport yourself at this rantipole rate!

SIR WILFULL.

No offense, aunt.

LADY WISHFORT.

Offense? As I'm a person, I'm ashamed of you—foh! how you stink of wine! D'ye think my niece will ever endure such a borachio! you're an absolute borachio.

SIR WILFULL.

Borachio!

LADY WISHFORT.

At a time when you should commence an amour and put your best foot foremost—

SIR WILFULL.

'Sheart, an you grutch me your liquor, make a bill. Give me more drink, and take my purse. *Sings.*

Prithee fill me the glass,
Till it laugh in my face,
With ale that is potent and mellow;
He that whines for a lass
Is an ignorant ass,
For a bumper has not its fellow.

But if you would have me marry my cousin, say the word, and I'll do't. Wilfull will do't; that's the word. Wilfull will do't; that's my crest. My motto I have forgot.

LADY WISHFORT.

My nephew's a little overtaken, cousin, but 'tis with drinking your health. O' my word you are obliged to him.

SIR WILFULL.

In vino veritas, aunt. If I drunk your health today, cousin,

353. laugh] *Q1, W1;* laughs *Q2.*

342. *rantipole*] ill-mannered. 344. *foh!*] an exclamation of disgust.

346. *borachio*] drunkard. The term is derived from the Spanish word for winebag.

350. *grutch*] grudge. 361. *overtaken*] overcome.

363. *In vino veritas*] In wine there is truth, i.e., drunkards frankly speak the truth.

I am a borachio. But if you have a mind to be married, say the word, and send for the piper; Wilfull will do't. If not, dust it away, and let's have t'other round. —Tony! —Odsheart, where's Tony? —Tony's an honest fellow; but he spits after a bumper, and that's a fault. *Sings.*

We'll drink, and we'll never ha' done, boys,
Put the glass then around with the sun, boys;
Let Apollo's example invite us;
For he's drunk every night,
And that makes him so bright,
That he's able next morning to light us.

The sun's a good pimple, an honest soaker; he has a cellar at your Antipodes. If I travel, aunt, I touch at your Antipodes; your Antipodes are a good, rascally sort of topsy-turvy fellows. If I had a bumper, I'd stand upon my head and drink a health to 'em. A match, or no match, cousin with the hard name? Aunt, Wilfull will do't. If she has her maidenhead, let her look to't; if she has not, let her keep her own counsel in the meantime, and cry out at the nine months' end.

MILLAMANT.

Your pardon, madam, I can stay no longer. Sir Wilfull grows very powerful. Egh! how he smells! I shall be overcome if I stay. Come, cousin.

Exeunt Millamant *and* Mrs. Fainall.

LADY WISHFORT.

Smells! he would poison a tallow chandler and his family. Beastly creature, I know not what to do with him! Travel, quotha! aye, travel, travel, get thee gone, get thee but far enough, to the Saracens, or the Tartars, or the Turks, for thou art not fit to live in a Christian commonwealth, thou beastly pagan!

SIR WILFULL.

Turks, no; no Turks, aunt; your Turks are infidels, and believe not in the grape. Your Mahometan, your Mussulman, is a dry stinkard. No offense, aunt. My map says that

375. *pimple*] boon companion.
376. *Antipodes*] the opposite side of the earth and its inhabitants.
387. *tallow chandler*] a maker or seller of tallow candles.
395. *dry stinkard*] a stinking non-drinker.

your Turk is not so honest a man as your Christian. I cannot find by the map that your Mufti is orthodox; whereby it is a plain case that orthodox is a hard word, aunt, and (*hiccup*) Greek for claret. *Sings.*

To drink is a Christian diversion,
Unknown to the Turk and the Persian:
  Let Mahometan fools
  Live by heathenish rules,
And be damned over tea cups and coffee!
  But let British lads sing,
  Crown a health to the king,
And a fig for your sultan and sophy!

Ah, Tony!

Enter Foible, *and whispers* Lady Wishfort.

LADY WISHFORT [*aside to* Foible].

Sir Rowland impatient? Good lack! what shall I do with this beastly tumbril? [*Aloud.*] Go lie down and sleep, you sot! or, as I'm a person, I'll have you bastinadoed with broomsticks. Call up the wenches. *Exit* Foible.

SIR WILFULL.

Ahey! Wenches, where are the wenches?

LADY WISHFORT.

Dear Cousin Witwoud, get him away, and you will bind me to you inviolably. I have an affair of moment that invades me with some precipitation. You will oblige me to all futurity.

WITWOUD.

Come, knight. Pox on him, I don't know what to say to him. Will you go to a cock-match?

SIR WILFULL.

With a wench, Tony? Is she a shake-bag, Sirrah? Let me

401. Turk and] *Q1;* Turk or *W1.*

412. the wenches] *Q1;* the wenches with broomsticks *W1.*

---

397. *Mufti*] Mohammedan priest.

407. *sophy*] the Shah of Persia.

410. *tumbril*] heavy cart.

411. *bastinadoed*] beaten on the soles of the feet.

420. *shake-bag*] large gamecock.

bite your cheek for that.

WITWOUD.

Horrible! He has a breath like a bagpipe! Aye, aye, come, will you march, my Salopian?

SIR WILFULL.

Lead on, little Tony; I'll follow thee, my Anthony, my Tantony. Sirrah, thou shalt be my Tantony, and I'll be thy pig.

And a fig for your sultan and sophy.

Exit singing with Witwoud.

LADY WISHFORT.

This will never do. It will never make a match—at least before he has been abroad.

Enter Waitwell, *disguised as for* Sir Rowland.

Dear Sir Rowland, I am confounded with confusion at the retrospection of my own rudeness! I have more pardons to ask than the Pope distributes in the Year of Jubilee. But I hope, where there is likely to be so near an alliance, we may unbend the severity of decorum and dispense with a little ceremony.

WAITWELL.

My impatience, madam, is the effect of my transport; and till I have the possession of your adorable person, I am tantalized on a rack, and do but hang, madam, on the tenter of expectation.

LADY WISHFORT.

You have an excess of gallantry, Sir Rowland, and press things to a conclusion with a most prevailing vehemence. But a day or two for decency of marriage—

WAITWELL.

For decency of funeral, madam! The delay will break

438. a rack] *Q1;* the rack *Q2, W1.*

---

423. *Salopian*] native of Shropshire.

425. *Tantony*] a corruption of St. Anthony, renowned for his triumph over gluttony. He was commonly represented in art as followed by a pig.

431. *retrospection*] act of looking back on the past.

432. *Year of Jubilee*] the year in which the Pope proclaims remission of the punishment imposed for sin. The year in which this play was first acted (1700) was a jubilee year.

439. *tenter*] tenterhook.

my heart; or, if that should fail, I shall be poisoned. My nephew will get an inkling of my designs and poison me; and I would willingly starve him before I die; I would gladly go out of the world with that satisfaction. That would be some comfort to me, if I could but live so long as to be revenged on that unnatural viper.

LADY WISHFORT.

Is he so unnatural, say you? Truly I would contribute much both to the saving of your life, and the accomplishment of your revenge. Not that I respect myself, though he has been a perfidious wretch to me.

WAITWELL.

Perfidious to you!

LADY WISHFORT.

O Sir Rowland, the hours that he has died away at my feet, the tears that he has shed, the oaths that he has sworn, the palpitations that he has felt, the trances and the tremblings, the ardors and the ecstasies, the kneelings and the risings, the heart-heavings, and the hand-grippings, the pangs and the pathetic regards of his protesting eyes! Oh, no memory can register.

WAITWELL.

What, my rival! Is the rebel my rival? 'A dies.

LADY WISHFORT.

No, don't kill him at once, Sir Rowland; starve him gradually, inch by inch.

WAITWELL.

I'll do't. In three weeks he shall be barefoot; in a month out at knees with begging an alms. He shall starve upward and upward, till he has nothing living but his head, and then go out in a stink like a candle's end upon a save-all.

LADY WISHFORT.

Well, Sir Rowland, you have the way. You are no novice in the labyrinth of love; you have the clue. But as I am a person, Sir Rowland, you must not attribute my yielding to any sinister appetite, or indigestion of widowhood; nor impute

---

452. *respect*] consider.

468. *save-all*] a device in a candlestick to hold the ends of candles so that they may be burned.

my complacency to any lethargy of continence. I hope you do not think me prone to any iteration of nuptials.

WAITWELL.

Far be it from me—

LADY WISHFORT.

If you do, I protest I must recede, or think that I have made a prostitution of decorums; but in the vehemence of compassion, and to save the life of a person of so much importance—

WAITWELL.

I esteem it so.

LADY WISHFORT.

Or else you wrong my condescension.

WAITWELL.

I do not, I do not!

LADY WISHFORT.

Indeed you do.

WAITWELL.

I do not, fair shrine of virtue!

LADY WISHFORT.

If you think the least scruple of carnality was an ingredient—

WAITWELL.

Dear madam, no. You are all camphire and frankincense, all chastity and odor.

LADY WISHFORT.

Or that—

Enter Foible.

FOIBLE.

Madam, the dancers are ready, and there's one with a letter, who must deliver it into your own hands.

LADY WISHFORT.

Sir Rowland, will you give me leave? Think favorably, judge candidly, and conclude you have found a person who would suffer racks in honor's cause, dear Sir Rowland, and will wait on you incessantly. *Exit.*

WAITWELL.

Fie, fie! What a slavery have I undergone! Spouse, hast

486. *camphire*] camphor, supposed to lessen sexual desire.
494. *incessantly*] instantly.

thou any cordial? I want spirits.

FOIBLE.

What a washy rogue art thou, to pant thus for a quarter of an hour's lying and swearing to a fine lady!

WAITWELL.

Oh, she is the antidote to desire! Spouse, thou wilt fare the worse for't. I shall have no appetite to iteration of nuptials this eight-and-forty hours. By this hand I'd rather be a chairman in the dog-days than act Sir Rowland till this time tomorrow!

Enter Lady Wishfort, *with a letter.*

LADY WISHFORT.

Call in the dancers. Sir Rowland, we'll sit, if you please, and see the entertainment.

Dance.

Now, with your permission, Sir Rowland, I will peruse my letter. I would open it in your presence, because I would not make you uneasy. If it should make you uneasy, I would burn it. Speak, if it does. But you may see by the superscription it is like a woman's hand.

FOIBLE [*aside to* Waitwell].

By heaven! Mrs. Marwood's; I know it. My heart aches. Get it from her.

WAITWELL.

A woman's hand? No, madam, that's no woman's hand; I see that already. That's somebody whose throat must be cut.

LADY WISHFORT.

Nay, Sir Rowland, since you give me a proof of your passion by your jealousy, I promise you I'll make you a return, by a frank communication. You shall see it; we'll open it together. Look you here. (*Reads.*) "Madam, though unknown to you"—Look you there, 'tis from nobody

500. iteration] *W1;* interation *Q1–2.*

509–510. by the superscription it is] *Q1;* the superscription is *W1.*

---

497. *washy*] watery.

502. *chairman in the dog-days*] bearer of a sedan chair in the hottest part of the summer.

that I know—"I have that honor for your character, that I think myself obliged to let you know you are abused. He who pretends to be Sir Rowland is a cheat and a rascal." —Oh, heavens! what's this?

FOIBLE [*aside*].

Unfortunate! all's ruined!

WAITWELL.

How, how, let me see, let me see! (*Reading.*) "A rascal, and disguised and suborned for that imposture." —O villainy! O villainy —"by the contrivance of —"

LADY WISHFORT.

I shall faint, I shall die, I shall die, oh!

FOIBLE [*aside to* Waitwell].

Say 'tis your nephew's hand. Quickly, his plot, swear, swear it!

WAITWELL.

Here's a villain! Madam, don't you perceive it? don't you see it?

LADY WISHFORT.

Too well, too well! I have seen too much.

WAITWELL.

I told you at first I knew the hand. A woman's hand? The rascal writes a sort of a large hand, your Roman hand. I saw there was a throat to be cut presently. If he were my son, as he is my nephew, I'd pistol him!

FOIBLE.

Oh, treachery! But are you sure, Sir Rowland, it is his writing?

WAITWELL.

Sure? Am I here? Do I live? Do I love this pearl of India? I have twenty letters in my pocket from him in the same character.

LADY WISHFORT.

How!

529. I shall faint, I shall die, I shall die, oh!] *Q1;* I shall faint, I shall die, oh! *Q2, W1.*

536. *Roman hand*] round and bold handwriting.
543. *character*] handwriting.

FOIBLE.

Oh, what luck it is, Sir Rowland, that you were present at this juncture! This was the business that brought Mr. Mirabell disguised to Madam Millamant this afternoon. I thought something was contriving, when he stole by me and would have hid his face.

LADY WISHFORT.

How, how! I heard the villain was in the house indeed; and now I remember, my niece went away abruptly, when Sir Wilfull was to have made his addresses.

FOIBLE.

Then, then, madam, Mr. Mirabell waited for her in her chamber, but I would not tell your ladyship to discompose you when you were to receive Sir Rowland.

WAITWELL.

Enough, his date is short.

FOIBLE.

No, good Sir Rowland, don't incur the law.

WAITWELL.

Law? I care not for law. I can but die, and 'tis in a good cause. My lady shall be satisfied of my truth and innocence, though it cost me my life.

LADY WISHFORT.

No, dear Sir Rowland, don't fight; if you should be killed, I must never show my face; or hanged—oh, consider my reputation, Sir Rowland! No, you shan't fight. I'll go in and examine my niece; I'll make her confess. I conjure you, Sir Rowland, by all your love, not to fight.

WAITWELL.

I am charmed, madam; I obey. But some proof you must let me give you; I'll go for a black box, which contains the writings of my whole estate, and deliver that into your hands.

LADY WISHFORT.

Aye, dear Sir Rowland, that will be some comfort; bring the black box.

WAITWELL.

And may I presume to bring a contract to be signed this night? May I hope so far?

LADY WISHFORT.

Bring what you will; but come alive, pray come alive. Oh,

this is a happy discovery!

WAITWELL.

Dead or alive I'll come, and married we will be in spite of treachery; aye, and get an heir that shall defeat the last remaining glimpse of hope in my abandoned nephew. Come, my buxom widow.

Ere long you shall substantial proof receive
That I'm an arrant knight—

FOIBLE [*aside*]. Or arrant knave. *Exeunt.*

[V] *Scene continues.*

Enter Lady Wishfort *and* Foible.

LADY WISHFORT.

Out of my house, out of my house, thou viper! thou serpent, that I have fostered! thou bosom traitress that I raised from nothing! Begone! begone! begone! go! go! That I took from washing of old gauze and weaving of dead hair, with a bleak blue nose, over a chafing dish of starved embers, and dining behind a traverse rag, in a shop no bigger than a birdcage! Go, go! starve again, do, do!

FOIBLE.

Dear madam, I'll beg pardon on my knees.

LADY WISHFORT.

Away! out! out! Go set up for yourself again! Do, drive a trade, do, with your three-pennyworth of small ware, flaunting upon a pack-thread, under a brandy-seller's bulk, or against a dead wall by a ballad-monger! Go, hang out an old frisoneer gorget, with a yard of yellow colberteen again. Do! an old gnawed mask, two rows of pins, and a child's fiddle; a glass necklace with the beads broken, and a

---

578. *buxom*] gay (the archaic meaning).

580. *arrant knight*] wandering knight.

580. *arrant knave*] downright knave. Foible plays on the word *arrant* (*errant*), using it in its later sense.

[V]

4. *weaving of dead hair*] i.e., making wigs.

6. *traverse rag*] tattered curtain.

11. *bulk*] stall.

13. *frisoneer gorget*] woollen neckpiece or kerchief.

13. *colberteen*] a kind of cheap lace.

quilted nightcap with one ear. Go, go, drive a trade! These were your commodities, you treacherous trull! This was your merchandise you dealt in, when I took you into my house, placed you next myself, and made you governante of my whole family! You have forgot this, have you, now you have feathered your nest?

FOIBLE.

No, no, dear madam. Do but hear me; have but a moment's patience. I'll confess all. Mr. Mirabell seduced me; I am not the first that he has wheedled with his dissembling tongue. Your ladyship's own wisdom has been deluded by him; then how should I, a poor ignorant, defend myself? O madam, if you knew but what he promised me, and how he assured me your ladyship should come to no damage! Or else the wealth of the Indies should not have bribed me to conspire against so good, so sweet, so kind a lady as you have been to me.

LADY WISHFORT.

No damage? What, to betray me, to marry me to a cast servingman? to make me a receptacle, an hospital for a decayed pimp? No damage? O thou frontless impudence, more than a big-bellied actress.

FOIBLE.

Pray do but hear me, madam; he could not marry your ladyship, madam. No indeed; his marriage was to have been void in law, for he was married to me first, to secure your ladyship. He could not have bedded your ladyship; for if he had consummated with your ladyship, he must have run the risk of the law and been put upon his clergy. Yes indeed; I inquired of the law in that case before I would meddle or make.

17–18. your merchandise] *Q1;* the merchandise *W1.*

---

19. *governante*] housekeeper.

32–33. *cast servingman*] discharged servant.

34. *frontless*] shameless.

41. *put upon his clergy*] A criminal who could read and write might escape sentence of death by claiming "benefit of clergy," a privilege originally restricted to clergymen.

43. *meddle or make*] have anything to do with the affair.

LADY WISHFORT.

What, then I have been your property, have I? I have been convenient to you, it seems! While you were catering for Mirabell, I have been broker for you? What, have you made a passive bawd of me? This exceeds all precedent; I am brought to fine uses, to become a botcher of secondhand marriages between Abigails and Andrews! I'll couple you! Yes, I'll baste you together, you and your Philander! I'll Duke's Place you, as I'm a person! Your turtle is in custody already; you shall coo in the same cage, if there be constable or warrant in the parish. *Exit.*

FOIBLE.

Oh, that ever I was born! Oh, that I was ever married! A bride! aye, I shall be a Bridewell-bride. Oh!

Enter Mrs. Fainall.

MRS. FAINALL.

Poor Foible, what's the matter?

FOIBLE.

O madam, my lady's gone for a constable. I shall be had to a justice, and put to Bridewell to beat hemp. Poor Waitwell's gone to prison already.

MRS. FAINALL.

Have a good heart, Foible; Mirabell's gone to give security for him. This is all Marwood's and my husband's doing.

FOIBLE.

Yes, yes, I know it, madam; she was in my lady's closet, and overheard all that you said to me before dinner. She sent the letter to my lady; and that missing effect, Mr. Fainall laid this plot to arrest Waitwell, when he pretended to go for the papers; and in the meantime Mrs. Marwood declared all to my lady.

---

46. *broker*] i.e., marriage broker.

49. *Abigails and Andrews*] waiting maids and menservants.

50. *Philander*] lover.

51. *Duke's Place you*] marry you in a hurry, as at St. James's Church in Duke's Place, notorious for irregular marriages.

55. *Bridewell-bride*] a bride in Bridewell Prison, where women offenders were often punished by being required to beat hemp.

MRS. FAINALL.

Was there no mention made of me in the letter? My mother does not suspect my being in the confederacy? I fancy Marwood has not told her, though she has told my husband.

FOIBLE.

Yes, madam; but my lady did not see that part. We stifled the letter before she read so far. Has that mischievous devil told Mr. Fainall of your ladyship then?

MRS. FAINALL.

Aye, all's out, my affair with Mirabell, everything discovered. This is the last day of our living together; that's my comfort.

FOIBLE.

Indeed, madam, and so 'tis a comfort if you knew all. He has been even with your ladyship; which I could have told you long enough since, but I love to keep peace and quietness by my good will. I had rather bring friends together than set 'em at distance. But Mrs. Marwood and he are nearer related than ever their parents thought for.

MRS. FAINALL.

Say'st thou so, Foible? Canst thou prove this?

FOIBLE.

I can take my oath of it, madam; so can Mrs. Mincing. We have had many a fair word from Madam Marwood, to conceal something that passed in our chamber one evening when you were at Hyde Park and we were thought to have gone a-walking; but we went up unawares, though we were sworn to secrecy too. Madam Marwood took a book and swore us upon it, but it was a book of verses and poems. So as long as it was not a Bible oath, we may break it with a safe conscience.

MRS. FAINALL.

This discovery is the most opportune thing I could wish. Now, Mincing?

92. verses and poems] *Q1;* verses and *omitted in W1.*

92–93. So as long as] *Q1;* so long as *Q2, W1.*

Enter Mincing.

MINCING.

My lady would speak with Mrs. Foible, mem. Mr. Mirabell is with her; he has set your spouse at liberty, Mrs. Foible, and would have you hide yourself in my lady's closet till my old lady's anger is abated. Oh, my old lady is in a perilous passion at something Mr. Fainall has said; he swears, and my old lady cries. There's a fearful hurricane, I vow. He says, mem, how that he'll have my lady's fortune made over to him, or he'll be divorced.

MRS. FAINALL.

Does your lady or Mirabell know that?

MINCING.

Yes, mem; they have sent me to see if Sir Wilfull be sober and to bring him to them. My lady is resolved to have him, I think, rather than lose such a vast sum as six thousand pound. Oh, come, Mrs. Foible, I hear my old lady.

MRS. FAINALL.

Foible, you must tell Mincing that she must prepare to vouch when I call her.

FOIBLE.

Yes, yes, madam.

MINCING.

O yes, mem, I'll vouch anything for your ladyship's service, be what it will. *Exeunt* Mincing *and* Foible.

Enter Lady Wishfort *and* Marwood.

LADY WISHFORT.

O my dear friend, how can I enumerate the benefits that I have received from your goodness? To you I owe the timely discovery of the false vows of Mirabell; to you the detection of the imposter Sir Rowland. And now you are become an intercessor with my son-in-law, to save the honor of my house, and compound for the frailties of my daughter. Well, friend, you are enough to reconcile me to the bad

105. or] *W1;* and *Q1.*

117–118. to you the detection] *Q1;* to you I owe the detection *W1.*

---

120. *compound*] make composition.

world, or else I would retire to deserts and solitudes, and feed harmless sheep by groves and purling streams. Dear Marwood, let us leave the world, and retire by ourselves and be shepherdesses.

MRS. MARWOOD.

Let us first dispatch the affair in hand, madam. We shall have leisure to think of retirement afterwards. Here is one who is concerned in the treaty.

LADY WISHFORT.

O daughter, daughter, is it possible thou shouldst be my child, bone of my bone, and flesh of my flesh, and, as I may say, another me, and yet transgress the most minute particle of severe virtue? It is possible you should lean aside to iniquity, who have been cast in the direct mold of virtue? I have not only been a mold but a pattern for you, and a model for you, after you were brought into the world.

MRS. FAINALL.

I don't understand your ladyship.

LADY WISHFORT.

Not understand? Why, have you not been naught? Have you not been sophisticated? Not understand? Here I am ruined to compound for your caprices and your cuckoldoms. I must pawn my plate and my jewels, and ruin my niece, and all little enough.

MRS. FAINALL.

I am wronged and abused, and so are you. 'Tis a false accusation, as false as hell, as false as your friend there, aye, or your friend's friend, my false husband.

MRS. MARWOOD.

My friend, Mrs. Fainall? Your husband my friend? What do you mean?

MRS. FAINALL.

I know what I mean, madam, and so do you; and so shall the world at a time convenient.

MRS. MARWOOD.

I am sorry to see you so passionate, madam. More temper

---

137. *naught*] immoral. 138. *sophisticated*] corrupted.
149. *temper*] equanimity, composure.

would look more like innocence. But I have done. I am sorry my zeal to serve your ladyship and family should admit of misconstruction, or make me liable to affronts. You will pardon me, madam, if I meddle no more with an affair in which I am not personally concerned.

LADY WISHFORT.

O dear friend, I am so ashamed that you should meet with such returns! [*To Mrs. Fainall.*] You ought to ask pardon on your knees, ungrateful creature; she deserves more from you than all your life can accomplish. [*To Mrs. Marwood.*] Oh, don't leave me destitute in this perplexity! No, stick to me, my good genius.

MRS. FAINALL.

I tell you, madam, you're abused. Stick to you? Aye, like a leech, to suck your best blood; she'll drop off when she's full. Madam, you shan't pawn a bodkin, nor part with a brass counter, in composition for me. I defy 'em all. Let 'em prove their aspersions; I know my own innocence, and dare stand by a trial. *Exit.*

LADY WISHFORT.

Why, if she should be innocent, if she should be wronged after all, ha? I don't know what to think—and, I promise you, her education has been unexceptionable. I may say it; for I chiefly made it my own care to initiate her very infancy in the rudiments of virtue, and to impress upon her tender years a young odium and aversion to the very sight of men—aye, friend, she would ha' shrieked if she had but seen a man, till she was in her teens. As I'm a person, 'tis true. She was never suffered to play with a male child, though but in coats; nay, her very babies were of the feminine gender. Oh, she never looked a man in the face but her own father, or the chaplain, and him we made a shift to put upon her for a woman, by the help of his long garments and his sleek face, till she was going in her fifteen.

163. shan't] *Q2, W1;* sha'not *Q1.* 166. stand by] *Q1;* stand *W1.*

163. *bodkin*] a pin-shaped ornament used by women to fasten up their hair.

164. *brass counter*] coin of base metal used as a token of payment.

166. *stand by*] undergo. 176. *babies*] dolls.

178. *made a shift*] used a trick.

MRS. MARWOOD.

'Twas much she should be deceived so long.

LADY WISHFORT.

I warrant you, or she would never have borne to have been catechized by him; and have heard his long lectures against singing and dancing, and such debaucheries; and going to filthy plays, and profane music-meetings, where the lewd trebles squeak nothing but bawdy, and the basses roar blasphemy. Oh, she would have swooned at the sight or name of an obscene playbook! And can I think, after all this, that my daughter can be naught? What, a whore? And thought it excommunication to set her foot within the door of a playhouse! O my dear friend, I can't believe it, no, no! As she says, let him prove it, let him prove it.

MRS. MARWOOD.

Prove it, madam? What, and have your name prostituted in a public court! Yours and your daughter's reputation worried at the bar by a pack of bawling lawyers! To be ushered in with an *Oyez* of scandal, and have your case opened by an old fumbling lecher in a quoif like a man midwife; to bring your daughter's infamy to light; to be a theme for legal punsters and quibblers by the statute, and become a jest against a rule of court, where there is no precedent for a jest in any record, not even in Doomsday Book; to discompose the gravity of the bench, and provoke naughty interrogatories in more naughty law Latin, while the good judge, tickled with the proceeding, simpers under a gray beard, and fidges off and on his cushion as if he had swallowed cantharides, or sat upon cow-itch.

191. my dear friend] *Q1;* dear friend *W1.*
196. *Oyez*] *O Yez Q1;* O Yes *Q2, W1.*
205. fidges] *Q1;* figes *W1.*
206. sat] *Q1;* sate *Q2, W1.*

---

196. *Oyez*] Hear ye, a cry used by court-criers to gain silence before making a proclamation.

197. *quoif*] white cap then worn by a serjeant-at-law.

201. *Doomsday Book*] the record of a survey of the lands of England made in 1085–1086 by order of William the Conqueror.

205. *fidges*] fidgets.

206. *cantharides*] a preparation of dried beetles used for medicinal purposes.

206. *cow-itch*] cowhage, a tropical vine, the pods of which are covered with stinging hairs.

LADY WISHFORT.

Oh, 'tis very hard!

MRS. MARWOOD.

And then to have my young revelers of the Temple take notes, like prentices at a conventicle; and after, talk it all over again in commons, or before drawers in an eating house.

LADY WISHFORT.

Worse and worse!

MRS. MARWOOD.

Nay, this is nothing; if it would end here, 'twere well. But it must, after this, be consigned by the shorthand writers to the public press; and from thence be transferred to the hands, nay into the throats and lungs of hawkers, with voices more licentious than the loud flounder-man's, or the woman that cries gray peas. And this you must hear till you are stunned; nay, you must hear nothing else for some days.

LADY WISHFORT.

Oh, 'tis insupportable! No, no, dear friend; make it up, make it up; aye, aye, I'll compound. I'll give up all, myself and my all, my niece and her all, anything, everything for composition.

MRS. MARWOOD.

Nay, madam, I advise nothing; I only lay before you, as a friend, the inconveniences which perhaps you have overseen. Here comes Mr. Fainall. If he will be satisfied to huddle up all in silence, I shall be glad. You must think I would rather congratulate than condole with you.

Enter Fainall.

LADY WISHFORT.

Aye, aye, I do not doubt it, dear Marwood; no, no, I do

209–210. all over] *Q1;* over *W1.*

---

208. *revelers of the Temple*] law students of the Inns of Court.

208–209. *take notes, like prentices at a coventicle*] The apprentices of dissenting tradesmen were required to take notes on sermons for the benefit of their employers.

217. *the loud flounder-man's*] A certain street vendor for many years distinguished himself by his forceful manner of crying flounders in the streets of London.

226–227. *overseen*] overlooked.

not doubt it.

FAINALL.

Well, madam, I have suffered myself to be overcome by the importunity of this lady your friend, and am content that you shall enjoy your own proper estate during life, on condition you oblige yourself never to marry, under such penalty as I think convenient.

LADY WISHFORT.

Never to marry?

FAINALL.

No more Sir Rowlands; the next imposture may not be so timely detected.

MRS. MARWOOD.

That condition, I dare answer, my lady will consent to, without difficulty; she has already but too much experienced the perfidiousness of men. Besides, madam, when we retire to our pastoral solitude, we shall bid adieu to all other thoughts.

LADY WISHFORT.

Aye, that's true; but in case of necessity, as of health, or some such emergency—

FAINALL.

Oh, if you are prescribed marriage, you shall be considered; I will only reserve to myself the power to choose for you. If your physic be wholesome, it matters not who is your apothecary. Next, my wife shall settle on me the remainder of her fortune, not made over already; and for her maintenance depend entirely on my discretion.

LADY WISHFORT.

This is most inhumanly savage, exceeding the barbarity of a Muscovite husband.

FAINALL.

I learned it from his Czarish majesty's retinue, in a winter evening's conference over brandy and pepper, amongst other secrets of matrimony and policy, as they are at present practiced in the northern hemisphere. But this must be

254. *Muscovite*] Russian.

255. *Czarish majesty's retinue*] Peter the Great had visited England in 1698.

agreed unto, and that positively. Lastly, I will be endowed, in right of my wife, with that six thousand pound, which is the moiety of Mrs. Millamant's fortune in your possession; and which she has forfeited (as will appear by the last will and testament of your deceased husband, Sir Jonathan Wishfort) by her disobedience in contracting herself against your consent or knowledge, and by refusing the offered match with Sir Wilfull Witwoud, which you, like a careful aunt, had provided for her.

LADY WISHFORT.

My nephew was *non compos*, and could not make his addresses.

FAINALL.

I come to make demands. I'll hear no objections.

LADY WISHFORT.

You will grant me time to consider?

FAINALL.

Yes, while the instrument is drawing, to which you must set your hand till more sufficient deeds can be perfected; which I will take care shall be done with all possible speed. In the meanwhile, I will go for the said instrument, and till my return you may balance this matter in your own discretion. *Exit.*

LADY WISHFORT.

This insolence is beyond all precedent, all parallel. Must I be subject to this merciless villain?

MRS. MARWOOD.

'Tis severe indeed, madam, that you should smart for your daughter's wantonness.

LADY WISHFORT.

'Twas against my consent that she married this barbarian, but she would have him, though her year was not out. —Ah! her first husband, my son Languish, would not have carried it thus. Well, that was my choice, this is hers; she is matched now with a witness. I shall be mad! Dear

---

268. *non compos*] not in his right mind.

272. *while the instrument is drawing*] while the legal document is being drawn up.

283. *her year was not out*] her first year of widowhood.

286. *with a witness*] the equivalent of *with a vengeance*.

friend, is there no comfort for me? Must I live to be confiscated at this rebel rate? —Here come two more of my Egyptian plagues, too.

Enter Millamant *and* Sir Wilfull Witwoud.

SIR WILFULL.
Aunt, your servant.

LADY WISHFORT.
Out, caterpillar, call me not aunt! I know thee not!

SIR WILFULL.
I confess I have been a little in disguise, as they say. 'Sheart! and I'm sorry for't. What would you have? I hope I committed no offense, aunt, and, if I did, I am willing to make satisfaction; and what can a man say fairer? If I have broke anything, I'll pay for't, an it cost a pound. And so let that content for what's past, and make no more words. For what's to come, to pleasure you I'm willing to marry my cousin. So pray let's all be friends; she and I are agreed upon the matter before a witness.

LADY WISHFORT.
How's this, dear niece? Have I any comfort? Can this be true?

MILLAMANT.
I am content to be a sacrifice to your repose, madam; and to convince you that I had no hand in the plot, as you were misinformed, I have laid my commands on Mirabell to come in person, and be a witness that I give my hand to this flower of knighthood; and for the contract that passed between Mirabell and me, I have obliged him to make a resignation of it in your ladyship's presence. He is without, and waits your leave for admittance.

LADY WISHFORT.
Well, I'll swear I am something revived at this testimony of your obedience; but I cannot admit that traitor. I fear I cannot fortify myself to support his appearance. He is as

288. *at this rebel rate*] in this high-handed manner.
289. *Egyptian plagues*] referring to the ten plagues visited upon Pharaoh, cf. Exodus 7–12.
291. *caterpillar*] i.e., vile fellow. 292. *in disguise*] intoxicated.

terrible to me as a Gorgon; if I see him, I fear I shall turn to stone, petrify incessantly.

MILLAMANT.

If you disoblige him, he may resent your refusal and insist upon the contract still. Then 'tis the last time he will be offensive to you.

LADY WISHFORT.

Are you sure it will be the last time? If I were sure of that! Shall I never see him again?

MILLAMANT.

Sir Willfull, you and he are to travel together, are you not?

SIR WILFULL.

'Sheart, the gentleman's a civil gentleman, aunt; let him come in. Why, we are sworn brothers and fellow travelers. We are to be Pylades and Orestes, he and I. He is to be my interpreter in foreign parts. He has been overseas once already; and with proviso that I marry my cousin, will cross 'em once again, only to bear me company. 'Sheart, I'll call him in. An I set on't once, he shall come in; and see who'll hinder him. *Exit.*

MRS. MARWOOD.

This is precious fooling, if it would pass; but I'll know the bottom of it.

LADY WISHFORT.

O dear Marwood, you are not going?

MRS. MARWOOD.

Not far, madam; I'll return immediately. *Exit.*

Re-enter Sir Wilfull *and* Mirabell.

SIR WILFULL.

Look up, man, I'll stand by you; 'sbud an she do frown, she can't kill you; besides—harkee, she dare not frown desperately, because her face is none of her own. 'Sheart, an she should, her forehead would wrinkle like the coat of a

337. an she should] *Q1;* and she should *Q2, W1.*

314. *Gorgon*] one of the three mythological sisters whose terrible aspect turned those who beheld them to stone.

324. *Pylades and Orestes*] Pylades was the devoted friend and traveling companion of Orestes.

cream cheese; but mum for that, fellow traveler.

MIRABELL.

If a deep sense of the many injuries I have offered to so good a lady, with a sincere remorse and a hearty contrition, can but obtain the least glance of compassion, I am too happy. Ah, madam, there was a time! But let it be forgotten. I confess I have deservedly forfeited the high place I once held, of sighing at your feet. Nay, kill me not, by turning from me in disdain. I come not to plead for favor; nay, not for pardon. I am a suppliant only for your pity. I am going where I never shall behold you more.

SIR WILFULL.

How, fellow traveler! You shall go by yourself then.

MIRABELL.

Let me be pitied first, and afterwards forgotten—I ask no more.

SIR WILFULL.

By'r Lady, a very reasonable request, and will cost you nothing, aunt. Come, come, forgive and forget, aunt; why you must, an you are a Christian.

MIRABELL.

Consider, madam, in reality you could not receive much prejudice; it was an innocent device, though I confess it had a face of guiltiness. It was at most an artifice which love contrived, and errors which love produces have ever been accounted venial. At least think it is punishment enough that I have lost what in my heart I hold most dear, that to your cruel indignation I have offered up this beauty, and with her my peace and quiet; nay, all my hopes of future comfort.

SIR WILFULL.

An he does not move me, would I might never be o' the quorum! An it were not as good a deed as to drink, to give her to him again, I would I might never take shipping!

346. your pity] *Q1;* for pity *W1.*

363. might never be] *Q1;* may never be *W1.*

---

338. *mum*] silence.

351. *By'r Lady*] By Our Lady.

363–364. *o' the quorum*] one of the justices of the peace constituting a bench.

Aunt, if you don't forgive quickly, I shall melt, I can tell you that. My contract went no farther than a little mouth-glue, and that's hardly dry; one doleful sigh more from my fellow traveler, and 'tis dissolved.

LADY WISHFORT.

Well, nephew, upon your account—ah, he has a false insinuating tongue! Well, sir, I will stifle my just resentment at my nephew's request. I will endeavor what I can to forget, but on proviso that you resign the contract with my niece immediately.

MIRABELL.

It is in writing and with papers of concern; but I have sent my servant for it, and will deliver it to you, with all acknowledgments for your transcendent goodness.

LADY WISHFORT [*aside*].

Oh, he has witchcraft in his eyes and tongue! When I did not see him, I could have bribed a villain to his assassination; but his appearance rakes the embers which have so long lain smothered in my breast.

Enter Fainall *and* Mrs. Marwood.

FAINALL.

Your date of deliberation, madam, is expired. Here is the instrument; are you prepared to sign?

LADY WISHFORT.

If I were prepared, I am not empowered. My niece exerts a lawful claim, having matched herself by my direction to Sir Wilfull.

FAINALL.

That sham is too gross to pass on me, though 'tis imposed on you, madam.

MILLAMANT.

Sir, I have given my consent.

MIRABELL.

And, sir, I have resigned my pretensions.

SIR WILFULL.

And, sir, I assert my right; and will maintain it in defiance of you, sir, and of your instrument. 'Sheart, an you talk of an

367. *a little mouth-glue*] an oral promise.

instrument, sir, I have an old fox by my thigh shall hack your instrument of ram vellum to shreds, sir! It shall not be sufficient for a mittimus or a tailor's measure. Therefore, withdraw your instrument, sir, or by'r Lady, I shall draw mine.

LADY WISHFORT.

Hold, nephew, hold!

MILLAMANT.

Good Sir Wilfull, respite your valor.

FAINALL.

Indeed? Are you provided of a guard, with your single beefeater there? But I'm prepared for you, and insist upon my first proposal. You shall submit your own estate to my management and absolutely make over my wife's to my sole use, as pursuant to the purport and tenor of this other covenant. [*To* Millamant.] I suppose, madam, your consent is not requisite in this case; nor, Mr. Mirabell, your resignation; nor, Sir Wilfull, your right. You may draw your fox if you please, sir, and make a bear-garden flourish somewhere else; for here it will not avail. This, my Lady Wishfort, must be subscribed, or your darling daughter's turned adrift, like a leaky hulk, to sink or swim, as she and the current of this lewd town can agree.

LADY WISHFORT.

Is there no means, no remedy to stop my ruin? Ungrateful wretch! dost thou not owe thy being, thy subsistence, to my daughter's fortune?

FAINALL.

I'll answer you when I have the rest of it in my possession.

400. a guard] *Q1;* your guard *Q2, W1.*

---

393. *fox*] a colloquial term for a sword.
394. *instrument of ram vellum*] legal document, written on parchment prepared from sheepskin.
395. *mittimus*] warrant of arrest.
395. *tailor's measure*] parchment used by tailors in taking measurements.
399. *respite*] delay.
401. *beefeater*] a yeoman of the royal guard.
408. *bear-garden*] arena for baiting bears.

MIRABELL.

But that you would not accept of a remedy from my hands—I own I have not deserved you should owe any obligation to me; or else perhaps I could advise—

LADY WISHFORT.

Oh, what? what? to save me and my child from ruin, from want, I'll forgive all that's past; nay, I'll consent to anything to come, to be delivered from this tyranny.

MIRABELL.

Aye, madam, but that is too late; my reward is intercepted. You have disposed of her who only could have made me a compensation for all my services. But be it as it may, I am resolved I'll serve you; you shall not be wronged in this savage manner.

LADY WISHFORT.

How! Dear Mr. Mirabell, can you be so generous at last? But it is not possible. Harkee, I'll break my nephew's match; you shall have my niece yet, and all her fortune, if you can but save me from this imminent danger.

MIRABELL.

Will you? I take you at your word. I ask no more. I must have leave for two criminals to appear.

LADY WISHFORT.

Aye, aye; anybody, anybody!

MIRABELL.

Foible is one, and a penitent.

Enter Mrs. Fainall, Foible, *and* Mincing.

MRS. MARWOOD (*to* Fainall).

Oh, my shame! These corrupt things are bought and brought hither to expose me.

Mirabell *and* Lady Wishfort *go to* Mrs. Fainall *and* Foible.

FAINALL.

If it must all come out, why let 'em know it; 'tis but the way of the world. That shall not urge me to relinquish or abate one tittle of my terms; no, I will insist the more.

436. bought and] *Q1; omitted in W1.*

FOIBLE.

Yes indeed, madam; I'll take my Bible oath of it.

MINCING.

And so will I, mem.

LADY WISHFORT.

O Marwood, Marwood, art thou false? my friend deceive me? Hast thou been a wicked accomplice with that profligate man?

MRS. MARWOOD.

Have you so much ingratitude and injustice, to give credit against your friend to the aspersions of two such mercenary trulls?

MINCING.

Mercenary, mem? I scorn your words. 'Tis true we found you and Mr. Fainall in the blue garret; by the same token, you swore us to secrecy upon Messalina's poems. Mercenary? No, if we would have been mercenary, we should have held our tongues; you would have bribed us sufficiently.

FAINALL.

Go, you are an insignificant thing! Well, what are you the better for this? Is this Mr. Mirabell's expedient? I'll be put off no longer. You thing, that was a wife, shall smart for this! I will not leave thee wherewithal to hide thy shame; your body shall be as naked as your reputation.

MRS. FAINALL.

I despise you, and defy your malice! You have aspersed me wrongfully. I have proved your falsehood. Go you and your treacherous—I will not name it, but starve together, perish!

FAINALL.

Not while you are worth a groat, indeed, my dear. Madam, I'll be fooled no longer.

LADY WISHFORT.

Ah, Mr. Mirabell, this is small comfort, the detection of this affair.

---

451. *Messalina's poems*] Messalina was the dissolute wife of the Roman emperor Claudius. Mincing, addicted to malapropisms, may have meant "miscellaneous."

463. *groat*] old English coin worth fourpence.

MIRABELL.

Oh, in good time. Your leave for the other offender and penitent to appear, madam.

Enter Waitwell *with a box of writings.*

LADY WISHFORT.

O Sir Rowland! Well, rascal?

WAITWELL.

What your ladyship pleases. I have brought the black box at last, madam.

MIRABELL.

Give it to me. Madam, you remember your promise.

LADY WISHFORT.

Aye, dear sir.

MIRABELL.

Where are the gentlemen?

WAITWELL.

At hand, sir, rubbing their eyes; just risen from sleep.

FAINALL.

'Sdeath, what's this to me? I'll not wait your private concerns.

Enter Petulant *and* Witwoud.

PETULANT.

How now? What's the matter? Whose hand's out?

WITWOUD.

Heyday! what, are you all got together, like players at the end of the last act?

MIRABELL.

You may remember, gentlemen, I once requested your hands as witnesses to a certain parchment.

WITWOUD.

Aye, I do; my hand I remember. Petulant set his mark.

MIRABELL.

You wrong him; his name is fairly written, as shall appear. You do not remember, gentlemen, anything of what that parchment contained? *Undoing the box.*

WITWOUD.

No.

---

478. *Whose hand's out?*] Who is making trouble?

PETULANT.

Not I. I writ. I read nothing.

MIRABELL.

Very well; now you shall know. Madam, your promise.

LADY WISHFORT.

Aye, aye, sir, upon my honor.

MIRABELL.

Mr. Fainall, it is now time that you should know that your lady, while she was at her own disposal, and before you had by your insinuations wheedled her out of a pretended settlement of the greatest part of her fortune—

FAINALL.

Sir! pretended!

MIRABELL.

Yes, sir. I say that this lady, while a widow, having, it seems, received some cautions respecting your inconstancy and tyranny of temper, which from her own partial opinion and fondness of you she could never have suspected—she did, I say, by the wholesome advice of friends and of sages learned in the laws of this land, deliver this same as her act and deed to me in trust, and to the uses within mentioned. You may read if you please (*Holding out the parchment.*)—though perhaps what is inscribed on the back may serve your occasions.

FAINALL.

Very likely, sir. What's here? Damnation! (*Reads.*) "A deed of conveyance of the whole estate real of Arabella Languish, widow, in trust to Edward Mirabell." Confusion!

MIRABELL.

Even so, sir; 'tis the way of the world, sir, of the widows of the world. I suppose this deed may bear an elder date than what you have obtained from your lady.

FAINALL.

Perfidious fiend! then thus I'll be revenged.

Offers to run at Mrs. Fainall.

504. inscribed on] *Q1;* written on *W1.*

SIR WILFULL.

Hold, sir! Now you may make your bear-garden flourish somewhere else, sir.

FAINALL.

Mirabell, you shall hear of this, sir; be sure you shall. Let me pass, oaf! *Exit.*

MRS. FAINALL.

Madam, you seem to stifle your resentment; you had better give it vent.

MRS. MARWOOD.

Yes, it shall have vent, and to your confusion; or I'll perish in the attempt. *Exit.*

LADY WISHFORT.

O daughter, daughter, 'tis plain thou hast inherited thy mother's prudence.

MRS. FAINALL.

Thank Mr. Mirabell, a cautious friend, to whose advice all is owing.

LADY WISHFORT.

Well, Mr. Mirabell, you have kept your promise, and I must perform mine. First, I pardon, for your sake, Sir Rowland there and Foible. The next thing is to break the matter to my nephew, and how to do that—

MIRABELL.

For that, madam, give yourself no trouble; let me have your consent. Sir Wilfull is my friend; he has had compassion upon lovers, and generously engaged a volunteer in this action for our service, and now designs to prosecute his travels.

SIR WILFULL.

'Sheart, aunt, I have no mind to marry. My cousin's a fine lady, and the gentleman loves her, and she loves him, and they deserve one another; my resolution is to see foreign parts. I have set on't, and when I'm set on't, I must do't. And if these two gentlemen would travel too, I think they may be spared.

PETULANT.

For my part, I say little; I think things are best off or on.

---

541. *off or on*] either way.

WITWOUD.

I gad, I understand nothing of the matter; I'm in a maze yet, like a dog in a dancing school.

LADY WISHFORT.

Well, sir, take her, and with her all the joy I can give you.

MILLAMANT.

Why does not the man take me? Would you have me give myself to you over again?

MIRABELL.

Aye, and over and over again; for I would have you as often as possibly I can. (*Kisses her hand.*) Well, heaven grant I love you not too well; that's all my fear.

SIR WILFULL.

'Sheart, you'll have time enough to toy after you're married; or if you will toy now, let us have a dance in the meantime, that we who are not lovers may have some other employment besides looking on.

MIRABELL.

With all my heart, dear Sir Wilfull. What shall we do for music?

FOIBLE.

Oh, sir, some that were provided for Sir Rowland's entertainment are yet within call.

A dance.

LADY WISHFORT.

As I am a person, I can hold out no longer. I have wasted my spirits so today already that I am ready to sink under the fatigue; and I cannot but have some fears upon me yet that my son Fainall will pursue some desperate course.

MIRABELL.

Madam, disquiet not yourself on that account; to my knowledge his circumstances are such, he must of force comply. For my part, I will contribute all that in me lies to a reunion. In the meantime, madam (*to* Mrs. Fainall),

547. for] *Q1; omitted in Q2, W1.*

550. you'll have time enough] *W1;* you'll have him time enough *Q1.*

542. *I gad*] i.e., by God.
550. *toy*] play.
563. *of force*] necessarily.

let me before these witnesses restore to you this deed of trust; it may be a means, well-managed, to make you live easily together.

From hence let those be warned, who mean to wed,
Lest mutual falsehood stain the bridal bed;
For each deceiver to his cost may find,
That marriage frauds too oft are paid in kind.

Exeunt omnes.

EPILOGUE

Spoken by Mrs. Bracegirdle

After our Epilogue this crowd dismisses,
I'm thinking how this play'll be pulled to pieces.
But pray consider, ere you doom its fall,
How hard a thing 'twould be to please you all.
There are some critics so with spleen diseased,
They scarcely come inclining to be pleased;
And sure he must have more than mortal skill,
Who pleases any one against his will.
Then, all bad poets we are sure are foes,
And how their number's swelled, the town well knows;
In shoals I've marked 'em judging in the pit;
Though they're on no pretense for judgment fit,
But that they have been damned for want of wit.
Since when, they, by their own offenses taught,
Set up for spies on plays, and finding fault.
Others there are whose malice we'd prevent;
Such who watch plays with scurrilous intent
To mark out who by characters are meant.
And though no perfect likeness they can trace,
Yet each pretends to know the copied face.
These with false glosses feed their own ill nature,
And turn to libel what was meant a satire.
May such malicious fops this fortune find,
To think themselves alone the fools designed;
If any are so arrogantly vain,
To think they singly can support a scene,
And furnish fool enough to entertain.
For well the learned and the judicious know
That satire scorns to stoop so meanly low
As any one abstracted fop to show.
For, as when painters form a matchless face,
They from each fair one catch some different grace;
And shining features in one portrait blend,

2. I'm *Q2, W1;* In *Q1.*

---

21. *glosses*] notes of explanation.
30. *abstracted*] separated from others.

To which no single beauty must pretend;
So poets oft do in one piece expose
Whole *belles assemblées* of coquettes and beaux.

---

36. *belles assemblées*] fashionable gatherings.

Appendix

Chronology

Approximate years are indicated by *.

Political and Literary Events	*Life and Major Works of Congreve*
1631 John Dryden born.	
1633 Samuel Pepys born.	
1635 Sir George Etherege born.*	
1640 Aphra Behn born.	
1641 William Wycherley born.*	
1642 First Civil War began (ended 1646). Theaters closed by Parliament. Thomas Shadwell born.*	
1648 Second Civil War.	
1649 Execution of Charles I.	
1650 Jeremy Collier born.	
1651 Hobbes' *Leviathan* published.	
1652 First Dutch War began (ended 1654). Thomas Otway born.	
1653 Nathaniel Lee born.*	

1656
D'Avenant's *THE SIEGE OF RHODES* performed at Rutland House.

1657
John Dennis born.

1658
Death of Oliver Cromwell.
D'Avenant's *THE CRUELTY OF THE SPANIARDS IN PERU* performed at the Cockpit.

1660
Restoration of Charles II.
Theatrical patents granted to Thomas Killigrew and Sir William D'Avenant, authorizing them to form, respectively, the King's and the Duke of York's Companies.

1661
Cowley's *THE CUTTER OF COLEMAN STREET.*
D'Avenant's *THE SIEGE OF RHODES* (expanded to two parts).

1662
Charter granted to the Royal Society.

1663
Dryden's *THE WILD GALLANT.*
Tuke's *THE ADVENTURES OF FIVE HOURS.*

1664
Sir John Vanbrugh born.
Dryden's *THE RIVAL LADIES.*
Dryden and Howard's *THE INDIAN QUEEN.*
Etherege's *THE COMICAL REVENGE.*

1665
Second Dutch War began (ended 1667).
Great Plague.

Dryden's *THE INDIAN EMPEROR.*
Orrery's *MUSTAPHA.*

1666
Fire of London.
Death of James Shirley.

1667
Milton's *Paradise Lost* published.
Sprat's *The History of the Royal Society* published.
Dryden's *SECRET LOVE.*

1668
Death of D'Avenant.
Dryden made Poet Laureate.
Dryden's *An Essay of Dramatic Poesy* published.
Shadwell's *THE SULLEN LOVERS.*

1669
Pepys terminated his diary.
Susannah Centlivre born.

1670
Dryden's *THE CONQUEST OF GRANADA*, Part I.

Born on January 24 at Bardsey, near Leeds, Yorkshire.

1671
Dorset Garden Theatre (Duke's Company) opened.
Colley Cibber born.
Milton's *Paradise Regained* and *Samson Agonistes* published.
Dryden's *THE CONQUEST OF GRANADA*, Part II.
THE REHEARSAL, by the Duke of Buckingham and others.
Wycherley's *LOVE IN A WOOD.*

1672
Third Dutch War began (ended 1674).
Joseph Addison born.
Richard Steele born.
Dryden's *MARRIAGE À LA MODE.*

1674–1681

Lived at Youghal and Carrickfergus in Ireland.

1674

New Drury Lane Theatre (King's Company) opened.

Death of Milton.

Nicholas Rowe born.

Thomas Rymer's *Reflections on Aristotle's Treatise of Poesy* (translation of Rapin) published.

1675

Dryden's *AURENG-ZEBE.*

Wycherley's *THE COUNTRY WIFE.**

1676

Etherege's *THE MAN OF MODE.*

Otway's *DON CARLOS.*

Shadwell's *THE VIRTUOSO.*

Wycherley's *THE PLAIN DEALER.*

1677

Dryden's *ALL FOR LOVE.*

Lee's *THE RIVAL QUEENS.*

1678

Popish Plot.

George Farquhar born.

Bunyan's *Pilgrim's Progress* (Part I) published.

Rymer's *Tragedies of the Last Age Considered* published.

1679

Exclusion Bill introduced.

Death of Thomas Hobbes.

Death of Roger Boyle, Earl of Orrery.

Charles Johnson born.

1680

Death of Samuel Butler.

Death of John Wilmot, Earl of Rochester.

Dryden's *THE SPANISH FRIAR.*

Lee's *LUCIUS JUNIUS BRUTUS.*

Otway's *THE ORPHAN.*

1681 Charles II dissolved Parliament at Oxford. Dryden's *Absalom and Achitophel* published. Tate's adaptation of *KING LEAR*.	
1682 The King's and the Duke of York's Companies merged into the United Company. Dryden's *The Medal*, *MacFlecknoe*, and *Religio Laici* published. Otway's *VENICE PRESERVED*.	Entered Kilkenny School, Kilkenny.
1683 Rye House Plot. Death of Thomas Killigrew.	
1685 Death of Charles II; accession of James II. Revocation of the Edict of Nantes. The Duke of Monmouth's Rebellion. Death of Otway. John Gay born. Crowne's *SIR COURTLY NICE*. Dryden's *ALBION AND ALBANIUS*.	
1686	On April 5, entered Trinity College, Dublin.
1687 Death of the Duke of Buckingham. Dryden's *The Hind and the Panther* published. Newton's *Principia* published.	
1688 The Revolution. Alexander Pope born. Shadwell's *THE SQUIRE OF ALSATIA*.	Returned to England.
1689 The War of the League of Augsburg began (ended 1697). Toleration Act.	

Death of Aphra Behn. Shadwell made Poet Laureate. Dryden's *DON SEBASTIAN*. Shadwell's *BURY FAIR*.	
1690	
Battle of the Boyne. Locke's *Two Treatises of Government* and *An Essay concerning Human Understanding* published.	Visited Ireland.
1691	
Death of Etherege. Langbaine's *An Account of the Dramatic Poets* published.	Enrolled on March 17 as law student in the Middle Temple, London.
1692	
Death of Lee. Death of Shadwell. Tate made Poet Laureate.	Published a romance, *Incognita*. Contributed poems to Charles Gildon's *Miscellany of Original Poems*. Translated the eleventh satire of Juvenal for Dryden's translation of *The Satires of Juvenal and Persius*.
1693	
George Lillo born. Rymer's *A Short View of Tragedy* published.	*THE OLD BACHELOR* produced at Drury Lane Theatre in March. *THE DOUBLE DEALER* produced at Drury Lane Theatre in December.
1694	
Death of Queen Mary. Southerne's *THE FATAL MARRIAGE*.	Commemorated the death of Queen Mary in *The Mourning Muse of Alexis*.
1695	
Group of actors led by Thomas Betterton leave Drury Lane and establish a new company at Lincoln's Inn Fields. Southerne's *OROONOKO*.	*LOVE FOR LOVE* produced at Lincoln's Inn Fields Theatre in April. Appointed Commissioner of Hackney Coaches. Published essay *Concerning Humour in Comedy*.
1696	
Cibber's *LOVE'S LAST SHIFT*. Vanbrugh's *THE RELAPSE*.	Visited Ireland and received an honorary M.A. degree from Trinity College in February.

1697	
Treaty of Ryswick ended the War of the League of Augsburg. Charles Macklin born. Vanbrugh's *THE PROVOKED WIFE.*	*THE MOURNING BRIDE* produced at Lincoln's Inn Fields Theatre in February.
1698	
Collier controversy started with the publication of *A Short View of the Immorality and Profaneness of the English Stage.*	Published *Amendments of Mr. Collier's False and Imperfect Citations.*
1699	
Farquhar's *THE CONSTANT COUPLE.*	
1700	
Death of Dryden. Blackmore's *Satire against Wit* published.	*THE WAY OF THE WORLD* produced at Lincoln's Inn Fields Theatre in March. In late summer and autumn, visited Belgium and Holland with Charles Mein and Jacob Tonson.
1701	
Act of Settlement. War of the Spanish Succession began (ended 1713). Death of James II. Rowe's *TAMERLANE.* Steele's *THE FUNERAL.*	*THE JUDGMENT OF PARIS*, a masque, performed at Dorset Garden Theatre in March.
1702	
Death of William III; accession of Anne. *The Daily Courant* began publication. Cibber's *SHE WOULD AND SHE WOULD NOT.*	
1703.	
Death of Samuel Pepys. Rowe's *THE FAIR PENITENT.*	
1704	
Capture of Gibraltar; Battle of Blenheim. Defoe's *The Review* began publication (1704–1713).	Collaborated with Vanbrugh and Walsh in *SQUIRE TRELOOBY*, a farce adapted from Molière's *MONSIEUR DE POURCEAUGNAC* and

Swift's *A Tale of a Tub* and *The Battle of the Books* published.
Cibber's *THE CARELESS HUSBAND.*

produced at Lincoln's Inn Fields Theatre.

1704–1705

Joint manager with Vanbrugh of the new Haymarket Theatre.

1705

Steele's *THE TENDER HUSBAND.*

Published *The Tears of Amaryllis.* Appointed Commissioner of Wine Licenses.

1706

Battle of Ramillies.
Farquhar's *THE RECRUITING OFFICER.*

1707

Union of Scotland and England.
Death of Farquhar.
Henry Fielding born.
Farquhar's *THE BEAUX' STRATAGEM.*

1708

Downes' *Roscius Anglicanus* published.

1709

Samuel Johnson born.
Rowe's edition of Shakespeare published.
The Tatler began publication (1709–1711).
Centlivre's *THE BUSY BODY.*

1710

Publication of first collected edition of Congreve's works, including *Semele*, an opera.

1711

Shaftesbury's *Characteristics* published.
The Spectator began publication (1711–1712).
Pope's *An Essay on Criticism* published.

1713
Treaty of Utrecht ended the War of the Spanish Succession.
Addison's *CATO*.

1714
Death of Anne; accession of George I.
Steele became Governor of Drury Lane.
John Rich assumed management of Lincoln's Inn Fields.
Centlivre's *THE WONDER: A WOMAN KEEPS A SECRET*.
Rowe's *JANE SHORE*.

Appointed an undersearcher of Customs and Secretary to the Island of Jamaica.

1715
Jacobite Rebellion.
Death of Tate.
Rowe made Poet Laureate.
Death of Wycherley.

1716
Addison's *THE DRUMMER*.

1717
David Garrick born.
Cibber's *THE NON-JUROR*.
Gay, Pope, and Arbuthnot's *THREE HOURS AFTER MARRIAGE*.

1718
Death of Rowe.
Centlivre's *A BOLD STROKE FOR A WIFE*.

1719
Death of Addison.
Defoe's *Robinson Crusoe* published.
Young's *BUSIRIS, KING OF EGYPT*.

1720
South Sea Bubble.
Samuel Foote born.
Steele suspended from the Governorship of Drury Lane (restored 1721).
Steele's *The Theatre* (periodical) published.

Pope's translation of Homer's *Iliad* dedicated to Congreve.

Hughes' *THE SIEGE OF DAMASCUS.*	
1721	
Walpole became first Minister.	
1722	
Steele's *THE CONSCIOUS LOVERS.*	Visited Bath with Henrietta, Duchess of Marlborough, and John Gay.
1723	
Death of Susannah Centlivre. Death of D'Urfey.	Birth on November 23 of Lady Mary Godolphin (afterward Duchess of Leeds), Congreve's daughter by Henrietta, Duchess of Marlborough.
1725	
Pope's edition of Shakespeare published.	Made his will on February 26, leaving most of his estate to Henrietta, Duchess of Marlborough.
1726	
Death of Jeremy Collier. Death of Vanbrugh. Law's *Unlawfulness of Stage Entertainments* published. Swift's *Gulliver's Travels* published.	Visited by Voltaire.
1727	
Death of George I; accession of George II. Death of Sir Isaac Newton. Arthur Murphy born.	
1728	
Pope's *Dunciad* published. Cibber's *THE PROVOKED HUSBAND* (expansion of Vanbrugh's fragment *A JOURNEY TO LONDON*). Gay's *THE BEGGAR'S OPERA.*	Wrote *Letter to Viscount Cobham.* In Bath from May through October with Henrietta, Duchess of Marlborough, and Lady Mary Godolphin.
1729	
Goodman's Fields Theatre opened. Death of Steele. Edmund Burke born.	Died on January 19 in his London lodgings in Surrey Street, off the Strand. Buried on January 26 in Westminster Abbey.

1730

Cibber made Poet Laureate.

Oliver Goldsmith born.

Thomson's *The Seasons* published.

Fielding's *THE AUTHOR'S FARCE.*

Fielding's *TOM THUMB* (revised as *THE TRAGEDY OF TRAGEDIES,* 1731).

1731

Death of Defoe.

Lillo's *THE LONDON MERCHANT.*

1732

Covent Garden Theatre opened.

Death of Gay.

George Colman the elder born.

Fielding's *THE COVENT-GARDEN TRAGEDY.*

Fielding's *THE MODERN HUSBAND.*

Charles Johnson's *CAELIA.*

1733

Pope's *An Essay on Man* published.

1734

Death of Dennis.

The Prompter began publication (1734–1736).

Theobald's edition of Shakespeare published.

Fielding's *DON QUIXOTE IN ENGLAND.*

1736

Fielding led the "Great Mogul's Company of Comedians" at the Little Theatre in the Haymarket (1736–1737).

Fielding's *PASQUIN.*

Lillo's *THE FATAL CURIOSITY.*

1737

The Stage Licensing Act.

Dodsley's *THE KING AND THE MILLER OF MANSFIELD.*

Fielding's *THE HISTORICAL REGISTER for 1736.*